Practicing Protestants

LIVED RELIGIONS

Series Editors David D. Hall and Robert A. Orsi

Practicing Protestants

Histories of Christian Life in America, 1630–1965

Edited by

LAURIE F. MAFFLY-KIPP

LEIGH E. SCHMIDT

MARK VALERI

The Johns Hopkins University Press

Baltimore

This book has been brought to publication with the generous
assistance of the Lilly Endowment.

2 4 6 8 9 7 5 3 1

The Johns Hopkins University Press
2715 North Charles Street
Baltimore, Maryland 21218-4363
www.press.jhu.edu

Library of Congress Cataloging-in-Publication Data
Practicing Protestants : histories of Christian life in America, 1630–1965 /
edited by Laurie F. Maffly-Kipp, Leigh E. Schmidt, and Mark Valeri.
p.   cm.
Includes bibliographical references and index.
ISBN 0-8018-8361-X (hardcover : alk. paper) —
ISBN 0-8018-8362-8 (pbk. : alk. paper)
1. United States—Church history. 2. Christianity and culture—United
States—History. I. Maffly-Kipp, Laurie F., 1960– II. Schmidt, Leigh Eric.
III. Valeri, Mark R.
BR515.P76 2006
280′.40973—dc22   2005032063

A catalog record for this book is available from the British Library.

CONTENTS

The History of American Christian Practice Project, a three-year collaborative enterprise under the sponsorship of the Lilly Endowment, set out to confront Christian practice as an aspect of American religious history. The twelve principal researchers for the project faced far more knots than we could ever hope to untangle in a single volume of essays, and there seemed to be no end of loops and twists in the threads we were following. Take one example: Jonathan Edwards's congregants in the early 1730s thought they knew, quite concretely, what Christian forgiveness meant. Forgiveness, in the Puritan mode, entailed a specific set of social obligations enacted within the context of a local church community. One was to forgive debts, to acknowledge faults, and to speak cordially. Adopting those practices, it was believed, eventually would instill the appropriate feelings of love within the heart of the individual. By the mid-eighteenth century, as colonial congregations increasingly came into contact with a world of transatlantic mercantile, cultural, and intellectual exchange that expanded their social and economic relations, understanding forgiveness as a discrete set of obligations to the local community became less viable. How could one forgive those beyond the bounds of the congregation—say, the native captors of women taken in warfare? Did God's imperative to forgive extend to those who were outside the immediate church, and, if so, how could such actions be demonstrated to others?

If forgiveness appears likely to be a particularly wooly element of Christian practice, consider the dilemmas involved in the seemingly more precise practice of prayer. In the early twentieth century, Protestant liberals and conservatives alike grappled with the "problem" of prayer: when, where, and how to do it. People did not seem to be praying as much as they once had, lamented Reuben Torrey and other leaders; and when they did pray, they altered the familiar evangelical forms in favor of ones more congruent with "modern" life. Prayer meetings were being shuffled off to more convenient hours, and families did not have the time they once had to engage in collective morning and evening prayers. Could people instead pray on their own during the commute to work or find a spare moment amid the bustle of a hectic office? In turn, did those sorts of prayers, timed for modern efficiency, necessarily demonstrate an attenuation of religious feeling or a decline of family piety?

Christian practice in America has always presented a series of quandaries rather than a stable set of ingredients. As these opening examples suggest, even those actions often considered quintessentially a part of the Christian life—sacrament, prayer, reconciliation—open up a host of questions, concerns, conflicts, and anxieties. These cases also suggest the importance of exploring practice and practices as historical issues. Were people really praying less in the 1920s, or was the practice of prayer taking different forms? Did self-help maxims, daily affirmations, and meditative techniques replace more familiar habits of petitionary prayer? Except for the obviously important historical work of exploring the continuities and discontinuities of religious practice, American historians have only occasionally made this province their own. With the notable exceptions of collections edited by David Hall, Colleen McDannell, and James M. O'Toole, there has thus far been only scattered attention to the conception of practice in the historiography of American religion.[1] The History of American Christian Practice Project brings questions about practice into more sustained historical and theoretical focus.

This collection of essays represents the central publishing venture of a larger collaborative enterprise that has involved more than twenty historians of American religion, practical theologians, and pastors in an exploration of the significance and usefulness of "practice talk" as a tool for understanding American Protestant life. The core working group of twelve historians, whose essays compose this volume, met five times between June 2002 and October 2004. In two of those meetings, we added to our group three practical theologians and pastors, Kathleen Cahalan, Robert Langworthy, and Craig Townsend. At various points along the way, we enjoyed the careful advice and formal commentary of Dorothy Bass, Richard Wightman Fox, Charles Hambrick-Stowe, and Albert Raboteau. At our first group meeting, in June 2002, we benefited from the presence of Edwin Gaustad; and at our third, in June 2003, from the participation of David Hall. At every meeting we had the assistance of Kathryn Lofton, at the time a doctoral student in American religious history, who added another critical voice to our discussions. Almost all of these scholars participated in our culminating conference, held at the University of North Carolina at Chapel Hill in October 2004, where Grant Wacker served as the keynote speaker. Thus, the volume is the fruit of an extended series of conversations, reflections, and debates—an exchange that we hope proves to be ongoing and of widening reach.

ACKNOWLEDGMENTS

This book would not have been possible without the generous support of the Lilly Endowment, Inc., as well as the sage counsel of those associated with it, particularly Christopher Coble, who shepherded the project from start to finish. Also, our home institutions—Princeton University, the University of North Carolina at Chapel Hill, and Union Theological Seminary of Virginia—supported our cross-institutional collaboration, as did numerous people at each school, including Louis Weeks and Daryl Sasser at Union, Anita Kline and Barbara Bermel at Princeton, and Hope Toscher at Chapel Hill. The acumen and energy of Kathryn Lofton, the chief coordinator of our meetings and exchanges, kept us moving and lifted our spirits at every turn.

Crucial to the shaping of our group endeavor were several senior historians who advised us at various points and in different capacities along the way: Dorothy Bass, Richard Wightman Fox, David D. Hall, Charles Hambrick-Stowe, Albert Raboteau, Ann Taves, and Grant Wacker. In our effort to forge a larger exchange between historians of American religion and theologians of Christian practice, we found wonderful interlocutors in Kathleen Cahalan, Robert Langworthy, and Craig Townsend.

We have been very fortunate to work with Henry Tom, Juliana McCarthy, and Anne Whitmore, our editors at Johns Hopkins University Press. We are also grateful to have David Hall and Robert Orsi as editors of the larger series in which this volume appears.

Above all, we are appreciative of the rich collegiality that this project has fostered. It has been a source of great satisfaction for us to work over the last four years with such a fine group of scholars, all of whom we now count as good friends. We trust that at least one practice has been fully vindicated by our research: namely, the practice of convening scholars to think collaboratively about their shared areas of inquiry.

Practicing Protestants

Introduction

LAURIE F. MAFFLY-KIPP

LEIGH E. SCHMIDT

MARK VALERI

Christian practice has always defied singular definition, particularly in the diversity and competition of America's religious marketplace. From the earliest days of colonial settlement, a Christian practice without controversy would have been difficult to find. The sacraments were, of course, among the most obvious points of contention: Were there seven of them, two, or none? Did the Lord expect the faithful to receive the communion elements while kneeling or sitting? Was baptism a rite reserved for adult believers only? Did full immersion in a river reenact the gospel or mock devotion? Then there was the calendar and the right ordering of Christian time: Was the Sabbath the only genuine feast day, and how was it to be hallowed? Should regular devotional rhythms and routines shape each day of the week? If so, were set prayers and printed meditations as worthy as more improvised wrestlings of the soul with God? For American Christians, who have not been the heirs of a single tradition of religious practice, the most vexing puzzle has been the nature of the Christian life and the practices that constitute it.

Recent Theories of Practice

The History of American Christian Practice Project began with more questions than answers about the historical import and theoretical underpinnings of religious practice as a construct. What exactly is included within this rubric? Why are so many academics and churchgoers talking about "practice" and "practices" these days? Is it a valuable analytic category for religious historians? If so, how might we begin to draw a "more comprehensive map of practices" over time—to use David Hall's formulation from his introduction to the volume *Lived Religion*?[1]

In order to answer such questions, we had first to make our way through an increasingly complex, multidisciplinary literature on practice. That growing body of scholarship involves the work of constructive theologians, social historians, moral philosophers, cultural anthropologists, and qualitative sociologists of the past three decades. We found it of heuristic value to divide that literature into two intellectual lineages. The first is the work of leading social theorists of practice—Pierre Bourdieu, Michel de Certeau, Catherine Bell, and Talal Asad among them. The second is the work of contemporary theologians—Dorothy Bass, Craig Dykstra, and Stephanie Paulsell, to name three—who have evinced a keen interest in revitalizing the Christian life through a sustained recovery of practices. These latter thinkers, in turn, have drawn on wider philosophical and ethical reconstructions of the virtuous life and its practices, including the work of Alasdair MacIntyre and Pierre Hadot. Though the two camps, social theorists and practical theologians, often stand in tension with one another, they both provided resources for our work.

Within the first camp, the critical emphasis is on the hegemonic, regulatory, and structuring character of practice. Pierre Bourdieu, for example, identified "habitus" as the system of "durable, transposable dispositions" through which people "give shape and form to social conventions." Bourdieu encouraged the study of practices as part of penetrating the "logic" of a whole social and cultural field.

> In reality, even in social formations where . . . the making explicit and objectifying of the generative schemes in a grammar of practices, a written code of conduct, is minimal, it is nonetheless possible to observe the first signs of differentiation of the domains of practice according to the degree of codification of the principles governing them. Between the areas that are apparently "freest" because given over in reality to the regulated improvisations of the habitus (such as the distribution of activities and objects within the internal space of the house) and the areas most strictly regulated by customary norms and upheld by social sanctions (such as the great agrarian rites), there lies the whole field of practices subjected to traditional precepts, customary recommendations, ritual prescriptions, functioning as a regulatory device which orients practice without producing it.[2]

Rather than framing practice in philosophical terms as a conscious attempt to embody moral excellence, Bourdieu argued that practice is regulated by exterior social conditions and maintained by conscious and unconscious submission to those conditions. At the same time, Bourdieu insisted on keeping enough improvisatory play within the prescriptive, regulatory field of practices to allow room for resistance, negotiation, and redirection. In Bourdieu's terms, practice was an inevitable aspect of social existence; practice was equated with the habits of body and mind, the customary acts and routine disciplines that formed the very texture of everyday life.

Attentive to Marxist and Foucauldian views of society in which individuals act within an arena of fundamental power differentials, these social theories of practice prove especially helpful at illuminating situations of conflict between prevailing groups and less powerful social actors. Terms like *domination, discipline, coercion,* and *constraint* fill this theoretical lexicon, capturing the note of suspicion toward the inculcation of practice. "Practice theorists are particularly attentive to the political dimensions of social relationships, especially with regard to how positions of domination and subordination are variously constituted, manipulated, or resisted," explains Catherine Bell. "Not surprisingly, practice theory has emerged in conjunction with greater attention to the lingering effects of colonialism, the political ramifications of routine cross-cultural encounters, and the various social effects of economic and cultural domination."[3] From this vantage point, the exploration of practice is, at bottom, an examination of the intricate exercises of power, the procedures of enforcement, the spaces of negotiation, as well as the subtle tactics of resistance.

This theoretical approach provides critical terms for describing and interpreting a wide range of actions, religious and otherwise. Within religious studies, the deployment of the category of practice has facilitated examinations of behavior beyond narrow constructions of ritual and liturgy, enabling scholars to move into the murky arenas of daily social encounter and everyday experience. Now, alongside the study of sacraments, memorial services, and public prayers, historians of American religion can also approach more mundane regimens and habits of the Christian body. An emphasis on practice, then, opens doors to an astonishing range of historical queries. How are routine habits of deference to God, ministers, and elders inculcated and enfleshed? How, in turn, are those patterns of authority and domination pried open, challenged, or nimbly evaded? How do the implicit rules that govern the relations between men and women within churches and homes operate? How are the bodily disciplines and postures of devotion instilled and enforced in the lives of children? Practice theory enjoins historians to see the Christian life within a dense pattern of cultural actions, dispositions, regimens, hierarchies, habits, resistances, and appropriations.

The second intellectual lineage, that of constructive theology and moral philosophy, offers a different purchase on the significance of religious thought and symbolism within communities of faith. Much of this scholarship, illustrated in the recent work of Dorothy Bass, Craig Dykstra, and Stephanie Paulsell, has been prompted by a perception of diminished practice and a desire to recover and encourage more meaningful processes of spiritual formation.[4] "Practices," Dorothy Bass explains at the outset of her influential collection *Practicing Our Faith*, "are those shared activities that address fundamental human needs and that, woven together, form a way of life. Reflecting on practices as they have been shaped in the context of Christian faith leads us to encounter the possibility of a faithful way of life, one that is both attuned to present-day needs and taught by ancient wisdom."[5] Whereas Bourdieu and Bell sought to describe the landscape of everyday experience and social action, Bass and other Christian interpreters of practice seek to form more virtuous or consecrated lives. They ask how contemporary Christians can cultivate sustaining religious practices in a postmodern world of fragmented identities and patchwork faiths. How can Christians practice their faith in a culture that offers so many alternatives, secular and religious, to Christianity? Proponents of a return to Christian practice come from both ecumenical and more conservative Protestant traditions, but all are convinced that in the self-conscious cultivation of particular types of traditional Christian habit lies the key to a renewal of the Christian life.

This resurgent emphasis on practice in American Protestant theology has received much of its inspiration from Alasdair MacIntyre's retrieval of Aristotle's virtue ethics. According to Aristotle, the good life does not consist of haphazard and unrelated acts of good conduct (for example, the American infatuation with random acts of kindness); moral excellence is achieved only through an intentional and full-orbed philosophy that constitutes a whole way of living in the world.[6] Philosophy as a way of life offers those patterns of proper conduct (or habits of virtue) that result in true human happiness. MacIntyre's reconstruction of that classical interpretation of the good life has proven highly resonant with leaders of Christian communities.[7] MacIntyre proposes to those leaders that virtuous behavior can be achieved in their members through the cultivation of traditions of moral excellence. In habituating themselves to good practices, community members can recover a confidence and belief in the traditions themselves. In an increasingly "post-Christian" world, where theology seems to have been pushed to the wayside, churches can cultivate habits of Christian practice, foster corporate identity, and eventually reinstall belief in the tradition itself. In short, people can be habituated into belief in the truths of Christianity through the practices of the Christian life.

In contrast to scholars such as Bourdieu and Bell, these church leaders have faith not only in practice but also in the Christian social world. If our first group of theorists assume that social structures are generally hegemonic, with resistance located in small-scale tactics of getting by or making room, Christian theorists view such regulatory structuring as largely humane, enabling, and supportive.[8] Happiness and virtue, they would say, are associated with a life of Christian discipleship through a religious community; the church and its leaders provide a structure that makes possible, rather than limits, true happiness. In this sense, elites and ordinary people (or clergy and laity) move toward a common and mutually beneficial goal. This constructive view rises not from a desire to unmask the asymmetries of power and the minutiae of discipline but from a hope of restoring power and regulation to the Christian life. The one approach interrogates discipline; the other celebrates it.

Yet, even the renewal of Christian practice bedevils its proponents with questions about the criteria for selecting and shaping current practices. According to most Protestant theorists of practice, the process of retrieval occurs through the careful culling of tradition based on an awareness of and appreciation for the history of Christian communities. What, exactly, is that "tradition" toward which Christians need to turn? It is at this point that the work of religious historians becomes especially salient. The recovery of the Christian way of life depends in large part on an agreed upon, constitutive set of historical *practices*. Protestant theorists of practice *need* history, because it provides the sources for those foundational habits and patterns of action that will lead to renewed faith. But, of course, they need histories of a particular kind, histories that yield kernels of insight about practice, that reveal what has shored up Christian identity in the past and what has produced sanctified and meaningful lives through the centuries. Though less likely, the histories could also recount what to avoid; they could be histories of patterns of practice that have produced violence, prejudice, disaffection, or boredom within Christian communities. The desired history is that of the "embodied wisdom" of Christianity on such mainstays as worship, prayer, Sabbath keeping, hymn singing, spiritual retreat, healing, and Bible reading.[9]

Such projects of recovery can too easily result in simplified and idealized narratives of practices sadly lost and then happily found; they depend largely on the discovery of recognizable practices that can be replanted in contemporary churches to flourish anew. In telling a story of recovery, what is significant about prayer and forgiveness, for example, is the common meaning they potentially present for Christians across time and place. Any disputes over that meaning or changes in the meaning over time are almost necessarily downplayed in the search for a usable past. In looking for relevant virtues and habits to reclaim from history, Protestant practitioners are at considerable risk of seeing their own prior assumptions, present values, and felt needs reflected back to them.

All of us involved in the History of American Christian Practice Project know this much: good histories alone will not create predictable or easy applications. The history of Christian practice yields irretrievable particularities more than irreducible commonalities; discontinuity is every bit as important as continuity; changes in the Christian life prove irrevocable. Still, we have not abandoned the proposition that fuller and more nuanced historical narratives may provide resources for reflection within contemporary Christian communities. Although the sweep of critical theories from Bourdieu to Bell holds considerable sway among our participants, we have remained deeply interested in the possibilities of a conversation among historians of American religion, constructive theologians, and practicing Christians. The historical pursuit of practice may be useful to both descriptions and prescriptions of the Christian life.

The theoretical imagining of Christianity as a way of life presents historians with a significant opportunity to take seriously—more so than do some of the social theories mentioned above—the relationship among theology, community structures, and individual agency. Because Protestant theorists do not immediately regard with suspicion the motives of communal leaders nor assume that the inculcation of particular practices is merely a flexing of institutional muscle, proponents of practice prod historians to leave ample room for the consideration of the thick interpenetration of beliefs and behaviors for all participants. For Protestant scholars of practice, questions about religious meaning are not wholly subsumed into questions of social power, and their theological and philosophical concerns thus act as an important counterbalance in the larger academic inquiry into practice. At a still broader level, we recognize that historical scholarship is constructive too, that its task is not confined to exposing the forgetfulness at the heart of historical memory or the invented-ness of the usable pasts Protestants (or others) create. As historians, we care as well about the embodied wisdom through which American civil and religious communities cohere or fragment.

In sum, we have taken a mediating stance between social analysis and theological appropriation of practice. Following the divergent promptings of these two theoretical camps, we hope to offer fuller descriptive accounts than have previously been written, ones that hold the hermeneutics of suspicion and trust in creative tension. As a scholarly group, we have worked with an understanding of practice that keeps it within the context of the instrumentalities and asymmetries of power and refracted through constructions of race, colonialism, gender, economy, sexuality, and spirituality. However, we have also interpreted practice as theologically informed acts that Christian communities have repeatedly nurtured and instilled over time. That is, we have also pursued the meaning of specific practices within a conception of Christianity as a whole mode of life, as a way of intentionally structuring relationships in this world and with the divine in order to embody Christian virtue and piety.

Protestant Practice in American History

A growing number of works in American religious history are calling attention to practice as an interpretive, and frequently ambiguous, rubric. Drawing on the social theory of practice and utilizing an ethnographic approach, these works maintain that practices both mediate religious culture (thereby regulating behavior) and express creativity, improvisation, and resistance. As Robert Orsi has put it, "practice" offers a rich, varied approach to religion: "the key words here are *tensile, hybridity, ambivalence, irony;* the central methodological commitment is to avoid conclusions that impose universality."[10] This scholarly emphasis on ambivalence and negotiation thus far has generated more thematic analyses than chronological conceptualizations. One recent anthology argues that diversity and instability in American religion can be captured best by assembling practices not by historical or confessional identity but by type of activity: praying, singing, teaching, healing, imagining, persuading.[11] Such phenomenological approaches yield important insights about the multivalent character of particular religious behaviors, but they do not move us toward a more nuanced comprehension of the development and transformation—that is, the historical contextualization—of religious practices in American life.

As we began to ponder how our collaborative research could help map change in American religious practices over time, we made the decision to concentrate our attention on Protestantism. Fully aware that further mapping of practice was necessary far beyond Protestant church life, indeed far beyond Christianity itself, we nonetheless thought that the best way for us to begin to sharpen the history of practice was to narrow our focus to one tradition, however internally diverse and conflicted that tradition was. Looking at the history of American Protestants, we discerned several recurrent themes or clusters of issues that fell into historical periodization. Thus, we have organized the following essays around four turning points: Puritan and evangelical practice in New England, 1630–1800; mission, nation, and Christian practice, 1820–1940; devotional practices and modern predicaments, 1880–1920; and liberal Protestants and universalizing practices, 1850–1965. Although these turning points do not exhaust the possible interpretive rubrics, they provide useful, and we think provocative, starting points for the creation of a historical map, a legend, of sorts, in which to locate contests over specific practices and practice more generally.

One final word about the essays before we elaborate on our turning points. Not every essay defines a traditionally recognized Christian practice. Part of our purpose is to expand the usual scholarly repertoire beyond preaching and the sacraments; we hope, though, to widen the lens without letting the familiar emphases fall from view. Many of the essays do, in fact, address traditional practices, albeit through nontraditional lenses. Each essay explores the ways in which other religious communities, cultural challenges, and social forces have compelled a reconsideration of religious behavior. We historicize practice by looking for continuities and discontinuities, probing for contingency and change in discrete historical moments. We hope thereby to situate the history of Christian practice in the context of American cultural history, to enrich the story of practices, and to suggest possible rereadings of American religious history itself.

Puritan and Evangelical Practice in New England, 1630–1800

The first of our historical turning points concerns the transition from Puritan to evangelical practice in New England, particularly as the Enlightenment took hold. Looking at a turning point compels consideration of what went before, in this case how eighteenth-century beliefs about practice derived from and diverged from earlier Protestant notions of comportment. Many sixteenth- and seventeenth-century Protestants, fleeing what they took to be a "practice-bound" church, avoided a generalized, singular definition of *practice*. The founders of the Protestant movement set out to "recover" a true reading of faithful Christian behavior from what they impugned as medieval ceremonialism, sacerdotalism, and ritualism. Medieval traditions, by John Calvin's reading, promoted Catholic practices as efforts to secure divine favor, thereby intruding on Christ's saving work. This critique shaped fundamental assumptions about practice in communities that became Protestant. Rather than "practice," reformers spoke of piety in everyday life, a "perpetual fast," in Calvin's terms, of self-sacrifice and discipline in opposition to the sacramental system. Many Protestants in seventeenth-century America expressed these assumptions in terms of the individual's duty to the local community. Religious leaders encouraged practices as integral to communal and visible discipline. They urged the embodiment of the Christian life in corporate duties of sobriety and charity, along with prayer and worship, that bound adherents into communities of solidarity.[12]

In the course of the eighteenth century, American Protestants began to modify their expressions of practice. They moved toward universal definitions of Christian being-in-the-world, grounded on interior affections and beliefs that linked individuals to a religious society that transcended local communities. Several demographic, social, political, and cultural developments shaped these new understandings. Encounters with French and Spanish Catholics, trade and warfare with Indians, and the presence of new residents of various faiths drawn by commercial opportunities from throughout the Atlantic world challenged assumptions about a fixed and homogenous social order. The rapid commercialization of the economy in Boston, New York, Philadelphia, and Charleston, and even inland trading centers such as Hartford and Albany, allowed for rapid social mobility and, moreover, for ease of long-distance communication of goods and ideas, tastes and religious sensibilities. The infusion of rationalist religious sensibilities, scientific discoveries, and a new moral philosophy based on natural law and individual affection, all of which were made widely available through new forms of print culture, offered alternatives to customary Christian formulations of the self and society, interior disposition and external deed. We use the term *Enlightenment* as a shorthand for the cultural coalescence of these varied forces—pluralistic, commercial, scientific, and philosophical.[13]

The first two essays in Part 1 probe in more detail this period of profound intellectual and behavioral transformation. Catherine Brekus examines devotional writing by focusing on Puritans and evangelical Calvinists in New England during the seventeenth and eighteenth centuries. Evangelicals inherited a seventeenth-century Puritan practice of spiritual self-reflection and journal writing as well as long-established Protestant assumptions about human sinfulness and self-deception. Yet, while retaining the practice of writing and the essential tenets of their spiritual forebears, they used a different grammar of religious experience. Inspired by the confluence of evangelical and Enlightenment cultures, which emphasized the individual's perceptions, sensation, and activism, evangelicals were more assured about their spiritual states than were Puritans. Evangelical devotional writing created a sense of continuity with the past, of stability in religious identity, along with adaptation to a new epistemology and form of activist self-fashioning. According to Brekus, the practice of writing by evangelicals mediated spiritual transformation under the guise of changelessness.

Mark Valeri's essay on how the well-known pastor and theologian Jonathan Edwards promoted forgiveness as a Christian virtue reinforces many of the same themes. Edwards frequently accepted Puritan teaching that compelled forgiveness as a social discipline, the maintenance of the local community through social deeds such as the remitting of debts and kind speech. From 1730 through 1750, however, Edwards found this Puritan paradigm of forgiveness increasingly problematic. New philosophical ideas challenged him to ground moral behavior in individual affection rather than communal duty; like other evangelicals of the day, he assimilated many Enlightenment categories. Frequent warfare with Indian tribes provoked him to consider a universal benevolence that transcended tribal identities. In this intersection of social and theological forces, Edwards began to reconsider and reconstitute the practice of forgiveness, bit by bit, as a conduit of solidarity between white New England Protestants and their Indian, French-allied, Catholic-convert neighbors.

Mission, Nation, and Christian Practice, 1820–1940

The essays in Part 1 demonstrate how religious behavioral continuity mediated dramatic social and intellectual changes for eighteenth-century Anglo-Protestants; the essays in Part 2 deal more directly with innovation and social power in the American Protestant past. This section begins in the early nineteenth century, a period that saw American imperial expansion westward, the creation of new religious communities, and renewed interest in evangelization and mission. Previous scholarship on this transformative political project, with its emphasis on the internal dynamics of national development, has focused principally on domestic Protestant revivalist practices. The nineteenth century, in particular, has been characterized largely as the century of awakenings and the various physical manifestations—from barking and falling down to itineracy and entrepreneurship—that attended them.[14]

We shift attention instead to the margins of this political enterprise, to geographical and cultural borders where Protestant practices ran up against religious others in the course of colonization and nation-building. This focus allows us to limn the various ways in which Protestant practice can be seen as a medium through which power has been asserted, contested, and resisted. Here we witness its encounter with nationalistic imperatives: the political, one might even say national, dimensions of cultural encounter, meetings that catalyzed practical improvisation as much as principled adherence to tradition. Yet, as in Part 1, we discover the extent to which Protestant apprehension of correct religious practice also has been molded by intercultural awareness, of Protestants in relation to others—be they Catholic, Mormon, Japanese, or Native American.

This is not the only lens through which Laurie Maffly-Kipp in Chapter 3 views missionary practice in Hawaii from 1820 through 1860, but it provides a crucial angle of interpretation for her. Protestant evangelists from the American Board of Commissioners for Foreign Missions (ABCFM) and missionaries from the Latter-day Saints (LDS) encountered in Hawaii daily realities and momentary necessities that compelled adjustments in their practice of mission. Hawaiian customs, from ritual dance and the use of intoxicants to clothing and sexual practices, challenged missionaries to adopt new behaviors in the islands. These accommodations necessarily entailed, Maffly-Kipp maintains, an engagement in the colonial enterprise as a nationalistic venture. Infused with confidence in the colonial enterprise, ABCFM missionaries distanced themselves from native customs and actively separated themselves from Hawaiian communities and customs. Less attached to American national identity— indeed, resistant to it—LDS missionaries developed a closer rapport with Hawaiian culture on its terms, offering a theology of non-American sacred destiny and innovative, ecstatic practices of healing and prophecy that allowed a different interface with natives. In both cases, the convergence of Christian beliefs, Hawaiian culture, and nationalist agendas inspired practical improvisation.

Roberto Lint Sagarena, in Chapter 6, and David Yoo, in Chapter 5, address the culture of nationalism more explicitly. Lint-Sagarena's topic is the development of Mission Revival architecture in California in the 1870s, especially the appropriation by Protestants of Spanish mission styles and the attendant revision of California history in terms of the triumph of a Franciscan (putatively liberal and proto-American) ethos over other forms of Catholicism. In this case, architectural practice literally framed a space for the coexistence of Protestant, Catholic, and American nationalist identities. It expressed a "curious ecumenism" whereby American Protestants interpreted Spanish settlers of California as proto-democratic, that is, participants in the national myth. The practice of building public structures that evoked a type of religiosity was concrete, so to speak, yet it also delineated an area of interpenetration between sacred and political ideologies.

Similar elements—religious architecture, nationalist sentiments, deep intellectual convictions—flowed together in the story of the Korean Christian Church in Hawaii during the 1920s and 1930s. In fact, David Yoo takes the nurture of nationalist identity in this setting as a practice in itself. Yoo shows that in the teaching and liturgies of the Korean Christian Church believers engaged a series of outside forces, especially American and Japanese attempts at colonial hegemony. In that engagement they developed new modes of worship, education, and political utterance. All of these were bound together by corporate discipline and a particular theology. Yoo's essay, like Lint-Sagarena's, reinforces the interpretive potential of practice as a realm for religious and political confrontation and innovation.

Michael McNally also addresses Christian missions in his chapter on the Ojibwe. Like Yoo, he views Protestant practice from the vantage of those who had, to a greater or lesser extent, newly embraced Christian practices as their own. In terms of specific practices, however, Christianization provoked intense communal concern and debate about the relative merits of Christian and native ways. Here, too, novel combinations of practices provided the means of negotiating dramatic cultural change. McNally argues that the honoring of elders as a religious practice was the very ground on which Ojibwe Indians struggled to resolve their standing vis-à-vis Christianity. Honoring elders affirmed their pre-Christian customs. Yet, as Ojibwe converts submitted to Christian eldership, they deviated from those customs, developing new ways of honoring elders, an "improvisation on old kinship structures."

Devotional Practices and Modern Predicaments, 1880–1920

In Part 3 we move back to beliefs and behaviors that might be defined more traditionally as spiritual practices—prayer, healing, and worship. Just as our first turning point involved struggles within and between Christian communities to adjust practices in new social and cultural conditions, so does this third set of essays, which tracks

modern predicaments encountered in the late nineteenth and early twentieth centuries. By "modern predicaments" we mean a matrix of intellectual and social changes
that compelled further reconsiderations of Christian practice. The ascendancy of
Darwinism and the modern physical sciences in the academy raised questions about
the cultural authority of the Bible, traditional Christian doctrines, and belief in miracles. Industrialization of the economy, new definitions of gendered social roles, and
the spread of a consumer ethos and urban commercial organization over the landscape rendered problematic the pursuit of customary patterns of devotion premised
on stable communities, extended families, and rural rhythms of labor.[15]

Traditionally, this period has been described in terms of a bifurcation within American Protestantism: modernists or liberals accommodated Christian belief and practice to these new conditions while sectarian movements, emergent Pentecostalism, and
militant fundamentalism resisted change. Our essays here belie such a straightforward
dichotomy. They show a subtle and sometimes surprising confluence of creativity and
continuity in response to larger cultural challenges. Focusing on the emergence of the
evangelical divine-healing movement that flourished among North American, British,
and European Protestants in a broad range of denominations during the latter decades
of the nineteenth century, Heather Curtis explores how practices such as meditation,
prayer, laying-on of hands, and anointing enabled participants in divine healing to
challenge a Christian devotional ethic that linked bodily suffering with spiritual holiness and valorized patient resignation as the proper Christian response to physical
affliction. By embracing a paradoxical understanding of the relationship between personal agency, ritual practice, and divine sovereignty, Curtis argues, proponents of faith
healing sought to modify the meaning and experience of illness and pain in the spiritual life. Practices of healing, within this context, helped people navigate the various
medical theories, gender ideologies, and religious idioms that influenced the ways in
which Protestant women and men in the late nineteenth century understood and experienced bodily infirmity and pursued physical and spiritual health.

Rick Ostrander sets practices of prayer in a related milieu for American Protestants
in the early twentieth century. Drawing a contrast between liberal and fundamentalist Protestants, Ostrander defines the context in terms of commercialization, the frantic pace of modern life, and scientific beliefs. Both groups, Ostrander concludes,
adapted prayer practices to such conditions. Liberal Protestants developed a flexible,
mobile, and spiritualized notion of prayer in accommodation to modern sensibilities,
while fundamentalists created special prayer meetings and rural retreats and conferences to safeguard the spiritual life from modernist incursions. Like faith healers,
these practitioners of prayer made innovations on received practices in the context of
cultural and social exchange, particularly as that exchange suggested the need to

affirm or modify deeply rooted ideas about divine power and human agency, divine immanence and transcendence, the laws of nature and the graces of miracle. In this case, practice mediated not only Christian identity and the culture of modernity but also theology and bodily activity.

Anthea Butler uses this last observation as a central insight into her subject. She probes how the worship practices in the Church of God in Christ (COGIC) mediated an innovative theology of sanctification (the necessity for personal holiness) through physical activities such as glossolalia, shouting, and dancing. The more frequently studied charismatic practices, Butler argues, cannot be understood apart from their connection to everyday moral regulation and communal demarcation. Butler shows that the improvised rhythms and bodily movements of COGIC worshipers represented both an adaptation to contemporary cultural forms and an expression of an underlying charismatic theology and concern for common discipline.

Liberal Protestants and Universalizing Practices, 1850–1965

The fourth part takes up the wider geographical and political contexts in which twentieth-century Protestant communities struggled with notions of practice. "Liberal Protestants and Universalizing Practices, 1850–1950," concerns itself not simply with the *facts* of social and religious diversity and encounter—patterns which, as we have seen, have been evident from the very beginning of the American Protestant story—but with the ideology of pluralism as a *practical* religious dilemma for liberal Protestants. One reaction to cultural encounter was to separate one's community from others (be they other Protestants or those of other faiths) by way of distinctive modes of religious practice. Another response, particularly for those Protestants who were colonized, occupied, or otherwise oppressed, was to use Christian practices to resist the dynamics of imperial control. Yet a third path emerged in the late nineteenth century, as liberal Protestants of European heritage sought their own means to reconcile Christian particularities with cultural difference through the construction of purportedly "universal" approaches to religious practice. Such strategies, in theory, could swathe all religious people in a cosmopolitan spiritual embrace. Liberal Protestants employed various ways of practicing religious univeralism, including liturgical and artistic movements and interfaith conferences. In hindsight, we may see the boundedness of their vision, but we must also note that this trajectory toward pluralistic ideals and the dilemmas of appropriateness in Christian practice that it prompted still concern liberal Protestant communities today.

Thomas Wentworth Higginson was a New England social reformer, Unitarian minister, and writer during the second half of the nineteenth century. He was also one of the first Americans to grapple with the practice of religious cosmopolitanism in a systematic way. He couched his response in the concept of "sympathy." Leigh Schmidt's essay on Higginson and the practice of sympathy among liberal Protestants at the end of the nineteenth century reveals explicitly universalizing encounters among different religious groups. Schmidt shows how the concrete acts associated with sympathy—concerted conversations with religious people from diverse traditions, the scientific study of religion apart from sectarianism, and the gathering in retreat centers—constituted a practical theology, an affective orientation in the territory of exchange, where quite distinct religious and social affiliations commingled.

Tisa Wenger focuses on dance as an innovation in Episcopal practices of worship. William Norman Guthrie, rector of St. Mark's-in-the-Bouwerie Episcopal Church in New York City in the 1920s, introduced "eurythmic worship" as a way to attract new members and resources to his inner-city parish. Guthrie, drawing on contemporary theories of comparative religion, claimed that a relevant Christianity must reach back to its pagan origins and that when he did so he found dance at the heart of religion. He believed that restoring dance to its proper place in Christian practice would ultimately make a truly universal Christianity possible. Wenger's essay illustrates the friction and debate provoked by innovations in Christian practice, and it suggests yet again the mediating role of practices and their reflection of the historical and cultural moment.

Sally Promey's discussion of liberal Protestants, the National Council of Churches, and arts professionals inside and outside the church looks at this type of encounter in the 1950s. Promey describes the close alliance between Protestant theologians such as Paul Tillich and modernist visual art as the inculcation of a practice of aesthetic discernment, which leads into a host of other activities, ranging from the use of art in sanctuaries to the production of materials for Christian education. We see here especially how the interface between religious communities and cultural movements sparked innovative and controversial practices. Liberals nurtured a "taste culture" of aesthetic discernment as a mediation of what they saw as the dehumanizing, commercial, totalitarian mass culture of the age. In that social and political context, they promoted modernist abstraction as a truly Christian expression of the free individual in a free world, and they contrasted artistic modernisms with another sort of Protestant visual culture that they disparaged as mass-produced and sentimentalized. Aesthetic discernment linked a very particular theological vision to quite specific artistic practices, defying any notion of secularization.

We do not intend our four turning points to establish a single narrative, much less a theoretical baseline. The historical particularities defy insertion into a cohesive schema of Christian practice. While talk of practice conjures material things, conceptual and literal geographies, familial relations, and daily epistemologies, the very localism and temporality of such matters confute historical and therefore theoretical generalization. Yet, we do think that these narrative clusters suggest ways in which to historicize practice, to recover the moments of interchange among received tradition, regulation, and power as one set of factors, and innovation, agency, and creativity as counterbalancing responses. By so historicizing practice, we hope to suggest movement, encounter, and transformation: perhaps as a heuristically useful backdrop against which to set other stories.

Our narratives illustrate the ways in which Christian practice in America has changed through its manifold encounters with the other, has defied categorical explanation, and may therefore be seen as all the more unbound by theoretical paradigms. Some of these paradigms, to return to our opening, limit our expectations of practice to regulation and power. Other paradigms dehistoricize practice by envisioning it as a recovery of Christian virtue in the midst of secularization and materialism. Historical particularity, in contrast, brings us to appreciate the confluence, in any one moment, of authority and innovation in a fidelity to the past accompanied by an adaptation to the present. Historical particularity as applied here knits together the history of Christian practice with the history of American culture and society.

PART I

PURITAN AND EVANGELICAL PRACTICE IN NEW ENGLAND, 1630–1800

CHAPTER ONE

Writing as a Protestant Practice

Devotional Diaries in Early New England

CATHERINE A. BREKUS

One morning in April of 1757, Sarah Osborn, a 43-year-old schoolteacher, rose with the first light of the sun, closed the curtains around her bed for privacy, and knelt on her bed in front of a small portable desk. With a few quick strokes of her penknife, she sharpened her quill, carefully dipped it in a pot of ink, and then began writing. "Stay with me," she wrote to God, her quill scratching against the page, "and Purge and cleanse me. Stay with me and quicken me. Stay with me and soport, socour, direct, and comfort me. Lord I cannot Let thee go. O withdraw not. Slay everything that would Provoke thee to withdraw, and abide with me." When she reached the end of the page, she gently sprinkled it with sand to dry the ink and then turned it over to continue writing.[1]

Osborn saw writing as a form of prayer and as one of the most important parts of her devotional life. From the early 1740s until the 1770s, when failing eyesight made it difficult for her to write, she wrote and stitched together more than fifty volumes of diaries, carefully marking each one with a number and a date. "I seem to Lie u[nder] necessity to improve my Pen if [I w]ill be at all Lively in religion," she explained. According to Samuel Hopkins, her minister in Newport, Rhode Island, she wrote between 5,000 and 15,000 pages, only about 1,500 of which survive.[2]

Many Protestants in seventeenth- and eighteenth-century New England wrote religious diaries. Few, if any, matched Sarah Osborn's sheer number of pages; but like her, they saw diary writing as a deeply meaningful discipline that could bring them into union with the Divine. Writing in the morning before the business of the day or, more typically, at night after all the chores had been done, they reflected on their sinfulness, their desire for salvation, and God's glory.

During the middle of the eighteenth century, the style of devotional writing changed, as Puritan piety gave way to a new evangelical style. "Evangelicals," it can be argued, created a more confident and activist form of piety that helped them cope with the changes that were transforming eighteenth-century New England culture. While Puritans had written diaries in order to determine whether they numbered among the elect, Osborn and other evangelicals expressed more certainty about their salvation. Although they were linked to Puritans by crucial resemblances, their diaries reflected new concerns. Rather than scrutinizing themselves for evidence of grace, evangelicals embraced the practice of devotional writing in order to cultivate Christian virtue within themselves, to identify how God was directing their lives, and, in some cases, to evangelize others.

Besides examining the differences between Puritan and evangelical dairy writing, this essay argues that religious practices, because of their illusion of stability, have often helped to mediate change. While scholars have explored practices as forms of discipline, sites of resistance, and building blocks for a more virtuous life (and all three kinds of interpretations are drawn on here), this essay is most interested in questions about how religious practices have mediated change over time. Practices have provided a reassuring sense of connection to the past during times of momentous social, political, and economic transformations. Ironically, although Christians have always been attracted to religious practices as a way to preserve tradition against the acids of change, in fact, practices have often served as a vehicle for theological innovation. When Sarah Osborn knelt on her bed in the mornings, pouring out her heart to God in written prayer, she thought that she was repeating a timeless ritual that linked her to earlier generations of Christians, even the prophets. In many ways, she was right. But her diaries also reflect the emergence of a new kind of Protestant faith that was born in the eighteenth century, a faith which was deeply shaped by the new ideas of the Enlightenment. Through the practice of devotional writing, she and other eighteenth-century Protestants laid the groundwork for an evangelical future while believing that they were simply continuing the Puritan past.

Searching for Grace: Puritan Devotional Diaries

When the first British settlers sailed to New England in the early 1600s, hoping to create a "city on a hill," many tucked sheets of foolscap, quills, and inkwells into their trunks to record their remarkable pilgrimage. John Winthrop, the future governor of the Massachusetts Bay Colony, brought two kinds of journals with him as he crossed the Atlantic: a volume of "annals" to record what happened on shipboard, and a private diary to record his interior religious experiences. When he made entries in his annals, he usually described himself in the third person as "the governor"; but in his "Experiencia," as he called his diary, he spoke in the first person as a contrite sinner who promised "to give myselfe, my life, my witt, my healthe, my wealthe to the service of my God & Saviour."[3]

Winthrop and the other men and women who settled in New England were dissenters from the Church of England. They had earned the name Puritans, originally meant as an insult, because of their complaints that the Church of England was a corrupt institution that needed to be purified. The English Reformation, in their opinion, had preserved too many Catholic beliefs and practices. Hoping to recreate the primitive simplicity of the early Christian church, they disdained anything that smacked of Catholic ritualism, such as making the sign of the cross and kneeling to receive the sacrament.

Yet, even though Puritans condemned the ritualism of the Anglican Church, they continued to embrace dozens of Christian practices, including family prayer, individual prayer, baptism, church attendance, fasting, almsgiving, Bible reading, and celebrating the Lord's Supper. As the heirs of John Calvin, who had helped lead the Protestant Reformation, they believed that humans could be saved only through divine grace, not their own good works; they insisted that religious practices were not salvational in and of themselves. "God will have mercie on whom he will have mercie," John Winthrop wrote in his diary. "There was never any holye meditation, prayer, or action that I had a hand in, that received any worthe or furtherance from me or anythinge that was mine." Nevertheless, Winthrop and other Puritans claimed that practices could be a *means* of salvation. As historian Charles Hambrick-Stowe explains, "in Puritan spirituality God did not come *because* someone engaged in a certain exercise; but if God was going to come, He would do so through the means of that exercise."[4] Instead of dismissing practices as mere forms, Puritans insisted that true Christianity demanded something more than an inward disposition. They believed that to achieve union with God, they had to "practice" their faith.

Given the Puritans' intense focus on the Bible, it is not surprising that they emphasized writing as an important religious practice. Influenced by the examples of Moses, Jeremiah, and Habakkuk, all of whom had been commanded to write ("Write thee all the words that I have spoken unto thee in a book," God ordered Jeremiah), they saw writing as an especially valuable means of grace because of its permanence.[5] Flawed by original sin, humans were too imperfect to remember all of their religious experiences, but if they committed them to paper, they could preserve them against forgetfulness. "Do not trust your slippery memories with such a multitude of remarkable passages of Providence as you have, and shall meet with in your way to heaven," advised John Flavel. "Certainly it were not so great a loss to lose your silver, your goods and chattels, as it is to lose your experiences which God has this way given you in the world."[6] Unlike prayer and other religious practices, writing led to the creation of material, permanent objects that could be objectively examined for signs of God's will.

God had commanded his prophets to write, but he had not told them to write *diaries*. So why were Puritans particularly drawn to the practice of keeping diaries, a relatively new form of self-expression in the seventeenth century? Although there is no simple answer to this question (and many Puritans preferred to express their devotion in other kinds of writing, especially poetry and memoirs), it is significant that diaries, with their chronological, dated entries, bear a striking resemblance to both travel logs and account books. Puritans may have borrowed the form of travel logs because they imagined life as a pilgrimage. (This must have been especially true for first-generation colonists who made the dangerous voyage across the Atlantic.) And they may have imitated account books because they saw diaries as a spiritual "accounting" of sin and grace.[7]

Puritans wrote devotional diaries for many reasons: to examine themselves for signs of grace, to heighten their appreciation of God's grandeur, and to fix their thoughts on God rather than the vanity of "the world." Instead of imagining their diaries as an opportunity for the free expression of individual creativity, as many Americans do today, the Puritans approached their diaries as a space for rigorous self-examination. Indeed, they did not understand writing to be a means of spiritual liberation (an idea popularized by nineteenth-century romantics) but of self-regulation. Although writing could certainly lead to moments of transcendent union with God, it more typically involved an anguished confrontation with the sinful self. Devotional writing was a difficult and painful discipline.

When Puritans sat down to write in their diaries, their main goal was self-examination. In the words of Cotton Mather, the most published Puritan minister, "Frequent SELF-EXAMINATION, is the duty and the prudence, of all that would *know themselves*, or would not *lose themselves*."[8] The questions Puritans asked themselves were always the same: What did they find when they looked into their hearts? Did they find any evidence that they numbered among the elect who had been predestined for salvation? Influenced by Francis Bacon, whose empirical method revolutionized the study of science, Puritans examined their lives with almost clinical detachment. As Michael McGiffert has noted, the diary of Thomas Shepard, a prominent Puritan minister, sounds oddly like a lab notebook or "a description of a scientific experiment." Scrutinizing his life for "evidence" of his relationship to God, Shepard repeatedly began his sentences with an empirical description of what he "saw" in himself. "I saw my own weakness," he lamented in 1641. And a few months later, "I saw myself very miserable because by my sin I had separated myself from God and turned my face from him."[9] Perhaps Shepard found it difficult to examine his life with such a dispassionate, critical gaze, but he subjected himself to the same discipline almost every night; he rarely went to sleep without first pondering the lessons he had learned about himself that day.

Although Shepard hoped to find convincing evidence of his salvation, he always feared the possibility of self-deception. Despite the growing influence of Francis Bacon, Shepard and other Puritans remained skeptical about humans' capacity to attain full knowledge of either the self or God. As historian Stephen Toulmin has shown, late-Renaissance thinkers tended to assume that doubt and ambiguity were an inherent part of the human condition, and it was not until the mid-seventeenth century, after the devastation and chaos of the Thirty Years War (1616–1648), that philosophers such as René Descartes and Gottfried Wilhelm von Leibniz began to construct a new, more reassuring world view based on rationality and certainty.[10] For most Puritans, however, such optimism about human knowledge seemed presumptuous, even arrogant. Because they prized religious humility above all else, they feared becoming too confident about their salvation. In historian Charles Cohen's words, Puritans alternated "between complacency and doubt; doubt spurs the desire for assurance, which encourages deeds that encourage faith, but assurance edges into presumption and inspires doubt."[11] The only way to cope with painful episodes of doubt, which they hoped would become less frequent as they grew closer to death, was to carefully search the self for "evidence" of true Christian faith. With the help of guides like Henry Scudder's *The Christians Daily Walke* and Thomas Hooker's "The Character of a Sound Christian in Seventeen Marks," they carefully examined their experiences for "marks" of their election.[12] "Examined my selfe by the signs of uprightness in Scudders *dayly walk,*" wrote Increase Mather, the distinguished pastor of Boston's Second Congregational Church; "I was not without Hope that a work of grace is wrought in my soul."[13]

When Increase Mather and other Puritans looked inward with "hope," they always found the same thing: *sin.* On page after page of their diaries, they lamented their corruption in a self-abasing language that shocks modern ears. (David Shields has remarked that modern Americans use this kind of radical language to criticize institutions, but rarely the self.[14]) Michael Wigglesworth, for example, filled his diaries with descriptions of his "wretched backsliding heart," "vileness," "carnality," "vanity," and "whoarish affections." Jonathan Mitchel bemoaned his "vile heart." Cotton Mather condemned himself as "filthy."[15]

Troubled by this self-abasing, punitive language, many critics have portrayed Puritan diaries as morbidly narcissistic. In 1878, Moses Coit Tyler, a literary historian, wrote: "It cannot be said that our ancestors failed to write diaries. Unluckily, however, the diaries that they wrote . . . were generally records of events which took place only inside of them; psychological diaries, more or less mystical and unhealthy; chronicles of tender, scrupulous, introverted natures, misled into gratuitous self-torture; narratives of their own spiritual moods of fluctuating hour by hour, of visitations of Satan, of dullness or of ecstasy in prayer, of doubts or hopes respecting their share in the divine decrees; itineraries of daily religious progress, aggravated by overwork, indigestion, and a gospel of gloom."[16] The Puritan practice of diary writing, in Tyler's opinion, was nothing more than an exercise in "self-torture."

Despite Tyler's disgust at the Puritans' "gospel of gloom," they wrote diaries not to wallow in the ugliness of sin but to heighten their awareness of God's "astonishing" grace. Although they always began their diary entries by examining their sinfulness, they ended by praising God for his perfection. Consider, for example, the case of Thomas Shepard, who wrote scores of pages lamenting his corruption. In 1641, in a typical entry, he grieved that he was "nothing else but a mass of sin and . . . very vile"; but instead of falling into despair, he expressed awe at God's goodness. "Immediately the Lord revealed himself to me in his fullness of goodness with much sweet affection," he marveled. "The Lord suddenly appeared and let me see there was strength in him to succor me, wisdom to guide, mercy in him to pity, spirit to quicken, Christ to satisfy, and so I saw all my good was there, as all evil was in myself." His self-abasement was not an end in itself but a means to a deeper appreciation of his utter dependence on a sovereign, majestic, merciful God. Of course, Shepard's blissful moments of assurance inevitably gave way to renewed doubts. However, writing was never solely a form of self-discipline for him but also an opportunity for transcendence.[17]

Besides using their diaries to examine themselves and to heighten their love of God, Puritans also hoped to overcome their temptations to "worldliness." By forcing themselves to write about their lives every morning or evening, they hoped to discipline themselves to fix their minds on God instead of on worldly pleasures, be they money, sex, or fame. Borrowing an image from Psalm 131 ("Surely I have behaved and quieted myself, as a child that is weaned of his mother: my soul is even as a weaned child"), many longed to be "weaned" from their "carnal" desires. Indeed, Puritan diaries are filled with lists of "resolutions," sometimes numbered, that reflect their intense struggle against "the world." Writing in 1711, Cotton Mather resolved to renounce the "Flesh," the "World," and the "Divel." "I rebuke, I restrain, I deny the *Flesh* in its Irregular Inclinations," he vowed. "I dream not of Happiness in the great Things of this *World;* I see nothing here will make me happy."[18] But the vehemence of his language betrayed him. As he knew, he was too human (he would have said "sinful") to conquer completely his desires.

The Puritans' most painful struggles involved "weaning" themselves from their attachment to loved ones. Puritan ministers often warned their congregations not to elevate fallen humanity above God. Although Christians could love friends and family, they were never to forget that their ultimate allegiance was to God. In the words of one minister, "To love them with a particular love, as things distinct from God, to delight in them merely as creatures; and to follow them as if some good, or happiness, or pleasure were to be found in them distinctly from what is in God: this is a branch of spiritual *Adultery,* I had almost said *Idolatry.*" In anguished diary entries, both ministers and lay people expressed fears of loving their spouses, children, or friends more than God. They did not want to be guilty of worshiping "false idols." When Cotton Mather's wife lay dying from the measles, he subjected himself to the strict discipline of writing in order to control his emotions. In a poignant entry, he wrote, "Those Words of my Saviour do much run in my mind; The Cup which my Father gives me, shall not I drink it? I would endeavor all possible Imitation of such a patient Submission unto the Will of God."[19] By writing in his diary, he tried to focus on his love of God rather than his "particular love" for his wife.

Puritans not only tried to "wean" themselves from family members, but from their love of life itself. Ultimately all devotional writing led to the same goal: preparation for death. In the pages of their diaries, Puritans asked themselves, over and over, whether they were truly prepared to die. "Think daily of thy death, and that last great account" advised William Perkins. If they numbered among the "elect," then they would be ready to forsake the pleasures of everyday life in order to be with God. When Thomas Shepard looked inward and found that his "heart was not prepared to die," he struggled to "wean" himself even further from the world. By forcing himself to write, he tried to determine whether he was ready for Judgment Day.[20]

Since the Puritans always expected their devotional writing to bring them anguish as well as joy, one wonders why they subjected themselves to such a strenuous regimen. There are no easy answers, but it is likely, as historian Michael McGiffert has argued, that Puritans gained a sense of assurance from their ability to sustain a "methodical, painful discipline" that most would have tried to avoid. The very fact that they managed to sit down day after day and take quill in hand to bewail their sinfulness may have seemed like "evidence" of their closeness to God.[21]

Puritans assumed that the path to God was always hedged with anxiety and suffering. This has sometimes been difficult for modern scholars to understand. Rather than exploring the religious reasons for the Puritans' willingness to subject themselves to a rigorous discipline, they have insisted that Puritans experienced writing as a kind of freedom—as an opportunity to construct new identities. For example, one historian has argued that John Barnard, a Boston carpenter, "actively constructed a personal piety" in his diary.[22] While this interpretation certainly holds a grain of truth, it distorts the more complicated story that Puritans told about themselves in their diaries.

Puritans repeatedly insisted that they were helpless to "construct" themselves—only *God* could give them a contrite heart—and they embraced the rigors of writing because it offered them the possibility of transcendence, not self-determination. Suffering, in their opinion, could be the means of redemption. As Thomas Shepard noted in his diary, some Christians wanted "to have joy and peace alway[s]," but in his opinion, "temptations, fears, and wrestlings" were also "good." In a single, forceful sentence that summed up the Puritan world view, he wrote, "the greatest part of a Christian's grace lies in mourning for the want of it."[23] Devotional writing always involved "mourning," but in the eyes of Puritans, it was a powerful means of grace.

Growing in Grace: Evangelical Devotional Diaries

It is impossible to identify a distinct date when the Puritan style of diary writing was replaced by an evangelical style. Religious practices tend to be so personally meaningful and so deeply woven into the fabric of churches that they rarely change within a single generation. Instead, they evolve gradually, creating the illusion that little has changed at all.

Because of this illusion of stability, the Protestants who wrote devotional diaries in the middle and late eighteenth century did not believe that they were departing in any way from their Puritan predecessors. And, at first glance, the similarities between Puritan and evangelical diaries are much more striking than the differences. In terms of their physical appearance, all of these diaries look much the same. In 1740, as in 1640, people wrote with quill pens on pages of foolscap, almost certainly imported from England, that they had cut into squares with a penknife. When the ink was dry on the pages, they stitched them together into booklets that were small enough to be tucked into a pocket.[24]

The resemblances are more than superficial. Theologically, eighteenth-century Protestants shared the Puritans' faith in total depravity, unconditional election, limited atonement, irresistible grace, and the perseverance of the saints; and as they searched for spiritual models, they often looked backward to the seventeenth century for inspiration. Indeed, because the religious revivals that took place during the 1740s led to a renewed interest in Puritan piety, many Puritan memoirs were published in new editions then.[25] Hannah Heaton, a Connecticut farmwife, confessed that John Bunyan's *Grace Abounding to the Chief of Sinners* "affected me much," and Sarah Osborn read a wide variety of personal narratives, including the diary of Elizabeth Bury, a Puritan woman whose papers were published posthumously. "I have always been helped by reading the Lives and experiences of others," Osborn wrote in her memoir. "Some times they have been blest to convince me of sin, some times to scatter doubts, and some times raised my affections into a flaim." She saved her highest words of praise for Cotton Mather, whom she deeply admired because he "humbly filld his diary with continual sensures upon himself." As she poured out her heart in her diaries, she hoped to imitate his example.[26]

John Cleaveland, a young Yale student studying for the ministry, wrote a journal that sounds so much like a Puritan diary of self-examination that it is almost startling. If it did not have a name and date on it, one could easily mistake it for a seventeenth-century text. As part of his preparation for ministry, Cleaveland kept a diary every day for three months in order to judge his spiritual progress. As he confessed in nearly every entry, he rarely experienced a "Sence of heavenly and Divine things," but despite his constant despair over his "vileness and Stupidity," he continued to subject himself to the painstaking discipline of self-examination. By forcing himself to confront his relationship to God each night before sleep, he hoped to eventually find a spark of grace in his soul. Nevertheless, like the Puritans who inspired him, he did not expect ever to attain certainty of his salvation.[27]

Despite important continuities with the past, the practice of devotional writing began to change during the eighteenth century. During the revivals that took place in New England during the 1730s and 1740s, a new kind of Protestantism began to flourish—a Protestantism that historians now describe as "evangelicalism." (To be clear, eighteenth-century Protestants did not describe themselves in self-conscious terms as evangelicals, but they seemed to realize that they stood on the brink of something new, and they settled on the adjective *evangelical* to describe their experiences. For example, after a night of prayer, Sarah Osborn wrote about feeling "true evangelical repentance.")[28] Since evangelicalism was not a single, coherent movement, any definition risks oversimplification, but, generally speaking, evangelicals tended to be more optimistic about their ability to determine whether or not they had been genuinely saved. As historian David Bebbington has explained, "Whereas the Puritans had held that assurance is rare, late and the fruit of struggle in the experience of believers, the Evangelicals believed it to be general, normally given at conversion and the result of simple acceptance of the gift of God."[29] Unlike Thomas Shepard, who had assumed that true faith entailed anxiety, evangelicals began to believe that they could be almost completely certain of their salvation. Although they still conceded the possibility of deception, most were able to pinpoint the exact time and place that they had been "born again." Nathan Cole, a farmer from Connecticut, began his memoir with the words, "I was born Feb 15th 1711 and born again Octo 1741."[30]

How and why did Puritans become evangelicals? Evangelicalism seems to have been a response to a sense of mounting crisis in the eighteenth-century Anglo-American world. Nothing seemed certain in mid-eighteenth century America: the expansion of the marketplace, the breakdown of social hierarchy, and increasing religious diversity presented individuals with greater personal choices than ever before.[31] First, a consumer revolution brought luxuries within reach of more people than earlier generations of Americans could ever have imagined. As Protestants experienced the pleasures of the marketplace, they seem to find it increasingly difficult to keep their vows to be weaned from the world or, in David Brainerd's more violent language, to be "crucified to all its allurements."[32] When Sarah Gill, the daughter of a prominent evangelical minister, strolled along the waterfront in Boston, she saw many tempting goods for sale—books, furniture, fine silver, silk, china—but as she sternly reminded herself in her diary, she had chosen to worship "The Cross of Christ," not "self gratifications," "Plenty, a full Table—Fine apparell, Delicacies."[33] Similarly, Jonathan Edwards reminded himself that he loved God more than Mammon. In a list of religious resolutions that he wrote in his diary, he swore, "I will not murmur, nor be grieved, whatever prosperity, upon any account, I see others enjoy, and I am denied."[34]

Second, many Protestants felt bewildered by growing religious diversity, which was the result of increased immigration to America as well as sectarian ferment within the colonies. Sarah Osborn traced her heritage back to the British Puritans, but she was surrounded by people of many different denominations: Roman Catholics, Quakers, Anglicans, Moravians, Baptists, and even a small group of Jews. (Touro Synagogue, the oldest synagogue in the United States, was built in Newport in 1762.)[35] While some people may have been intoxicated by this new religious freedom, others seem to have found it confusing. With so many choices, how could one be sure of making the right decision? After a conversation with "some serious good sort of people" who were Seventh-day Baptists, Osborn wrote a letter to a trusted minister asking him to help her defend the custom of keeping Sunday as the sabbath. "I seem much more confused than usual," she admitted.[36]

Evangelicals were also troubled by new currents of religious ideas. Although few American ministers were as radical as England's Samuel Clarke, who challenged the doctrine of eternal punishment, or Daniel Whitby, who complained that the entire idea of original sin was "exceeding cruel, and plainly inconsistent with the Justice, Wisdom, and goodness of our gracious God," a quiet revolution had begun to take place in America's churches. Evidence suggests that the change happened from both the top down and from the bottom up. For example, at the same time as the Reverend Samuel Webster was condemning the doctrine of infant damnation as cruel, ordinary Christians began drifting away from older ideas of innate depravity. As Jonathan Edwards complained, many of his congregants mistakenly described their children as "innocent." By the early nineteenth century, Protestantism had been subtly transformed by a growing faith in human goodness and compassion.[37]

To be clear, few eighteenth-century Protestants could have precisely identified the structural changes that were reshaping their world. Just as modern Americans only vaguely glimpse the larger forces transforming our culture—including the rise of global capitalism, the resurgence of religious conservatism, and the ongoing scientific revolution—most early Americans found it difficult to articulate exactly what was changing and why. Nevertheless, they could not help but feel the reverberations of these larger intellectual and socioeconomic changes in their daily lives. When Sarah Gill tried to curb her desire for the luxuries of the marketplace, when Sarah Osborn puzzled over whether Baptists as well as Congregationalists were good Christians, and when Jonathan Edwards felt as if he had to vigorously defend a doctrine that had once been widely accepted, they gave voice to the subtle shifts taking place in everyday life.

Hoping to make sense of these changes, eighteenth-century Protestants turned to a traditional practice: writing. Since many early diaries seem to have been lost, it is difficult to know how widespread the practice of devotional writing was, but historian David Shields has speculated that it became especially popular in the mid-eighteenth century—even more popular than it had been among the Puritans. There are many likely reasons for this, including the excitement generated by popular revivalism. People tend to write diaries when they feel as if something dramatic has happened in their lives.[38] But it also seems possible that evangelicals were especially attracted to diary writing because it seemed to link them to the past. Throughout Christian history, practices such as writing or prayer have been particularly appealing because of their quality of timelessness. Growing numbers of evangelicals may have turned to diary writing because it helped them to feel anchored at a time when the world seemed to be adrift.

In some ways, evangelicals responded to the changes around them by intensifying an inherited Puritan language. Troubled by the growing faith in human goodness, they took the Puritan rhetoric of sinfulness and depravity to a new extreme. "How perverse and stubborn is my will," Susanna Anthony exclaimed. "How dark and blind my understanding! How carnal my affections! Alas, what pride; what hypocrisy yet remain! How little faith, love, humility, repentance, new obedience, sincerity, and holy conformity to God, is to be seen in my soul! So that I am even ready to cry out, I am altogether as an unclean thing; that there is nothing but wounds and bruises, and putrifying sores; that the whole head is sick and the whole heart faint." (Others saw Anthony very differently; she was widely admired for her Christian selflessness.)[39] Hannah Heaton's language was even stronger: she longed to "fly out of this blind withered naked sore stinking rotten proud selfish self love into the arms of a lovely jesus." Not even Michael Wigglesworth, perhaps the most self-abasing of the Puritans, sounded quite so hostile to the self.[40]

But in a world that seemed to be cut adrift from its traditional moorings, Protestants also began to construct a new kind of faith in their diaries, a faith that simultaneously resisted and accommodated the changes that were reshaping New England culture. In the most surprising transformation, evangelicals began to use a new vocabulary to describe their relationship to God; they adopted a language of sensation, experience, and certainty that was inspired by the intellectual movement known as the Enlightenment. At first glance, this language seems puzzling, especially because so many historians have portrayed the Enlightenment, with its emphasis on reason, and evangelicalism, with its heart-centered piety, as warring forces in eighteenth-century America. According to historian Henry May, for example, the Great Awakening, as the mid-eighteenth-century revivals became known, marked a battle between "The Age of Reason and the Age of Enthusiasm."[41] Yet, even though Protestants resisted the strands of Enlightenment thought that led to deism or skepticism, they were deeply attracted to the Enlightenment's faith in experiential knowledge. "All our knowledge is founded" on "EXPERIENCE," proclaimed John Locke.[42] Faced with a crisis of certainty (how could one know the "truth" in an increasingly commercial and pluralistic world full of so many choices?), they increasingly based their faith on experience as well as on inherited creeds. Whether or not we agree with historian David Bebbington that "the Evangelical version of Protestantism was created by the Enlightenment," it is hard to ignore the affinities between the two movements. Ironically, evangelicals defended themselves against the rationalist strains of the Enlightenment by embracing an equally "enlightened" language of experience, assurance, and proof.[43] With a new confidence in the authority of first-hand experience, they claimed that believers could "feel" and "know" whether they had been transformed by divine grace, as in this account by David Brainerd: "I was spending some time in prayer and self-examination and the Lord by his grace so shined into my heart, that I felt his love and enjoyed full assurance of his favor for that time and my soul was unspeakably refreshed with divine and heavenly enjoyments. At this time especially as well as some others sundry passages of God's Word opened to my soul with divine clearness, power and sweetness so that I *knew* and *felt* 'twas the Word of God and that 'twas exceeding precious."[44]

Since Puritans had also scrutinized their lives for signs of divine grace, evangelicals did not view their focus on experience as a break with the past. However, they approached the question of personal religious experience with a significantly different epistemology. Unlike the Puritans, who had always been fairly skeptical about what they could genuinely know about themselves or God, evangelicals were far more optimistic about human knowledge. According to Jonathan Edwards, for example, converts gained a new spiritual "sense" that was just as real as the physical senses of hearing, seeing, smelling, tasting, and touching.[45] As he recorded in his "Personal Narrative," he felt that new, immediate sense when reading a biblical passage that particularly moved him: "there came into my soul, and was as it were diffused through it, a sense of the glory of the divine being; a new sense, quite different from anything I ever experienced before."[46] (Edwards was influenced by both Anthony Ashley Cooper, third earl of Shaftesbury, and Francis Hutcheson, who argued that all humans have an innate moral sense that helps them distinguish good from evil. Although Edwards rejected this positive view of human nature, he still agreed that knowledge came from sense perception.) *Sensible* became one of the most common adjectives in evangelicals' diaries. Hannah Heaton "had sensible communion with god"; Sarah Osborn experienced a "sense" of God's "excellence, glory and truth"; and David Brainerd "found a sensible attraction of soul after him." While praying, he had felt "sensible sweetness and joy."[47]

Evangelicals filled their diaries with descriptions of their experience. "Blessed be God for the experience of His Mercy truth and faithfulness recorded in this Book," Sarah Osborn wrote on the cover of her 1757 diary. Because the word *experience* has become such a common part of our language today, we may find it difficult to hear its revolutionary cadences. We tend to use the word *experience* as a synonym for individual subjectivity, and we describe our experiences in the same way as our feelings, as interior and private. But in the eighteenth century, *experience* had a more objective, scientific connotation, and evangelicals believed that they could make discoveries about both themselves and God by examining their lives. Indeed, like natural philosophers who adopted the Newtonian method in order to verify their findings, they often described their faith in scientific terms as "experimental": it could be validated by concrete, measurable experience. According to Sarah Gill, for example, she had been "experimentally convinced" of the justice of eternal punishment.[48]

As these examples suggest, the most important differences between seventeenth-century Puritans and eighteenth-century evangelicals lay in their attitudes toward knowledge and assurance. Of course, the older language of anxiety and doubt did not entirely disappear. In a dark moment, Gill wrote: "I find my self at an Utter Uncertainty about my spiritual state."[49] Similarly, when Experience Richardson, a Massachusetts woman, reflected on her life on her forty-second birthday, she lamented, "I think I don't feel so much grace as I felt when I was sixteen years old. Tis a bad sign."[50] But the dominant mood was far more optimistic. While one can find expressions of *both* anxiety and assurance in seventeenth- and eighteenth-century diaries, the scale tipped toward anxiety in the seventeenth century (with some individual converts nonetheless expressing certainty), and toward assurance in the eighteenth century (with some converts still continuing to express doubts). When Susanna Anthony subjected herself to the discipline of self-examination, she wrote a sentence that would have stunned Thomas Shepard or Cotton Mather: "Through the free, rich, sovereign grace of God, I have these evidences so clear, that I can as well deny my own existence, or that my soul is immortal, or that I ever performed a rational act or exercise: I may as well doubt of these, as of the spiritual exercises of grace, which appear as real, and as constant, as the acting of my rational powers." Given her confidence, it is perhaps surprising that she continued to search herself for "evidences of grace," but as she explained, she hoped that her written self-examinations would give her "strength against an hour of temptation."[51] If she were ever tempted to doubt, she would be able to calm her fears by reading her diaries.

Strict Congregationalists, or Separates, were the most radical wing of eighteenth-century evangelicalism, and they took the emphasis on certainty to an extreme. While moderates believed they could find objective signs of divine grace, they were also careful to maintain a stance of humility. A sovereign God was ultimately beyond human understanding. In contrast, Separates claimed that true Christians were absolutely sure of their conversion. Indeed, the Separate Church in Mansfield, Connecticut, insisted that "all Doubting in a Believer is sinful, being contrary to the Commands of God and hurtful to the Soul, and an hinderance to the Performance of Duty," and in nearby Canterbury, Separates claimed that "Assurance is of the Essence of Faith."[52] When Nathan Cole, a Separate, wrote an account of his conversion, he filled it with declarative statements of fact: "I saw," "I was sure," and "I knew": "Now *I saw* that I must Suffer as well as do for Christ; now *I saw* that I must forsake all and follow Christ; now *I saw* with new eyes; all things became new; A new God; new thoughts and new heart; Now I began to hope I should be converted some time or other for *I was sure* that God had done some great thing for my soul; *I knew* that God had subdued my stubborn heart; *I knew* my heart would never rise so against God as it had done."[53] While he continued to struggle with intermittent episodes of doubt after his conversion (reminding us, once again, that the language of assurance and anxiety always coexisted), he insisted that true Christians ideally should be "sure" of their salvation.

Although more moderate evangelicals remained too "Puritan" to use this bold language of certainty (and they loudly complained about the Separates' arrogance), they, too, believed that experiential knowledge of God was possible.[54] By writing diaries, they hoped to create material objects that would offer objective evidence of their salvation and God's goodness. Hannah Heaton confessed, "Sometimes in my darkness when i have read things in my diary that i had forgot it has seemd strengthning & quickning to me." Similarly, Sarah Osborn reread her diaries whenever she felt tempted to despair. Because she was a poor woman who was her family's sole financial support, she often wondered how she would buy food or pay rent, but in her most fearful moments, she studied her diaries and underlined passages for easy reference.

Addressing God directly, she wrote: "My own experience has ever Provd to me, that thou art the God that has fed me all my Life Long—the God that didst never Leave me upon the mount of difficulty, but always appeard and wrought deliverance." She believed that her diaries offered convincing *proof* that a loving God would never abandon her.[55]

Freed from the theological concerns about assurance that had vexed the Puritans, evangelicals adapted the practice of devotional writing to new purposes. Rather than searching for evidence of their election, they hoped that writing diaries would help them to become better Christians. Sarah Prince hoped that her diary would "excite" her "to make Progress in Religion," and Experience Richardson thought that writing would help her to "watch & pray" as she battled to overcome her sins of "pride & vain glory."[56] Although writing remained a painful confrontation with the sinful self, evangelicals believed that it could help them to become more virtuous. As Mark Valeri argues elsewhere in this volume, in his study of the practice of forgiveness, evangelicals believed that truly moral behavior required an interior, godly disposition, not simply external actions. Hence it is not surprising that they viewed writing as an exercise not only in soul searching but in character building as well.

In another break with the past, evangelicals tended to be so confident about their salvation that they thought their life stories could serve as models, however flawed, for others on the Christian path. The Puritans had treated their diaries as strictly private documents, sometimes ordering them to be destroyed at death. Despite the popularity of John Bunyan's *Grace Abounding to the Chief of Sinners*, only a small number of Puritans' personal writings found their way into print, almost all posthumously. In contrast, evangelicals seem to have seen their diaries as a form of evangelism as well as personal devotion, and many seem to have wanted their words to become public. While some shared their manuscripts with friends, others bequeathed them to children. For example, Susanna Anthony allowed members of her women's prayer group to read some of her pages, and Hannah Heaton imagined that her children would read her words after her death. "My dear children," she wrote in her diary, "I leave you here a little book for you to look upon that you may see your mother's face when she is dead and gone."[57] Sarah Osborn seems to have hoped that her diaries would be read by future Christians. On the cover of one of her diaries she wrote, "I commite it to the disposal of providence." Perhaps she hoped that just as Puritan diaries had once inspired her, her diaries would someday inspire others.

The sharing of diaries, whether in published or manuscript form, offers an important clue to solving the puzzle of how evangelicalism spread so quickly in the mid-eighteenth century. Each individual Protestant did not invent a new kind of religious style on his or her own; it happened in communication with like-minded believers.

While tracing the ultimate roots of this new style is difficult (Did it come from leaders? Did it emerge more popularly, from the "bottom up"?), it is clear that evangelicalism spread through many different communication networks: oral sermons and testimonies, published theological tracts, religious periodicals, and, of course, shared diaries.[58]

By the end of the eighteenth century, Osborn and many other Protestants had helped reshape an older Puritan faith in order to meet the challenges posed by religious pluralism, the growth of the market economy, and the Enlightenment. Despite their admiration for the Puritans, these Protestants cultivated a more optimistic, evangelistic style of piety that was built on a new confidence in human knowledge. When Susanna Anthony tried to clarify how deeply she had been changed by her conversion, she explained, "My mind was enlightened."[59]

The emergence of a new, evangelical world view had subtle but important effects on every aspect of eighteenth-century Protestantism. Perhaps if evangelicals had realized that they were creating a new type of religiosity, they would have been alarmed, but because their religious practices seemed to connect them to the past, they were able to ignore the theological shifts that had begun to separate them from their Puritan heritage.

Diary writing continued to be an important Protestant discipline throughout the nineteenth and twentieth centuries, and it has become increasingly popular in recent years. Bookstores around the country sell blank books designed for diary writing, "guided" journals with quotations or exercises that are designed to stimulate writing, and instructional books on how to "journal," as personal writing is popularly called.[60]

This new form of journal writing seems to be a response to a pressing sense of religious crisis in American culture today. At a time when growing numbers of Americans describe themselves as "spiritual" rather than "religious" and when mainstream Protestants have expressed deep anxiety about declining church membership rates, consumerism, and the breakdown of civic life, individual believers have once again turned to traditional religious practices in order to make sense of their changing world. Today, however, unlike in the eighteenth century, theologians and ethicists are more self-conscious about the power of religious practices and have deliberately tried to revitalize them—and create new ones—to meet the religious needs of the twenty-first century. Dorothy Bass, for example, has urged Christians to reclaim the practice of keeping the Sabbath, and Stephanie Paulsell has written a book about honoring the body.[61] Perhaps we are standing in the midst of yet another Protestant transformation, a transformation that is once again taking place through the subtle malleability of Christian practices.

CHAPTER TWO

Forgiveness

From the Puritans to Jonathan Edwards

MARK VALERI

In 1740, the Reverend Jonathan Edwards fretted about the state of affairs in his town, Northampton, Massachusetts. The son and grandson of New England ministers, he had recently led many townspeople into a period of spiritual awakening and would later achieve fame as a defender of Calvinist revivals. Yet he worried that such religious fervor had not engendered, as he had hoped, a society of love and concord. In a particularly biting sermon from that year, he accused many of his parishioners of being "content to put on a religious face in the meeting house or at private religious meetings" while continuing to "enjoy their covetousness and their pride, and their malice and envy, and their revenge" in public "behavior."

Such hypocrisy was troubling, he continued, because it appeared to legitimate the enemies of godliness. Critics of evangelical Protestantism, from liberal clergy in Boston to freethinking rationalists in Glasgow, demeaned it as emotion without moral substance, sensuality and superstition masked as devotion. To promote revival, Edwards declared, people should care less about their reputation for attending worship and more about their conduct "among men." They should in fact "excel other people in a just and righteous, humble, meek, peaceable, quiet loving conversation one among another." They should be "far from all revenge and ill will, all living in love, studying to promote one another's good," and "apt to forbear with one another, apt to forgive one another." Edwards repeated this last admonition: his people should be "forgiving one another, retaining no grudge against any." If they showed forgiveness, they would "make" doubters "believe that there is indeed something in our profession. It will have a greater tendency to convince the world about us . . . ten times [more] than all our private religious meetings, and it will stop the mouths of them that ben't convinced."[1]

Edwards's exhortations point to a transformation in the conception and practice of forgiveness in New England's churches in the eighteenth century. He followed the standard lexicon of Christian virtues when he urged forgiveness, but his sense that he needed to argue its necessity, and the way in which he explained its operation, distinguished him from the previous generation of pastors. Edwards's concern for order and concord in his town bespoke a customary—and what we might label puritan— idea of forgiveness as a means to solidarity in the local community. In this setting, forgiveness denoted a specific behavior ("quiet conversation," in the above sermon) defined by the pastor and regulated through corporate moral supervision. Yet Edwards overlaid such social rules with a rhetoric of interior dispositions or moral states ("far from ill will" and "living in love"). This alerts us to a second strand in Edwards's preaching, which we might call evangelical. Employing the language of the critics of experimental Calvinism ("them that ben't convinced") he parsed forgiveness as a benevolent inclination that, contrary to what the detractors said, derived from evangelical conviction. This conception pointed toward the union of individuals in a widespread moral community. Edwards came to envision a practice of forgiveness that transcended the local community—that even crossed national and ethnic boundaries.

Edwards never made a complete transition from Puritan to evangelical conceptions of forgiveness. He often wove together Puritan and evangelical themes, stressing one or the other at different times, often maintaining both at the same time. He continued to aspire to local control over his parishioners' behavior even as he reoriented his ideas around internal moral states and cosmopolitan ideas of social solidarity. How should we understand Edwards's ambiguity? He modified the Puritan practice of forgiveness as he encountered social schism and religious disputes in his town, new social sensibilities attending a vigorous commercial and legal culture, religious skeptics who disparaged Calvinism as morally offensive, a growing international network of evangelicals, and conflict between English and Indian residents of New England. Such encounters propelled Edwards into what Pierre Bourdieu has identified as "the whole field of practices subjected to traditional precepts and customary recommendations" yet freed for "improvisations." In this in-between space, a realm defined by neither pure regulation and customary (Puritan) teaching nor pure innovation and (evangelical) interiority, Edwards reoriented his understanding of forgiveness without producing an entirely new conception of it.[2]

Edwards's story shows how the modern history of the Christian practice of forgiveness turns on the complex interaction between customary regulation and the innovations called for by specific social and cultural realities. Indeed, our contemporary discussions about religion, forgiveness, and social conflict—energetic and profuse as they are—must deal with a similar set of negotiations, albeit in quite different social circumstances. They face the same sort of competing claims that Edwards confronted in early modern New England: the relationships of public acts to interior affection, local loyalty to universal compassion, particular religious convictions to public encounters between different peoples.

Customary Practices of Forgiveness

Like New England's Puritan ministers, Edwards derived one reading of forgiveness from his pastoral concern to maintain discipline over the local community. Many American Puritans, to be sure, identified themselves with a widely dispersed network of English Dissenters and European Calvinists. Boston divines Increase and Cotton Mather, for example, were well known for their engagement in imperial politics and cosmopolitan, learned culture in the 1680s and 1690s. Yet, by inculcating Christian practices, most Puritans turned to local, neighborly relationships. Samuel Willard, a Boston minister active toward the end of Puritan dominance in New England and the most accomplished theologian there before Jonathan Edwards, summarized nearly a century of Puritan teaching on the topic. "The word" *forgiveness,* Willard wrote at the close of the seventeenth century, "properly signifies to send a thing away; to remove it from one; it is used for a Man's remitting of a servant, or a Debtor, by taking off his Servitude or obligation from him." Thus, forgiveness was a taking away, in this case, the removal of previously incurred obligation or debt. Willard's terms were precisely social, his illustrations economic. Forgiveness was the public act of releasing a servant from his indenture or a debtor from her contract. It had to do with social affairs in the immediate community.[3]

Puritan preachers typically included two reasons and one condition for the exercise of forgiveness. The first reason, quite simply, amounted to scriptural admonition. New Testament writers exhorted Christians to forgive. The second reason required a more elaborate explanation. Christians ought to forgive their enemies—interpreted as those who had harmed them—on the pattern of divine pardon. The early-seventeenth-century Cambridge teachers William Perkins and William Ames, along with first-generation New England pastors such as John Cotton and latter-day Puritans such as Willard, maintained that forgiving others was a logical and moral necessity for those who had been forgiven by God. Christ forgave sinners when they were guilty and incapable of restitution for sin. Believers trusted in this pattern of forgiveness. They affirmed that forgiveness ought to be bestowed on others without merit or compensation. The social practice of forgiveness expressed one's credence in the Protestant doctrine of justification by faith alone. To refuse to forgive one's personal enemies was, perforce, to reject this pattern, instead expecting punishment, restitution, or reparation for past debts or offenses. Those who refused to forgive could not, the-ologically speaking, trust that Christ would forgive them. By this logic, the church could make forgiveness of others a requirement for membership.[4]

The divine pattern of forgiveness did not, however, compel Christians to forgive enemies who intended to maintain their offense into the future. That was pure non-sense. Forgiveness concerned the past, not the future; it could not release the offen-der from future debts. It presumed a past offense and the offender's intention to make a break between the past and the future. Even God demanded repentance. So, Puri-tan writers asserted that contrition was a prerequisite for being pardoned by neigh-bor, church, or God. This condition did not imply contractual notions of mutual ob-ligation. According to theory, the offender paid the offended nothing for previous misdeeds: all debts were canceled. Repentance conveyed merely the intention (not the guarantee) to commit no such offenses in the future.[5]

When expounding on forgiveness, many established Puritan writers treated it as a practical embodiment of belief. The most extreme case of this, as in many things, was Cotton Mather. He described forgiveness chiefly in terms of social acts: to "*do good* unto those neighbors, who will speak ill of you," by which he meant to speak well of them, to refrain from taking a rumor-monger or critic to court for libel, to abate the financial obligations of poor debtors rather than sue them. Other Massachusetts pas-tors, such as Peter Thacher and John Danforth, did not flatten out forgiveness into mere deed, as Mather sometimes appeared to do, but they did parse it in terms of acts. Addressing contentions among Boston churches, especially the schismatic formation of new congregations, Thacher wrote of "requisite Actions," including gentle conver-sation, kind conduct, and restraint from legal recrimination. Danforth also empha-sized cordial speech. The real Christian "banishes away all Bitterness," by which he meant verbal assault, "Clamour, and Evil-Speaking." The Christian also relinquishes "Long Possessed Rights" for the sake of amity.[6]

For these Puritans, forgiveness controlled contention and compelled submission to the local community. Spiritual advice manuals and public proclamations from the seventeenth century portrayed social division as a catastrophe for New Englanders. Preachers of fast-day and election sermons, backed by leading laity and magistrates, argued that the civil order depended on the extent to which New Englanders obeyed the divine mandate to solidarity. Rituals of forgiveness offered one a means of cohe-sion. Unforgiving behavior, in contrast, invited divine judgment and erosion of the commonweal. In this context, forgiveness took on a political valence.[7]

Treating forgiveness as social obligation and external behavior, New England's leaders did not hesitate to compel its performance. Through the 1650s especially, church leaders held disciplinary trials that concerned, among other matters, cases of

conflict between neighbors. Puritans might well have found a model for such discipline in Calvin's Geneva, where the Consistory excommunicated parishioners who
held grudges, maintained disputes, or refused to express forgiveness by public gestures such as speeches of reconciliation, bodily embraces, or attending church with
one's previous enemy.[8] Church bodies in Massachusetts and Connecticut admonished members to speak kindly of previous enemies, refrain from pursuing business
partners or commercial debtors in court, and stifle the urge to complain against one's
critics. Alarmed by the prospect of civil litigation concerning such matters, the First
Church of Boston declared in 1649 that "none of the members" were to "goe to law
one with another without" the "Consent" of the church meeting, where charity and
forgiveness trumped legal prerogative.[9]

Despite these admonitions, after the Restoration in 1660 New Englanders increasingly turned to civil courts to adjudicate social disputes. The imposition of a legal system supervised by royal officials, an increase in the number of non-Puritan residents,
and expanding commercial opportunities pushed the church into the background as
an arbiter of social relationships. Forgiveness receded from records of disciplinary trials, virtually disappearing by 1740. Mention of debt relief or obligations to charity, injunctions against verbal recriminations, admonitions to neighborly reconciliation,
and excommunication for violation of these duties dropped off precipitously. Cases
of civil litigation rose correspondingly.[10]

Many churches nonetheless continued to enforce the practice of forgiveness, as
public conduct, through sacramental discipline. During the early eighteenth century,
New England's pastors responded to increasing social divisions by requiring people
to express forgiveness in the professions, or "relations," of faith that they gave before
being admitted to the Lord's Supper. The First Church of Haverhill, Massachusetts,
for example, obliged one Thomas Jonson to acknowledge his censoriousness and criticism of neighbors before he joined the congregation. He declared that he not only
desired "all whom I've wronged or injured at any time to forgive me" but also desired
"to forgive all that have injured me at any time as I expect to be forgiven of God." Such
language became nearly formulaic in the Haverhill Church—an indication of its importance there.[11]

Many congregations required acts of forgiveness not only to join the church but
also to maintain membership. The Haverill congregation excommunicated one John
Bradley for "using bad language" and for "Contention." To be readmitted, he provided
the following confession of "fault": "I thot my self very much wronged and abused
and provoked by my brother [fellow church member] that contended with me. Yet I
acknowledge 'twas a shame that I have been in such an ill frame towards him; that I
could not love and forgive him. I desire to forgive him, and pray God to forgive him;

and to forgive me."[12] At the church in Medfield, Goodwife Hope Lovel requested "to come to the Table of the Lord in obedience to Christ." Her profession focused on forgiving her neighbors in the most specific, even material terms: "I hope I can heartily forgive all whom I have been ready to think have wronged, and injured me, and heartily wish their prosperity in this world, and more especially that they may be happy in the world to come." Jonathan Edwards's father, Timothy Edwards, encouraged similar testimonies to forgiveness in his church at East Windsor.[13]

Edwards between Custom and Change

Following his father, Jonathan Edwards frequently drew on this Puritan paradigm, especially in his early years in Northampton (1730–1735). Provoked by factionalism, quarrels, and disputes there, he turned to the sacraments in asserting his pastoral authority. Under his grandfather, Solomon Stoddard, the Northampton church had abandoned strict tests for admission to the Lord's Supper, the very tests illustrated by the "relations" discussed above. Edwards nonetheless argued during the 1730s that individuals should at least scrutinize their own behavior before participating in Communion. According to him, the Bible required spiritual regeneration for admission to the Lord's Table, and good social acts attended regeneration. So, efforts toward social virtue, such as forgiveness, remained, by his reading, a standard for sacramental participation even if the church (by dint of an overly lax policy) could not exclude people from the table.[14] In a 1731 sermon, he preached that "persons should particularly examine themselves before they come to the Lord's Supper whether or no they don't entertain a spirit of hatred or revenge towards their neighbor. If a man has such a spirit . . . and gives vent to it, it renders him unfit to attend the sacrament. . . . Persons, therefore, should particularly examine themselves whether or no they have forgiven their enemies . . . so as never to design to do anything to gratify a revengeful spirit."[15]

Edwards implied that many of his own parishioners had forgotten how much a Christian profession, and therefore sacramental privileges, entailed the obligation to forgive others. Many older, longstanding members of the Northampton congregation, he claimed in another sermon, chafed at the rapid entrance of new believers into the church during surges of revival in the 1730s. Old-timers had established their social positions in the town and congregation through years of "religious performances." Many of the recently awakened, in contrast, had made the transition from dissolute sinner to respectable church member through only an afternoon's experience. So "Old seekers," according to Edwards in 1735, engaged in "quarreling" out of an attitude that was legalistic and commercial—they were "indignant" that new believers offered no payments for their "debts." Such spiteful people, Edwards chided, ironically owned less grace than the new converts whom they disparaged.[16]

Edwards never relinquished his responsibility to compel his parishioners to enact forgiveness. Later in his career, he did deemphasize the local community and its quite specific social obligations; he came to embrace a transatlantic, even universal, fellowship of moral solidarity based on virtuous affections rather than on congregational discipline. Yet even then he retrieved the Puritan agenda, perhaps ambivalent about his loss of local authority. Even as he extended his ministry beyond Northampton, to preach in other towns and correspond with fellow evangelicals throughout the British Atlantic, he continued to exhort his own congregation to cordial speech, political concord, debt relief, and submission to his pastoral oversight. In the late 1740s, Edwards in fact redoubled his efforts to institutionalize moral discipline at home. He attempted to close Communion in Northampton to the unworthy, those who exercised inadequate self-scrutiny, urging them to remove themselves from the Lord's Supper. When his parishioners resisted and ousted him from the Northampton pulpit, Edwards argued that their betrayals were, ironically, unforgivable. His parting words to them predicted his vindication and their punishment by God. His resentment, he intimated, was only proper, because they had never repented, had never even suggested that they were sorry for their mistakes. They had broken covenant with God and their pastor, and thus endangered their society and their souls.[17]

Edwards inherited a system of sacramental discipline premised on the assumption that external conformity to communal rules and regulations trained interior affections. Puritan teaching held that the church shaped individuals' intentions to forgive others even as it compelled forgiving behavior. Sincere sentiments of pardon—the mental state of generosity toward one's moral and material debtors—attended conciliatory behavior. Edwards's reflections on the relationship between internal state and external act, to be sure, elude simple generalizations. As early as the 1720s, he had contemplated the complex relationship of motive, affection (eighteenth-century moral philosophers used the term to mean moral disposition or inclination), and public act in the experience of forgiveness. He did not settle on any one rule for the connection between deed and disposition. In the early 1730s he nonetheless retained a Puritan model that urged forgiveness as a behavior that brought about, and to that extent preceded, inner intentions to pardon one's moral debtor.[18]

Take, for example, his early 1730s sermon on Matthew 5:44, Jesus' admonition to love enemies. Edwards used highly affective language throughout his exposition and exhortation, but he bracketed the most emotion-laden passages with claims that correct doctrine obliged believers to practice forgiveness whatever their feelings. Forgiveness was, he argued at the beginning of the sermon, a Christian duty incumbent on all believers by virtue of their profession of faith. It sealed their membership in the local congregation. The conclusion of the sermon settles on public incentives regardless of internal dispositions. Edwards admitted that people might not feel love for their enemies. They should nonetheless behave in a loving manner, he declared, quickening the pace of his prose with a series of active verbs:

> [Do not] allow a contrary spirit to shew itself in any outward exercises. . . . don't vent an ill will by telling against him, reviling of him, ridiculing of him, and publishing his faults. [If] you feel the stirring of a revengeful spirit, cross it as much as you can. Seek opportunities to do your enemy good and strive with yourself in those things if you carry an ill and revengeful spirit; 'tis to be hoped that in this way it will be mortified; and if you do good to your enemy, it is to be hoped that it is the way you may attain to love him.

In other words, Christians should behave against their ill-dispositions, and love might well follow on good deeds. To be sure, Edwards did not muster the specificity of seventeenth-century preachers. He included no exhortations to abate debts or relinquish civil claims. He did, however, plead for a social practice that defied contrary feelings and only subsequently might produce the proper emotions.[19]

Universalizing Forgiveness

From the height of the revivals (1735 through 1744) on, however, Edwards gradually modified the emphasis in his preaching on forgiveness. Never completely jettisoning the Puritan attention to local issues, moral discipline, and public deed, he nonetheless focused more intently on the affective dimensions of forgiveness and its connections to a wider moral community. He even began to reconfigure his formulation of the relationship between forgiveness as external behavior and interior disposition, arguing that the former followed from the latter.[20] He culminated his 1748 *Treatise on Religious Affections* with the claim that public acts of benevolence derived from a conversion of moral disposition. True believers, he wrote, were "united to the people of Jesus Christ as their people," had affections of "forgiveness of those that have injured them, and a general benevolence to mankind," and so fulfilled "rules of meekness and forgiveness, rules of mercy and charity." Visible, enacted benevolence "is an evidence to others of their sincerity in their profession, to which all other manifestations are not worthy to be compared." Like other virtues, forgiveness gave public expression to inner sentiments of grace: compassion, benevolence, humility, and self-sacrifice.[21]

Admittedly, Edwards's writings merely hint at a rearrangement of the order of deed and disposition; he did not give an explicit formula. Even a mere hint, however, suggests a change in agenda. He increasingly imagined a moral community uncoerced by Puritan disciplinary measures, unbounded by local and customary affiliations, yet joined together by the disposition of benevolence. Perhaps he had become disenchanted with Northampton, its familial loyalties, recurrent factions, and resistance to religious reform. Spiritual revival intimated the potential for a moral community that transcended particular congregations, towns, and parochial discipline. Itineration, vast publication networks, and plans for a transatlantic "Concert of Prayer" all bespoke a more expansive network of moral solidarity. In encountering even the first intimations of this network and its difference from local communal frictions, Edwards began to improvise on the received ideal of forgiveness.[22]

Edwards's turn to the affections also signaled his engagement in and debate with a moral-philosophical, rather than strictly evangelical, community. He became particularly interested in the so-called Moral Sense school of the Scottish Enlightenment. Moral Sense writers, such as the third earl of Shaftesbury and Francis Hutcheson, grounded moral judgment on interior sentiments of virtue and vice. These sentiments linked individuals to the natural moral law. The moral law, discovered by reason, encoded a universal ethic that individuals knew instinctively, in inchoate form: benevolence constituted the prime virtue and merited reward (conversely, unjust and mean self-interestedness composed the chief vice and merited punishment). Edwards noted that many Enlightenment moralists critiqued evangelical Calvinism as irrational and even vicious. Calvinist notions of divine election, salvation by faith alone, and the Atonement contradicted ordinary sentiments of justice, reason, and the moral law. It inverted benevolence and inhumane moral judgments.[23]

Edwards urged his people to disprove these skeptics by good behavior; more to the point, he also set out to demonstrate that the doctrines of evangelical Calvinism offered a stronger motive toward humane behavior than did the beliefs of its detractors. During the 1730s and 1740s especially, Edwards addressed critical moralists in their own terms: the inner sense or disposition to benevolence. To return to his sermon on Matthew 5:44, Edwards argued, "Christian morality greatly excels the morality of the Heathen Philosophers." As he glossed this contrast, he deconstructed the claims of the deist and skeptical moral philosophers. Their systems, he insisted, lacked compassion because they rested moral judgment on common sentiment and natural law, which clouded motives to bestow mercy and forgiveness. "The light of nature," he maintained, "seems to suggest" that "iniquity ought to be Revenged." Skeptics and scoffers "have no knowledge of a superiour Invisible being to whom it belongs" to take care of such matters as "justice"; they must conclude that it is a human duty to avenge, rather than forgive, moral offense. Christians, however, and especially Calvinists, trusted in providential power over human affairs. As private individuals they had no need to avenge wrongs, seeing that God was both willing and capable to exact vengeance. Also, being Calvinists, they could not predict the ultimate spiritual state of anyone. So, freed from the obligation to procure justice for themselves, believers could embrace the mandate to forgive, and thus to make solidarity with all human beings.[24]

In later writings, Edwards elaborated on this argument. Evangelical doctrines such as the Atonement, he mused in his private philosophical notebooks from 1744 through 1752, implied a more complete version of human solidarity and a more powerful practice of forgiveness than did the ethics of the Scottish and English Enlightenments. He once again compared Christian teaching on forgiveness to that of writers who defined ethics in terms of natural law. They so followed the rule of reward and punishment that they minimized forgiveness as a moral imperative. "Natural theology," Edwards wrote, "afforded no hope of forgiveness after sinning" because "the law of nature promises" no "pardon for sin." So, contemporary ethicists such as Francis Hutcheson and other "Deists can never show, on their principles" of natural law, "any release from past debts."[25]

Although Edwards did not put it in these terms, he implied that the urbane opponents of experimental Calvinism dispensed with forgiveness in favor of an ethic of contractual obligation. He might have had in mind here the congruence between Enlightenment ethical systems and what to him appeared to be an increasingly inhumane market culture. Moral Sense philosophers and their American admirers emphasized benevolence, compassion, honor, and the like, which supposedly bound individuals into networks of social solidarity. Yet these sentiments, as Hutcheson's student Adam Smith would later make explicit in 1759, concerned merit and demerit, praise or retribution; they tracked the ledger of social debts. They obliged individuals to the inflexible principles of equity and justice that were embedded in the natural moral law. For Shaftesbury, Hutcheson, and Smith, natural morality left little room for the seemingly irrational dynamics of sacrificial atonement, faith, and pardon. This explains why forgiveness did not enter into their moral vocabulary. They never explained the concept or urged its practice in their moral treatises.[26]

Edwards turned the Moral Sense stress on benevolence—the affective sympathy of one human being with all other humans—against Enlightenment critics of Calvinism by arguing that benevolence necessitated forgiveness and that forgiveness implied the truth of divine redemption, the logic of Christ's sacrificial death and offer of justification by faith. The very doctrines derided by anti-Calvinists provided a more secure basis for benevolence than the so-called natural law. Evangelical belief could, as it turned out, reach beyond provincial or commercial loyalties to offer an expansive and generous moral community. Edwards later would make this a central assertion of his treatise *The Nature of True Virtue*.[27]

Taking benevolence beyond the local corporatism of old New England, Edwards intimated that individuals ought to extend forgiveness not only to their immediate neighbors and fellow church members but also, ultimately, to every human being. In the dynamic conclusion to his sermon on Matthew 5, he maintained that all people, Christian or not, shared the same human nature, the same moral corruption, the same potential for conversion, and the same fitness for benevolence, which is to say for being forgiven.

> We ought to pity and love our Enemies as companions in injury . . . [and] notwith-
> standing their injuries to us love them as our fellow Creature and partaker with us of the
> same human nature. . . . We ought to have a universal benevolence to mankind . . . [and
> so] when we see them unjustly hurting us, and injuring and abusing us, we are to con-
> sider that there is just the same corruption of nature in our hearts, the same spirit of evil,
> of malice, which we see in them. . . . We [especially] ought not to hate them, for we don't
> know but that God has a design of mercy towards them. We ought not to hate them, for
> we don't know but that God has from all Eternity put his love upon them [and that]
> Christ shed his precious blood for them and bestowed his own Image upon them. . . .
> We don't know but that they are to be our Companions in Glory.

This is a particularly charged passage (the repeated "we ought not to hate . . . for we don't know," resolved into surprise and recognition), and it indicates the direction towards which Edwards was moving: love and hate, universal benevolence, invisible brotherhood.[28]

This conceptual shift had remarkable implications for Edwards's recommendations on how New Englanders ought to practice forgiveness. It both informed and was prompted by Edwards's confrontation with what in eighteenth-century New England was the most dangerous form of the other, French-allied, often Catholic, Indians. In 1740 he preached on a notable occasion associated with this issue. It was the visit of his cousin Eunice Williams to her family in Longmeadow, Massachusetts. Eunice had been captured by a Mohawk tribe thirty-six years earlier, in an infamous raid on the town of Deerfield. Raised among her captors, she spoke no English. She had a Mohawk husband and children. She already was a celebrity of sorts, the subject of a best-selling account by her father and of frequent speculation about her conversion to Catholicism. Her much-awaited return and her refusal to resettle in Massachusetts caused anguish, even shock.[29]

Edwards was among the first to see her, at family gatherings during two of her three visits to Longmeadow, where her brother Stephen Williams was pastor. Soon after one meeting, Edwards preached a series of three sermons. His subject was "keeping God's commands . . . under trials." The word *trial,* as he used it, had two meanings: trial as a pain to be endured and trial as a test of one's guilt or innocence. Much of the sermon addressed the temptations to betray God under physical pressure. Here he issued an appeal to his cousin Eunice: she ought to convert to Protestantism despite the possibility of persecution by her tribe in Canada. Yet, most strikingly, Edwards spent the last sermon addressing New Englanders who did not suffer Indian captivity, the family members and neighbors of Eunice Williams. They too, Edwards averred, were under trial as to whether they would keep God's commands. In their case, the command at issue was "Christ has forbidden us to revenge ourselves for injuries."

Edwards included admonitions for neighbor to forgive offending neighbor, but his words hardly could have been heard apart from common sentiments to avenge Mohawk atrocities like the capture and conversion to Catholicism of Eunice Williams and her alienation from her English family. If "you have a fair opportunity in your hands to avenge yourself," to "humble" your enemy "upon his unworthy treatment of you," and "to forego the opportunity seems very difficult to you, and you think if you do so it will be the way to encourage him in his injuriousness," then "let the consideration of what you have heard" of Christ's command stay your hand. "Your safest way and the surest way to defence and vindication and prosperity and honor is" to "consider what God says: 'Vengeance is mine; I will repay it.'" Furthermore, "if you take vengeance into your own hands, God will leave it with you to manage it for yourself as you can, and may probably unexpectedly strengthen your adversary against you, and turn on his side."[30]

If Edwards's listeners heard him in the way I have suggested, then they must have been astonished. He claimed that God might turn out to be a patron of Eunice Williams's captors. Warfare between English settlers and their Indian enemies was, as it turned out, not merely a stage for God to enact his control over nations. It also was a stage for believers to display benevolent affections, even forgiveness, beyond their communities in extraordinary measure.

Later in his career, when he had been ousted from Northampton (in part because of the opposition of the Williams family), Edwards became a pastor to a mixed Indian and white congregation in the village of Stockbridge. During the last of the colonial wars, the so-called French and Indian War, refugees from frontier outposts crowded into Stockbridge. One Sunday morning in 1754, during worship, Indians attacked and killed three English residents of the village. Yet Edwards continued to insist on the possibility of forgiveness. He included here not only Housatonics, who had not gone to war against the English, but also Mohawks who had settled in the area. Edwards brought many of them into Communion. He increasingly ruminated on the religious sensibilities and natural moral virtues of Indians, and he held out the prospect, even during the French and Indian War, of a divine peace that would override human conflict and unite those "weary of contention" into a human community of "friends."[31]

Preaching to his Indian parishioners, Edwards pointedly offered an idea of forgiveness that transcended tribal and national identities. "There is forgiveness offered to all nations," he claimed, because it was Christ's "design of making other nations his People." Similar language suffused one of Edwards's baptismal sermons: "'tis the will of Christ that all nations shall be taught," towards which end Christ offered pardon to "all alike." By including Housatonics and Mohawks in his scope of forgiveness, Edwards urged them, as he had urged his townspeople, to embrace the mandate to forgive as an affection that linked them to other tribes and to English settlers. As a baptismal vow, his Indian converts were to "profess universal forgiveness and good will to mankind."[32]

Concluding Thoughts

Edwards's preaching to the Stockbridge Indians delimits, perhaps, the most creative implication of his reconsideration of forgiveness. He made other applications of the evangelical paradigm as well, urging a transatlantic union of love and understanding among believers, exhorting the awakened to spread benevolence and mercy in their mixed societies, and informing New England that the true nature of Christian existence was conformity to heaven, where saints from every conceivable tribe experienced perfect peace and union without punishment, payment, or revenge.[33] In all of this he demonstrated the expansive possibilities of an evangelical discourse of affections. He engaged current intellectual and social trends, transforming the practice of forgiveness, in conversation with Enlightenment critics and in the context of an increasingly fractious and conflict-ridden public order. He realized that New Englanders no longer operated in close-knit communities defined by kinship obligations and parochial filiopieties.

This is not, however, the whole story. Edwards never resolved his ambivalence about Puritan and evangelical practices of forgiveness. He recognized and even rued the loss of social specificity and local discipline over moral practices. A transitional figure between Puritan and evangelical America, he remained enough of a Puritan to retain customary loyalties, to the New England town and tribe, the gathered church, and Anglo-American Protestantism as a national as well as spiritual construct. He never imagined that the political implications of forgiveness might include anything less than complete support for the British Empire and its war against Catholicism, France, and her Indian allies.[34]

In the swirl of eighteenth-century social and cultural change, evangelicals like Edwards made innovations on practices such as forgiveness; but they did so bit by bit, slowly, ambivalently. To refer to Bourdieu's trope once again, Edwards operated in the "field of practices," where regulation (Puritan discipline in the local community) and improvisation (the creation of new forms of forgiveness centered on interiority and cosmopolitan sensibilities) coexisted. Poised in between, Edwards's efforts mark the emergence of an evangelical style of practice but not the stable fixture of that style.

Current writing about forgiveness contains similar ambiguities. Several commentators encourage recovery of a traditional practice of forgiveness, rooted in the Christian church and fostered through communal discipline. Other writers insist that such a recovery depends on individuals' appropriation of theological concepts of redemption and divine forgiveness. Several social theorists debate the relationship between interior disposition and external deed. Yet another set of analysts question the usefulness of grounding a social virtue like forgiveness on any specific religious world view. Other moralists debate the relative virtues of forgiveness, repentance, justice, and moral responsibility. However much it is urged by such writers, especially in a world of ethnic conflict and retributive wars, forgiveness resists static formulation. Such moral deliberation and ambivalence have a long history.[35]

PART II

MISSION, NATION, AND CHRISTIAN PRACTICE, 1820–1940

CHAPTER THREE

Assembling Bodies and Souls

Missionary Practices on the Pacific Frontier

LAURIE F. MAFFLY-KIPP

In the 1850s, George Q. Cannon, a future apostle in the Church of Jesus Christ of Latter-day Saints (LDS), journeyed as a missionary to the Sandwich Islands (now Hawaii). Braced for a hostile reception from the natives, Cannon was dismayed to find that other Christian missionaries proved to be his most stubborn opponents: "Everything was done to have them [the residents] shun us," he wrote, "to inspire them with suspicion, to make us unpopular. These influences, with those vicious and destructive practices which are fast hurrying the nation to extinction, were against us." Beyond simple frustration, his words suggest a complex tangle of social dynamics: hostility between other Christians and the newly arrived Mormons; the use of local peoples as pawns in a larger colonial battle; and, perhaps most significantly, a keen awareness of the political significance of local religious practice. Cannon objected not to native ways but to the Euro-American Catholic and Protestant "practices" he saw as damaging to both indigenous and American cultures. "The Sandwich Islander is being destroyed and blotted from the face of the earth," he continued, "by too much of what is called in Babylon, civilization."[1]

Some of this may not seem surprising. The history of Christian missions has always been animated by the dissonance between religious precepts and local practices and with the effort to adapt European (and later Euro-American) Christian ideals to different cultural realities. What is unusual here is the fact that Mormons did not equate Euro-American practices and politics with Christian faith. In a curious reversal that would have shocked many Protestant and Catholic evangelists, Cannon equated "civilizing" not with Christianizing but with a descent into moral corruption. From the first days of LDS missionary outreach in the 1830s, Mormon evangelists identified themselves as Christian but not quite American. They took pride in the notion that they were a "peculiar" people, at odds with many of the dominant and taken-for-granted practices of evangelical Protestants. What features of their mission fueled this peculiarity? How can we begin to understand the practical differences that distinguished Mormon missionaries from their Protestant counterparts? One major difference was political: the conflicts that had occurred between Mormons and the United States government kept the Sandwich Islanders from automatically associating the Mormons' proselytizing activities with imperial power. But many more material calculations—economic, ecclesiastical, and theological—distinguished Mormon strategies of evangelization from Protestant tactics.

Exploration of Cannon's experience, and the experiences of early American Christian missionaries more generally, prompts new ways of thinking about the relationship between Christian beliefs and American cultural norms, religious piety and national practice, as they were forged in this period of early American imperial expansion. Disentangling this complex web of activities may help us better understand how two Christian traditions—Mormonism and evangelical Protestantism—could be at once so similar and yet so utterly different. Springing from similar backgrounds and sharing a common set of cultural practices (including an emphasis on the practice of evangelism), practitioners of these two traditions nonetheless engaged in missionary practices that were—at least in their initial phases—radically divergent. Many dimensions of this new religious dynamic emerged in the first heyday of missionary work on the Pacific, between 1820 and 1870. What did "civilizing" mean, for Latter-day Saints, for Protestants, and for Pacific peoples? And how did these cultural encounters, and the new ways of acting and believing that emerged from them, reshape Christian practices in this era?

Scholarly study of Christian missions has focused on the theoretical and ideological bases for evangelization, that is, the work of communicating and transplanting beliefs. Evangelism, looked at in this way, would seem to present a fairly straightforward (if still difficult) task. The term itself, drawn from the word Greek word *evangel,* or "good news," refers to the messenger of the Christian Gospel, the bearer of God's word. The practice of *evangelizing,* then, means to bring news of the gospel. Most nineteenth-century American missionaries, Protestant and Mormon alike, would have agreed with the common sense wisdom of Louisa Pratt, a Mormon in Tahiti in the 1840s, who characterized her work as that of "teaching children of nature whose minds were dark, to know and love truth."[2] Missionaries communicated beliefs to those who had not yet heard the gospel message.

But, accepting Pratt's self-description at face value causes us to miss the many small tasks and everyday routines that composed the work of evangelization. Missionary labor was nothing if not faith put into action, a series of encounters and activities in which the received wisdom of theology and doctrine was constantly tested and modified by the necessity of the moment. Lucy Thurston, wife of one of the first Protestant clergy in the Sandwich Islands in the 1820s, remarked that missionary life elicited from her a new kind of improvisatory sensibility: "We had entered a pathway that made it wisdom to take things as they came,—and to take them by the smooth handle."[3] Examining the logic of those everyday practices, in turn, however fragmentary and provisional they seem, introduces us to what Michel de Certeau refers to as the "practice of everyday life," the minute-by-minute calculations that human beings make as they are faced with constantly changing circumstances. It is the underlying logic of such "tactics," rather than the claims of truth made by participants (or contemporary historians), that reveals the repertory of possibilities for behavior within a given situation.[4]

In a missionary context, one of the most important everyday practices was the identification of activities and behaviors as "Christian" and "non-Christian" (most often called "heathen" or "disgusting" by the missionaries). Just as George Cannon limned the distinction between true civility and "destructive" behavior, American missionaries were constantly on the alert for outward signs of irreligious conduct, both among themselves and among their potential converts. Living on the geographical margins of American culture forced continual confrontations with the behavioral boundaries of Christianity itself: What is Christian practice? Which elements are essential to it and which dispensable? What is worth fighting over and what not? Here we can see in stark terms the logic of the calculations made, rather than simply the content of the choices themselves, granting us a perspective on religious experience that is related to—but separable from—the vantage offered by an examination of Christian or native beliefs in isolation.[5] In turn, a better comprehension of the logic of Christian practice in the past may enable a clearer appreciation of how such negotiation takes place in the present.

Another area of negotiation—the wrestling with Christianity and cultural difference—is particularly salient here. The multivalent encounter of natives, Mormons, and Protestants in the Pacific further complicates this story and illuminates the linkages to American nationalism that formed an integral part of Protestant self-awareness. It is easy to forget that the American missions movement—both Protestant and Mormon—was intimately bound up with the early development of the United States as a political entity. Just as these Christian missionaries were learning to distinguish themselves from other peoples in the field, they were simultaneously learning, and practicing, what it meant to be a citizen of a sovereign and powerful nation. How those two identities—religious and national—were intricately linked is a major theme of this story. Protestant evangelicals firmly believed that Christianity in the United States represented the acme of religious history and that true progress necessitated spreading their religious beliefs and practices to as many people as possible.[6] For evangelicals, appropriate Christian practice included more than the right kinds of church organization or baptismal rites; it also comprised the assumption that God had ordained the U.S. government as the appropriate political vehicle for Christian societies. Many Protestant leaders, therefore, saw no conflict of interest in combining their spiritual and political activities, since both furthered the cause of Christ on Earth. For example, a number of missionaries from the American Board of Commissioners for Foreign Missions (ABCFM), an organization founded in 1810 and composed primarily of Congregational and Presbyterian clergy, left their clerical callings to work as federal agents in the Sandwich Islands, and being in such local settings emboldened many more to "represent" U.S. interests, either formally or informally.

In this context, then, it is especially revealing to look at how Christians who were less or differently committed to the American experiment separated the gospel mission from the patriotic one. As Ann Stoler has noted, *colonialism* is a term that is often used quite carelessly; it tends to frame all cultural interactions in terms of their relation to state power, but it obscures the fact that denominational enterprises (not to mention non-Protestant traditions) sometimes quite consciously distinguished themselves from national entities. If this was true occasionally of American Protestants, it was even truer of Mormons, who in the mid-nineteenth century saw themselves as the victims of United States imperialism. For Latter-day Saints, the truth of the gospel message was often inimical to American beliefs and behaviors. Their "religious grammar," comprising both attitudes and practices, had diverged dramatically from that of their Protestant colleagues.[7] Comparing Protestant and Mormon missionary practices, then, highlights the ways their different relationships to American political identity affected their encounters with native peoples.

Christian Sorties into the Pacific

By the time George Cannon began his mission, Protestant efforts in the Pacific had been underway for nearly six decades. Following swiftly on the success of the first British explorations of the area, the London Missionary Society (LMS) in 1797 dispatched three delegations to the South Seas, with thirty emissaries designated for the island of Tahiti alone. In 1814, the evangelical organization established a second mission, in New Zealand. The following year King Pomare II reconquered Tahiti. When he declared Christianity the national religion, the floodgates to missionary and mercantile enthusiasm opened wide. Americans, encouraged by news of the receptiveness of islanders to evangelical teachings and eager to begin their own efforts, geared up for a Pacific mission. Under a tacit agreement with their London counterparts, American Protestants concentrated their efforts north of the equator while the LMS remained in the islands to the south. Roman Catholics began to arrive in the region only after 1841, when the French asserted control in the Society Islands. Before that time, Pacific Christianity remained decidedly Protestant.[8]

In the fall of 1819, seven young couples and four American-educated native Hawaiians departed the United States for the Sandwich Islands under ABCFM auspices. In doing so, they launched a missionary effort that lasted until 1853, when the islands were declared officially "Christianized." In the intervening years, twelve different missionary parties left New England for the Pacific Basin, where they planted evangelistic outposts, schools, and small communities of Euro-Americans on all of the islands. One of their number, Henry Cheever, reported in 1856 that between 1820 and 1844 the ABCFM had commissioned sixty-one male and sixty-seven female missionaries who had organized twenty-five independent native churches, which had received 31,409 members. In addition, the Protestants had established 403 public schools and printed a total of 22,061,750 pages of translated scripture and other texts on their local printing presses.[9]

Mormon missionaries arrived relatively late in this era of religious migration, and they entered immediately into arenas of religious and civil conflict. Between 1843, when the first three elders departed for the Society Islands, and the 1890s, when the Church of Jesus Christ of Latter-day Saints experienced tremendous success among the Maori of New Zealand, LDS missionaries visited every major Polynesian island group. These fields were part of a larger sphere of Pacific enterprise for the nineteenth-century church that included California, the west coast of South America, Samoa, Tonga, New Zealand, and Australia. By 1852, when local political events abruptly ended the missionary venture in the Society Islands, the Mormons had baptized several thousand natives scattered over dozens of islands, and claimed a larger membership than did the LDS Church in Scotland, one of its more successful European fields. By 1889, the Honolulu branch of the church probably was larger than any other outside of Utah, with 891 members. By 1913, nearly a quarter of the native Hawaiian population claimed membership in the LDS. In New Zealand, by the 1890s, nearly 10 percent of the Maori population professed the faith.[10]

All of these American missionaries, Protestant and Mormon, would have used much the same language to describe the "good news" of Christian salvation that they were bearing to Pacific peoples. Yet their enterprises were vastly different in practice. It is in a closer examination of evangelistic design that we begin to see the dissimilar logic behind these Christian missionary practices and the correspondingly disparate decisions made about daily interactions with indigenous cultures.

Protestant Practices of Evangelization

Protestant missionary training, such as it was in the early nineteenth century, began with formal education. The majority of male ABCFM missionaries were recent products of theological programs such as Andover Seminary, where they received grounding in history, philosophy, biblical languages, and doctrine. Women studied at Mount Holyoke or other seminaries that inculcated a classical education befitting a missionary wife. Aspiring evangelists learned little about strategies of proselytization in school, although by the 1840s students could glean something about life in the islands from the published journals of former missionaries and explorers. Young, newly ordained, and often newly married to a woman who also longed to serve God in a foreign field, these Protestants had enthusiasm and energy, but they generally knew very little about the societies they would enter. To these children of settled, predominantly middle-class families from the Atlantic seaboard, the Pacific loomed as an ideal conjunction of spiritual challenge, adventure, and economic opportunity.[11]

One certainty they carried with them was an assured knowledge of the correlation between Christian belief and "civilized" behavior. American Protestant missionaries were reared in a world in which, ideally at least, a prior and interior disposition of faith animated one to act in certain ways. While a good evangelical would never have argued that Christian behavior was a sure indication of one's salvation, it was certainly the case that a heart changed by a conversion experience would lead an individual to love godly conduct. A truer test of faith came through the narration of the salvific experience and an articulated conviction of God's salvation. Still, outward signs served as markers of the many distinctions that informed the lives of antebellum evangelicals: civilized, Christian people generally dressed, spoke, and acted in a particular fashion that "uncivilized," non-Christians did not follow. Through newspaper articles and periodical literature circulated by tract societies, evangelicals learned a repertoire of aesthetic and moral terms with which to describe the behavior of the uncivilized: *ugly, polluted, barbaric, despicable.*

These evangelical judgments were bolstered by the air of inevitability that animated their understanding of Pacific native lifestyles. Native cultures trod an inexorable road to extinction, according to reigning Euro-Protestant understandings of ethnology and cultural evolution. Thus, they were, even if reformable, still part of a dying way of life, a demise that missionary outreach was intent on abetting. Christopher Herbert has argued persuasively that missionary intimacy with Pacific peoples was inherently "treacherous," in that the desire to bestow the gift of Christian conversion was "inseparably linked to a broad and deliberate effort to dismantle" local cultures.[12] Alongside a belief that all souls could receive grace through conversion, missionaries expressed a millennial certainty that these peoples, as a whole, would not inherit the earth. Evangelicals varied considerably, of course, in the zeal with which they forecast this cultural genocide in the service of spiritual regeneration, but it is striking how many, like Henry Cheever, stated the principle quite baldly: "Be it that many of them as individuals may be converted and saved, they cannot survive much longer as nations. The decree has gone out against them—prophecy must be fulfilled."[13] More than simply a hard fact to be accepted, this was, for Cheever, a cause for celebration. "Through their acceptance of the [Gospel], although they now become extinct, the prophecy will be made good, that *in him (Christ) shall all nations of the earth be blessed.* . . . With thanks and everlasting joy the ransomed Hawaiian, the Indian, the Hottentot, the South Sea Islander . . . shall come up to the general assembly and church of the first-born."[14] Ultimately, native habits and practices would not endure; they would give way to the civilized culture of Christianity.

Yet, these "vanishing" cultures could not help but attract the immediate attention of newly arrived evangelicals. Among the first things missionary diarists and correspondents noted were the activities that set apart Christians from native peoples. Lucy Thurston, embarking from Boston in October 1819 to begin life in the Sandwich Islands, illustrated the distinctive blending of categories by which she would judge Hawaiians: "We cut loose from our native land for *life,* to find a dwelling place, far, far away from civilized man, among barbarians, there to cope with a cruel priesthood of blood-loving deities, and to place ourselves under the iron law of *kapus* requiring men and women to eat separately."[15] Anxious to substitute her own gender-based categories for the "barbaric" practices of the natives, Lucy's sentiments suggest that correct behavior, piety, and gender relations were intimately linked. She equated civility with a particular form of Christianity (non-priestly, non-blood-loving, and non-polytheistic) and a distinctive style of interaction between men and women. As luck would have it, the law of *kapus* was lifted just months before Thurston's arrival, leaving Protestants free to substitute their own gender-based customs. Another missionary, Mary Alexander, invoking aesthetic discernment as a moral category, lamented the discrepancy between the physical beauty of the landscape and the spiritual ugliness of its inhabitants: "As we gazed at the island in the evening light, it baffled comprehension, that beings so vile should be placed in scenes so beautiful."[16]

Like their British Protestant colleagues to the south, early ABCFM missionaries aimed to instill both civilization and Christianity among native peoples, but on the ground, civil behavior and comportment frequently took precedent over the subtler work of soul saving. This prioritization led to an overwhelming concern for—one might even say an obsession with—proper practice. Protestants were fascinated by indigenous ways and described them in detail. In volumes that would serve as precursors to modern ethnographic method, missionary diaries typically began with a chapter or two detailing traditional myths and legends, relating stories of human sacrifice (more common in the South Sea Islands), and depicting priestly rites.[17] Henry Cheever included in his reminiscences intricate drawings of "old Hawaiian idols," giving his readers an even more vivid "glimpse of the besotted idolatry which the aborigines of this Island Kingdom of Hawaii were then addicted to, and of the moral state of Hawaii as it was."[18] William Ellis, a British missionary whose four volume *Polynesian Researches* (1830) portrayed in exquisite detail the "peculiar character and engaging habits" of South Sea Islanders and whose work was read and quoted by missionaries, explorers, and novelists for decades thereafter, justified his labor as a chronicle of the work of missionaries "under the Divine blessing," who had "transformed the barbarous, cruel, indolent, and idolatrous inhabitants," rendering his subjects "comparatively civilized, humane, industrious, and Christian people."[19]

Why go on in such detail about these "despicable habits"? Presumably, the goal was to illustrate the distance the indigenous people had traveled toward civilization and Christian behavior. But the description and exemplification in these works, like the domestically produced captivity narratives and dime novels that they resembled, became a customary evangelical activity that served several important cultural purposes. First, it gave voice to the Euro-Protestant (sometimes prurient, particularly when it helped to raise money) fascination with the "uncivilized," and it reflected an abiding desire to police the boundaries between appropriate and inappropriate conduct. Perhaps more important, the emphasis on native habits and practices in these volumes divulges a fundamental truth of the missionary experience: Despite the ambition to inculcate right *belief,* deeds—and the passage from one set of *practices* to another— were often the only markers available for missionaries to gauge conversion. In fact, missionaries spent far less time worrying about beliefs than they did regulating conduct. A. W. Murray of the London Missionary Society expressed the dilemma well:

> The first thing that claims the attention of a missionary to a people of a strange tongue on reaching his field of labor is the language. . . . He and they dwell, as it were, apart; though living, it may be, in close proximity, they are really strangers to each other. . . . We could not speak a language which the natives could understand, but we could act one which they were not slow to comprehend. The language of deeds is intelligible even to pagans.[20]

Evangelization, then, entailed the inculcation of a new grammar of activity, since actions were easier to regulate and measure than were the internalization of abstract ideals.

Ideally, native converts would cross the threshold to civility and Christian living with the help of God's grace, and would rapidly begin to act accordingly. A few natives seemed to live up to this standard. Exemplary in this regard was Bartimeus, a blind native who had become a model Christian. Henry Cheever depicted the convert as someone who initially could hardly have been a more profligate sinner, displaying all of the characteristics of the uncivilized: he was rescued after having been buried alive by his mother (thus he did not have a loving maternal influence); he had "filthy" habits; he hardly wore any clothing (in traditional Hawaiian style); he was addicted to *awa*, the traditional narcotic drink of the islands; and he danced the "licentious" hula. "He was fast wearing himself out in the service of Satan," Cheever remarked. After his conversion, however, Bartimeus's conduct changed dramatically. The first sign of progress was that he refused to dance the hula when asked by the local chiefs; soon thereafter, he set out to memorize the Bible (since he could not read), and eventually became a preacher, able to produce a scriptural passage from memory for almost any occasion.[21] How Bartimeus might have described his faith was considerably less important to the missionaries, if only because it was less easily comprehended than was the evidence of his changed behavior.

Or so the missionaries thought. Apparently they trusted the evidence of their eyes more than their fledgling translating abilities, or perhaps they assumed that appropriate behavior would eventually stimulate right belief. Still, native appearances could also deceive. At the very least, exchanges over religious practice revealed the difficulty of interpreting even the simplest gestures. The classic example of gift giving illustrates this point. In an important sense, evangelistic practice entailed the sharing of gifts. Missionaries brought gifts that they hoped would aid in civilizing their native charges and would eventually usher them into the broader Christian community, which, as Protestants saw it, was a precious gift in and of itself. Chief among their offerings was Euro-American clothing, the wearing of which could both bestow civility (through the covering up of body parts, which demonstrated Christian modesty and appropriate sexual practice) and mark the wearer as a member of the fellowship. When native communicants were clad in bonnets, boots, and long dresses—a custom that seems absurd to modern eyes—they practiced Christian virtue and indicated their new social status. In the eyes of the missionaries, this eagerness to don heavy muslin garb substantiated the native desire for the many blessings of the Christian life. Gifts, in other words, brought whole worlds of meaning along with them.[22]

Evidence suggests that natives thought of gift giving as a reciprocal process, an exchange that should be of mutual benefit to both parties, and which needed to respect the integrity of each side. Sometimes, then, Protestant gifts—even heavy muslin gowns—seemed like a beneficial trade. Euro-American goods were bartered avidly in

Pacific island communities, and their use often figured into indigenous displays of status that neatly conjoined the interests of missionaries and natives. Such was the case when, shortly after the Thurstons arrived in Hawaii in 1820, the royal family made it clear that they loved the new clothing the missionaries were willing to provide. When the king held a feast to commemorate his late father, Kamamalu, one of his wives asked Lucy Thurston if she might borrow one of her dresses to wear for the occasion. Lucy took this query as a sign of success, as an acknowledgment of a common understanding of what appropriate dress signified, yet it is quite likely that this successful exchange was merely a happy coincidence of interests, an act that simultaneously conferred status in the eyes of local subjects and met Euro-American requirements for proper feminine modesty. Similarly, some natives expressed great desire to possess the Bible and other American books, probably because they saw them as a desirable symbol of a novel technology, which thus conferred on the owner a local eminence.[23] Hawaiian leaders, praised by ABCFM promoters as among the first to convert to the Protestant cause, saw missionary customs as fashionable ways to distinguish themselves from their subjects. When Asa Thurston requested that the king allow some of the natives to attend religious instruction, the king ordered that "none should be taught to read but those of rank, those to whom he gave special permission." As Lucy recalled, "To do *his* part to distinguish and make them respectable scholars, he dressed them in a civilized manner."[24]

The conferral of gifts as a means of evangelization did not always end so cheerfully, particularly if natives believed that the missionaries had not lived up to their promises. Did island leaders recognize that Protestants understood their own donations of clothing and service as far superior to anything the natives could offer in return? It is difficult to say, but it is clear that locals often insisted on receiving their due. When William Alexander first arrived in the Marquesas, he was delighted by the greeting extended to him by Hape, the local chief. But as the visit continued over a period of weeks, Hape grew angry that the missionaries had not cured him of his sickness and brought him presents. He acceded to their wishes for a time, but soon his patience ran out and he ordered the missionaries to depart. Hape apparently did not conceive of the exchange as an open-ended invitation for the Protestant minister to transform local practice; it only made sense to him if it were mutual and if it kept intact the social and religious values of his own society.[25]

In the long term, of course, conversion was not a gift at all, at least not in the sense of a mutual exchange. It required forsaking all remnants of what the missionaries took to be native "religious practice," including participation in healing ceremonies, the ritual use of *awa*, expressed loyalty to indigenous practitioners, and the worship of local deities. It also entailed forsaking a host of customs that evangelicals associated with uncivilized behavior: dressing immodestly, polygamy, extramarital sexual activity,

and traditional dances (regarded as leading to—or celebrating—promiscuity). In return, converts would be educated in the habits of reading, praying, and church attendance, as well as the more abstract virtues of industry, frugality, and modesty. In most
cases, missionaries had to settle for whatever bits of compliance they could get; the
practical divide between native Christians and non-Christians remained frighten-
ingly narrow and hard to decipher. Civilized practice was *not* a sure guide to inner
transformation, and motivation was often impossible to pinpoint. Henry Cheever
wondered about a group of natives who "now clothe their nakedness quite decently . . . wherever foreigners are. . . . But the truth is, when found out, they too often manifest little or no shame. The blush of virtue, the genuine feeling so well described in the old Roman word *pudor* . . . you seldom see."[26] Even something as
seemingly straightforward as church attendance consisted of hundreds of smaller gestures and actions that did not always conform to the missionaries' expectations. Mary
Alexander described a service she attended in the Marquesas in 1833, where her husband preached to a very large audience.

> The big bread-fruit tree that had been used as a cook-house was now used as a church.
> The ladies sat under its shade on chairs, while the natives rushed around in noisy con-
> fusion. The preaching was no easy task. The natives would smoke and talk and mimic.
> Some would lie and sleep, some laugh and talk, some mock and excite laughter; here one
> would sit smoking a pipe, there one twisting a rope; often there was such confusion that
> the preacher could scarcely hear himself speak. Not unfrequently the half of those pres-
> ent would arise and go off laughing and mocking. They were ready to gnash on us with
> their teeth when we told them their gods were false.[27]

The stark truth here became apparent: Although the missionary objective was the inner transformation of the native soul, outward conduct was the only regulable feature
of local cultures. But even monitored behavior, closely watched, revealed an abun-
dance of subtler activities that complicated, contradicted, or even defied the civilizing process. Civilization, as a practice, could slide through one's fingers like the sand
under one's feet.

Protestant Tactics of Cultural Separation

While missionaries tried to change the habits of natives, they found that life in the
islands changed their own practices. It is easy to miss the extent to which Protestants
had to modify and transform themselves in order to evangelize abroad, particularly
because missionaries themselves either denied or were not conscious of the many al-
terations their work necessitated.

These tacit transformations are demonstrated most clearly by the lengths to which missionaries went to place themselves *above* local cultures. Protestant *clergy*, of course, saw themselves as set apart by their calling to the ministry, a distinction that was easily conflated with a cultural and racial separation from local peoples. They took their cue from their British counterparts, who had years of experience dealing with native peoples in the Pacific and elsewhere in the British Empire. By the time the ABCFM arrived on the Pacific scene, evangelical missionaries of the LMS had moved beyond their more charismatic, first-generation roots and were quickly establishing themselves economically and educationally within island societies. The second-generation clergy often exacted a tax from local peoples to pay for their missionary expenses. Generally they were well-educated men who saw their sacred calling as something that set them apart from the objects of their labor. For both social and ideological reasons, they favored the separation of the cultures. Socially, British missionaries in particular tended to style themselves as "English gentlemen," given their years of theological schooling. They lived apart, engaged their missionary pupils as servants, and maintained a lifestyle marked by as much British-derived refinement as they could manage. Ideologically, they favored limiting their encounters with natives to discrete moments of preaching and teaching, because it reinforced what they saw as the appropriate line of demarcation between the sacred and the mundane elements of life. At least one missionary made a policy of never letting natives enter his house because of his fear of their corrosive influence upon his children. In turn, missionaries policed this psychic and physical distancing amongst themselves, frowning upon compatriots who took native wives or who mingled too freely with local people. Such cultural mixing was seen as a betrayal of the imperial cause. It may also have been an indication of the anxiety surrounding the prospect of deep cultural engagement.[28]

American missionaries, although removed from the aristocratic patterns of imperial British culture, adopted similar tactics of separation. They believed that the necessity for this distancing was obvious to local people, as Henry Cheever explained: "Hawaiians know the wants of foreigners are more than theirs, are glad to have it so, and would be unwilling that their teachers should live like themselves."[29] That missionaries often held positions as quasi-governmental officials only enhanced this distance. In many Pacific islands, as Anna Johnston has noted, evangelists served as the founding Euro-American settlers, who brought with them the first symbols and institutions of colonial administration and economic power.[30] For political and religious reasons, then, missionary life came to exhibit a distinctive mixture of communal love and discrete cultural partitioning, as Euro-Americans struggled to find a comfortable and safe stance to take with respect to natives.

Fear of intimacy with natives was a constant undercurrent of evangelical reportage. Missionary women in particular, whose lives were the most circumscribed geographically and who worked in constant physical proximity to local people, commented on the overwhelming sensation of being surrounded and examined by the intrusive gaze of native onlookers. Their Euro-American customs begat considerable native curiosity. Lucy Thurston remarked that after their arrival, throngs of natives peered in her windows and doors at all hours, anxious to look at her and see how she lived.[31] The Presbyterian Mary Alexander, describing a year-long sojourn from Hawaii to the Marquesas in the 1830s, conveyed the impression that the natives were not only watching but were waiting to violate her home: "At first our doors and windows were crowded almost to suffocation by the savages gazing at us. Our cooking was done outside. . . . Sometimes the natives would take the food out of the kettles by hooks, and carry it away."[32] The violence and eroticism of her vivid descriptions makes it clear that Alexander felt keenly these native practices as fundamental personal intrusions.

> They would often thrust bamboo sticks, with hooks, through our lattice windows, to take whatever they could reach. We often awoke at night to find them with their poles thrust through the windows, taking clothing or anything they could get, or pulling up the thatch to take whatever they could reach, sometimes not one only, but a gang of thieves stealing at the same time from different parts of the house. . . . I dared not look at them, for I was sure to see a look that would fill me with disgust and horror.[33]

Few missionaries expressed their fears of violation as graphically as Mary Alexander. But native curiosity led to increasing missionary anxiety, and most evangelicals soon felt the need for regulation of their necessarily intimate relations with local peoples.[34] Protestant practices of proscription, in turn, took many forms, including psychic, instrumental, and spatial attempts to separate various elements of their lives from those of natives. Euro-American clothing, food, music, and material objects were imbued with sacred significance simply by virtue of marking the fraught but essential boundary between civilization and barbarism. Divine power, for missionaries, lay in the ability to control and demarcate closeness to native cultural practices and, by extension, to natives themselves. Even pastoral duties were circumscribed by a fear of crosscultural intimacy. Many clergy tried not to meet with natives outside of teaching, preaching, and catechesis, and within the worship service itself certain social distinctions took root as a way of appropriately delimiting power within the church community. William Alexander described the first meeting he attended after his arrival in Honolulu in 1832. Over four thousand people were present to hear Hiram Bingham preach under an enormous, open-air thatched roof. Alexander noted with interest that teachers and chiefs sat on benches while everyone else sat on the floor.[35]

Patterns of labor presented another opportunity to reinforce distinctions of rank. Euro-Americans employed natives as domestic laborers to manage the practical needs of their families. Henry Cheever described the situation of the Reverend Mr. Green on Maui: "He told them before he went that they must raise wheat for his breadstuff, and immediately they began . . . and have succeeded in furnishing the best bread eaten at these Islands. He tells his *lunas,* persons appointed for this purpose, when he wants anything, and forthwith they do all the *paipaiing* (stirring up) among the people, and it comes."[36]

Ministers couched this reliance in terms of local hospitality and the exigencies of ministerial support, but it is also clear that missionary families relied heavily on local laborers, resulting in a particular kind of domestic intimacy based on a clearly delineated power relation. Lucy Thurston, who was one of the first Euro-American women to arrive in Hawaii when she landed there in 1820, devoted considerable space in her diary and letters to relatives in the States to discussion of native laborers. In 1835, after fifteen years in the mission field, Lucy commented with satisfaction on the social reversals among her workers. A native family lived in a house in their compound, she related in a letter back to the States, "they give us their services," including bringing food and water and cooking. "He, who under the old dispensation, officiated as priest to one of their gods, now, under a new dispensation with commendable humility, officiates as cook to a priest and his family."[37]

Even the architecture of missionaries' homes and workplaces reflected their desire for demarcation from local cultures. Church structures and schools were separate from the compounds that housed the families of missionaries, and the arrangements of the domestic enclosure articulated an elaborate set of relations. Lucy Thurston described her homestead in Kailua where she raised her four children, emphasizing proudly that it conformed to her image of how such a complex should look: "The large house and yards have distinct accommodations, for household natives, the work of the family, for native company, and schools." The large number of household helpers lived in a thatched hut in the backyard, and the children's enclosure lay deep within the grouped wooden-framed dwellings, accessible only through the parental bedroom: "I . . . am still porter to the only door that leads into the children's special enclosure, and have the satisfied feeling of their being safe, beyond the reach of native influence."[38]

As Lucy Thurston's comments indicate, the welfare of missionary children represented the greatest danger of the lack of appropriate separation of cultures. Lucy initially did not heed the advice of LMS clergy to keep Euro-American children entirely away from natives. She insisted on keeping her children at home with her, and did not send them away to be educated in the States, as did other missionary families. In the beginning, she recalled later, "Native youth resided in our families, and so far as was consistent, we granted them all the privileges of companions and of children." But after several years, "our eyes were opened to the moral pollution which, unchecked, had here been accumulated for ages." Cultural contact, for missionaries, brought with it a new order of potential spiritual harm. "I had it ever in my heart," remarked Lucy, "the shafts of sin flying from every direction are liable to pierce the vitals of my children." For Lucy, the dilemma was stark: "Are missionaries with their eyes open to the dangers of their situation, to sit conscientiously down to the labor of bringing back a revolted race to the service of Jehovah, and in so doing practically give over their own children to Satan?"[39]

In turn, moral disorder had to be counteracted creatively with new practices. Lucy determined that

> the first rule to be attended to with regard to children is that they *must not speak the native language*. It is an easy thing to *make* such a law, but it is a mother's duty to guard it from being violated, and to form in her children *fixed habits* of doing as they are required. It of course, follows, that they are never left to the care of natives after reaching the age of prattling. No intercourse whatever should exist between children and heathen.[40]

In 1841 missionary families founded Punahou School, an academy intended to educate Euro-American children apart from the corrupting influences of the natives.[41] And finally, in what may have been the most ironic step taken in the development of Pacific Protestant missions, Lucy determined to keep her children at home on Sunday mornings and give them private religious instruction, after her teenaged daughter complained about having to attend her father's sermons when she could not understand the language in which he preached.[42] The structure of Pacific Christian communities, and even the most basic patterns of missionary life, were transformed by the overwhelming desire to avoid cultural alteration.

New forms of intimacy and contact in the missionary encounter led to novel practices among Protestant missionaries as they sought to establish a degree of separation from their native charges. Not infrequently, their efforts precipitated the further circumscription of their own lives. If a common stereotype of missions is the sometimes violent regulation of native life, equally striking is the image of missionary children living as virtual prisoners within the compound walls, unable to interact with natives in any way. Lucy Thurston expressed the doubleness of this limitation in her own life: "The ladies were limited to the free use of their own houses and yards. To go beyond domestic premises, like *prisoners* or like *queens,* they must have an escort, and proceed with limited freedom." She took her first walk alone through the local village after having lived there for four and a half years.[43] As a Christian colonizer living among the colonized, Thurston and her female colleagues constructed a world that was physically, psychically, and ultimately religiously separated from its local context; consequently, their own religious practice changed dramatically to fit the contours of their racial and sexual anxieties.[44]

Mormon Practices of Evangelization

A photograph of the Latter-day Saints Laie Chapel in Hawaii, taken at its dedication in 1882, does not look that different from the photographs of Protestant missionary settings of the same time. A large, wooden frame building with a steeple, symmetrically placed windows lining both of its longer sides, and a white picket fence delineating its yard. Out front on the lawn is gathered a large group of the faithful: men with long, white beards, wearing three-piece suits and straw hats, with pocket watches and canes, and women in long-sleeved, ankle-length white dresses and hats. They seem confident and happy, taking pleasure in their success. On the face of it, one might be tempted to conclude that Mormon and Protestant missionaries were doing much the same thing—creating American Christian civility in a tropical setting. Moreover, Mormon missionary rhetoric evidences a similar degree of alienation from the natives. Yet this community differed substantially from its Protestant counterparts in the islands. Their missionaries no doubt considered themselves as much refugees as evangels. Their chapel was situated in a gathering place designed to house the faithful of Zion in their last days on Earth; its borders held out the sins of the world around them, both Christian and native; and they knew themselves to be—indigenous and Euro-American alike—a saving remnant of the House of Israel.[45]

When Joseph Smith sent missionaries to other parts of the globe, his primary intent was to gather them together back in the earthly Zion; there, the chosen people, brought in from all corners of the world, were to build God's kingdom on earth. According to a series of revelations received by Smith in the early 1830s, the lost tribes of Israel were to be gathered together again under the "tent of Zion," and he sent out messengers to do just that. Persecuted by other Americans and forced to flee across the continent, early members of the church embarked on missions with a message of liberation from earthly oppression more literal and material than that offered by Protestants. Young, poor, mostly uneducated, and trained with little more than the tidings of Smith's prophetic witness and a story of a maltreated community, Mormon missionaries arrived in the Pacific to save the souls of the Lamanites, one of the lost tribes of Israel, which they believed had settled in the Pacific Islands after an ancient journey by boat from the Holy Land.

It is difficult to gauge the power of this liberatory message for natives, but clearly, it resonated in a way that distinguished Mormon evangelists from their Protestant colleagues, who were perceived as—and often were—representative of American governmental power. It is likely that the Mormons' story of worldly persecution and principle of the gathering offered Pacific Islanders a prominent place in a community of believers, one that many found desirable. Mormons even told them of a book—the first missionaries had no translated texts—that purported to recount the story of their common ancestors. In 1851, Louisa Pratt reported speaking, at a meeting of women in Tahiti, about the origins of the Book of Mormon. Significantly, one of the natives asked "if the ancient Nephites were Europeans. I told them they were the ancient fathers of the Tahitians. At this they appeared greatly interested, and wished to learn more about the book."[46] Whether it was the congenial practice of storytelling, the materiality of the book, or the personalized message that most attracted the attention of local peoples we will never know, but many did warm to foreign guests who proferred a common founding story. It is likely, too, that Mormon embodiment of imperial persecution lent an immediate kinship to the interaction, since the Saints communicated a legacy of discrimination that surely resonated with natives who were rapidly being overtaken by European and American imperial forces. Parley Parker Pratt described the Mormons, in his first Pacific mission pamphlet, as a people "disfranchised, robbed, plundered, dispersed, slandered in every possible way, and driven to the mountains and deserts of the American interior."[47] One might think such a self-portrait a strange way to attract followers, but it held potential reverberations for almost every indigenous group in the nineteenth-century Pacific.[48]

Yet, necessity as much as ideology compelled Mormon missionaries from the beginning to live differently among the natives than did other missionaries, composing a culture of intimacy rather than distance. The first LDS emissaries to the Sandwich Islands assumed that they were setting off to preach to whites, but after encountering fierce responses they realized their tactics would need to change. George Cannon, the leader of the mission, recalled seeking a revelation from God that would guide them. His answer came in the form of the divine disclosure that local natives were members of the House of Israel and needed to hear of the restoration of the gospel through Joseph Smith.[49] This presented a problem, since surely the LDS leaders did not intend that their missionaries convert Hawaiians and have them all emigrate to Utah? The theological, ecclesiastical, and social dilemmas represented by this shift included the mandate to gather in Zion, the need for access to the temple for sacramental purposes, and deep-seated racial and cultural difference, and they would remain at the center of Mormon practice in the Pacific for the next sixty years.

More immediately, though, LDS missionaries faced utter poverty. As part of a church still in its institutional infancy and more focused on building up Zion in Utah than on consolidating its interests in the Pacific, they had no formalized missionary structures to support them. George Cannon, along with a group of men barely old enough to shave, arrived on Maui without enough money to afford a roof over his head. Not being able to pay for a rooming house, he and his companions rented a "native house," the term for the most primitive of dwellings that had neither a floor nor a solid roof. It was, in other words, a thatched hut much like that occupied by most islanders. The native owner, taking pity upon the group because they were white, managed to secure a table and three chairs, at which they ate the local fare cooked by their landlord.[50] If poverty enforced proximity to native peoples, so too did the challenge of language acquisition. Addison Pratt lived among the natives in the Society Islands as a teacher, but because he was simultaneously trying to learn the local language, he was forced into a role reversal, attending school himself and going to services conducted by natives.[51] For at least the first decade, most LDS missionaries traveled from place to place, rooming with friendly locals, living on native food such as poi and fish, and taking odd jobs.[52] Their lack of resources compelled the Saints to conform to local practices and power dynamics, rather than immediately attempting to change them.

Unlike Protestant ministerial vocations, Mormon ecclesiology did not set apart a priestly class or provide a mandate for religious distinction through prior training or education. All male members of the LDS church, when called by the Prophet, were expected to serve as messengers of the good news. As a lay movement without ministers, the church did not distinguish certain people as particularly qualified for sacred duties; indeed, as soon as a man joined the church he could be asked to carry out important obligations as a member of the priesthood. In the early years, men were summoned to callings with little advance notice. Benjamin Johnson, for example, sent on a mission to the Sandwich Islands in the 1850s, had ten days to prepare himself for departure and make arrangements for his three wives and eight small children at home. The Mormon tradition, frequently modified and renewed by continuing revelation from God through the Prophet, was in itself a work in progress. As natives joined the Pacific Island churches, they were quickly given church offices and dispatched as missionaries themselves to speak to other natives. This practice elevated indigenous leaders within the community in fairly short order. Thus, professionalization did not loom as a separating feature in the relationship between natives and missionaries.[53]

Another encouragement to intimacy with native peoples came in the devotional activities of the faith. Mormon missionaries offered practices that meshed relatively easily with at least some indigenous sacred traditions. While Saints, like Protestants, required the renunciation of *awa* and hula dancing and encouraged the donning of "modest" Euro-American clothing, their sacramental practices were filled with a charismatic spirit that held a distinctive appeal. Protestant labor most often consisted of preaching (proclaiming and interpreting the Bible), teaching language skills (in order to facilitate individual comprehension of the Scriptures), some singing of hymns, and catechesis (a study of lessons and precepts derived from biblical truths). Evangelicalism was, by any measure, a text-based religious movement, albeit one that relied on the most progressive British and American educational techniques.[54] By the mid-nineteenth century, Protestants had translated the gospel widely and circulated copies of the Bible in the vernacular throughout their fields of labor. For many natives the association of Protestant missionaries with European and American culture was a strong asset, particularly among those peoples who looked upon the acquisition of new technologies (literacy being chief among them) proffered by their missionary neighbors as valuable.[55]

Cognizant of the potency of skills they could offer alongside the gospel message, Mormons were anxious to communicate by means of the printed word, a concern attested to by early publishing efforts in Great Britain, Australia, and Hawaii. Missionaries reported handing out tracts wherever they went, and many spent the better part of their days disseminating the few copies of the Book of Mormon or the works of Orson Pratt and his brother, Parley P. Pratt, that were available to them. But lack of resources in the Pacific arena again forced improvisation. In Tahiti, the few books furnished to the missionaries had been distributed to Americans and British on passing ships, leaving none for indigenous communicants. Even in the first years of involvement in Australia, although language was not an issue, the mission was so poorly supplied that the two local copies of the Book of Mormon were read aloud in meetings at the Sydney Branch. As David Whittaker has noted, the real problem was not simply the accessibility of literature but the fact that it was only obtainable in English and thus was quite useless in the native context.[56]

Although the American Saints lamented this state of affairs, the dearth of texts had the effect of encouraging a different quality of relationship with their native charges. Forced out of their books, missionaries paraphrased, they told stories, they testified, they prayed, and they sang, utilizing precisely the kind of communicative techniques familiar to members of an oral society. Louisa Pratt lamented the lack of privacy that the work entailed but marveled at the apparent enthusiasm of the Tahitians for this approach: "The house for the first two months was nearly always thronged at night with the people talking reading and singing." Her husband, Addison, noted that "All the Pacific Islanders have a great desire for learning psalms and hymn tunes. . . . when they once learn a tune, they never tire of singing it. They will collect at a neighbor's house at dark and sing a new tune over and over till midnight."[57] The Pratts also used local feasts as a way to mark and celebrate the reorganization of time, something apparently motivated by native desires. Louisa reflected that "every little turn in their affairs must be celebrated by a feast, even to changing the Sabbath."[58]

Other aspects of Mormon spiritual practice also resonated with traditional native ways. Most of the Protestant evangelists in the region were Calvinist and therefore harbored a deep suspicion of religious enthusiasms, eschewing the manifestation of spiritual gifts in the present age as heretical. Latter-day Saints, in contrast, cultivated the gifts of the spirit, and their necessary lack of emphasis on written materials only highlighted this distinguishing characteristic. As Pacific mission president Parley Pratt declared in an 1854 circular, "this Christianity of the New Testament is a system of visions, angels, revelations, prophesyings, gifts, miracles, etc. Such a system you can never oppose—it speaks and acts for itself; its votaries know what they experience, see, hear and feel."[59] Throughout early Mormon missionary accounts, perhaps the most often reported scene was that of a healing by a missionary. James Brown, serving in Tahiti, recounted extensively his experiences anointing and healing the sick, and preaching "on the signs, gifts of angels, etc."[60] Healing was also an important means by which missionary wives could interact with native women. Having brought along her consecrated oil, Louisa Pratt was in constant demand: "The females had great faith in the oil," she observed. They repaid her for her ministrations with food and other gifts, cementing the bonds of reciprocity.[61]

Because of their belief in continuous revelation, Mormon missionaries put more stock in prophecy and visions than did their Protestant counterparts; this was another feature of the LDS faith that had structural parallels in traditional native beliefs and practices. Peter Turner, a Methodist missionary in Tonga, expressed frustration that the natives wanted more "mystical" and "visionary" accounts of religious experience than he felt comfortable providing. His charges said that they had visions of heaven and Christ, and they wanted an opportunity to speak with him about such spiritual manifestations. Turner, however, could only instruct them to be suspicious of these experiences.[62]

Mormons, in contrast, not only brought a faith that encompassed and legitimated the expression of spiritual power by the individual but brought with them word of a latter-day prophet. Louisa Pratt hung pictures of Joseph and Hiram Smith on the wall in her bedroom and was startled that "all the People on the Island came to look at [them]." She described how one evening a man left a group of visitors to look at one of the pictures: "he kneeled before it in order that the painting might come in range with his eyes. . . . For a quarter of an hour he looked steadfastly upon it, I believe without turning his eyes." Louisa did not assume that this represented an act of worship; she concluded that "he wished undoubtedly to imprint the lineaments of the features upon his mind."[63]

Mormons had more physical proximity with natives than their Protestant counterparts, by necessities of their underfunded circumstances and through more shared
exercises of devotion. One needs to be careful not to overstate this familiarity. American Mormons shared with other missionaries a sense of cultural superiority that
reared its head from time to time. As several historians have noted, the prophetic call
to preach to the Lamanites encoded a double message: on the one hand, missionaries
carried an announcement of salvation and future hope; on the other, they reminded
converts that they were degraded, uncivilized creatures who had fallen from the
virtues of their ancestors.[64] Throughout the history of outreach in the Pacific, LDS
missionaries also voiced tremendous unease with many indigenous practices, and
they vacillated between promoting assimilation of the natives into the ways of "civilization" and the guarded incorporation of local practices into the church.[65] George
Q. Cannon slept on bare floors, but he consistently asserted the need for an unclouded
direction of influence from the missionary to the missionized: "The Lord sends His
Elders out to teach and not to be taught," he insisted. "The man who goes out expecting the people to whom he is sent, to teach, enlighten and benefit him commits a
great blunder. He does not understand the nature of his priesthood and calling."[66]

Yet, "going native" did not present the same degree of repulsion and fascination
for Mormons that Protestants articulated. While American Mormons occasionally invoked the distinction between "civilized" and "uncivilized" behavior, such language
was far less common within the Mormon community. Although Cannon touted the
need for native "enlightenment," he also defended the eating of dog meat as a most
delicious and satisfying meal; and he claimed that, although initially he was repelled
by the taste of poi, he prayed to God to make him find it palatable, and his wish was
granted. Quite a few Mormon missionaries married native women and girls (one as
young as thirteen), an action that did not seem to provoke ill will among their Mormon colleagues.[67] On the contrary, the adaptation to native ways at times was met
with a particular admiration. Louisa Pratt recalled seeing Brother Grouard, an early
missionary to Tahiti, who had been in the field for seven years and had married a native woman: "He had acquired an air of dignity an sobriety very nearly similating
him with a Catholic monk; his eyes were sunken apparently with sorrow and his whole
appearance was grave and majestick. I had seen him in the vigor of youth and thought
him a gay lively man, now his look was full of wisdom and years."[68] While he may
have lost some of his youthful zest, Pratt's comments do not convey the sense of dis-
sipation and depravity that Protestants associated with whites who "went native."

Some cultural boundaries, such as marriage, could apparently be crossed. But as
was true for Protestants, other divides were more charged: The easier compatibility of
Mormon religious practices and indigenous customs raised the specter of the confu-

sion, or even purposeful mixing, of the two modes of religious practice. Mormonism offered ways to build upon the native past, but it also was seen by the natives to have powers like those of traditional spirits, and this the missionaries found disconcerting. LDS workers in the field complained that natives seemed to move casually back and forth between Mormon rituals and native customs. Worse yet, some apparently couldn't tell the difference between the two. In Tahiti, James Brown related that he had baptized a couple and then healed their young infant of an illness. A short time later, he watched as an older couple entered the room, walked over, kissed the baby, "then went through some ancient heathen ceremony that I could not understand." When the baby died less than an hour later, Brown asked the parents to explain what had happened. They told him that the couple "had power with evil spirits, and had afflicted [the baby] in the first place." Brown's priesthood had apparently broken their power, and "they could not reunite it with the babe until they could come and touch it; and when they had done that, the parents and all concerned lost faith, and could not resist the influence that came with the old pair of witches."[69] While Brown was uncomfortable with this mixing of religious powers, it is clear that the natives were not; pragmatic in their beliefs, they chose to accept the work of whichever healer seemed most powerful.

The tactics of Mormon and Protestant missionaries, each driven by their own internal logic and necessary improvisations, engaged native practices in very different ways. It is tempting to conclude that Protestants, with their greater resources, attention to social hierarchy, and focus on an educated clergy, held less appeal to the natives. Mormons, to be sure, did have the initial edge, by dint of their relatively democratic local organizational structure and their charismatic practices, not to mention their utter lack of the resources that kept the Protestants at greater social distances from local communities. The Saints also had a political edge, by virtue of their attempts to distinguish themselves from the culture and politics of the United States. It was, however, through the opportunity to build their own "Zion" in the Pacific that Mormons began to reconstruct the very social hierarchies that they had left behind.

The Flight from Babylon

American Latter-day Saints may have criticized the natives, but a more insidious Babylon lurked nearby. Like George Cannon, who asserted that the Sandwich Islanders would have easily accepted the gospel had they not been seduced by the vicious ways of the Gentiles, Saints frequently blamed degradation among the indigenous people on the influence of European and American Protestants. Mormons simultaneously valued the fact that Protestants had laid the groundwork for the reception of the restored gospel in the islands but also blamed all defects in the process on prolonged exposure of the natives to corrupt Gentiles. Unlike Protestant missionaries, who were believers in original sin and censured the natives for "uncivilized" behavior, the Mormons did not adhere to the doctrine of the Fall. Sinfulness, they believed, could be brought about more readily by social context—namely, the evil influences of Protestant communities on local cultures—than by individual waywardness. This critique of Euro-American civilization left a way out, a means by which LDS missionaries could condemn practices but still see the local peoples as relatively blameless. They decided that the natives were among the persecuted remnant, just like North American Mormons; in this respect, they shared a common fate that the missionaries understood. They therefore hoped that service "in the Kingdom" would rid native peoples of their wicked ways.[70]

The behavior of Protestant missionaries toward Mormons in the islands only reinforced the reputation of the United States as a modern-day Babylon. Throughout the 1850s, Protestants in the Sandwich Islands threatened natives who showed interest in the Mormons, and LDS missionaries themselves came under verbal attack from local evangelical ministers.[71] Clearly, in many instances this persecution led natives and Mormons to see themselves in common cause—against a political as well as a religious oppressor. It also prompted LDS missionaries to urge that native Saints gather in communities on the islands, even if they could not travel to Zion itself, in Utah. Briefly during the 1850s in Lanai, and beginning again in the 1860s in Laie, Mormon leaders encouraged native converts to gather with them in communities where, much like the Saints in Utah, they organized themselves into self-sustaining economic units. Benjamin Johnson, the first counselor in the mission presidency, was appointed to negotiate for land on Lanai in 1853 in order to separate the faithful from "their corrupt surroundings." Naming the resulting town "Joseph" and the valley in which it resided "Ephraim," the Saints split into "pioneer" groups and began to plan, build, and dig.[72]

Tactics of separation, then, also figured largely in the Mormon approach to evangelization. Initially, at least, it was God's chosen people—native and white alike—who were to distance themselves from the evils of the world emanating primarily from Europe and America—the modern-day Babylon. Their rhetoric of community development mirrored the westward trek of the Saints to the Salt Lake Basin: In Lanai in 1854, twenty-one white LDS settlers joined fifty native Saints and, dubbing themselves "pioneers," established a new colony. The military-style organization so reminiscent of the early years of Utah settlement led to a leveling and mingling of interests in the church-owned community and in a necessary interracial intimacy among believers. Homes and churches were constructed simply, in the native style. In some respects, Mormons in this early gathering sought a common mode of life that combined indigenous spatial and architectural practices with a pioneering American communal ethic. Yet, signs of cultural tension quickly emerged. Trouble surfaced initially when native laborers refused to work according to the schedules and standards set by the missionaries. Elder Ephraim Green's journal is peppered with complaints about the "laziness" of his native charges. He vowed that he "would have given up on them if they were not descendants of Abraham, Joseph, and Lehi and therefore full of promise and favored with blessings of the Lord."[73] The fledgling community, never intended as a permanent settlement, was forced to close in the late 1850s when Mormon favor in the eyes of the Hawaiian government dwindled.

The next attempt to establish a Polynesian Zion, the gathering at Laie in the 1860s, was considerably better organized, supported, and centrally controlled from Utah. This time, an emphasis on the inculcation of appropriate LDS customs and teachings—Mormon civilization—was considerably more in evidence. As before, the LDS Church owned the colony property and created a land-holding system to rent shares to native workers. But church leaders divided settlers much more clearly into Euro-American and indigenous cadres. Migrants from Utah equipped with particular skills arrived to serve as teachers. Natives and *haoles* (whites) attended separate schools and church services, a decision justified on linguistic grounds. Ecclesiastical separation followed spatial separation; whereas initially native converts were led by their own elders, a series of clashes over indigenous religious practices in the 1870s—one involving the growing of *awa* as a cash crop, the other concerning the "erroneous practices" of native members of the priesthood—led to the curtailing of the use of native elders in the missions, further distinguishing indigenous from American Saints.[74] Not only had the gathering devolved into separate religious spheres, but leadership within the native community was increasingly curtailed and controlled by white colonists. In important respects, the era of relative communal intimacy had vanished.

Is the Mormon trajectory simply a story of the inevitable routinization of charisma, the move from a dynamic, spirit-filled and egalitarian movement to a bureaucratic and hierarchical church? Or, do we attribute it to a creeping racism among members? Both are in part the case. When a colony of Hawaiians moved en masse to Utah in the 1910s, they were housed in a separate area outside of Salt Lake City on a self-subsistent farm called Iosepa, and one is hard-pressed to understand their isolation as anything other than church-sponsored segregation.[75] Like almost all Protestant churches in the United States by 1900, Sabbath morning had become a segregated time for Mormons.[76] But equally significant in this comparison is that Mormons had an adapted (and adaptive) theology that incorporated Pacific peoples into an unfolding sacred story, an ecclesiology that encouraged a relatively isolated community, and a perception of Protestantism as an enemy that seemed, for a time, more dangerous than any native "barbarism." By the end of the 1800s, as Mormons reached a détente with the United States, the practices of the former Babylon gradually became their own. Yet, Pacific cultures remained important to the Mormon self-understanding: one need only recall that the first LDS temple outside of Utah was consecrated in Hawaii in 1917 to recognize that symbolically, if not numerically, Polynesia represents a critical sphere for LDS history. Today, the Polynesian Cultural Center on the island of Oahu provides a Mormon-sponsored homage to the Pacific world, embodying the sunnier side of a region that contained both peril and promise for early missionaries.[77]

The contrast between Protestant and Mormon approaches to evangelization also illuminates in sharp detail both the specific "Christian" practices each group understood as part of its repertoire of civility and the particular points of conflict, those treacherous behavioral boundaries that they dared not cross. Life in the mission field significantly changed the meaning of many activities, such as eating and dressing, that, when juxtaposed to native alternatives, became significant touchstones for Christian conduct. Finally, for both groups, varying strategies of intimacy with and separation from other cultures led to a fearful dance of fellowship in which the dictates of theology, church teaching, and political expediency struggled for the lead alongside personal fears and desires. Their Christian practices were shaped by many factors; sometimes they were improvised; and almost always, they brought missionaries and natives alike into untraveled territory.

It is difficult not to wonder, too, if there aren't other lessons to be learned in this tale of righteous missionary activity. Within decades of the founding of the United States, groups emerged that longed to spread lessons of a religiously based civility to other peoples around the globe. Protestants and Mormons, to be sure, used different strategies to do so, defining community in diverse ways, but both were animated by a vision of a unified, international Christian fellowship, an alliance based on common belief and practice that would transcend political divisions. Yet in both instances (and others), missionary strategies, molded by both religious ideology and improvisatory ingenuity, drew from the best instincts of Christian generosity only to rebuild the very walls they had set out to topple. Obsessed with the righteousness of their cause and its relationship (positive or negative) to the nascent domestic political experiment, American evangelical fervor in the mid-nineteenth century was already consumed in the labyrinth of its best and worst fantasies.

Such critical blindness to practical effects has lingered in our heritage. As our nation continues its quest to be the bearer of the civic religion of democracy, how should we enact "civility" or require it in others? Where, indeed, are the outer limits of our definitions of moral practice, and how do we separate morality from "Americanness," however we define it? What are the particular strategies by which we approach and separate ourselves from other individuals or societies, and what are the practical flashpoints of those interactions? Pluralism within a national or international community is an enticing but elusive goal, and our nation is still plagued by a startling lack of reflexivity about our own moral and "civil" strategies. Do we really understand what sorts of everyday practices will produce the intimate communities we most ardently desire?

CHAPTER FOUR

Honoring Elders

Practices of Sagacity and Deference in Ojibwe Christianity

MICHAEL D. MCNALLY

It is everywhere apparent, even in Bob Dylan's voice on his recent albums, that youth is evading the baby boomer generation. As that generation matures, its parent generation has become the very old. Today, many Christian faith communities find themselves graying along with the population as a whole. In a contemporary culture that valorizes youth, an economy and society that relegate the old and retired to the margins, and after nearly two hundred years of what Thomas Cole has identified as a twofold *demeaning of aging,* many of us hunger for fresh ways of imagining aging as a meaningful process and evaluating afresh the worth and relevance of what the old and their ways of knowing have to offer the common good.[1]

We might yearn to reclaim a golden age of American religion when the young respected their seniors, but a closer reading of the American past finds Christians displaying a deep and seemingly perennial ambivalence concerning the spiritual meaning of their own aging and how a Christian should properly regard the authority of the old.[2] While the Fifth Commandment's injunction to honor father and mother, and the interpretive tradition that extends "father and mother" to include all one's elders, ground this most basic of kinship obligations in God's will, it has never been clear how the authority of elders should square with other configurations of Christian authority: that of the learned, the clergy, the prophet, or the born again. What is more, never has old age uniformly lived up to the wisdom and venerability that are so consistently expected of it. Still, one can find rich veins of Christian practice within American communities that distinguish themselves in their disciplined regard for the authority of old age, resources that can help reimagine the possibilities of what the old and their wisdom have to offer the common life.

The Ojibwe people (variously known as Ojibwa, Chippewa, Anishinaabe), indigenous to the upper Great Lakes region, are one community with a longstanding regard for old age, its religious significance, and its authority. Perhaps this will come as no surprise, given the romantic image of the wise old Indian that popular culture reinforces.[3] But if Native American communities do succeed in distinctively honoring elders, it is emphatically not because they *naturally* do so. Instead, honoring elders has required hard work, the disciplined labor of moral teaching and ritualized decorum that create the authority of elders through practices of *deference*. In turn, this has led to the exercise of a way of knowing, itself practical in nature, in practices of *sagacity* also performed in the idiom of ceremonious decorum, practices of speech, silence, and discernment. While oral history and early accounts suggest that eldership thus constituted and exercised surely held sway in aboriginal days, more striking still is how Ojibwe communities have doggedly held onto—even accentuated—their maxim to "honor elders" amid the momentous and rapid changes since contact with Euro-Americans and their microbes, missionaries, and money.

The aim in this essay is to *denaturalize* Ojibwe eldership by looking at its cultural history and by demonstrating how it became an American Christian practice pivotal to a distinctive Ojibwe articulation of the Christian tradition in Ojibwe life. To fulfill this aim, the essay examines a watershed period during which practices of eldership accrued new meanings and took on new urgency. From the late 1860s to 1900, an intensive reservation-era encounter with missionaries under formal U.S. policies of Indian assimilation introduced new loci of cultural authority that challenged that of elders, but persisting practices of eldership in the spaces of Ojibwe Christianity conferred on that movement a kind of integrity. At such moments, when the difficulty of honoring elders is clear, Ojibwe eldership can be most instructive to nonnatives seeking different models for imagining aging and eldership. Ojibwe people struggled to honor elders while living in multiple worlds and amid challenges of dislocation, poverty, and patriarchy that worked against that goal.

These distinctive practices are not inevitably tied to the culture of a relatively small Christian community. They have something to say to a wider circle. From the perspective of Alasdair MacIntyre, Dorothy Bass, and others, these Ojibwe practices can be seen as significant examples of how formal practices and cultivated mental disciplines can generate, shape, and sustain the moral, experiential, and meaning-seeking inner life of religion. In this respect, the following discussion parallels those in this volume concerned with devotional practices, moral disciplines, and spiritual formation.

Examining Ojibwe deference and sagacity in the late nineteenth century can also enlarge our appreciation for how religious practices offer an apt medium through which to see how native and other people maintain lives of integrity and meaning under the confines of missionization and colonization. Such practices made possible the living of lives at once Christian and Anishinaabe—and this is to say made possible Ojibwe Christianity. In this latter respect, social theorists of practice identified in this volume's introduction provide important clues to the reading of Ojibwe sagacity. John and Jean Comaroff's studies of the ironic products of missionary exchanges with southern African peoples and Michel de Certeau's attention to the ways that people whose lives are largely structured by forces well beyond their own control assert themselves into and between those structures through what he calls the "production of consumption" alert us to the social theorists' suspicion that practices are always implicated in the disciplines of social power. They also give us an appreciation for how practices often become the only available medium for religious self-determination.[4]

Such assertions are admittedly only those of a "relative cultural freedom," as Robert Orsi observed, and Certeau notes that they are by definition largely invisible to an official view that sees only the consumption of the determining structures.[5] The invisibility of ritualized Ojibwe hymn singing hardly betokens the relative insignificance of subtle improvisations and gestures that interrupt the flows of assymetrical power.[6] In fact, their significance is perhaps in inverse proportion to visibility, their roots tapping deeply through fissures in the foundations of missionary discipline to the lifegiving soils beneath. As in Chapters 3 and 6 of this volume, for example, this examination of seemingly inconsequential practices suggests that religious practices may have as much to do with *making do* as with *making meaning*, as much to do with mediating the power structures of the social world as with mediating "worldview" and "ethos" (to use Geertz's famous formulation), or the inner and outer life of religion.[7]

Eldership in Ojibwe Tradition

In order to tell how this aspect of Ojibwe cultural history has changed over time, one must first establish something of the relationship between the outward practices constituting eldership and an Ojibwe world view. For many of us, "honor the elders" may sound flat at first, perhaps even cliché. But even a brief consideration of Ojibwe tradition suggests how the practices that promote this Ojibwe virtue refer to a sophisticated world view that gives it shape and depth in at least three ways.[8]

First, practices of honoring elders have been situated in an understanding of the natural circle of life, *bimaadiziwin*, as an ultimate concern. Because the tradition has been oriented toward the profundity of living well in this world rather than emphasizing the next, old age itself has marked a kind of religious attainment, fruit of the mindful and artful exercise of proper relations among human and nonhuman (plant, animal, spirit) members of that circle of life.[9] To grow old has been seen as tantamount to becoming more fully human in an Ojibwe sense, more fully *Anishinaabe*.[10]

Crucially for our purposes, *eldership* implies old age but does not denote a fact of biology. Community recognition as an elder has not been simply an entitlement for
those of great age. No traditional rite of passage has marked entrance into this age set
nor has there been equal regard for all old people. An elder, it might be said, has been
a sort of ideal type to which a community has agreed that some correspond more
closely than others. As with Confucius, who publicly considered himself no sage even
while performing the part, Ojibwe elders have exercised eldership in ways that have
had to be recognized by the community as worthy performances.

Secondly, what's at stake in honoring elders should be seen in light of the ultimacy
of an Ojibwe notion of kinship, sacred community. As in the Confucian tradition, the
well-ordered society for the Ojibwe has been an aesthetic and spiritual as well as ethical matter, and Ojibwe society has come into being through the graceful exercise of
practices of decorum that recognize and constitute proper kin relations. Thus seen,
practices of deference have been more than the mere etiquette they may appear at
first glance to be. They have been ritualized means for the constitution of the properly ordered community. In the complex designations of Ojibwe kinship terminology,
which provide a map for appropriate relationships among individuals, elders as a class
are everyone's relatives, everyone's teachers, everyone's responsibility. Suggestively,
there is a homology between the kinship terms for elders and the kinship terms employed to claim relations with spirits, who are generally addressed as Grandmother
(*nookoomis*) or Grandfather (*nimishoomis*). This logic certainly has been manifest in
the key ceremonialized gesture of offering elders tobacco (*akawe asemaa*) when seeking their counsel or favor, for this gesture has been elemental to the creation of right
relationship with spirits.

Thirdly, in this primarily oral tradition, cultural and religious authority has been
vested broadly in elders. As with other native traditions, no sacred text or stratified
class of authorized interpreters is in place to give more particular shape to tradition.
Indeed, the Ojibwe have hastened to ensure that matters of sacred knowledge remain
secure in the oral tradition, beyond the reach of books and the unauthorized eyes who
might see them. It has been *elders* who have been deemed to hold traditional authority, who have been authorized to determine what tradition is. The primary arena for
the exercise of this authority has been public speech. In a primarily oral culture, those
whose speech commands an audience exercise authority. Elders have been welcome
to speak whenever, wherever, and however they wish. Interruptions and even questions posed midstream have been considered more than bad manners; they are disre-
spectful in a fundamental sense to the structures of cultural authority. Deference,
then, has been no mere matter of etiquette but a set of practices that has ceremonialized elders' privilege as teachers. The listeners are not to presume to know what ques-

tions to ask, much less the answers, and even if it seems to them that an elder has strayed far afield from the matter at hand, or from her or his competence, the burden is on the listener to appreciate what might nevertheless be learned.

Ojibwe Elders' authority to speak has extended to their privilege to grant permission for others to speak. In formal discourse, people have made certain to establish their own authority by pointing to that of an elder or circle of elders who directed them to say or do what they are saying. Indeed, it seems that the bulk of public speaking has come from younger members of the community, but it must be noted that their authority has derived from elders, who have watched their words and actions carefully and intervened when necessary.

That elders in an oral tradition should be stewards of a community's traditional knowledge is, of course, to be expected. What is counterintuitive is that the authority of elders in oral traditions has allowed for, even embraced, religious and cultural change. Elders ought not to be conventionally understood as mere reservoirs that have accrued more tradition because they've lived many moons. Neither should they be construed simply as conservators of the status quo, bulwarks against change. Instead, it is in the peculiar religious authority of elders, constituted in and through practices of deference and sagacity, that tradition and innovation could have come together and where cultural change could have retained a kind of integrity on Ojibwe grounds. If tradition is what elders say it is, then it is to the practices of elders' authority that we must turn to grasp the subtlety with which continuity and change have been woven together in Ojibwe history.

Christianity and Chaos

The structures of Ojibwe cultural and religious authority were deeply challenged by missionary Christianity and the social dislocations that accompanied it, but ultimately they were not replaced, as missionaries had hoped they would be. Indigenous religious practices could authorize within the faith some measure of freedom to navigate new social and religious worlds of missionary encounters on native terms. Indeed, the continued practices of deference and sagacity provided Ojibwe Christians with key integuments between their tradition and their practice of the Christian tradition.

The late nineteenth century brought the Ojibwe more than the diminution of their lands. Reservation social structures cleared the ground for a fuller Ojibwe engagement with the Christian tradition and fostered a problematic relationship between subsequent generations of *Anishinaabe,* their collective past, and the elders who represented it. From the 1870s until the 1920s, U.S. policy promoted the cultural assimilation of

Indians and the private allotment of tribal lands into family farms to be owned by male heads of nuclear households. These policies established English-only boarding schools to remake the children, removed from the strong bonds of kin and the seasonal round, and prohibited the public practice of indigenous ceremonies, giveaways, and dances.

Plainly, assimilation policies served to undermine the traditional cultural authority of elders as the emblems of the very traditions such policies were meant to eradicate. In 1898, a missionary at the Leech Lake reservation observed, "In many respects the old people are the greatest sufferers by the onward sweep of progress. They cannot adapt themselves to the new order, and yet the old is vanishing from their grasp."[11] But it was less the content of assimilation policy than the social chaos it caused which proved to be the deeper challenge to eldership. Displacement, dispossession, poverty, and the diseases, like tuberculosis, associated with these conditions brought alarming social fragmentation and violence to Ojibwe communities, taking their toll, in turn, on the very kinship structures on which the traditional authority of elders rested.

Diseases endured by the strong proved fatal for young children and the elderly. In his informal census of the White Earth reservation in 1880, an Episcopal priest remarked that there were fifty more deaths than births at White Earth. "The Indian of today," he wrote, "does not reach the same old age of the red man of 100 years ago. . . . There are now but five or six old men on the reservation."[12]

Those who survived to old age were difficult to support in the lean years of the late nineteenth century. Traditional subsistence based on moving with the seasonal rounds was more difficult to obtain for people legally confined within reservation boundaries. Congress routinely failed to apportion the treaty annuities due Ojibwe people. Timber companies were leveling the habitat that housed game. A series of dams on the headwaters of the Mississippi, built to improve navigability downstream, flooded entire villages in the flat terrain and, more ominously, laid waste to their staple food, wild rice.[13]

In these colonizing circumstances, distinctions of gender, age, lineage, and band accrued new meanings and new ramifications. Factions emerged. Drunken skirmishes among kinsmen proved deadly. Men and women interacted in ways unknown to previous generations.[14] Tensions among generations, too, took on new valences and had greater ramifications in the reservation era. Generation gaps appeared, and regard for the elderly was broken by glaring examples of its opposite. Pauline Colby of the Leech Lake mission in the 1890s remarked, "I have looked in vain for the reverence for the aged that is accorded [by the southwestern Indians]. Our aged ones, especially the women, expect but little consideration, and get less."[15] Her language invites skepticism about a timeless romanticized image of elders venerated by their people;

but it also bears witness to the difficulties that faced Ojibwe people who were trying to honor their elders in those difficult years of tuberculosis, hunger, and broken promises, and perhaps to an increasing slippage between rhetoric and actual practice.

One is tempted to view the elders who did remain in the midst of this new world order of social chaos as dogged adherents to tradition. Instead, as historian Rebecca Kugel has shown, it was elders who had invited key changes to tradition in the first place. Kugel documents how the traditional authority of elders, especially male elders, had become deeply challenged in the 1850s and 1860s by younger generations of more militantly anticolonial "warriors" following charismatic leaders like Hole in the Day.[16] Kugel notes that traditional Ojibwe society always had involved some balance between the civil authority of the *ogimaag,* elder male leaders typically referred to in English as "chiefs and head men," and the military authority of warriors, comprising younger men. Times of peace and times of hostility had called for different kinds of community leadership, and Ojibwe society had emphasized the wisdom of such a balance. But in the 1850s and 1860s, militant warriors criticized elder leaders for their accommodationist posture toward Euro-Americans. After considerable deliberation, they signed treaties, invited missionaries to live among them, and sought the agricultural capital and schools they judged to be indispensable to their community's future.[17]

When the Episcopal bishop Henry Benjamin Whipple told a council of Ojibwe elders in 1862 that the Ojibwe must transform their lifeways else be doomed by the encroachment of civilization, one elder agreed in this regard: "You have spoken true words—we are poor—we are growing poorer. We feel the Great Spirit must be angry with us or our people would not fade away—our young men used to take advice of our old men and our old men spoke good words, but they don't do it now."[18]

This was more than a perennial complaint of an older generation for the loss of respect; the elder observes that the social breakdown is in part on account of elder men's abandoning their customary responsibilities. A balance that recognized the occasional importance of the authority of warriors but that in general privileged the circumspection and diplomacy of elders had become polarized into competing structures of authority with respective factional alignments, and the realignment had privileged the warriors' rigid approach to asserting a boundary between tradition and change. The warrior leaders claimed followers largely from among the Métis descendants of Ojibwe unions with French or English fur traders, most of whom identified with Roman Catholic missions. By contrast, the *ogimaag* drew followers largely from the ranks of "full-blood" Ojibwe, a significant number of whom identified with the Episcopal mission, although a good number of "full bloods" opposed Christian affiliation altogether.

Ironically, elder *ogimaag* who had cast their lot with the new tradition of Protestant Christianity found still further challenges to their authority from within the
Christian tradition itself, at least as it was promoted by missionaries.[19] Along with
other agents of assimilation policy, these missionaries maintained that Ojibwe tradition and "Christian civilization" were incompatible, and they viewed elders as the
standard bearers of those problematic traditions. For missionaries, the task of making Christians out of these people would require hierarchical configurations of authority: educated young converts would need to be placed over their unschooled elders, men over women, and especially clergy over laity. To this end, missionaries
hastened to wed their clerical authority with the power of the reservation agents and
the annuity payment systems on which Ojibwe people increasingly depended. Payments entitled to Ojibwe under treaties were fashioned into monetary rewards for
Sabbath-keeping and other churchly practices. For starving people, it paid to practice
the new customs.

Ojibwe Christianity was no straightforward outcome of missionary design, however. Time and again, a distinctively Ojibwe Christianity would slip through the many
cracks of missionary and reservation discipline, and this distinctive Christianity was
formed through the medium of practice.[20] As Maffly-Kipp shows in Chapter 3 of this
volume, missionary discipline itself was often cobbled together from what was possible in the field, a matter of compromises with theoretical directives from headquarters. But with a proclivity for thinking of "religion" in terms of practices, Ojibwe people asserted themselves through practices in distinct ways. Ojibwe Christians spoke of
Christianity itself in terms of practice; they called it *Anami'aawin,* "prayer." Likewise,
their term for Ojibwe Christians, *Anami'aajig,* "those who pray," identified that community with its practice of spoken prayer. Although a sharp boundary was drawn between Christianity and Ojibwe "paganism" by missionaries, who vigilantly maintained it by their discipline, clearly the *Anami'aajig* did not conceive of this new
complex of practices and beliefs as a bounded system, antithetical to the beliefs and
practices of Ojibwe tradition.[21] In a time of rapid change, many Ojibwe people practiced *Anami'aawin* as a form of Ojibwe tradition, one that took its place among other
Ojibwe ceremonial complexes. For them, *Anami'aawin* could negotiate the maintaining of core value commitments of Ojibwe tradition with the innovations necessary for the community's continued material and cultural survival.[22]

To the extent that *Anami'aawin* could negotiate tradition and innovation, it did so
in no small part because its articulation took place soundly under the authority of elders. Again, eldership, which one would expect to be a predictably conservative force,
turns out to be identifiably involved with cultural change. Ojibwe tradition at any
given point is what elders say it is, within bounds guaranteed by broader circles of

consensus. Thus, the authority of tradition is really an authority granted to and exercised by elders, through a complex of practices that can be distinguished in terms of decorum that privileges what elders have to say and practices of sagacity through which elders' authority is staged and ceremonialized and thus conformed to established tradition. The point here is that such practices do not simply *recognize* an authority that is already there but that they themselves constitute the authority by virtue of ritualizing it. The anthropologist Maurice Bloch, studying the culture of the Merina of Madagascar, has appreciated that ritualized oratory by elders is a matter of political authority. Attending less to the content of things said than to the stylized form of their saying, Bloch notes how the placement of speakers in a room, their cadences and silences, and their comportment constitute authority.[23] It is important, then, to examine the contours of Ojibwe Christian regard for the aged and their authority as rendered visible in such practices.

The particulars of this decorum are often quite subtle, ironically most apparent in the missionary archives when their unstated rules have been violated. The practices of sagacity have largely to do with oratory, ways of speaking and remaining conspicuously silent that betoken deliberateness, command an audience, and set the terms for public discussion.

The practices associated with deference include ways of speaking and listening that privilege elders' voices and elders' authority to delegate the right to speak. Deferential decorum also involves complex codes of the extension of hospitality and formalized gift giving, offerings of tobacco for elders' counsel, and practices of decision making that take the needs of elders and children into account first. Again, such practices seem at first glance less consequential, less remarkable, than they have proved to be. But the historical Ojibwe engagement with Christianity, wherein the authority of native elders met challenges of clerical and bureaucratic authority from without and prophetic authority from within the Ojibwe tradition, clearly show how such practices of decorum markedly ceremonialize their authority. And it is here where the practices of decorum, those constituting deference and those constituting sagacity, helped make possible the negotiation of continuity and change, of tradition and Christianity, that one could argue helped enable the Ojibwe to survive as a distinctive people.

To be sure, missionaries noted the influence of *ogimaag* in the collective "conversion" of those band members who followed their leadership. At Red Lake in the 1870s, for example, an entire village followed Madweganonind into baptism and affiliation with the Episcopal mission. Within three years of the baptism of the "old chief" (here *old, akiiwenzii,* is an honorific but also applies to the *ogimaa*'s biological age, for he was born around 1800) ninety of the one hundred fifteen villagers had been baptized, and forty-five had become Episcopalian communicants. One missionary boasted that this was "a larger number proportionately by far than in any other place in the U.S."[24]

But if missionaries recognized that they had to contend with certain prominent elders, they dismissed older Ojibwe in general as intractably bound to habit, custom, and language and consequently poor candidates for the cultural revolution they saw as necessary to the adoption of a Christian way of life.[25] Instead, Episcopal missionaries sought to cultivate an indigenous church by identifying promising young Ojibwe men, removing them to boarding schools for education in the English language and Christianity, and eventually ordaining them as deacons to evangelize their kinsmen, under the supervision of a nonnative diocesan official. Historians have seen in these efforts the answer to why Episcopalians outperformed a range of other Protestant missionary efforts among Minnesota's Ojibwe.[26] But clearly, in the late nineteenth century, it was key elders, both men and women, who were at the center of efforts to make the Christian tradition their own in the more familiar Ojibwe idiom of religious practice.

Practicing Deference and Sagacity in *Anami'aawin*

Sustained practices of deference and sagacity may have been familiar to Ojibwe who became involved in the Christian movement, but they carried a new charge of contestation in the reservation environment circumscribed by missionaries and agents who equated the Christian life with the "civilized" life. This element of contestation is visible in at least three contexts: as lay Christian sodalities articulated anew the familiar forms of kinship organization, as key lay elders asserted their leadership, and in Ojibwe clergy's continued high regard for their elders.

The distinctive Ojibwe Christianity produced by the *Anami'aajig* took shape not so much in the chapels and schools of the mission as in the semiautonomous spaces in which indigenous sodalities of men and women repaired a torn Ojibwe social fabric in new, distinctively Christian, improvisations on old kinship structures. Importantly, these gatherings provided spaces of orality, out of earshot of the missionaries, who determined the written record. As a result, precious little written evidence survives of their activities, but under closer examination, the force of the subtle practices, which missionaries noted only in passing, can be seen.

In the early 1870s, Ojibwe elders at White Earth suggested to Bishop Whipple that lay societies of men and women should be formed for the purposes of "encouraging one another in the faith." Whipple agreed, authorizing and directing his field missionaries to promote such societies on established Methodist models for nurturing

lay devotion. In the Methodist fashion, they called the men's groups singing and praying bands and the women's industrial societies.

In 1881, John Johnson Enmegabowh, the first Native American Episcopal priest and
the one who anchored the mission at White Earth, spoke of having two classes of
"young men" at White Earth village, numbering between twenty-five and thirty, joined
by "some of our chiefs," referring to the *ogimaag*. There were also at this time two societies of women at White Earth village. Each group had its own spiritual "chiefs," elder men and women, respectively, who directed the ritualized exchange of songs and
ideas, gave counsel, and settled disputes that arose.[27] And it is in these sodalities that
we can best see the persistence of eldership practices in Ojibwe Christianity.

Consider the case of Shaydayence (Little Pelican), one of the elder advisors of the
young men's sodality at White Earth village. It was he who sought Bishop Whipple's
endorsement of the singing and praying band idea in the first place, and the sequence
of actions is revealing. Lay societies were encouraged by the mission church, but they
were established under elders and, it seems, at the initiative of key elders like Shaydayence. Indeed, in a funeral eulogy for Shaydayence, Whipple identified him as the
"real, recognized leader of the Christian community" at White Earth; and acknowledging this as a continuation of leadership, he added, "as he had before been of the
heathen."[28] This elder was, to be sure, an exceptional leader, representative more of
the ideal of eldership than of elders generally. Still, he perhaps best exemplifies the
way some elders finessed the transition to Christian practice with integrity on Ojibwe
grounds.

Prior to their removal to White Earth reservation in 1868, Shaydayence served the
Gull Lake band as its principal spiritual leader. He was the preeminent leader of the
Midewiwin society in that band and a *jiisakii*, a healer and diviner who engaged in a
shamanic ceremony colloquially referred to as the "shaking tent."[29] Episcopalian missionaries remembered Shaydayence as having once been the "prime minister of Satan," a bitter opponent to James L. Breck's initial establishment of the St. Columba
mission at Gull Lake in 1852.[30] But even the "antichristian" leader committed his son
Nabiquan to the care of the mission in order to become "learned in the learning of
the Egyptians."[31] Displaced along with most of his community several days' journey
away to White Earth, Shaydayence reported that there he became "excessively devoted . . . to firewater. I was very quarrelsome, and was repeatedly cut and stabbed by
my fellow Indians in drunken quarrels, when I knew nothing about it."[32] He recovered himself, however, and in 1875 became baptized at the estimated age of sixty-four.
For the remaining eleven years of his life, he was the principal spiritual elder of the
Anami'aajig.

With a Christian affiliation, Shaydayence continued his vocation of spiritual counsel and healing. His plain assertion in practice of the continuity between Ojibwe and Christian traditions of leadership bespoke the continued recognition of his authority by Ojibwe and missionaries alike, as well as the nondogmatic nature of his spiritual way of knowing. Even as a spokesman for the *Anami'aajig*, he relied extensively on the herbal, ritual, and musical knowledge he had mastered as a *Midewiwin* initiate. His visits to fellow Ojibwes, either alone or with the young men's band, typically took place at sickbeds or deathbeds. And although he had formally parted ways with the *Midewiwin*, his healing as a Christian was hardly limited to spiritual prayer. J. A. Gilfillan, the archdeacon in charge of the Ojibwe missions, noted that Shaydayence was "also a great believer in the efficacy of medicine accompanied with prayer, and gives many instances of the wonderful recoveries it has caused; but to give medicine without prayer he abhors."[33] His mobilization of the gospel, herbal knowledge, and confident manner were all part of the same healing art.

Other elders also held influence among the *Anami'aajig*. At White Earth's Pembina band village, the nascent *Anami'aajig* community requested authorization from the bishop to form a men's band under Wagejigezhick and a women's band under Ogeshiyashik, his wife. Interestingly, their request, dictated to deacon George Johnson, was glossed for the bishop by Gilfillan with a concern about keeping the elder woman's authority in its place within his own clerical chain of command. He advised the bishop, "If you merely write: *I hereby authorize the women of Pembina settlement to form a women's band under Mrs. Waygidjigizig under the superintendence of Rev. Geo. B. Johnson* that will be sufficient."[34]

Also at White Earth village, a middle-aged woman, Kakabishque, conveyed to the bishop via Gilfillan that "appointed leaders of Bands have chosen one among ourselves whom we would wish to take general leadership of us, namely Susan Roy."[35] Another elder, Equay me do gay, baptized Suzanna Wright, was one of the initial Christians at Gull Lake. She was daughter to Waubojiig (White Fisher), a renowned *ogimaa* there prior to the removal to White Earth, sister to the *ogimaa* Waubonoquod, and aunt to deacon Charles Wright Nashotah. A group calling itself the Committee of Mazigishik's Band at White Earth village reported that they had taken as their advisors the *ogimaag* Waubonoquod, Tecomigizhik, and Joe Critte [Charette].[36] At Leech Lake, both women and men met under the "spiritual charge" of the elder, Kegiosh, a blacksmith in his eighties, and Susan Bongo, daughter of a trader who was a mixed blood descendant of a runaway African American slave. It was observed that Kegiosh always spoke first at the gatherings, and directed the proceedings.[37]

While these advisors were not the civil leaders who signed treaties, those *ogimaag* were also important to the leadership of these sodalities, further suggesting the groups' import as reconstituted Ojibwe social units. These societies made celebrated expeditions to preach and exhort near and far. They visited the sick and dying and pooled resources and labor to make their communal way in their new agrarian world. A leader of the Young Men of White Earth village reported that they had "visited to the sick man Tecomighizhick and to our fallen friend Makaque and to another fallen man." They also visited "Gahgige ash, sick man and five acres of land was planted for him."[38]

The most regular activity of the sodalities was assembling in evening prayer meetings, which they did as often as four nights per week. In their meetings, they ate, prayed, sang, shared food and clothing, organized mutual aid, and served as professional mourners for others in the community. Missionary accounts of the devotional meetings note their ritualized nature, especially the stylized nature of the oratory, its pacing and sequencing with song and prayer, and the consistent prominence of elders.

> In all these meetings the method of procedure is the same; meet about nightfall, begin with singing a Chippewa hymn, then prayer, then another hymn, then the leader names the one who is to speak, after he or she sits down another hymn, then another speaker is named and so on until 9 or 10 o'clock when the meeting is closed with prayer. The speakers are nearly all middle aged or elderly men or women. There is never any excitement or extravagance . . . but solemnity. In these meetings they seem to find most of their joy—they have no other parties nor meetings but only those connected with religion.[39]

Rebecca Kugel has identified these societies as key to the "process of social regeneration," and to be sure, they were more than narrowly religious confraternities. In the new world of reservation and mission, they reiterated familiar structures of Ojibwe kinship, not least of which was eldership, that made their new life possible. Without them, Kugel writes, "the experiment with Christianization and agriculture would have amounted to little."[40]

While they applauded the contribution lay societies made to conversion, missionaries worried about their lack of control over the groups and about the centrality of these evening meetings to the rhythms of native Christianity. A clergyman at Leech Lake complained to the bishop that prayer meetings had eclipsed official worship at the mission station in importance among his Ojibwe charges. "Since we came here," Edwin Benedict wrote, "we have endeavored to make these poor people understand the difference between the value of Public Divine worship to almighty God and prayer meetings of a few persons. We have therefore allowed them . . . but too many meetings of this kind in a week would to my estimation prove rather an injury than good to them."[41] Such comments are telling reminders of the social politics with which practices could be charged in missionary encounters. In these *Anami'aajig* sodalities the authority of Ojibwe elders was perpetuated, despite the challenges of social dislocations, assimilation policies that undermined the value of traditional ways, and clerical authority.

Practices of Sagacity

Missionaries consistently reported the centrality of elder Christians' oratory in their attempt to show the vitality of Christian life. Shaydayence's stature rested on his ability to speak well, from the heart and with the bearing of an elder. "Talking had always been his forte," Gilfillan averred.[42] He was hailed, not because he took on the aspect of an evangelist, but because he continued to speak with the pacing, ceremony, and authority befitting an Ojibwe elder. "In whatever company he was, the conversation was sure to take a religious turn," it was said about Shaydayence. "He persuaded so spontaneously and almost unconsciously and with such a genuine enthusiasm that it seemed perfectly natural, and just the proper word in the proper place."[43] The archdeacon even expressed unusual regard for Ojibwe speech practices, such as ribald humor, that would ordinarily provoke a missionary's rebuke. "He frequently gravitated towards spiritual things having first established his conversations with a joke and a laugh," Gilfillan observed. "What would have sounded strained and forced and would have been disgusting from anyone else sounded as natural as breathing from him."[44]

To speak well was not just to have something important to say but to have demonstrated a mastery of the decorum that gave importance and authority to whatever was said. Even a non-Indian missionary could sense Shaydayence's mastery of ceremonious social interaction: "his manners are exceedingly polite, almost courtier like; I marvel at the gracious words which proceed out of his mouth."[45] As Maurice Bloch's observations of elders' councils in Madagascar suggest, the formalization of speech can mean much more than good manners; it betokens an appeal to elders' traditional authority which one cannot substantially challenge, because the authority is constituted in the form, not the content, of what is said.[46] To his native auditors, Shaydayence's mastery of the practices of oratory framed *whatever* he said in terms of a recognized traditional authority.

Speaking well, in Ojibwe terms, included the authority to delegate public speech, and Shaydayence ritualized the exercise of this authority to tangible effect as well. At devotional meetings of Ojibwe Christians, Gilfillan observed, "he soon took the place of leader, speaking first himself, naming the speakers in succession, correcting any wild statements made, and being the life of the whole meeting. He always had the right word to say; it did not seem as if they could have any meeting without him."[47]

The authority of a speaker's words was not always in proportion to the quantity of those words. In fact, the measure of oratorical authority had much to do with an elders' cultivated art of maintaining silence and listening well. Madweganonind of Red Lake, for example, "spoke but few words. No one ever heard him make a speech. He listened to all that was said, and when at the end of it he summed it up in a few words and told them what ought to be done, his decision was final."[48]

In Shaydayence's case, listening was an art to be cultivated because it reflected the profound Ojibwe commitment to humility, especially as it concerns knowledge of the sacred. "He never could read a word[,] but he had listened so attentively to the Bible when it was read that though he could not give chapter and verse, the soul of the message was in his heart, and in his eloquent way he made it seem real to his listeners."[49] Indeed, prior to the reservation era, missionaries frustrated by a lack of Ojibwe conversions nevertheless routinely observed the polite manners with which Ojibwes listened to them. In his earlier days, Shaydayence may have challenged Episcopalians at Gull Lake, but even then it was clear that he took seriously his dialogue with them. Indeed, this is largely because of the commitment on the part of certain Ojibwe elders to the Episcopal mission, evidence itself of a cultivated pragmatic wisdom with little room for dogmatic thinking. Here again, the traditional authority of elders relied less on the content of tradition than on the formally constituted authority of elders to determine what the tradition would be in a particular circumstance. Constituted through practice rather than with reference to content, this authority was no airtight mechanism for the conservation of tradition but left considerable room for improvisation.

In this light, we can appreciate that those *ogimaag* who "converted" did not do so hastily or merely as a byproduct of a strategic alliance decision. The sincerity of conversion did not, however, bespeak a doctrinaire repudiation of all things previously believed and practiced.[50] The deliberation, the listening, and the discernment were perhaps indicators of quite the converse: a cultivated ability to do a novel thing well on Ojibwe terms. For example, in 1869, a Gull Lake *ogimaa*, Nabuneshkung, respectfully "offered his house for services . . . even though he was not converted." Urged to "renounce his heathenism and Grand Medicine," the *ogimaa* made clear his intention to convert but told the native deacon, "I am preparing for it. I do not want to go into it half hearted, and unprepared for the great battle. When I wanted to follow the warpath I have never gone unprepared. I studied and imagined the hard battle before me."[51] Part of this cultivated ability to do a novel thing well involved proceeding according to Ojibwe patterns of discernment and decision making that inspired consensus. There was certainly dissent and division among members of the community in these years, and the *ogimaag* led the people, but not by decree. They led by listening and persuading groups of the wisdom of a given course of action. A missionary at LaPointe, Wisconsin, observed out of frustration in the 1830s that "constantly you hear individual Indians in new potential mission territories, declining to render an opinion until they meet in council."[52] At the helm of such councils were elders. "The headman [*ogimaa*] acts more as an advisor than as a king, if he is a man of energy and independence, he often acquires considerable influence. But if he is not, or if for any reason he is unpopular with his band, they do not much regard him."[53]

Such cultivated practices of listening and discernment gave to Ojibwe Christian sagacity a broad-minded posture that stood in contrast to the missionaries' more dogmatic views of the necessary link between Christianity and Anglo-American culture. In the early 1880s, for example, a millennial movement emerged at White Earth and Red Lake around an Ojibwe prophet and self-declared Ojibwe incarnation of Christ. This man, Abitageshig, taught a transformative ceremonial dance, performed around the Prayer Drum, which he said had been spelled out to him in a vision. This movement did not incite violent anticolonial action, but it did pose a considerable challenge to the *Anami'aajig* movement, as many Ojibwe Christians became swept up in its practices, despite disavowals of drumming and dancing.[54] The choreography and musical accompaniment of the dance were the fruit of a prophetic vision, but because it was prefaced by a Christian prayer, it had received a policy of engagement if not support from the Benedictine missionaries there. The abbot in charge of the mission had reportedly even blessed the drum.[55] Significantly, broad-minded elders affiliated with the Episcopal mission joined the Roman Catholics in not viewing this dance in dogmatic terms. The young men's sodality at Pembina approached their advisor, the elder Meshakikishig, about how best to respond to the inducement "to attend and join in [these dances]." With the elder's advice, the sodality "thought it politic to allow the other young people to dance at stated intervals, always of course, keeping the two ideas, devotion and amusement, distinct." Meshakikizhig, in turn, sought advice on the matter from the Métis Episcopal priest C. H. Beaulieu, who took issue with the elder and opined "strongly and clearly against any heathenish practices whatsoever."[56]

Attentive listening was related, in Shaydayence's case, to a regular practice of contemplative silence, another practice befitting elders and one that could give the few words that were spoken still further esteem. Gilfillan noted that even though Shaydayence's Christian life occupied only his final eleven years, he had developed a "deep knowledge of spiritual things," which "were the subjects of his incessant contemplation and prayer, and the action of the Holy Spirit on natural abilities of the very highest order enabled him to arrive at those things independently without ever having been taught them or heard them from others."[57]

Shaydayence's contemplation met with his continued practice of praying, as an elder, on behalf of the community. Shaydayence's speech commanded audiences, but it clearly was regarded also as particularly effectual. He was hailed for taking prayer extremely seriously. Shaydayence's healing practice rested on the esteem given him as one who prays over the sick, and his whole life as a Christian seemed to involve conspicuous acts of intercessory prayer.

Practices of Deference

Public expressions of sagacity also implied deference. The ritualization of deference was made visible in the ways Ojibwe Christians approached their elders and extended hospitality to them. The continued relevance of such practices of deference is clearer still when nonnative missionaries reflected on their breach of such social codes.

The offering of tobacco to elders (*akawe asemaa*), for example, apparently remained a consistent part of *Anami'aajig* practice, if one that made missionaries so uneasy that they seldom wrote of it, given its association with "pagan" practices of offering to spirits. Their discomfort did not keep the missionaries from duplicating the practice, but with a cultural adjustment. In 1897 at Red Lake, during the customary Christmas giveaway by the church, "the sick and the aged . . . each received a warm piece of clothing or a packet of tea, and some of the old men a pipe and packet of tobacco."[58] Evidently, some missionaries deemed it unbecoming for elder women to receive tobacco too, although tobacco smoking and chewing remained an important part of older women's lives. Pauline Colby, an Episcopal missionary at Leech Lake, wrote of sending, as a gesture of respect and care, "a ration of flour, sugar, salt, and tobacco to an old pagan woman, grandmother of some Christian Indians."[59] Preliminary to a formal council with Ojibwe *Anami'aajig* leaders and *ogimaag*, while on his tour to the northern missions, Bishop Whipple handed out cigars. Such actions were strategic maneuvers in treaty making, but they did honor the authority of the Ojibwe dignitaries in attendance.

Codes of hospitality to elders and others may have been so elemental to Ojibwe life that their practice within the Ojibwe community receives little mention in the missionary record. It is implied in the complex of "visiting" that developed in reservation years, a social practice that enabled the *Anami'aajig* to fashion a broader community consciousness that extended beyond local ties of kin, village, and reservation.[60] Nonnative missionaries sometimes learned of such conventions by their own breaches of them. Gilfillan recognized his own learning curve concerning Ojibwe hospitality. For example, when the Red Lake *ogimaa* Madweganonind came to White Earth village, some sixty miles to the south, Gilfillan took pains to provision him and put him up in a nearby Ojibwe home, "installing him, as I thought, comfortably, there." Several hours later, Gilfillan noticed

> a long thing like a log, lying on the snow in front of my woodpile—it was the depth of winter and it was cold—and found it was the Old Chief lying there wrapped in his blanket. He had taken that way of apprizing me that his quarters, or else the food, in the one room log cabin of the Indian were not altogether satisfactory. I took the hint, and for the remainder of their stay, he and his brother were my honored guests, as they ought to have been from the first.[61]

According to a detractor, such conduct was more a pattern than an exception with Gilfillan, owing to his wife's reported intolerance of having native people as guests in her home.[62] Like the Protestant missionaries in the Pacific islands, boundary maintenance of this sort could prove urgent for missionaries uneasy about their own border crossing.

Pauline Colby, by contrast, seemed to treasure her role as caretaker of elderly Indians at Leech Lake. When a policy change dictated that a civil servant take over her directorship of the home for the aged that she had established, she wrote that she surrendered the job "rather reluctantly, for though I have more work than I can do justice to, I have found a vast deal of satisfaction in making the old creatures as comfortable as it is possible for them to be."[63]

Evidence of Ojibwe Christian adaptation of the practice of deference is perhaps best seen in the way clerical authority was squared with that of lay elder leaders. Although the younger Ojibwe deacons who were trained in English and the Bible were stationed in each reservation village and credited by Episcopalian sources as the main engine of evangelism there, the final authority in these *Anami'aajig* communities rested, as it long had, upon the shoulders of key elders. Indeed, the younger clergy seemed to hold authority within the community only as it was quietly delegated to them by *ogimaag* and other elders.

Obviously, the clerical authority of young male deacons represented a challenge to traditional religious authority when they had exchanges with elders within and without *Anami'aajig* circles. In 1880, a "Sunday School for the aged" was conducted by "the young men." Gilfillan wrote: "When the young Indian clergymen spoke to the old men on the subject of religion, they were very often surprised by the reply: 'You are only a child; you do not know anything; I ought to teach you, instead of your setting yourself up to teach me; I have lived a long time and learned a great deal.'"[64] Gilfillan added that "this was in accordance with Indian notions and did not take into account the fact that knowledge of books and some other things had something to do with obtaining wisdom, as well as age. Latterly, as the Indians begin to perceive this, that rejoinder has not been so common."[65] But, within the sodalities of the *Anami'aajig,* deacons deferred to the authority of their elders.

Almost from the first to last, the deacons were sons, nephews, or close cousins of the prominent *ogimaag* and were thus possibly cloaked, in Rebecca Kugel's reckoning, in a "quasi-hereditary" authority.[66] Perhaps this hereditary authority was accentuated by the dearth of elders at the time and the breakdown of clan system. Although each of the deacons was trained in the English language by Gilfillan and Enmegabowh with the Bible as their sole text, their correspondence, which is scant, suggests that the deacons worked in an Ojibwe-language world. Most wrote their official correspondence in Ojibwe; only Charles Wright Nashotah's correspondence goes beyond broken English.

Scattered in various villages throughout the White Earth, Red Lake, and Leech Lake communities, the leadership network of Ojibwe deacons helped foster a shared consciousness across traditional band lines and more recent reservation lines that proved strategic under U.S. Indian policy. Still, their leadership was soundly woven into the fabric of and was dependent upon the leadership of *ogimaag* and elders in their respective communities.[67]

Authority and the Deacon's Strike of 1882

The *Anami'aajig* may have imagined the clerical authority of Enmegabowh, the first Ojibwe Episcopal priest, and the deacons as being delegated by elders, but the missionaries understood it in terms of a missions hierarchy; the latter took pains to ensure that clerical authority trumped the authority of lay elders and that, in the crucial case of Enmegabowh, diocesan authority exceeded that of native clergy. In 1882, tensions came to a head when the Ojibwe deacons staged a strike, leaving their posts and conspicuously canceling worship for months. At first glance, the affair appears to be about wages and unequal treatment of native clergy, but a closer look reveals how seriously the Ojibwe community regarded the mission's disrespect for elders, especially Enmegabowh.

At the center of the strike was J. A. Gilfillan. As the bishop's archdeacon for Ojibwe missions, Gilfillan was charged with financial, pastoral, and disciplinary oversight of the deacons and their mission stations. Perhaps it was canonically appropriate that Gilfillan refer very few matters up the chain of command to the bishop, but the Ojibwe *ogimaag* and other elders came to view Gilfillan as an obstacle rather than an asset to their access to Whipple, who had earned their respect and could bring his national influence to bear on their behalf.

Gilfillan took pains to discipline what he viewed as an Ojibwe constitutional proclivity toward idleness, pride, and backsliding. As the bishop's gatekeeper, Gilfillan did not hesitate to exercise a paternalistic judgment that, among other things, considered elders to be the most intransigent among a whole people he deemed children. This became clearest in his pattern of subverting the requests of native elders. In 1881, Gilfillan clarified the broken English of a letter penned for a Pembina band *ogimaa* by the Ojibwe deacon George Johnson with this gloss: "He wishes a paper from you to Waygidjigizig, the chief of that settlement, authorizing him to hold that part of the reservation against white intruders, settlers. That of course does not amount to anything, but it is well to gratify him."[68] When Suzanna Roy, elder leader of the women's guild at White Earth village, appealed to the bishop for financial support, Gilfillan added a cover note urging Whipple otherwise: "You are exceedingly kind to Mrs. Roy in sending her the $10. . . . [The Roys] were better able to earn everything they want than almost any other family."[69] When the esteemed *ogimaa* Manidowab appealed to the bishop to secure the "fitting" of his house as Washington officials had promised, Gilfillan glossed the letter, which he himself had transcribed, as follows: "If Isaac [Manidowab] were not very lazy he could fix up his own house. He is nothing of a worker nor ever will be and the only thing is to keep him gently alive till he dies."[70] Gilfillan added that Manidowab's wife had recently defected to the "Romish Church, the only defection of that kind we have had for some years, so *that* does not make for their being very worthy of help."[71]

Ojibwe Christians took seriously such disrespect for elders. More than bad manners, it challenged the continued practice of *Anishinaabe* community within the Christian tradition. Ojibwe deacons demonstrated this concern physically. With the support, if not the instigation, of the elders cited above, they withdrew from their posts to protest Gilfillan's inappropriate exercise of power toward them, toward their elders, and perhaps especially toward their elder in the priesthood, Enmegabowh, with whom Gilfillan vied for authority as the clerical leader of the *Anami'aajig.*

Tensions had been rising between Gilfillan and Enmegabowh for some time. In 1880, Gilfillan had confronted Enmegabowh for soliciting support directly from contacts he had made on his various travels in the East, without the authorization of Gilfillan or the bishop. They may have had a point, but the controversy implies deeper tensions concerning *Anami'aajig* autonomy, for the appeals Enmegabowh had made were for clothing, food, and capital purchases the Ojibwe needed to survive. For his part, Enmegabowh had been stirring animus against Gilfillan. The mission physician had warned the bishop to cease supporting Gilfillan, given his bad reputation among the Ojibwe. "The leading Indians at White Earth, Wild Rice River, Red Lake, and Leech Lake all have the same name for him—liar."[72]

In November 1882, Charles Wright Nashotah, the deacon at Leech Lake, notified

Gilfillan that he had left his post and was calling for a renewed investigation into the sexual misconduct of a nonnative priest there and for the replacement of the sub-Indian agent and a schoolteacher at Leech Lake, a retired missionary named S. G. Wright, who purportedly was harassing Ojibwe women. Nashotah's claims also concerned the double standard being applied to the native clergy, for Gilfillan had made haste to discipline deacons John Coleman and George Johnson (Enmegabowh's son) for fathering children deemed illegitimate by Anglo-American reckonings of marriage.[73]

Gilfillan explained the matter to the bishop in terms of Charles Wright Nashotah's own idleness and his having had "too much prosperity" so soon after having been an uncivilized "blanket Indian."[74] Several weeks later Gilfillan suggested that the bishop dismiss a letter from the deacon's brother-in-law, an influential Leech Lake trader, because it "is Chas. Wright all over. It is dictated by Chas Wright's jealousy, who wishes to force out Mr. Benedict that he may be sole lord there."[75]

In the ensuing months, however, as all but two of the deacons left their posts in agreement with Nashotah, Gilfillan admitted to the bishop that the deacons had "held councils" a year earlier at White Earth, during the treaty payment, and that their stated objectives were higher pay and advancement to the priesthood. Advancement to the priesthood meant much more than a bump in pay that could allow the Ojibwe leaders to cease hunting and gathering to provide for their families. As priests, the *Anami'aajig* leaders would be free of Gilfillan's supervision, and not just about church matters, for Gilfillan controlled the deacons' access to the passes Indians needed to travel off reservation.[76] In his representations of the affair, Gilfillan discloses the significant threat to his own clerical authority posed by Enmegabowh, by this time clearly an elder as well as a priest: "Of course when a man of the age and influence of Rev. Mr. Johnson [Enmegabowh] leads astray his younger brethren, it is hard to make headway against it. It is a pity to see the aged Aaron, the priest of the Lord, fashion the idol calves to lead the people back to Egypt, but so it is. He does it through an unfounded jealousy of me, thinking if they all resign it will force my resignation as the cause."[77] Gilfillan did not see the affair in terms of a crisis of authority but represented the strike to the bishop in terms of a personal animosity borne of Ojibwe greed. "The immediate object is more pay," he wrote, "and they think that I stand in their way and that if I were removed they would have it all their own way."[78] "When these poor heathen get their eyes opened," Gilfillan added, "they do not see straight for some time."[79]

Gilfillan urged the bishop's discretion about his comments, in any correspondence with Enmegabowh, whose personal relationship with Whipple had several decades on Gilfillan's. He recognized Enmegabowh's implicit authority over Ojibwe missions and the precarious nature of his own authority compared with that of Enmegabowh: "I hope also that you will not write anything severe to Rev. Mr. Johnson," Gilfillan wrote, "as it would make him bitter against me as the author."[80] Ironically, Gilfillan reported that he and Enmegabowh had yet to talk directly about the matter: "Our friendly relations remained undisturbed, though I still have the same opinion as to what caused all this. I have confidence that he can undo all this if he wish, but forbear speaking to him about it."[81] In his fourth attempt, the following January, to contain the fallout from the affair, Gilfillan revealed that the strike might indeed have stemmed from his blocking Enmegabowh's role as elder and priest: "I have never attempted to exercise the least supervision or superintendence over Rev. Mr. Johnson in any way shape or manner, considering him entirely exempt from me, and he receives his salary direct. I have not even known for, I believe, three years past what it is."[82] Gilfillan even confessed his own reluctance to "forbid" Enmegabowh to make unauthorized appeals for funds for fear that "it might hurt his feelings for a younger person to rebuke him."[83]

Conclusion

In the end, although the bishop chose not to intervene, and hence not to alter the formal structure of the mission, an understanding apparently was reached among Enmegabowh, the deacons, and a chastened Gilfillan about how far the archdeacon's authority could range within that structure. In the aftermath of the affair, Gilfillan even argued against the Leech Lake missionary priest's proposal that Nashotah receive exemplary punishment.[84] But the strike did reveal a deep tension between missionaries and Ojibwe Christians in their reckoning of religious authority, and ever since then Ojibwe Christians have persisted in practices of deference and sagacity that privilege the authority of lay elders and that distinguish *Anami'aawin* with a supple capacity to integrate Christianity and native tradition, despite claims by many others that Christianity and Ojibwe tradition are mutually exclusive.

While this essay cannot encompass the twentieth-century cultural history of honoring elders, a personal anecdote can attest to the continued, perhaps accentuated, significance of the nineteenth-century terrain explored above. While drafting this chapter, I was approached by a member of the Minneapolis cathedral, which had commissioned new stained-glass windows. Interested in honoring the contribution to the diocese of Ojibwe Christians, she had persuaded her committee to include among the proposed windows one celebrating Enmegabowh, recently approved for inclusion in *Lesser Feasts and Fasts,* the Episcopalian calendar honoring notable Christians, in a dramatic celebration at the denomination's triennial convention in Minneapolis. Her committee had solicited the approval of two key Ojibwe clergy in the diocese for what she thought was sure to be their hearty endorsement, but she was perplexed when they strongly recommended that any window honoring Enmegabowh be complemented by a window honoring Madweganonind, the elder leader of the nineteenth-century Red Lake community. Having clarified the matter and confirmed my hunch with one of the Ojibwe priests in question, I suggested to her that too much exclusive attention on Enmegabowh ran the risk of making of him a kind of trophy, being conspicuously displayed by a church eager to assuage its own ambivalence about Ojibwe missions and making a loyal churchman out of a man whose commitment to *Anami'aawin* had led him to challenge boldly the missionary structures that so often undermined the authority of his people and its elders. But with the complement of a window of Medwagononind, people would learn that it was through the sagacity of such lay elders as he, and the practices of deference that honored the authority of this sagacity, that Ojibwe Christians could inflect their understanding of the gospel and the Christian life with the fundamental commitments of the *Anishinaabe* way.

The wider circle of Christians can certainly be instructed by their example. Ojibwe people's persistence in and improvised adaptation of these practices of deference and sagacity enabled this group of Christians to make room within the confines of the orthodoxies and institutions of the established church for Christian lives of integrity, meaning, and purpose that accorded with their most important traditions. More particularly, those of us who are constrained to rethink aging and what it might mean for community are instructed by their example of the healthy exercise of ways of knowing that are perhaps distinctive to elders and that can flourish to enrich our common life. The Ojibwe Christian example may suggest that, under the right conditions, elders' ways of knowing may be less bound to orthodox and dogmatic understandings of the past than convention, and perhaps one or two of Bob Dylan's lyrics themselves, tell us.

CHAPTER FIVE

Nurturing Religion Nationalism

Korean Americans in Hawaii

DAVID K. YOO

Two features of the architecture of the Korean Christian Church in the Liliha Street neighborhood of Honolulu stand out for their nationalistic symbolism. The first is the entrance to the church, a replica of an ancient palace gate in Seoul. This distinctive and colorful passageway into the church was the pride of the congregation when the building was dedicated in 1938. Although somewhat faded by the years and the elements, the gateway stood the test of time until 2000, when the entire building was demolished as a result of structural problems.[1]

The second nationalistic architectural feature, a statue of Syngman Rhee (1875–1965), stands in the center of the campus. The plaque accompanying the imposing figure of Rhee identifies him as the father of South Korea and the founder of the Korean Christian Church. Rhee is best known as the first president of the Republic of Korea (South Korea), but he also spent more than forty years in the United States as a student, exile, and leader within the immigrant Korean American community. Rhee and the Korean Christian Church both served as important if controversial anchors in the immigrant community in the Hawaiian Islands and throughout the Korean diaspora.

The gateway, the statue of Rhee, and other nationalistic elements of the Korean Christian Church as a whole illustrate how religious nationalism functioned as a Christian practice in the United States. Less identifiably religious than practices such as prayer and meditation, religious nationalism nevertheless has a rich and varied legacy within the history of the United States. When religious nationalism is discussed, it is often in the context of an American civil religion and signifies an understanding of the United States as the nation destined to be God's New Israel.[2] Providential destiny, however, has been open to multiple interpretations. As historian Albert Raboteau has pointed out, the very meaning of the nation itself could vary radically depending upon one's circumstances. What British colonists heralded as the New Israel constituted for African slaves the New Egypt.[3] Korean Americans, along with many others who ventured to these shores around the turn of the twentieth century, shaped and defined their experiences in the United States through religious traditions and institutions that they transplanted and made anew. Like African Americans, most Korean Americans claimed a Protestant Christianity that set them within the dominant religious tradition of the nation. Yet, by virtue of race, they were set apart from their European American counterparts.

The case of the Korean Christian Church in Hawaii, then, complicates the landscape of Protestant Christian practices in the United States by reminding us that practices such as religious nationalism have been influenced by constructs of race. Korean Americans have been one of the groups marked as religious and racial others, and such categories of difference have been used to define normative, white Americans. Leaders and members of the Korean Christian Church dealt with at least three interrelated dimensions of race. The first Koreans in Hawaii saw themselves as a repository of Korean identity in the face of Japanese colonialism in Korea. Korean Americans were aware of the systematic efforts by Japan to erase and absorb Korea into its empire. Though racial categories were never fixed, it is clear that Korean Americans understood themselves to be preserving Korea as a distinct people and nation through what could be termed a community of memory.[4] At the same time, Korean Americans in Hawaii found a racial legacy in the United States that lumped them with other Asians and extended to them discriminatory policies and stereotypes. Finally, Korean Americans faced the enduring racial markers that have been reserved largely for Native Americans, African Americans, and Latinos.[5] These racial formations reflect the ways in which Korean Americans in Hawaii represented both an exile and an immigrant community.

If analysis of the Korean Christian Church illustrates how Christian practices are racialized, then also evident is the politicization of these practices. The Korean American religious nationalism that took shape in Hawaii brought together Protestantism and politics in ever widening circles, radiating from the local to the international, and intricate webs that connected those contexts. The practice of religious nationalism entered into the local politics of Korean Americans in Honolulu and the Methodist missions in the Hawaiian islands. Furthermore, many Korean Americans had strong ties to American Protestant missions in Korea and to the important role such missions had played and continued to play in the development of modern Korea. Finally, the practice of religious nationalism formed an integral part of a diasporic independence movement that not only spoke to the efforts to free Korea from Japanese colonial rule but that also involved an American empire with vital interests in East Asia as well as in the Hawaiian Islands.

In the case of Korean American religious nationalism, what identifiable forms did the practice take? How were racial and political nationalisms manifest in particular practices? Four subpractices suggest how religious nationalism took shape in this context: self-determination, education, social services, and the nationalist marking of the physical landscape. Self-determination, a concept that gained wide currency in President Woodrow Wilson's Fourteen Points speech in 1918, stressed the sovereignty of nations.[6] As a practice, Korean American self-determination was reflected in a sensibility or world view rooted in a legacy of Protestant nationalism in Korea that made its way to Hawaii through migration. Along with this sensibility, self-determination lay behind the tensions between Syngman Rhee and his compatriots and the Methodist missions in Hawaii. The eventual break with the Methodists and the formation of the Korean Christian Church as an independent entity represented a foundational act of self-determination that girded the religious nationalism of the church. Self-determination, in its conceptual and applied dimensions, profoundly shaped the religious nationalism within this community.

Church-related education emerged as an important locus for the practice of religious nationalism. The creation of church-sponsored private schools for boys and girls, through the Korean Christian Institute, indicated the importance placed upon the training of Christian nationalists. The Korean Christian Institute put into practice Rhee's vision of cultivating future Christian leaders, even as his own education in Korea and the United States had shaped his views of religion and self-determination. In this essay, the parameters of Christian practice include the founding of church institutions and the teaching of certain curricula.

In its social services, the church also cultivated a religious nationalism. The Korean Christian Church established the Korean Old Men's Home to care for aging men who had worked in the sugar cane fields. Religious nationalism in the form of racial pride and religious convictions prompted the church to take care of its own. The Korean Christian Church also provided key leadership to the Women's Relief Society, a social service collective in the islands with strong church ties. The Relief Society enabled many of the women to work for the local community and their homeland in the name of God.

Finally, the specific architectural choices manifested in the Honolulu church façade and in the statue of Syngman Rhee illustrate how religious nationalism was practiced on the physical landscape. In both examples, members of the church gave physical expression to the religious nationalism that they embodied and sought to live out.

The definitions of *practice* illustrated in this chapter emphasize the ways practice functions as a conduit of exchange between the church and society and culture. Issues of power, negotiation, and resistance enter into the story. The sensibilities or dispositions that informed practices are a critical element of the analysis of how religious nationalism was part of the lived religion of Korean Americans in Hawaii.[7] In the case of the Korean Christian Church, members were positioned between societies and cultures and were racialized as the other within two colonial contexts. Korean Americans in Hawaii were a transnational community that maintained important ties to people, institutions, and events in Korea while fashioning a new life in a territory of the United States. Like the essays by Laurie Maffly-Kipp (Chapter 3) and Roberto Lint Sagarena (Chapter 6), this chapter explores the ways in which histories of Christian practice complicate notions of what is meant by the term *American*. Furthermore, by incorporating nationalism into the canon of Christian practices, this chapter addresses what the editors refer to as the interpenetration of spiritual and temporal activity. While a fundamental power differential framed colonial and postcolonial experiences, this story accentuates how a group of men and women carved out their own identity as Korean Americans and Christians in Hawaii. It emphasizes how this people made their own history even as they contended with the constraints of circumstances often beyond their control within a crucible of shifting encounters and exchanges.

As a case study, an examination of the Korean Christian Church enables us to enter territory relatively uncharted in the study of American religion. While some work has been conducted on the religious life of Korean Americans in the post-1965 era, very little attention has been paid to their earlier history, which dates to 1903.[8] Furthermore, the locale of Hawaii removes us from typical religious history landscapes. How many histories of American religion account for the territorial experience? While the story of such a singular church pushes us deep into the local, the geography and cultural identity of that church will keep this narrative international. Most of the Koreans who left their homeland were part of a global migration of individuals who were sought for their labor. In this case, the first stop on their route was the sugar plantations covering the Hawaiian Islands. Along with these laborers came Korean ministers, who not only helped establish churches, but who also represented denominational ties to American Protestant missionaries and organizations. Although unmoored from their home country, the new Korean laborers in Hawaii entered a nexus of peoples, institutions, and ideas that facilitated a vital religious and cultural exchange between Korea and the United States. Situating the story of Christian practice within that migrant world of transition and encounter will necessarily press us beyond obvious regional borders and postcolonial presumptions.

Protestant Nationalism in Korea

The practice of religious nationalism among Korean Americans, especially in the areas of self-determination and education, was an adaptation of the Protestant nationalism they practiced in Korea. Historian James Grayson suggests that Protestant Christianity has been one of the two most important influences on Korean history in the last century, along with Japanese colonial rule (1910–1945), and that the two were intricately intertwined during the first half of the twentieth century.[9] The contact and exchange that took place between Koreans and American missionaries in the peninsular nation set the groundwork, particularly in terms of sensibility or world view, for the religious nationalism practiced by Korean Americans in Hawaii.

Protestant missionaries, primarily Methodists and Presbyterians, constituted the initial and an important ongoing American presence in Korea from the 1880s; in fact, the lines dividing God, nation, and commerce were often blurred, because missionaries worked in all of these realms, sometimes simultaneously.[10] Relationships forged between missionaries and the royal family in Korea enabled Americans to establish schools, hospitals, and churches that provided structures for interaction between Koreans and Americans. In other words, at these sites, Koreans were directed in practices of learning that would form the basis for how they envisioned and lived out their religious nationalism. The intermingling of Western medicine and American educational curricula under the larger rubric of the Christian faith meant that Korean Protestants were putting together elements of a new world view to help them interpret and navigate the tumultuous change and loss unfolding before them. Ideas of reform, democracy, and liberation were embedded in the education and in the way the biblical texts were studied. By going to school and church, then, many Koreans forged a Protestant nationalism.

The American Protestant missionary strategy to educate both the elite and non-elite segments of the Korean population encompassed a large cross-section of society. The emphasis on teaching non-elites in the vernacular Korean language stood in stark contrast to the longstanding classical Chinese education that was reserved for the upper class. The decision to educate those traditionally excluded fostered in many new converts and students a democratic impulse that fueled religious nationalism and influenced views about the role of women in society.[11] This impulse carried over to the Korean American community in Hawaii, where it was manifested in a strong penchant by plantation laborers to seek education for their children, male and female. Education in Hawaii initially took place under the Methodist missionary educational system, which mirrored the schools Americans had established in Korea. The educational practices of the Korean Christian Church, while representing a divergence from the Methodist missions, nevertheless also borrowed from them.

For elites, like Syngman Rhee and other nationalist leaders, the educational experiences at places like the Methodist Pae Chae School in Seoul spawned in them a religious nationalism that advocated widespread societal reforms and spiritual renewal that would be critical for the future of their beleaguered homeland. The Independence Club, established in 1896 by former and current students at the Pae Chae School, served as an important forum for the religious nationalism brewing at the turn of the century. Philip Jaisohn, a convert to Christianity and eventual expatriate physician in Philadelphia, was a key figure in the club. He and others expressed their views through publications and discussion groups that proved formative to many future Korean American leaders as they envisioned and lived out their religious nationalism.[12]

Within this environment, various strands of nationalism took root in Korea. Some of them identified closely with a Protestant Christianity that had both indigenous and foreign elements.[13] Influenced in part by American Christian resistance to Japanese colonialism, many Korean leaders and non-elites formed their understandings of nation and God simultaneously.[14] How Korean Christians made sense of their nationalism varied. Some leaders found in the Bible a message of liberation that fostered a religiously based form of nationalism and activity that they viewed as consistent with claims of Christian faith upon all of the created order. The combination of religion and nationalism, according to Wi Jo Kang, could and did result in radical thinking and action, including violence.[15] Other Christian leaders in Korea, however, began to separate the affairs of state from those of religion, as a means of preserving the church's ability to continue its work as Japan tightened its imperial grip over Korea. According to one study, an influential strain of Protestant-influenced nationalism stressed the internal, spiritual renewal of the Korean people as critical for independence and self-rule. Such a notion resonated with the Confucian heritage of leading Korean thinkers and gave Christianity an influence that extended beyond those who became converts.[16]

One finds in Korea during this tumultuous period, then, multiple views of how Christians were to relate to their times. Protestant Christianity, reflected in its ideas, texts, and institutions, became an important means by which some Korean converts and leading thinkers envisioned reform for their homeland and, in the aftermath of annexation, independence. The directions that Christianity took in Korea influenced how Koreans understood both their faith and the appropriate relation of church and state. Protestant nationalism in Korea was varied and vital, but it could divide as well as unite. For better or worse, Korean religious nationalism in Hawaii would suffer from a major internal split. Different visions, each with antecedents in strains of Korean Protestant nationalism, would lead to deep antagonisms that polarized the Korean American community. One faction was led by Syngman Rhee and was based in the Korean Christian Church, while the other group was headed by another patriot and Christian Yong-man Pak and was tied to the Korean Methodist Church. Both Rhee and Pak were products of Methodist mission schools in Korea, and they had served time in prison together for their nationalist activities. In many ways, the two groups and churches possessed similar practices and sensibilities when it came to their religious nationalism, but issues of personalities and particular strategies drove a wedge between them.[17]

The religious nationalism practiced in Hawaii by Korean Americans owed much to its specific history and ongoing connections to Protestant nationalism in Korea. The role that education had played in fostering a religious nationalism for both elites and non-elites in Korea was reflected across the spectrum of the Korean American population in the islands. Practices would be configured to take into account local concerns, but the ties to Korea were important in developing a sensibility and providing real structure for the practices themselves. The importance of Protestantism in Korea for Korean Americans in Hawaii was also directly linked to American Protestant missionaries and their denominational structures. For some men and women, the decision to migrate to Hawaii was literally influenced by missionary encouragement to venture forth. Others, especially Korean students, were able to attend colleges and seminaries in the United States with direct sponsorship by missionaries. In Hawaii, most Koreans encountered a church that in one way or another was a version of the missions they had left in their homeland. In many ways, Koreans were leaving one colonial setting for another.

Koreans in Paradise

The reasons why people choose to migrate from their homeland to another place are complex, but religion, nationalism, and religious nationalism certainly influenced the journeys of Koreans to Hawaii at the turn of the twentieth century. The majority of the 7,500 Koreans who entered the islands between 1903 and 1905, and the picture brides that followed from 1910 to 1924, did so to work in the sugar cane plantations. American owners of the plantations sent recruiters specifically to Korea with the hopes that they could tap into the nationalism of Koreans by suggesting that they offset the growing labor monopoly of Japanese workers in Hawaii.[18] Recruiters called upon missionary contacts in order to gain entry to the community and asked the Korean government's permission to recruit laborers, but they found it very difficult to convince Koreans to leave. So, recruiters looked again to the missionaries. Methodist pastor George Heber Jones in Inchon, Korea, told his parishioners about the virtues of Hawaii and the promise of establishing a church there and carrying on Christian work. The fifty or so men and women who responded to the call made up nearly half of the first shipload of Koreans to Hawaii, who arrived on the S.S. *Gaelic* in January 1903.[19] The elements of religion and nationalism are readily evident in this migration. Religious nationalism was also a factor for leaders like Syngman Rhee, who was chafing under Japanese surveillance and harassment and for whom Hawaii was a desirable destination. The sponsorship of American Protestant missionaries enabled many of these leaders to secure passage out of Korea.

Not surprisingly, Christianity played a prominent role in the lives of Koreans as they began to settle into life on the islands. According to one study, by 1906 there were already thirty-six Korean Methodist churches in Hawaii.[20] Estimates suggest that between 40 and 60 percent of the first wave of immigrants (1903–1905) were Christians.[21] By World War II, the Koreans in Hawaii were overwhelmingly Christian. The Korean Methodist Church and the Korean Christian Church had approximately 1,000 members each, representing the two largest Korean American congregations in Hawaii.[22]

In the early years of Korean migration, the Methodist missions dominated the religious landscape in Hawaii. The prominent role of Methodists derived in part from comity agreements by which major American Protestant denominations agreed not to violate certain territorial boundaries. While many converts to Christianity in Korea had Presbyterian roots, the lack of a Presbyterian church in Hawaii meant that most Koreans attended Methodist churches. Those with Episcopal ties attended St. Luke's, but in terms of numbers and activity, the Methodists knew no rivals in the early years. Since the Methodists were also a major force in missions in Korea, networks linked Korean Christians and American missionaries in the islands.

Virtually all Koreans who emigrated to Hawaii started their lives there on the plantations. In the grueling and dehumanizing context of plantation life, these men and women were quickly introduced to racialization in an American colony. The fact that these laborers were adherents of the same religion as the owners, many of whom had their own missionary ties, did little to alleviate the exploitation of the Koreans. Race and economics trumped religion. Koreans represented about 11 percent of the workforce in 1905. The workday ran from 4:30 a.m. until 4:30 p.m. with only a half-hour break for lunch, six days a week for $16 a month. Koreans left the fields for Honolulu as soon as they could;proportionately with other plantation workers, they were among the quickest to leave the plantations.[23] The first stop for those departing the plantations for Honolulu was the church. The churches were at the heart of the community; there one could gather information about housing, jobs, and news from Korea, including the fight for independence. Religious nationalism infused the life of the churches.

Church-sponsored education played an important role in the religious nationalism among Korean Americans in Hawaii, even if fostering such sensibilities and practices was not an intended outcome of mission educators. The Compound School, founded in 1906 by the Methodist mission, was established as a boarding school for Korean boys and offered a primary education through the eighth grade, in English as well as in Korean. Many students who otherwise would have had difficulty acquiring an education benefited from the school. A number of the graduates went on to public and private high schools in Honolulu, and some continued their studies at the College of Hawaii and on the mainland.[24] The Compound School also provided an opportunity for students from different islands to share common experiences and develop a sense of community.[25] A product of this educational process was a heightened sense of being Korean, in part fostered by immigrant parents and churches concerned about the homeland but also reinforced by the treatment and status of Koreans struggling to survive in an often inhospitable setting. The issue of religious nationalism itself would become a point of controversy within the structure of the Methodist missions.

The Korean School Controversy and Syngman Rhee

The transnational religious politics of Korea followed the men and women who left their homeland for Hawaii. In 1912, the Reverend John Wadman, superintendent of the Hawaii mission of the Methodist Episcopal Mission, received funds from the Japanese consulate for mission work that included the Korean Compound School. When news of the source of the funds circulated in the Korean community, angry Koreans wanted to refuse the monies as adding insult to injury after the annexation of Korea by Japan in 1910. Wadman may have been concerned about offending the Japanese consulate and the substantial Japanese population that was also part of the Methodist missions in Hawaii. Perhaps for this reason or perhaps to exert mission authority and discipline, Wadman stated that the donation had been given in good faith and that it was indeed appropriate to apply such funds for the Compound School. Many of the students went on strike and refused to attend the school. Wadman, sought the assistance of Syngman Rhee, who was held in high regard by missionaries in Korea, to resolve the controversy.[26]

The timing of John Wadman's request worked well for Syngman Rhee. He had been studying in the United States since 1904 and had returned to Korea in 1910. After a brief stint as the general secretary of the Korean YMCA, he was looking for an opportunity to get back to the United States. Japanese control had grown considerably since he had departed to study in the United States, and Japan had annexed Korea a few months prior to Rhee's return to Korea. Rhee believed that he could do more for Korea in exile than at home. Using the pretext of attending a Methodist conference in the United States, he evaded Japanese authorities and arrived in Hawaii in 1912. He was indeed able to help diffuse the controversy over the school funds.[27]

In the story of religious nationalism of Korean Americans in Hawaii, it is critical to recognize the convergence of religious nationalism in the person and life of Syngman Rhee. The exiled leader represented a transitional figure in modern Korean history. Trained in the Chinese classics, Rhee also studied in Methodist mission schools. His education brought him into contact with reformers like Philip Jaisohn and with a world view steeped in religious nationalism. His exercise of that religious nationalism through the Independence Club and in other venues ran afoul of the royal court, and in 1899 Rhee was jailed under a life sentence for sedition. American missionaries used diplomatic channels to try to protect and free their former student, and these efforts, along with changes in the political climate in Korea, led to Rhee's release in 1904.

Rhee read and wrote during his prison years, and he fully embraced his religious convictions through a conversion to Christianity. His major work of prison writing, *The Spirit of Independence: A Primer of Korean Modernization and Reform,* is largely focused on the need for reform in turn-of-the-century Korea. Though the text does not address religion in much detail, there is a telling passage near the end of the text that makes a case for the nation of Korea taking on Christianity as a foundation. He wrote in part, "We must adopt this religion as the basis of everything."[28] One hears in these words the stirrings of a religious nationalism that would soon gather momentum.

Education would be a major catalyst of that momentum. Missionaries arranged for Rhee to leave for the United States soon after his release from prison. Rhee earned a Bachelor of Arts from George Washington University, a Master of Arts from Harvard University, and a Doctor of Philosophy from Princeton University. He was the first Korean to receive an American Ph.D. (Politics, 1910).[29] It seems plausible that Rhee further developed his views on religious nationalism during these years, since he was often invited to the home of Woodrow Wilson, who was the president of Princeton while Rhee was there, and may have learned something of the future U.S. president's stance on self-determination. In addition to politics, Rhee studied Christian theology at Princeton Seminary, where he lived in seminary housing and was taught by prominent Christian leaders such as Charles Erdman.[30]

With his credentials as a Christian, a highly educated man, and one who had suffered hardships for his homeland, Rhee assumed a position of leadership within the Korean American community in Hawaii from the outset. His presence may have helped smooth over the controversy over the Japanese consulate funds, but it was not long before his religious nationalism, mixed with his authoritative style, embroiled the Methodist missions and the Korean American community in further controversy. Rhee had been made principal of the Korean Compound School. In this capacity, he had the means to assess the conditions of the Korean immigrant communities throughout Hawaii. He discovered that many Korean girls were receiving an inadequate education, and he proceeded to recruit them to board at the Methodist-run Susanna Wesley Home. He intended to instruct them together with the boys at the Compound School, but the Methodists questioned the wisdom of coeducation. Those in charge of the Wesley Home blocked the girls from attending, and the first signs of strain emerged.[31]

A change in leadership of the Methodist missions added to the conflict when Wadman was replaced by the Reverend William Fry in 1914. Rhee and Fry clashed over the mission of the Compound School, as well as over the issue of coeducation. Fry objected to use of the school and the church for what he considered political purposes.[32] Rhee and other Korean Americans, however, saw their nationalist activities as part and parcel of their Christian faith. Although Rhee had enjoyed the support and guidance of many American missionaries and educational institutions, he represented in his religious nationalism a movement that often placed Korean Protestants in tension with their missionary counterparts. Perhaps the most compelling example of this divergence is that American missionaries—and Japanese authorities—in Korea were caught completely unaware by the massive, nonviolent declaration of independence by Koreans on 1 March 1919. Korean Protestant clergy were prominent signers of the declaration, and it is unlikely that the event could have occurred without the church institutions and networks that helped coordinate the uprising.[33]

The conflict over the proper place of politics in religion gave rise to the emphasis on self-determination by Koreans in Hawaii, as Rhee urged immigrants to take a strong stand for complete autonomy. In addition to chafing under criticism of nationalistic education in the church-run school, Rhee and other Korean immigrants resented mission control of the Compound School, since they supported it with their hard earned dollars. Fundraising proved to be another sore point, as Rhee had collected monies for students during a tour throughout the islands but had also reaped mission disapproval, for not having received proper authorization for the solicitations.[34] In response to the resistance he had met from the Susanna Wesley Home, Rhee circumvented the mission by starting the Korean Girls' Home, which would become the Korean Girls' Seminary in 1915. Rhee resigned his position as principal of the Compound School the following year and helped establish the Korean Christian Institute, for the education of boys and girls.

An act of self-determination, the founding of the Korean Christian Institute also marked the key place of education in the religious nationalism of Korean Americans in Hawaii. The very naming of the school as Korean Christian underscores the linkage between religion and nation. The curriculum, teachers, and classroom spaces reflected the fact that education, nationalism, and the church went hand in hand for many Korean American youth. Children learned Korean language, history, and patriotic songs, but they also sang Christian hymns. Often their teachers were lay evangelists or pastors. Much of the instruction that students received took place in Sunday school classrooms and church sanctuaries. Korean American–run schools nurtured patriotism not only in the students but in the parents and other adults who formed the audiences for oratory contests held throughout the islands.[35]

At the Korean Christian Institute, Rhee and his followers could practice a religious nationalism free from the constraints of missionaries. The admonishments against mixing politics and faith conveniently overlooked the pro-Japanese stance of some missionaries, who gave tacit approval of the annexation of Korea and the racialization of Koreans as an inferior people. The Institute, in contrast, was to be a vanguard for the new Korea. Rhee instructed his students: "You are Americans by birth, but you are Koreans by blood. Someday you will be builders of new Korea. Mingle yourselves with Korean boys and girls. Study hard the Korean language and Korean history if you truly love your fatherland. Do not marry foreigners."[36] A proper education would produce the kinds of men and women who would lead Korea in the future.

The efforts of Rhee as principal of the Compound School and then as lead instigator of the Korean Christian Institute did not, however, win him the approval of all Korean Americans in the islands. As much as some immigrants were drawn to the authoritarian patriot, others remained within the Methodist fold and clearly did not agree with Rhee's methods, even if they were largely sympathetic to his religious nationalism. The controversies surrounding Syngman Rhee would create deep fissures within the Korean American community. The religious nationalism that precipitated the break with the Methodists and creation of the Korean Christian Institute would have further consequences for religious life in Hawaii in the creation of the Korean Christian Church.

The Korean Christian Church

The establishment and subsequent life of the Korean Christian Church gave the fullest expression to the practice of Korean religious nationalism. At first glance, the origins of the church can be attributed to the controversies and clashes with the Methodist missions; and yet, the creation of the Korean Christian Church can also be viewed as the outgrowth of a religious nationalism that began in Korea and adapted to the particular circumstances in Hawaii. The commencement of the first congregation itself was a foundational practice of religious nationalism. A sensibility and national and religious legacy coalesced in the decision to start a church without ties to the missionaries who had introduced them to the Christian faith. In turn, the new congregation would serve as an umbrella for other practices, reflected in the social services offered by and the physical landscape of the Korean Christian Church.[37]

In the autumn of 1916, Syngman Rhee and about eighty other Korean Americans interested in breaking from the Korean Methodist Church began to meet. The New Church people, as they were known, formed the Central Korean Christian Church in December of 1918.[38] The Reverend Chan-ho Min, former pastor of the Korean Methodist Church in Honolulu, took on the duties of founding pastor. When Min received the call to this position, he was in Los Angeles, where he had gone for graduate study at the University of Southern California. He and his family arrived in Hawaii in the early part of 1919, and for ten years, Min and his wife, Mollie, helped set the foundations for the church in Honolulu and for branches in Oahu, Maui, and Hawaii. Eventually, Korean Christian Church congregations would also be established in Los Angeles and in Korea. An administrative umbrella organization, the Korean Missions Incorporated, guided the work of the church, including the ordination of ministers.[39]

The social services sponsored by the Korean Christian Church also exemplified its religious nationalism. A case in point is the Korean Old Men's Home founded in 1929 to serve the growing number of elderly men who had long labored on the sugar cane plantations. Young and hopeful when they arrived in the islands, these men over time had borne in their bodies the costs of years of grueling labor and in their spirits the effects of unfulfilled dreams. Biblical injunctions to care for the elderly meshed with Confucian notions of filial piety. The men were given housing and limited board and medical attention. The care was humble by modern standards, but it was significant, since many of these men had no other means of support.

In caring for these old-timers, church members also exhibited a pride that helped fuse religion and nation. The church sponsored dinners and other events, such as pioneer recognition ceremonies to honor the sacrifices that these men had made in Hawaii. They demonstrated faithfulness to the church through their service; they showed patriotism for their homeland by sending funds to support the Korean independence movement. These practices of religious nationalism sought to honor the past but also were meant to instruct the younger generation about how Korean Americans in Hawaii might live out their convictions.

It comes as no surprise that women were active in nearly every aspect of social service in the congregation. This included serving the local church and community, but many Korean Christian Church women also took part in and provided key leadership for larger efforts, like the Korean Women's Relief Society. Although the society attracted Christian and non-Christian women from throughout the Korean American community in Hawaii, church women played the major roles in the activities of the organization. The society gave women a means of providing leadership for their respective congregations and for the larger Korean American community in Hawaii.

The Korean Women's Relief Society started in March of 1919 when forty-one representatives of various Korean women's societies throughout the islands met in Honolulu to merge their efforts. The massive, nationwide, nonviolent independence demonstration in Korea on 1 March of that year created a ripple effect among Koreans abroad. The primary aim of the Relief Society was to provide support for women and children in Korea and for the provisional government in Shanghai. In addition, it supported political activities in the United States and Europe that pertained to Korean independence.[40]

The society also provided a vehicle for Korean American women to engage with a range of political, education, and religious issues in Hawaii by taking an interest in the needs of local Korean American communities. Helen Chung, a stalwart member of the Korean Christian Church, remembered that her mother and other ladies helped other needy families in Honolulu. "There was such a spirit of giving back then," Chung remembered of her days as a young girl, "and my mom and the others worked hard all day and then came to the church at night to make kimchee and other food to sell so that they could raise funds for the church and for Korea. People would come by the church all the time, not just on Sundays, and whenever you needed to find someone, you usually could find them there."[41] Evident in Chung's memories is the devotion to the homeland that the church inculcated through everyday practices such as making food and raising funds. In 1946, despite the aftermath of World War II, the society managed to send over 700 tons of goods to Korea.[42] The rendering of social services through the Korean Old Men's Home and the Women's Relief Society illustrates how the Korean Christian Church put its religious nationalism into practice.

Religious nationalism also manifested itself in the individual lives of church members, like Nodie Kimhaikim Sohn, who emerged as a key leader within the immigrant community in Hawaii. Her activities and loyalties were closely tied to Rhee and the constellation of organizations that he helped establish. Sohn came to the islands with her family at the age of seven in 1905, and a series of migrations and misfortunes left her and her mother without family there. Rhee took an interest in Nodie Sohn, helping her to continue her education in Hawaii and then arranging for her to attend the

Wooster Academy and Oberlin College in Ohio. She graduated in 1922 with a B.A. in political science from Oberlin and returned to Hawaii to take the post of superintendent of the Korean Christian Institute.

Sohn's post at the institute was the first of a string of leadership positions that extended her influence throughout the Korean American community. While she held top spots in gender-specific organizations, such as chairwoman of the Relief Society, she also served as a trustee of the Korean Christian Church, an officer of the independence movement organization Tongjihoe (Comrade Society), and as superintendent of the Korean Old Men's Home.[43] In her social service and leadership, Sohn epitomized the sensibility and practice of religious nationalism within the context of the Korean Christian Church.

Landscaping Practices

The physical landscape of the Korean Christian Church has borne witness to its religious nationalism. Particularly striking was the gateway mentioned earlier, to the main sanctuary at the Liliha Street church, that replicated the entry to an ancient palace in Seoul. The façade paid tribute to the long and rich history of Korea. The gateway, however, was more than a mere reference to the past, since it physically and symbolically fused religion and nation by serving as the primary entry way into the worship space. As members and visitors made their way into the church, they were reminded by the architecture of the ties that bound them to their faith and to their ancestry in Korea. The very existence of the church and its ministries proclaimed that God was on the side of the oppressed and disenfranchised. The message of liberation in the biblical exodus was very much alive in the hopes that the church members had for their homeland as it struggled under Japanese annexation. In the early years of the church, the gateway also stood as a reminder that Korean Americans in Hawaii were torchbearers for their homeland as Japan sought to absorb and erase Korea into its empire.

The dedication service for the gateway and sanctuary in April of 1938, covered by the Honolulu press, marked the occasion with considerable fanfare. Members took great pride in the fact that the experiment of creating an independent church had proved viable. The new building had cost the princely sum of nearly $45,000.[44] Members had scraped together their funds, and the building benefited from donations by wealthy friends, contacts credited to Rhee. Apparently, the break with the Methodist Church earned Rhee and his compatriots the favor of an elite network of Congregational ministers and missionaries, such as the Yale-trained W. D. Westervelt, who lent support to the budding Korean Christian Church.[45]

However, the liberating message of religious nationalism of Korean Americans had run up against resistance or indifference from some European Americans whom Rhee and others had hoped would help their cause. This was one reason why, by the late 1930s, morale in the new church was low. So, celebrating the accomplishment of dedicating a new church building and its gateway must have buoyed the spirits of those involved. In multiple ways, the gateway both expressed and fed the religious nationalism of the Korean Christian Church.

The statue of Syngman Rhee, also mentioned at the opening of the chapter, is placed high on a granite pedestal near the fellowship hall named in his honor. Rhee is shown dressed in traditional Korean clothing and holding what might be an open Bible in his left hand. His right arm is raised and extended as if to bless those beholding the statue. A more recent addition to the church landscape, the statue was dedicated on 15 August 1985, forty years to the day after the end of Japanese colonial rule in Korea. Religion and nation were bound together in this individual. The plaque on the pedestal reveals this melding by identifying Rhee as both the father of the Republic of Korea and the founder of the Korean Christian Church.[46]

Further evidence of the religious nationalism on display can be found near the base of the statue. Engraved in the stone is text from the Letter of Paul to the Galatians: "For freedom Christ has set us free; stand fast, therefore, and do not submit again to a yoke of slavery." Korea was no longer under the yoke of the Japanese, and church leaders seemed to be sending a message that Christ was to be credited for this liberation. By virtue of the subject of the statue, however, the church also emphasized that God had used his servant Syngman Rhee as a principal agent of this freedom. Church members sought in their commemoration to serve notice that the nationalism of their leader was steeped in Protestant Christianity. One can read the statue as a tribute to the man whose leadership of the organizations and activities affiliated with the Korean Christian Church modeled the religious nationalist vision he had for all of Korea. The statue testified that what had begun in Honolulu had extended across the Pacific to the Korean peninsula. The ascendancy of Rhee to the presidency of Korea could be attributed as the fruit of decades of practicing a religious nationalism in the context of the Korean American community. It is as if the statue physically confirmed what Rhee had written in prison about Christianity: this religion needed to be "the basis for everything."

The church building and the Rhee statue captured in wood, steel, and stone the religious nationalism that animated the dispositions and actions of Korean American Protestants in Hawaii associated with creation of the Korean Christian Church. The landscape of the church campus has served as a reminder to members and those passing by of a historic and enduring religious nationalism.

Summary and Conclusions

The migration of Koreans to Hawaii and the events connected to the founding and history of the Korean Christian Church demonstrate the inner workings of religious nationalism as a Protestant Christian practice. Instrumental to the discussion in this essay has been an understanding of Christian practice as sensibility and as lived religion. Korean Americans gave expression to their religious nationalism in the Hawaiian Islands as an adaptation of the Protestant nationalism forged in Korea under the religious, racial, and political pressures of a nation undergoing colonization by Japan. American Protestant missionaries and the institutions and ideas that they introduced provided much of the material for a Protestant nationalism that stressed self-determination, education, social services, and the physical landscape. Figures like Syngman Rhee embodied and envisioned the practice of religious nationalism. Not without controversy, the practice of religious nationalism resulted in a break with the Methodist mission and the creation of the Korean Christian Church as an independent entity.

The case of Korean American Protestants and their practices contributes some important points to the story of religion in the United States. Located far from the North American continent, Hawaii and its modern history underscore the fact that colonialism is very much part of the nation's past. The experiences of Korean Americans serve as only one example that the mixing of religion and colonialism was not the exclusive preserve of Europe. The United States laid claim to Hawaii then extended its reach throughout the Pacific into the Philippines and to East Asia.

The story of religious nationalism presented here also complicates standard racial dichotomies in American religion and history. The racial dynamics of the black-white divide, while not completely absent in Hawaii, prove less helpful in deciphering the racial formations that emerged there. The practices of Korean American Protestants addressed intra-Asian (Korea and Japan) race relations, as well as an American territorial colonialism in the islands. Majority and minority racial labels have been inverted on the islands, where Asians are the most populous group.[47] In terms of geography, the Korean American case moves us off the mainland, but also contributes to the effort to reclaim a religious legacy in the U.S. West, a region generally portrayed as devoid of religion.[48] Another geographical dimension the story of Korean Americans adds is a blurring of the divide between East and West. American missionaries in Korea helped spawn an indigenous Protestant nationalism that then emigrated and adapted to local conditions on the edges of the United States.

Like the binaries of black/white and East/West, the practices presented here call into question assumptions underlying the term *American*. On one level, the religious nationalism of those immigrants was directed towards Korea; on another level, some of the fervor of Korean Americans for their homeland was in response to the legal and extralegal forms of marginalization and dehumanization that they experienced in the United States. Korean Americans provide an example of the racial legacy of the United States in which certain groups, such as Native Americans, African Americans, and Latinos, have been used to differentiate who is and is not normatively American. The self-determination that resulted in the formation of an independent Korean Christian Church not only resisted Methodist control, but also represented an alternative version of religion, race, and politics to that offered by the missionaries and plantation owners.[49]

Religious nationalism held together the precarious transnational position occupied by Koreans in Hawaii during the early decades of the twentieth century. For Koreans who emigrated, and especially for those associated with the Korean Christian Church, the practice of a religious nationalism enabled them to find meaning and direction for their lives.

CHAPTER SIX

Re-Forming the Church

Preservation, Renewal, and Restoration in American Christian Architecture in California

ROBERTO LINT SAGARENA

Throughout U.S. history, American Christians have bemoaned the contemporary state of Christian belief and practice. Following the U.S.–Mexican War and the military conquest of the far Southwest in 1848, this Christian complaint took on a unique shape. As Anglo-American Protestantism arrived in a region with a recent Latin-American Catholic past, calls for Christian renewal became problematic as they highlighted the region's distinctive heritage. In this part of the the United States, the earliest Christian forbearers were Franciscans and Jesuits, not Puritans and Pilgrims. However, the American need for a history that legitimized their respective conquests offered the opportunity for a symbolic reconciliation between Protestantism and Catholicism, which emerged alongside a new form of nativism.

American fascination with the colonial mission churches (particularly in southern California) resulted in broad-based support for the restoration and preservation of monuments to the Catholic past as emblems of early American Christianity. This valorization of the Spanish missionary past created a new regional history that simultaneously allowed for a critique of Mexican religiosity, rationalized the outcome of American annexation, and gave Americans a new set of Christian exemplars that could be "recovered and restored."

Protestant Encounter with a Catholic Past

The first thorough description of Mexican California to reach general audiences in the United States was Henry Dana's immensely popular autobiographical adventure story *Two Years Before the Mast* (1840). Like many mid-nineteenth-century American Protestant visitors, Dana was generally critical of resident Catholic clergy and laity while voicing enthusiasm for the architecture of the region's adobe mission churches. Over the course of the nineteenth and twentieth centuries, American fascination with the missions would grow dramatically as the buildings' unfired adobe bricks became weathered and decayed, lending them the appearance of great antiquity. The rapid disintegration of these church buildings provided ripe material for American Christians' imaginations, for the ruins offered both historical solemnity and great interpretive possibilities both in the creation of a new history of the region and as powerful emblems of a "primitive" Christianity.[1]

The first mission that Dana saw was at Santa Barbara, where a church was built in 1815, the same year Dana was born in Cambridge, Massachusetts. To the nineteen-year-old sailor's eyes, "the Mission [was] a large and deserted looking place, the outbuildings going to ruin, and everything giving one the impression of decayed grandeur."[2] Such a gothic description became common to American narratives about the missions, adding an embedded ethical dimension to their history. The fact that these "stately monuments" had fallen into disrepair was taken by many Americans as evidence of the moral failure of Mexican rule, prompting critical commentaries about Mexican authorities' "secularization" of the colonial missions established by the Spaniards.

The term *secularization* here refers to the process of raising a Catholic mission church to parish status and replacing the "regular" clergy, from the religious order that had founded the mission (in this case Jesuits and Franciscans), with "secular" (diocesan) clergy. In 1749, King Ferdinand VI of Spain had ordered the secularization of all missions under his dominion in the New World. This edict was followed by the expulsion of the Jesuit order from the Spanish Empire in 1767 and a series of other reforms limiting the privileges of the clergy. As a result, the power and influence of the religious orders declined and the nature of Catholic missionization in the final years of the Spanish Empire in the Americas was permanently transformed. Under these new policies, tax-paying settlements were established and authority over Indian converts was transferred from ecclesiastical to civil authorities.[3]

Initially, the missions of Alta California had been founded largely to defend the Spanish imperial frontier against Russian and British incursions.[4] The last major Spanish missionization effort launched after Ferdinand's secularization reforms, the Alta California missions' future was clouded from the first. The document that ordered their establishment, the *Reglamento De La Nueva California* (1773), also contained the orders for their prompt secularization and transfer to civil rule.[5] The secularization of the missions of Alta California began in earnest in the early 1830s, shortly after Mexican independence, in 1821, and the founding of the last mission in the California chain, San Francisco Solano, in 1824.[6]

Henry Dana first saw Santa Barbara's mission only a few months after it had been secularized, tempting him to offer an American evaluation of the role of Mexican "misrule" in the "tragedy" of secularization. Dana wrote:

> Ever since the independence of Mexico, the missions have been going down; until at last a law was passed, stripping them of all their possessions, and confining the priests to their spiritual duties; and at the same time declaring all the Indians free and independent *Rancheros*. The change in the condition of the Indians was, as might be supposed, only nominal; they were virtually slaves, as much as they ever were. But in the Missions the change was complete. The priests have now no power, except in their religious character, and the great possessions of the missions are given over to be preyed upon by the harpies of the civil power. . . . The change had been made but a few years before our arrival upon the coast, yet in that short time the trade was greatly diminished, credit impaired, and the venerable missions going rapidly to decay.[7]

Dana's writing is remarkable as a statement of both reproach and regret about the decline of Catholic order in Mexican California made by a Harvard-educated, Protestant New Englander. Here, Dana manages to draw from the Black Legend his own observations about the harsh realities of mission life faced by Native American Christian neophytes. In describing the missionary decline, Dana can articulate his contempt for Mexican civil authority and cast aspersions on the clergy as slaveholders while simultaneously empathizing with them as Christian "victims" of Mexican civil authorities.

Dana's reading of the decline of the missions became a powerful and influential model for Americans' perceptions during and after the U.S.-Mexican War (1846– 1848). Early American reviews of the Franciscans' interactions with Indians at the missions were mixed, but even authors who, like Dana, were appalled at their treatment saw the secularization of the missions as terrible. Those with a more sympathetic view of the priests saw the secularization of the missions as an even more heinous act. For example, during the war with Mexico, Joseph Revere, the grandson of Paul Revere, described the secularization of the missions in much the same way as Dana had, but he also bemoaned the loss of the influence of the Catholic clergy upon the indigenous population. In his wartime diary, *A Tour of Duty in California* (1848), he wrote:

> Upon a small elevation at no great distance, we saw the ruined towers of an old church, and also some walls built of adobe, which had evidently enclosed extensive and commodious buildings, now fallen into utter decay. This was the ancient mission of Carmel, which in common with all the other missions, had been suppressed by an act of the Mexican Congress for reasons which I am unable to disclose. . . . This consecrated spot, so long the abode of holy men, is now the property of a private person, and has fairly "gone

to grass." Whether the surrounding Indians are any the worse Christians, or the more troublesome neighbors, may be easily guessed by those who know that Catholic missionaries exert a more wholesome influence over the aborigines than any others.[8]

Positive assessments of the Franciscan missionaries, like Revere's, became increasingly common after the war, as the missions were adopted as American ruins by settlers and tourists. The fact that the 1869 (and subsequent) editions of Dana's book revised his numerous references to the mission Indians as slaves to the more neutral term *serfs* is telling of changes in late-nineteenth-century American attitudes that were increasingly positive towards California's Catholic missionaries.[9]

As romantic American portrayals of the Spanish Franciscans and their missions proliferated, animus towards the Mexican implementation of secularization grew in direct proportion. This trend accelerated, and by the 1870s American authors in California commonly portrayed the missions and missionaries in positive terms, praising their paternalism towards the Indians and damning the "greedy" effects of "Mexican" secularization, even though secularization was explicitly a goal of Spain's enterprise. These tropes formed the basis of a genre of mission history that has remained immensely popular and influential for well over a century. An early example of this literature is Elizabeth Hughes's *The California of the Padres; or, Footprints of Ancient Communism,* published in 1875. Although she praised the padres' accomplishments using an odd blend of communism, feminism, and near pantheism, Hughes lauded the mission system in a very typical American fashion by telling her readers, "The Indians had all their wants supplied, and lived in peace and plenty." She bemoaned the fact that the missions' endowment, the California Pious Fund, was taken by the "hungry office-seekers and politicians" of the Mexican government and that "as the Fathers lost their influence on the community . . . everything went into decay."[10]

Hughes's book is noteworthy for praising "our friends the padres" for achieving their conquest of California "in the face of the greatest difficulties, not so much by power of force as by the feminine power of love and inspiration." Like many authors after her, Hughes would clearly ascribe negative aspects of colonization and Mexican rule to secular greed and idealize the religious altruism of the padres as a valuable historical legacy that Americans should claim. Hughes and many of her contemporaries imagined the Spanish conquest of California as having been a purely spiritual one. And, this refinement of the American understanding of the region's history had great implications for the way the region's present was understood; the American conquest of California was portrayed as a renewal of the Spanish Franciscan conquest, that is, as a legitimate, peaceful, and inevitable progressive transition towards a perceived greater civility, industry, and piety.

The Importance of Religious Intent in Conquest

While Americans came to picture California's early Spanish missionaries as pious men distinct from the secular corruptions of civil authorities, American Catholics (and in time, most Americans in California) came to see themselves more clearly as the legitimate heirs to the religious aims and accomplishments of the Franciscan padres. American settlement was defined as a civilizing project that would elevate religiosity in California after a dark period of decay under Mexican rule. The 100th anniversaries of many of the missions during the 1870s provided Americans with an opportunity to publicly celebrate their emerging vision of California's history and to practice Christian calls for a return to an earlier faith.

For example, the 1877 centennial celebration of the founding of Mission Saint Francis de Assis (better known as San Francisco's Mission Dolores) was a grand affair that attracted a crowd of more than 5,000 people, including such dignitaries as California's governor (the "president of the day") and the Mexican, Spanish, Russian, Portuguese, Chilean, and Costa Rican consuls. The presence of civil and religious dignitaries as well as a large Protestant showing among the celebrants bespeaks the broad appeal and importance that the history of the missions and the padres already held for Californians at the time.

California's Archbishop Alemany opened the festivities with a speech honoring the missions' founders. After providing numerous examples of the protection and instruction of Native Americans by priests in the Americas, he cited William Prescott's depiction of Queen Isabelle as the "Indians' excellent friend and protector" as final proof of the benevolence of the Franciscans' conquest of California. Alemany translated the Spanish conquest of California as the inheritance of all Americans by telling his audience, "Well may California be proud of her heroic disinterested Christian pioneers, who in a short time transformed numberless barbarous tribes into comparatively well-civilized Christian communities; and well may we echo to-day with sweet strains of joyous melody the solemn Te Deum intoned here for the first time one Hundred years ago."[11] By establishing the Franciscans as California's pioneers, with no reference to lay Spanish or Mexican settlers, Alemany reiterated the idea that California's conquest had been a strictly religious one. And, by doing so he was able to make a more powerful and less contentious claim to his audience about the legitimate succession of the American Catholic Church to the missionary fields of the early Spanish Franciscans after a war of conquest.

The best-received, and lengthiest, speech of the celebration was given by John Dwinelle, who was a Protestant attorney and local historian. His lecture provides insight into the curious ecumenism present in American versions of the missions' history. Dwinelle told the assembled celebrants, "Precisely one hundred years ago, in the year 1769, the colonization of California had its beginning; but it was a religious, not a civil or political colonization; and its origin, aims and results are to be treated as the work of the Roman Catholic Church. As a Protestant, with my fellow Protestants, I come here not to sing fulsome praises to the Roman Catholic Church, but to render her a due meed of honor."[12]

This opening statement displays the principal elements of the rhetorical strategy employed by Protestants to overcome any incongruities that might have been perceived in their celebration of the Catholic missions' history: a repetitive insistence on the religious character of the original conquest of California. Dwinelle reiterated that, "the colonization of California was not civil, but religious. Its plan was not so much to bring citizens into California, as it was to convert the native savages of California into Christians. . . . The religious character of this colonization is most emphatically and accurately described [by the] Hon. Alpheus Felch, one of the first judges on the United States Land Commission in California."[13] Dwinelle's reliance on an American Land Commissioner as an authority on the nature of the Spanish colonization and conquest of California is quite revealing of what was at stake. By establishing the original colonization of California as a religious enterprise, the legitimacy of the presence of lay Spanish and Mexican settlers who were not Franciscans was undermined. In this schema, what tied one to the place was a religious connection—that is, a connection between "genuinely" Christian people.

Dwinelle underscored the connections between Americans and the Franciscans by painting the padres as industrious and refined men who might feel at home in upper-class American social clubs. He claimed that, "the Franciscan Friars, who superintended these establishments, most of whom were from Spain, and many of them highly cultivated men, statesmen, diplomatists, soldiers, engineers, artists, lawyers, merchants, and physicians, before they became Franciscans, always treated the neophyte Indians with the most paternal kindness."[14] In contrast, he claimed, Mexican Californio—Spanish settler—merchants could be "characterized by the exuberance of their noses, their addiction to the social game called monté, and the utter fearlessness with which they encountered the monster *aguardiente* [alcoholic spirits]." Motivated by "rancor and greed," these private traders "were both constant and persistent in their denunciations of the monks who had charge of the Missions."[15]

The implications of Dwinelle's presentation are made clear in his condemnation of the Mexican government's "theft" of the mission's endowment and the Californios' "criminal" secularization of the missions. If the original conquest of California was religious and Mexican settlers' culpability in the decline of religion was obvious in the secularization and decay of the missions, then Mexican civil society could be seen as both illegitimate and morally bankrupt. For Americans, their own conquest and occupation of California was deemed legitimate precisely because they valued the missions' history and sought to connect themselves with it.

Dwinelle ended his speech to great fanfare and an ovation by a very enthusiastic audience. But, after the applause and cheers of Americans had subsided, the aged Mariano Vallejo stepped up to the podium to provide an alternate view of the missions' history. After a tribute to the efforts of the Franciscan missionaries, he mounted a defense of Mexican civil authorities that turned the tables on the American historical presentations of the day and obliquely criticized the American conquest of Mexican California. Pausing after his discussion of the merits of the Franciscans, he said,

> And, now, permit me to make a few remarks in defense of the good name of some of the individuals who governed this country during the Mexican Administration, whose reputation has been sometimes wantonly attacked; while nothing has ever been said against the Governors, under Spain who preceded them. . . . That the Mexican Governors robbed the Missions is an absurdity. . . . Castro, Gutierrez, Chico, Alvarado, Micheltorena, and lastly Pio Pico, all had to contend with revolutionary elements. The priests had disappeared, the neophytes had left the Missions and had gone away to the villages of the gentiles, and the government, under such circumstances, had to take possession of the lands which were claimed by the Missions, through the power which it possessed, and in order to defend the country against an *invasion with which it was threatened.*[16]

In short, Vallejo blamed the negative effects of the secularization of the missions on the American invasion of California. He argued that if not for the war, then perhaps the missions and their lands would not have been auctioned for proceeds to support the defense of the territory from hostile American invaders.

But Vallejo's most damaging assertion against the history presented by Americans was a denunciation of the idea that the colonization of California was strictly religious. He pointed out that,

> it is necessary to bear in mind that the Spanish flag waved over California, and that the priests did no more than comply with the orders of the King, at the same time that they looked for their own protection and that of the Missions, soldiers being constantly engaged in protecting the Missions, and in continuous campaigns for the purpose of keeping the Indians under subjection. Without those soldiers, the Indians would have risen immediately against the Missions, and all the white inhabitants would have inevitably perished.[17]

Vallejo held that, the opinion of Americans and their land commissioners aside, a strictly religious conquest did not and could not have occurred.

Doubtless his American audience would have been given a great deal to think about had they understood Vallejo, but he delivered his comments in Spanish without a translator.[18] There is no record of a response from Bishop Alemany or any other Spanish speakers in attendance, but the English speaking audience politely applauded his concluding remarks and admired the poise and dignity of the old "Don" as he left the stage.

Spanish Missions Made American

As political and economic power shifted into the hands of the growing population of American settlers, the region's urban environments were quickly and dramatically redefined. Old adobe buildings were torn down and more typically American wooden structures were erected, giving southern California's towns a new appearance. Writing in 1874, a reporter and California booster by the name of Benjamin Truman enthusiastically described this change, telling his readers, "Los Angeles is at present—at least to a great extent—an American city. Adobes have given way to elegant and substantial dwellings and stores; the customs of well-regulated society have proved to be destructive elements in opposition to lawlessness and crime; industry and enterprise have now usurped the place of indolence and unproductiveness."[19] Similarly, an 1875 essay in the *Santa Barbara Weekly* newspaper commended that community's complete metamorphosis, claiming, "Santa Barbara has now emerged from her transitional state, she is no longer a Spanish, but an American town."[20]

These transformations of California's urban environments were mirrored in architectural changes at the missions. The necessary restoration of decaying mission buildings offered a chance to add Americanizing features to some of the churches' façades, patterning them after New England churches. Priests at Mission San Juan Bautista hired carpenters newly arrived from the East Coast to modernize their church with a New England steeple and belfry in 1865.[21] Similar but more extensive renovations were begun at Mission San Luis Obispo in 1868, resulting in a complete makeover of the entire front of the church by 1880: a New England steeple was added, the red roof tiles were removed, and the structure was covered with wooden clapboard siding. And even more dramatically, when Mission San José was damaged in an earthquake in 1868, the original adobe structure was completely leveled and a wooden Gothic Revival church was built over the colonial foundation.[22]

But, the Americanization of mission architecture did not reflect any dampening of enthusiasm for the Spanish Franciscans and the missions themselves. Rather, it was a concrete expression of Americans' appropriation of the Spanish colonial past; just as

Americans on the Atlantic seaboard could point to a Puritan heritage, Americans on the Pacific coast began to claim a morally equivalent Franciscan heritage. By the 1870s, Californians felt secure enough about the Americanness of the padres and their missions to employ them as romantic emblems of their state and, perhaps more importantly, understand them as Christian exemplars. In 1876, at the centennial celebration of the Declaration of Independence in Philadelphia—the most American of celebrations—the California exhibit proudly represented the state's past through a collection of picturesque watercolors of the missions.[23]

Romance Spurs Renewal

On 20 December 1881, well-known writer Helen Hunt Jackson made her way into the city of Los Angeles aboard a Southern Pacific Rail Pullman car. Local newspapers reported that the author had come to write a series of essays on the area for *The Century Magazine*.[24] Within a few years, Jackson's California writings would further shape the way Americans in southern California articulated their sense of place and understood the state's religious past.

In 1883, *The Century* published Jackson's "Echoes In The City Of The Angels," an essay that recounted the city's history and gave an "insider's" tour of the remains of its Spanish and Mexican past. She wrote: "The city of the Angels is a prosperous city now . . . but it has not shaken off its past. A certain indefinable, delicious aroma from the old, ignorant, picturesque times lingers still, not only in its byways and corners, but in the very centres of its newest activities."[25]

"Echoes" was largely inspired by conversations with Antonio and Mariana Coronel, a nostalgic Californio couple who provided a great deal of anecdotal material for Jackson's depictions of southern California. She portrayed winning the couple's friendship as an entrée into the bygone world of the Californios, recounting, "Whoever has the fortune to pass as a friend the threshold of [the Coronels'] house finds himself transported, as by a miracle, into the life of a half-century ago."[26] American readers were greatly intrigued by her seductive display of California's romantic past. She claimed that a visitor could never,

> know more of Los Angeles than its lovely outward semblances unless he have the good fortune to win past the barrier of proud, sensitive, tender reserve, behind which is hid the life of the few remaining survivors of the old Spanish and Mexican regime. Once past this, he gets glimpses of the same stintless hospitality and immeasurable courtesy which gave to the old Franciscan establishments a world-wide fame. . . . In houses whose doors seldom open to English speaking people, there are rooms full of relics of that fast-van-

ishing past,—strongholds also of a religious faith, almost as obsolete, in its sort and degree, as are the garments of the aged creatures who are peacefully resting their last days
on its support.[27]

Jackson seduced her readers with the implication that if they hurried out to California, they too might catch a glimpse of what remained of its exotic and pious
Catholic past, that the premodern romance that had attracted American tourists to
the stately churches of Catholic Europe could also be found in a domesticated form
in America's Far West. Also published in 1883 by *The Century* was Jackson's "Father Junipero and His Work," a biographical essay about the life of Father Junipero Serra
(1713–1784), the Franciscan president of Alta California's chain of missions.[28] This
was the first and most influential hagiography of Serra to be read widely outside of
California; shortly after its publication, Little Brown and Company began reprinting
the article for use in public schools across the country and continued to do so until
1902.[29]

Helen Hunt Jackson's own enthusiasm for California's Spanish Franciscan missionaries was, perhaps, surprising, given that she was brought up in a strict Congregationalist family in Amherst, Massachusetts, and her depictions of Catholic clergy in
earlier European travel writings had often been negative.[30] But, in "Father Junipero
and His Work," Jackson made a crucial distinction between Catholics in general and
members of the Franciscan order in particular. Citing "a Protestant biographer of St.
Francis," she claimed that the Franciscans, like their order's patron, were motivated
by a Christian selflessness so great that "Cardinals and Pope alike doubted its being
within the possibility of human possibility."[31] By stressing the missionaries' Franciscan identity over their Catholic one, she made a distinction that helped to make them
and their history more palatable to Protestant Americans.

Although Jackson drew most of her factual material from a translation of Francisco Palou's 1781 Spanish biography of Serra, her narrative portrayal of the missionary and his fellow Franciscans was a very American one; it condemned the Mexican
secularization of the missions and bemoaned the churches' decayed condition. She
called for efforts at restoration, remonstrating "both the Catholic Church and the state
of California," for allowing Mission Carmel, the burial site of Father Serra, to "be left
to crumble away."[32] Jackson denounced this neglect as a shameful lack of respect for
the Franciscans' selfless spiritual missionization of California and their civilizing influence upon the Indians.

Jackson went even further than most of her predecessors by favorably comparing
California's past with that of states on the Atlantic seaboard. She told her national audience:

There was a strange difference, fifty years ago, between the atmosphere of life on the east and west sides of the American continent: On the Atlantic shore, the descendants of the Puritans, weighed down by serious purpose, half grudging the time for their staid yearly Thanksgiving, and driving the Indians further and further into the wilderness every year, fighting and killing them; on the sunny pacific shore, the merry people of Mexican and Spanish blood, troubling themselves about nothing, dancing away whole days and nights like children, while their priests were gathering the Indians by thousands into communities and feeding and teaching them.[33]

Thus, Jackson's idealized portrayal of the Franciscans articulate a moral indictment of her fellow Americans for their treatment of the indigenous peoples. And, Jackson was the first nationally read author to cast the Spanish Catholic missionaries as moral exemplars for all American "decedents of the Puritans." Quoting historian John Dwinelle, she admonished her readers:

"If we ask where are now the thirty thousand Christianized Indians who once enjoyed the beneficence and created the wealth of the twenty-one Catholic missions of California, and then contemplate the most wretched of all want of systems which has surrounded them under our own government, we shall not withhold our admiration for those good and devoted men who, with such wisdom, sagacity, and self sacrifice, reared these wonderful institutions in the wilderness of California. They at least would have preserved these Indian races if they had been left to pursue unmolested their work of pious beneficence."[34]

The popularity of Jackson's writings about California's Catholic past reached their height in her wildly successful romantic novel *Ramona* (1884). Its nostalgic descriptions of Californian piety cemented American conceptions of the region's past and provided the newcomers arriving during the state's cycles of real estate booms with a sense of regional identity tied directly to a Christian past. The building rush in southern California attracted many young architects from San Francisco. The work of Willis Polk, John Galen Howard, William P. Moore, Ernest Coxhead, John C. Pelton, W. J. Cuthbertson, and Joseph Cather Newsom would be deeply influenced by their exposure to southern California's mission architecture. The popularity of *Ramona* was fanning Americans' fascination with the missions into a heated passion. Like many in the growing crowds of visitors to the old churches, these architects sketched and painted the churches, observing their forms and admiring elements of their design.[35]

The missions' "beauteous decay" was the source of much of their aesthetic appeal. As a result, many of the adobe churches had endured the forty or more years since the American conquest without repairs and were nearing complete collapse. Early preservation efforts by Catholic priests had focused on maintaining the structural integrity of the mission buildings, usually with little concern about retaining the building's original appearance. But, as the missions assumed the role of regional emblems, southern Californians began to take an interest in grooming their "stately ruins," and they insisted on historical authenticity in their repair and restoration. In 1889, Los Angeles city librarian Tessa L. Kelso organized the Association for the Preservation of the Missions, with the help of the newly founded Historical Society of Southern California. Both groups organized educational tours of the missions that at once served to inculcate American versions of the missions' history and to raise funds for their preservation.[36]

Just when mission preservation efforts were beginning to come into vogue, the speculative financing that had been driving southern California's building boom gave way to a bust. As construction dwindled, many boom towns became ghost towns and architects returned to work in more economically stable San Francisco, but their exposure to the romantic enthusiasm for the missions in southern California would inspire attempts to create a distinctive new architecture for the state.[37]

The articulation of a Californian style of architecture had been attempted as early as 1883. That year, rail baron Leyland Stanford commissioned landscape architect Frederick Law Olmsted and the architectural firm of Shepley, Rutan and Coolidge of Boston to build his university in a manner that was "an adaptation of the adobe building of California." But the end result, Stanford University's brown sandstone buildings, more closely followed the Mediterranean Romanesque style more familiar to the Boston architects than the style of the whitewashed adobes of California.[38]

Less than a decade later, in 1890, San Francisco Bay area architect Willis Polk, returning from his sojourn in the Southland, published sketches for "An Imaginary Mission Church of the Southern California Type" in the architectural periodical *Architecture and Building*. In doing so, Polk presented the design of the adobe missions for serious consideration and imitation by the broader American community of architects. He made use of his southern California sketches to assemble a building that drew architectural elements from several different missions, adding the novel feature of a tower over the nave. His imaginary church was revolutionary; for the first time, stylistic elements from the missions were divorced from specific church buildings and employed as an architectural vocabulary of forms, echoing the Gothic Revival façades.

This breakthrough coincided with early deliberations about the style to be employed in the construction of the building representing California at the Chicago World's Fair (World's Columbian Exposition) in 1893. Polk and other architects who had worked in southern California published a number of essays in *Architectural News* and *California Architect and Building News* that carefully considered the best design elements of California's missions. Their stated hope was that these papers would be "both timely and useful in the proposition to represent this semi-Spanish Renaissance in the Architecture of California's buildings at the coming Columbian Exposition."[39]

The Californian World's Fair Commission held two contests for designs for the state's building. The first produced an eclectic mix of entries, none of which were deemed distinctly Californian enough. As a result, the California commissioners limited the second competition to designs in an as yet "unknown conglomerate style of . . . Moorish and Old Mission" that, it was hoped, would be more evocative of life on the Pacific coast.[40] A. Page Brown produced the winning entry. In his design for a large, 144-by-435 foot, building, Brown borrowed elements from the missions at Santa Barbara, San Luis Rey, and San Luis Obispo and added a "Moorish" central tower. It was to be constructed out of metal and wood with a sheath of plaster of Paris molded around fibrous jute cloth, quickly and economically providing the semblance of adobe.

The *California Monthly World Fair's Magazine* enthusiastically claimed that Brown's building would place its visitors "face to face with the California of Yesteryear. . . . We will have a building whose architecture is all our own, which will take the beholder back to the days when the Fathers, with their old Missions, started the march of civilization in the Golden West."[41] Upon completion, the *Official Guide to the World's Columbian Exposition* described Brown's building as having,

> carefully followed the old mission style in the design, but has interjected enough of the more ornate Moorish to relieve the somewhat somber effect of the old adobe church, while giving the required light and roominess. Outside, there is a clear story with a great flat central dome as the crowning feature, and a roof garden to heighten the semi-tropical appearance. . . . On the four corners and flanking the dome, are towers designed after the mission belfries, and in them are swung some of the Old Spanish bells that have outlived the padres and their crumbling churches.[42]

In 1895, Tessa L. Kelso retired from her position as city librarian and left the then-moribund Association for the Preservation of the Missions leaderless. But, the same year (and with encouragement from Kelso) Charles Lummis established a new preservation group, which would take on the task of preserving the missions; it was known as the Landmarks Club. While he had inherited the membership rosters of the earlier association, Lummis initially found little popular support for his efforts to restore the most decayed of the missions. Catholic priests had worked to preserve those missions that continued to serve as churches, but they had largely ignored the mission buildings that were ruins.[43] Because for both Catholic and Protestant Americans the historical significance of the Franciscan churches centered on their secularization and decay, any restoration threatened to undermine their role as crumbling monuments to "Mexican misrule."[44]

While many turn-of-the-century southern Californian Protestants were willing to romanticize Spanish Franciscan missionaries in the past, bringing ruined Catholic churches back to life in the present was another matter altogether. Lummis wrote in his memoirs, years later:

> It seems incredible to me now what uphill work it was to arouse any interest whatsoever in this [mission preservation] cause. In the first place a tidal wave of the thrice-damned A.P.A. (Pre-cursor to the Klu Klux Klan) had swept over California and religious bigotry (on the one side) was intense. Absurd as it seems, it is a literal fact that thousands of otherwise sane business men and citizens in Los Angeles firmly believed that the Catholics were drilling every night in the basement of the cathedral to rise and massacre the Protestants. The fact that the cathedral had no basement cut no figure at all.[45]

In order to assuage the common anti-Catholic sentiments of the time and court Protestant participation in the Landmarks Club, it was crucial that mission restoration be cast as the preservation of *civic* historical monuments. The Landmarks Club ultimately gained the widespread favor of the region's Protestants, in part as a result of Lummis's repeated assertion in *Land Of Sunshine* that "those mighty piles belong not to the Catholic church but to you and me, and to our children and the world. They are monuments and beacons of Heroism and Faith and Zeal and Art. Let us save them—not for the Church but for Humanity."[46]

But, the missions' Catholic past was still central to their significance for Americans, and a mission building divorced from its religious identity held little historical or cultural significance. This was something that Lummis came to realize during his acquisition of the chapel of the *asistencia* at Pala as he later recounted.

> A squatter name Veall "jumped" the Pala Mission and homesteaded most of the valley. His wife Kanaka, was a good Catholic, but Veall was a rabid A.P.A. Somehow, however, he had liked me in the old days when I went down there hunting and photographing. . . . I suggested to him one day that maybe he should sell it to me. . . . So in a few weeks I was the happy possessor of the Pala Mission. What a beautiful thing if the Landmarks Club could have a mission of its very own, a public park, with all its value as a monument of tradition and romance and achievement, but without any other "strings" whatever. But at the next meeting of my associates when I wanted to expiate on this dream, my tongue went flat, and almost to my own surprise I said, "Damn it boys! Pala wasn't built for a landmark or a park, but for a temple! I think we would be fences with stolen goods to keep it!" To my delight there wasn't a hem or haw. Not one of us was a Catholic, but we

all felt this certain fitness and reverence—as no one could help feeling who had worked so long in the presence of the work done by those great Apostles.[47]

For the club to turn the chapel into a secular building would be to commit the much-critiqued sin of California's Mexican regime. In the end, the chapel at Pala was sold to Catholic Archbishop Montgomery for the price that Lummis had paid for it plus the promise of a ten-year lease on the chapel, during which time the club would effect its restoration as a functioning church.

Thus, the promotion of mission preservation contained contradictory impulses: on the one hand, many Californians sought to establish the missions as civic monuments for all Americans; on the other, many dreamed of revitalizing these individual buildings in service to a living Catholic faith. These competing interests were productive, however. Restoring churches that had "fallen victim" to Mexican secularization became a progressive and patriotic civic act, one that allowed preservationists to reinforce Americans' understanding of their conquest of California as an echo of the Franciscan's earlier "spiritual conquest." Mission restoration legitimized the American inheritance of the state and thereby forged an ecumenical base of support for the Landmarks Club's work from among the region's religious leaders. Shortly after the restoration of the chapel at Pala began, an ad for the Landmarks Club in *Land Of Sunshine* reported:

> A course of lectures on behalf of the Club is now inaugurated. Rt. Rev. Geo. Montgomery, Bishop of Los Angeles and Monterey, opened the course December 28, with an extremely instructive lecture on the "Secularization of the Missions." It is notable that the work of preserving our historic landmarks is alike generously encouraged by this Roman Catholic bishop and by the Episcopal bishop of Los Angeles, Rt. Rev. Joseph H. Johnson, who shared the platform and prefaced the lecture with a cordial address. The old bigotries fall away before the joint interest of educated Americans to save the historic and the artistic.[48]

Though the leadership of the Landmarks Club was largely male, its foot soldiers and main organizers were primarily wealthy, white, Anglo-Saxon, Protestant women. One of the club's most prominent female members, Eliza Otis, known as "California's Beloved Mission Poet," who was wife of Harrison Grey Otis (publisher of the *Los Angeles Times*), perfectly captured the tone of the club's civic-minded ecumenism in a recruitment ad in the *Times*. She wrote:

> Catholicism and Protestantism are looked on generally as opposing forces, but here each had its work of preparation to accomplish, and each did it well, and today they stand face

to face without a thought of conflict. Puritanism commends the work accomplished by those early Mission Fathers, and comes here to sow and to reap in the soil which they made ready for the larger and grander life of this later century. The work proposed by the Landmarks Club, "to conserve the missions and other historic landmarks of Southern California," is a most commendable one and should have the hearty support of every public-spirited citizen of the state.[49]

No Catholic was more admired by the largely Protestant, silk-gloved members of the Landmarks Club than Father Junipero Serra. In a manner similar to their promotion of the preservation of the Catholic missions, Landmarks Club members launched a campaign for the canonization of Junipero Serra. Lummis himself inquired of Father Zephyrin Englehardt, a Franciscan historian and caretaker of the mission archives at Santa Barbara, why the Roman Catholic Church had not already declared Serra a saint and what the probability of its happening soon might be. In a letter to Englehardt in 1909, Lummis wrote, "This man [Serra]—whom, as a historian, I count foremost among all missionary pioneers and administrators of the New World—should have the proper recognition. It isn't for me to meddle with the programme of the church; but I have a right to work as an American and a Protestant and a Californian in recognition of the hero whom not even the A.P.A. seems to hate."[50] When Englehardt expressed his doubts about the likelihood of Serra's beatification, much less canonization, Lummis seemed all the more determined and enthusiastic about his cause. He responded to Englehardt, "I am a good deal disappointed at the improbability that we can secure the canonization of Junipero Serra. . . . However, I am a somewhat obstinate person; and am going to keep at this until whipped off the circuit. We have vague whispers of miraculous affairs; and I am going to trace them down."[51]

Sadly for the Landmarks Club's cause, Lummis was unable to document any miracles attributable to Serra. But, as a result of the Club's efforts, Serra's sainthood became a matter of public interest and regional pride for many Californians, regardless of their denomination. And, eventually, a controversial movement for Serra's canonization would emerge within the Catholic Church, its deliberations relying, in part, on the testimony of Protestant historians of the missions.[52]

The endorsement of Serra as an American hero and of the missions as public monuments not only worked to promote preservation efforts, it also supported Mission Revival architecture as the rightful and definitive style for the region. In the first decades of the twentieth century, designers of southern California's city halls, the Carnegie libraries, public schools, and resort hotels relied heavily on mission stylings. The Southern Pacific and Santa Fe rail lines rebuilt the region's rail depots exclusively in Mission Revival style. One historian reports that for each southern California house "done in the New England style . . . there [were] a thousand of the 'Mission Architecture.'"[53]

Even missions that were restored by the Landmarks Club were given a revival treatment; because of their advanced deterioration, their restoration often became a matter of imaginative reconstruction. Lummis recruited Sumner P. Hunt and Arthur B. Benton, famous Mission Revivalists, as the Landmark Club's architects "on account of their particular understanding and sympathy with the Mission architecture." And, while Lummis insisted on authenticity in the restoration of the missions, often, entire sections of the church buildings to be restored provided little evidence of their original form and were redesigned by the club's architects, blurring the line between the Franciscan mission designs and Mission Revival architecture.[54]

By far the most striking use of Mission Revival style, however, was its regular appearance in the design of southern California's Protestant churches. Lummis rightly boasted that the Protestant acceptance of the style was due in fair measure to the ecumenical influence of the Landmarks Club's preservation work. He noted: "It is quite common in California to see a Methodist or Baptist church calmly adopting the identical lines of the old Franciscan Missions—which of course makes them better architecture than their denominational brethren. The world do move! The Mission architecture is as Catholic as the Pope himself. Yet when the Landmarks club began its crusade, it is safe to say that not a Protestant church extant would have 'stooped to Romish architecture.'"[55] Preservationists' portrayal of "Old Mission Romance" as public history allowed the designers of Protestant churches to participate in the architectural vogue and integrate their houses of worship into what had become the region's signature style, without troubling themselves overmuch about its Catholic inspiration. And, as Mission Revival became ubiquitous in southern California, Protestant churches that were built in the style became the most dramatic signs of Americans' use of a Latin American–Catholic past as a moral anchor for the Anglo-Protestant present. There could be no stronger emblem for Americans' having claimed historical and moral continuity with the Franciscans' conquest of California than the widespread use of Mission Revival stylings in Protestant churches.

PART III

DEVOTIONAL PRACTICES AND MODERN PREDICAMENTS, 1880–1920

CHAPTER SEVEN

"Acting Faith"

Practices of Religious Healing in Late-Nineteenth-Century Protestantism

HEATHER D. CURTIS

At five minutes before seven o'clock on a winter evening in the year 1879, Sarah Mix knelt at the bedside of Mrs. Herbert Hall. For months, Hall had been confined to her bed with what she described as "enlargement of the spleen, inflammation of the bowels, and falling of the uterus." Her doctors had given her no hope of recovery, and she had begun to prepare herself to die. But Hall's friends were not willing to give up. Having read in the local newspaper about some "wonderful cures" through faith and prayer, these friends prevailed on Hall to send for Sarah Mix, an African American woman from the neighboring town of Wolcottville, Connecticut, whose ministry with the sick was becoming increasingly well known throughout New England.[1]

When Mix arrived at Hall's residence in West Haven, Mrs. Hall was so ill that she could not lift her head from the pillow. After ushering everyone from the room, Mix encouraged Hall to believe that God would raise her up from the "bed of death." Then she began to recite a "very simple prayer" asking God to "remove the pains and all inflammation." Next, Mix anointed Hall with oil in the name of the Lord, and laid hands upon her bowels and heart, beseeching God to heal both body and soul. "As she drew her hand over my bloated body," Hall recalled, "I felt the swelling going down." Finally, Mix bade the sick woman to "rise up and walk." At that moment, Hall got out of bed, dressed herself and went down to the kitchen, startling her family so much that one of her sisters fainted in surprise.[2]

From the beginning, many Christians have engaged in the practice of healing. While most, if not all believers have embraced Jesus as healer, the doctrines and rituals associated with this aspect of the Christian faith have varied widely and have often occasioned heated controversy. Similarly, although Christians repeatedly have culled a common repertoire of healing practices from their scriptures, the meanings they ascribe to prayer, laying-on of hands, and anointing with oil, as well as the cultural and theological work being accomplished in these rituals, are always shaped by historical and social circumstances. Throughout the nineteenth century, for example, debates over the place and practice of healing in the Christian life proliferated as shifting theological and cultural currents prompted a widespread rethinking of the relationship between bodily illness and spiritual health, and these debates helped generate a panoply of health reform and healing movements, such as Grahamism, hydropathy, homeopathy, Spiritualism, and Christian Science. As many historians have observed, these diverse movements presented alternatives to the regimens of "regular" or "orthodox" medicine and also to the devotional ethics of "orthodox" or "reformed" Protestantism, both of which disciplined their subjects to embrace patient endurance of affliction as the pathway to physical health and spiritual holiness. Scholars of American religion have long been attuned to the revisionist efforts of movements like Spiritualism, Christian Science, and New Thought, groups that are often classified as "outsider" or "alternative" religions in relation to Protestant evangelicalism. However, historians have only recently begun to take note of how divine healing, an extremely popular movement that flourished among late-nineteenth-century evangelicals, like Mix and Hall, worked to transform the way in which Christians contended with suffering.[3]

Exploring the complex manner in which advocates of divine healing or "faith cure" described and enacted the enigmatic relationship among human agency, ritual practice, and divine sovereignty in the healing process affords an opportunity to observe how participants in this movement contributed to a wider effort to modify the meaning and experience of pain in the Christian life.[4] According to proponents of divine healing, overcoming illness and its effects upon the flesh required an ability to translate belief into behavior. To be healed, they contended, was to believe that God had banished sickness from the body and to act accordingly, regardless of any sensory evidence to the contrary. The practice of healing, therefore, involved training the senses to ignore lingering pain or symptoms of sickness and disciplining the body to "act faith" by getting out of bed and serving God through active engagement with others. For the ailing women and men who espoused this perspective, participating in practices such as meditation, prayer, laying-on of hands, and anointing helped foster the requisite mental habits, corporal behaviors, and spiritual dispositions that faith in divine healing demanded. Within this context, practices of healing operated as tools for the spiritual formation of the self and as tactics for contending with the various gender norms, medical discourses, cultural debates, and religious idioms that shaped the experiences of pain, illness, and health during this period.

As a transatlantic and interdenominational movement, divine healing influenced a broad and diverse segment of late-nineteenth-century Protestant Christianity. During the 1870s and 1880s, faith healing was a frequent topic of debate and discussion among Methodists, Baptists, Presbyterians, Congregationalists, Episcopalians, Adventists, and various other evangelicals throughout the United States, Great Britain, and Europe. Converts to faith cure included prominent members of the Methodist Holiness movement and reformed Higher Life movement: Episcopal layman Charles Cullis (1833–1892), a homeopathic physician who founded and directed a network of health, welfare, and healing institutions in Boston; the Reverend John Inskip (1816–1884), Methodist leader and president of the National Camp Meeting Association for the Promotion of Holiness; Presbyterian minister William E. Boardman (1810–1886), author of the popular tract *The Higher Christian Life;* the Reverend A. J. Gordon (1836–1895), pastor of Boston's Clarendon Street Baptist Church and an important figure in late-nineteenth-century evangelical movements such as temperance, foreign missions, and D. L. Moody's revivals; and A. B. Simpson (1843–1919), a Presbyterian pastor who would eventually become the minister of the nondenominational Gospel Tabernacle in New York City and the founder of the Christian and Missionary Alliance.[5] While the majority of apologists for faith healing were male ministers, women also served as leaders and played key roles in shaping the movement's theology and practice. Among them were Mary Mossman (c. 1826–after 1909), who established and operated a healing home at the popular Holiness seaside retreat in Ocean Grove, New Jersey; Elizabeth Baxter (1837–1926), author, preacher, and cofounder of the Bethshan house of healing in London, England; S. L. Lindenberger, "house mother" of a large faith home in New York City; and Sarah Mix (1832–1884).[6] As African American leaders, Mix and her husband Edward were somewhat exceptional. Although many African Americans participated in divine healing (evangelist Amanda Berry Smith was a sometime devotee), individuals of northern European descent dominated the movement's leadership ranks.[7] Similarly, while faith cure appealed to both poor and wealthy citizens, leaders tended to be well-educated members of the middle and upper classes. Finally, although faith healing flourished in both rural areas and cities, urban centers, such as London, New York, Boston, and Philadelphia, became hubs of the movement's organizational activity.[8]

Throughout the 1870s, divine healing spread primarily through the ministries of itinerant evangelists such as Sarah Mix and her mentor Ethan O. Allen (1813–1902), a Methodist layman who traversed the northeastern United States laying hands upon the sick and praying for their recovery.[9] Lay people, like Mrs. Herbert Hall, also contributed to the movement's growth, by penning and publishing narratives describing their experiences of physical and spiritual restoration. Thousands of these testimonies appeared in popular religious newspapers such as the Methodist *Guide to Holiness*, in periodicals established for the express purpose of promoting divine healing, and in widely circulated anthologies like Mix's *Faith Cures, and Answers to Prayer.* By the early 1880s, divine healing had begun to take institutional shape, with the regular inclusion of healing services at camp meetings and faith conventions, the founding of faith homes for invalids who desired to seek healing in a nurturing environment, and the publication of treatises defending faith cure theology. The movement's widespread popularity became apparent in June of 1885, when more than fifteen hundred representatives from at least nine countries gathered in London for the International Conference on Divine Healing and True Holiness.[10]

"Acting Faith": Human Agency and the Performance of Healing

As one of the earliest proponents of divine healing in the United States, Sarah Mix exercised a profound influence upon the movement's understanding of the role that human action played in the process of healing. Mix began her ministry with the sick in her hometown of Torrington, Connecticut, in December of 1877. The news of her activities spread quickly "to towns and villages, and cities and states." Responding to invitations like the one she received from Mrs. Hall's friends, Mix journeyed to the residences of invalids throughout New England. She also invited petitioners to stay at her own home for brief periods of time while they sought relief from sickness. When personal contact proved impossible, Mix carried out her ministry through correspondence, assuring ailing sufferers from as far away as Genesee County, Michigan, and Devonshire, England, "God has promised to raise up the sick ones," and encouraging them to claim the promise contained in chapter 5, verse 15 of the New Testament Book of James, which reads, "The prayer of faith shall save the sick, and the Lord shall raise him up." "If you can claim that promise," Mix wrote to Carrie Judd, one of her invalid correspondents, "I have not the least doubt [that] you will be healed."[11]

But what did it mean to claim the promise? Mix went on to explain that in order to be healed, Judd must not only pray and believe, but act. First, she was to demonstrate her trust in "God and His promises" by laying aside "all medicine of every description" and by refusing to call upon physicians. Second, she was to begin praying for faith. Finally, on the afternoon of Wednesday, 26 February 1879, Judd was to "pray for herself" while the female prayer meeting at Mix's house in Connecticut also made her "a subject of prayer." "I want you to pray believing and then *act faith*," Mix wrote. "It makes no difference how you feel, but get right out of bed and begin to walk by faith."[12]

When Judd first read Mix's instructions, she "was tempted to smile unbelievingly."

Several years earlier, at the age of nineteen, a fall on an icy sidewalk in her hometown of Buffalo, New York, had rendered Judd completely bedridden. Suffering from what she described as "spinal difficulty," "a most distressing hyper-acuteness, called hyper-aesthesia," and "blood consumption," she remained confined to her room, unable to move without assistance. Although Judd received treatment from "the most skillful physicians," she was not expected to live. After such a dire prognosis and so many months of "confirmed helplessness," how did Mix expect her to arise and walk, Judd wondered. Despite her initial skepticism, Judd determined to give Mix's prescription a try. At the appointed hour she prayed for "an increase of faith"; then she "turned over and raised up alone, for the first time in over two years." Through active obedience to Mix's directives (which echoed Jesus's own commands in the gospels), Judd overcame her doubt not only in word but in deed. Healing was a matter of faith put into practice.[13]

Over the next few weeks, Judd continued to perform acts of faith that had been impossible for her prior to 26 February: she walked around her room and up and down the stairs, she visited neighbors, and she began to study and write without suffering the headaches that had so troubled her during her illness. By mid-March, the rector of the local Episcopal church to which Judd and her family belonged testified that the former invalid appeared to be "in perfect health."[14] Several months later, Judd composed a brief narrative of her healing which was published in the local newspapers. The article "attracted so much attention," Judd later recounted, "that it was copied into many other papers, and finally reached England, where it was published in the Christian Herald." Encouraged by the "hundreds of letters" from inquirers who wanted to know if her story was true, and also from "sufferers who saw the account and took courage," Judd composed *The Prayer of Faith*, which contained several accounts of healing, including her own, and "Bible teaching on the subject." Published in 1880, this book rapidly became one of the foundational texts of the divine healing movement in North America and abroad. Soon, Judd sensed a call, not only to write her story, but also to offer public testimony, first at prayer meetings, then as a "woman preacher" in churches, and eventually at national camp meetings and worldwide conventions.[15]

By acting her faith, Judd was transformed from a helpless invalid who "lay gasping faintly for breath" upon her cot to an energetic worker who was able to undertake the active ministries to which she felt ordained by God. Throughout her long confinement, Judd had struggled with the notion that she could best serve God by passively resigning herself to ongoing invalidism or even death. When she first became incapacitated, Judd felt "a deep regret that I had been obliged to give up all my plans for a fine education, and my ambitions for the future." Even when her physicians despaired of her recovery, Judd refused to believe that her earthly work was done. "I feel that I have a mission yet," she told her mother, Emily. Drawing upon the devotional ethic that had shaped her own experiences of pain and affliction, Emily Judd gently suggested to her daughter that her mission might be to "lie here and suffer and be an example of patience to others." This was a message that Carrie could not accept. "No, Mother," she replied, "I mean an *active mission*."[16]

This exchange between mother and daughter exemplifies a change; the image of the suffering servant as the epitome of Christian sainthood was less compelling to young persons of Carrie Judd's generation than it had been for their parents. By the 1870s, a shift had begun in many of the theological, cultural, and economic conditions that had lent authority to the notion that sickness and pain ought to be patiently endured as blessings sent or permitted by God for the sufferer's sanctification. A widespread and ongoing effort to emend the doctrinal heritage of the Calvinist tradition, for example, encouraged many Protestants to question the idea that God had ceased to work miracles after the apostolic age—a key tenet of Reformed theology—and to challenge the corollary belief that sickness was a godsend that ought to be accepted with thanksgiving. Similarly, the growing tendency to emphasize God's benevolence and mercy among eighteenth- and early-nineteenth-century moral philosophers, ministers, and social reformers made belief in God's afflictive providence less palatable for Protestants of both liberal and evangelical leanings.[17]

At the same time, mounting dissatisfaction with "heroic" medical techniques (blistering, bleeding, and the like) coincided with the development and proliferation of new technologies for the alleviation of pain, enabling late-nineteenth-century Christians to envision an alternative to a devotional ethic that valorized acquiescence as the appropriate response to physical distress. The discovery of analgesic agents, such as ether, chloroform, and nitrous oxide, undercut the notion that bodily suffering was an inescapable reality of human existence. By the 1870s, the use of anesthesia was widespread among American and European physicians of every class, and patients facing surgical operations or chronic conditions clamored for palliative remedies of all kinds.[18] The pervasive enthusiasm for pain-killers made passive acceptance of suffering seem not only needless but sometimes even pathological. Anyone who "chose to hurt," as historian Ariel Glucklich has put it, "had to be, in some sense, abnormal." Because pain had become "naturalized and medicalized," she explains, it had lost much of its currency as a "spiritual and religious" phenomenon.[19]

Transformations in the economic realm also affected the way Christians of Judd's generation interpreted and responded to suffering. Middle- and upper-class concerns about the rising demands of consumer capitalism in the latter decades of the nineteenth century contributed to a growing unease with the ideal of the passive sufferer as the paragon of Christian virtue. During these decades, many began to see the virtue of self-restraint, which had helped middle-class entrepreneurs succeed in the smaller-scale capitalism of the antebellum period, as a hindrance to personal advancement and broader economic growth. Related worries about perceived threats of over-civilization and neurasthenic paralysis engendered increasing suspicion of spiritual frameworks that associated sanctity with sickliness, weakness, and inactivity. In the view of certain cultural critics, passivity and physical frailty were symptoms of a disease that needed to be cured if modern civilization was to succeed, not characteristics of Christian holiness that ought to be cultivated.[20]

Finally, vigorous debates over the meaning and performance of "manly" and "womanly" virtue in this period unsettled assumptions about the relationship between physical suffering and spiritual blessing. As Gail Bederman has observed, the ideals of manliness based on self-denial which had helped to create and shore up middle-class consciousness in the antebellum era became increasingly problematic within the overlapping contexts of economic instability, rising consumerism, challenges to the political authority of Anglo-American men from women and foreign immigrants, and a growing fixation with the virility of the male body. The emergence of "muscular Christianity" in these years represented, in part, an attempt to elevate vitality and strength over serenity and submission as the exemplary traits of the spiritual virtuoso.[21]

Notions of female Protestant sanctity were also in flux during the latter decades of the nineteenth century. For Emily Judd, Carrie's mother, a devotional ethic that promoted passive resignation as the appropriate Christian response to pain had resonated with prevailing gender norms that associated true womanhood with self-sacrifice and submission. According to influential interpretations of the "domestic ideology" that shaped so many discussions of women's nature and role in society during the antebellum period, the ideal woman was a devoted wife and mother who delighted in denying herself for the sake of others and who achieved sanctification precisely through the physical, emotional, and spiritual suffering that self-abnegation and submission engendered.[22]

By the time Carrie Judd reached maturity, however, both the gender ideals and the devotional norms that had provided her mother with a framework for comprehending and coping with pain had become less authoritative as material improvements in women's lives eroded several key assumptions of the domestic ideology. Greater participation in higher education, urban life, and certain sectors of the growing economy, for example, helped stretch the boundaries of women's sphere beyond the home. Legal reforms gave women expanded property rights and easier access to divorce, and offered alternatives to submission as the proper posture of women in relation to their male kin and social contacts. The physical education movement advanced a view of the female body as "naturally healthy, not feeble, and saw suffering as an aberration not as an inevitable consequence of being female." By the 1870s, historian Nancy Theriot has persuasively argued, these developments, among others, called into question the "feminine script" that emphasized self-denying motherhood, innate feminine frailty, and the consequent necessity of female suffering and submission. For women of Carrie Judd's age group, Theriot contends, the attainment of physical and spiritual health might involve "self-control" rather than self-sacrifice and "purposeful action" rather than passive submission.[23]

Within this broader arena of cultural, social, economic, and theological change, divine healing offered an alternative to an inherited model of Christian sanctity that seemed increasingly unsatisfying on multiple fronts. By emphasizing the role of human agency in the process of healing, the practice of acting faith presented individuals like Carrie Judd with a strategy for surmounting the afflictions that beleaguered their bodies, as well as a means for rewriting the script that linked the pursuit of health and holiness with passive endurance of suffering. To act faith was to alter one's own experience of physical pain and to participate in a larger effort to transform the meaning of affliction and its place in the Christian life.

"The Use of Means": Practices and the Problems of Healing

Testimonies of healing like those published in *Triumphs of Faith*, the journal Carrie Judd founded in 1881 for the promotion of divine healing and Christian holiness, proclaimed that remarkable things happened when sick people acted faith. After earthly remedies had been tried and found wanting, when physicians and family members had given up hope, invalids who had been bedridden for years rose up and walked. The deaf heard and the blind received their sight. Even modest endeavors resulted in a great deal of awe. For Mrs. R. W. Fuller, standing upon her feet long enough to dress and wash herself was "as wonderful . . . as a trip to Europe would be to some."[24]

While testimonies like Fuller's highlight the astonishing, if everyday, feats accomplished through acting faith, they also show that empowerment often came at a price. If acting faith enabled individuals to perform astounding deeds, it did not always relieve the pain from which they longed to be released. Although some declared that their bodies were immediately and completely restored as soon as they stepped out upon their beliefs, others acknowledged that their symptoms failed to disappear and confessed that acting faith caused them considerable discomfort. When Mattie Littell, who had lain prostrate for almost three years obeyed the command to "arise and

walk," for example, she admitted that the exertion caused her "great pain." Upon reading the biblical command, "'Be careful for nothing,'" Urwin Sterry, who suffered from
sciatica, headaches, back pain, and lameness, worried that he had been too cautious
in his actions, and so, he wrote, "I . . . pushed right ahead *in the name of Jesus,* pain or
no pain, and I suffered . . . terribly." For some, attempts to act faith failed altogether.
One young woman whom Sarah Mix visited tried to get out of bed on a number of
occasions, but "each attempt made had resulted in paroxysms of distress."[25]

Stories like these created a pressing problem for the divine healing movement.
While the practice of acting faith enabled many men and women who were weighed
down by debilitating illnesses to reengage in social and familial life, go back to work,
and pursue all sorts of projects that had previously seemed unimaginable, it also
caused serious confusion and doubt among those who had difficulty ignoring the
pain that continued to plague their bodies. When Emma Whittemore, who suffered
from chronic back problems, heard Carrie Judd offer her testimony of healing, for example, she scoffed in disbelief at the notion of acting faith by denying sensory evidence. "I could not . . . perceive how anyone was justified in stating that he or she was
healed by faith before it could be experienced by sight or feeling," Whittemore declared.[26]

Leaders of the divine healing movement acknowledged that claiming healing and
acting faith, regardless of the ongoing occurrence of painful physical symptoms, required a leap of faith for individuals living in what members of the movement saw as
an increasingly materialistic and rationalistic milieu. Indeed, many advocates of faith
cure maintained that disregarding the testimony of the senses ran directly against the
grain in a "worldly" culture that appealed to and even cultivated sensory pleasures.
The tantalizing array of consumer goods, the world of fashion and display, the ever-
expanding selection of stimulating food, drink, and drugs—all of these pressures con-
spired to focus an individual's attention on things material, including the desires and
discomforts of the flesh. Not only were the sensual enticements of the surrounding
society difficult to resist, but the pervasive skepticism that characterized the culture
seemed impossible to circumvent. To overlook observable or sensible phenomena in
an environment that increasingly valued empirical evidence as the arbiter of truth was
no easy task, these evangelicals avowed, and certainly not an endeavor that a person
could accomplish solely on her own initiative.[27]

Proponents of divine healing insisted that only an influx of the Holy Spirit could,
as one adherent put it, "bring us to abstain from the sight of our eyes, and the hearing of our ears, and to see God over against the odds, whatever they be." God, not the
individual, was both the "author and finisher" of faith; the one who enabled the believer to take "no notice" of the "pains and symptoms" that continued to afflict the

body, and to act accordingly. "Christ has provided for the redemption and restoration of the human mind," wrote S. A. Lindenberger during her tenure as overseer at Berachah house of healing in New York City. "He will deliver from all evil thoughts, and then He will come in His indwelling presence and hold captive our thinking." Divine healing, in other words, involved not only the restitution of physical health, but also a reformation of the mental faculties.[28]

While leaders like Lindenberger emphasized the primacy of divine power in altering a person's perceptual framework, they also asserted that human beings could engage in certain practices that would encourage the process of epistemological transformation. Drawing heavily upon the works of classic mystical authors such as Jeanne-Marie Bouvier de la Motte-Guyon and François de Salignac de La Mothe-Fénelon, as well as upon the devotional writings of contemporaries like John G. Whittier and Phoebe Palmer, proponents of divine healing commended various forms of meditation as a means for making the mind receptive to the redemptive influence of the Holy Spirit. In her book on faith healing, Lindenberger encouraged her readers to prepare themselves to receive the mind of Christ by engaging in contemplative prayer. "You will be helped by holding your mind in stillness and keeping it a blank, waiting for His thoughts, and as you form the habit it will become easier and easier, until you are established in this way," she declared.[29] Mary Mossman, in her autobiography, *Steppings in God; or, The Hidden Life Made Manifest,* cited the teachings of numerous spiritual writers who stressed the importance of seeking, as her contemporary Thomas Upham put it, "a perfect coincidence of the finite mind with the Infinite" through the practice of contemplation. In order to "receive the manifestation of healing," Mossman suggested, we must "pass on into deeper spiritual life and affiliate more with the Divine mind concerning us." When our minds are brought into agreement with God's mind, she explained, "we no longer see the old man with its fleshly desires and diseases, but the new man created in Jesus Christ, and in the new life which we by faith receive we press on to apprehend all that for which we are apprehended of Christ Jesus. . . . Receiving life and light from this higher plane, we lose sight of material things." Although she often "seemed to be very ill," Mossman insisted that by "seeing *Jesus only*," she was able to disregard the feelings of her flesh, concentrating instead upon "wonderful manifestations of God's loving care."[30]

For those seeking healing of body, mind, and soul, "looking unto Jesus" was the "watchword," Mossman contended. Indeed, this catchphrase appeared in countless texts commending faith cure. In a widely circulated article entitled "The 'Look on Jesus,'" for example, pastor Otto Stockmayer (1838–1917), one of the principal advocates of divine healing in Switzerland, exhorted his readers, "Obey thy God, and contemplate Jesus." Meditating on Christ was necessary, Stockmayer argued, because of contemplation's power to shape perception. "When we fix our eyes upon an object, we put ourselves in contact with it, we place ourselves under its influence, we allow it to act upon our hearts," he explained. "Looking around about us, as well as constantly looking at ourselves, cannot but awaken and nourish evil in us," he continued. "The world which man carries within him . . . as well as the world that surrounds him, keeps him always a captive, he feels himself chained to visible things." Only by setting his sights on Christ could a man gain release from the sensations that imprisoned him. To gaze at Jesus, Stockmayer affirmed, was to look away from one's self and one's surroundings, to focus attention on the eternal rather than the temporal, to deny the physical in favor of the spiritual. Contemplating Christ, in other words, reoriented a person's perspective so that certain realities suddenly became visible while other things were obscured from view. As Anna Prosser, one of Carrie Judd's close associates, intoned in her testimony of healing, "Since my eyes were fixed on Jesus, / I've lost sight of all beside, / so enchained my spirit's vision, / looking at the crucified."[31]

Acquiring and maintaining such a singular focus on Jesus was, these writers argued, a difficult endeavor that required practiced vigilance on the part of believers. Although some might succeed in disengaging their minds from the web of sensory stimuli and empirical explanations that fettered their faith through the practice of contemplation alone, most people needed additional aid in order to break free from the ties that bound them to believe and to act according to the physical appearance and sensate experience of their bodies. Acknowledging, as always, that Christ was the one who would liberate the sick from their captivity, advocates of divine healing encouraged sufferers to participate in rituals that would facilitate the process of separation from the surrounding culture and from what Stockmayer called "the covetousness of the senses." Searching the Scriptures for insight, these evangelicals identified three practices that were "given of the Lord" as "means" of healing: "united prayer," (sometimes called "believing or prevailing prayer") as commended in Matthew 18:19; "laying-on of hands," as described in Mark 16:18; and "anointing with oil," as commanded in James 5:14–15. Bolstered by biblical authority, these three practices became the principal ritual framework through which proponents of faith cure promoted and sought divine healing for body, mind, and soul.[32]

For the sufferer whose consciousness of pain and commitment to an empirical epistemology made it difficult to trust God's promises for healing, let alone act upon them, these additional practices fostered a focus on God that eclipsed tangible experience. When Charles Cullis prayed with a city missionary from Chicago, laying his hands upon her and anointing her with oil according to the instructions in James 5:14, for example, this woman, who had struggled with sickness for years and who feared that perhaps "faith healing" was "not of sound doctrine," "lost sight of everything save

Christ." Doubts disappeared as the "holy ghost was filling me unutterably full," she wrote. The indwelling presence of God, she implied, banished all thoughts of unbelief, as well as her awareness of her physical sufferings: "My bodily ailments were not in my mind. . . . I rose and walked out of the room, downstairs, into the street, and with very little aid seated myself in the carriage."[33]

In addition to directing an invalid's mental attention heavenward, the practices of united prayer, laying-on of hands, and anointing served as ceremonies that opened a person's body to the transforming power of the Holy Spirit. "Laying on of hands," one proponent declared, "is like opening the door to let Christ in. Anointing with oil . . . is bringing the patient where Christ can touch him." Ironically, perhaps, the practices that involved physical contact—the laying-on of hands and anointing with oil— sometimes prompted particularly potent, even sensate experiences of God. When Ethan O. Allen offered prayer and laid hands upon Mrs. W. J. Starr, she felt what she later described as "an intense heat and moisture over the surface of my body, until at length my whole being was permeated by this divine healing power." Immediately, Starr declared herself healed and rose from her bed. Sarah Battles, of North Adams, Massachusetts, experienced a similar sensation when she sought the prayers of Sarah and Edward Mix. "When Mrs. and Mr. Mix laid their hands upon me, anointing me with oil in the name of the Lord, as we are commanded in the fifth chapter of James," she recounted, "I felt a thrill go through my whole being and knew that I was healed of my malady." Ruth L. King related her experience at the hands of Charles Cullis in comparable terms: "When Dr. Cullis prayed with and anointed me, I felt the power of the Holy Spirit like a great wave of peace, from the crown of my head to the soles of my feet. It was indescribable." For each of these individuals, the hands of a faithful believer, whether laid upon the affected parts of the flesh in prayer or upon the forehead for anointing, served as a conduit for the influx of divine energy.[34]

While not everyone who received prayer through the laying-on of hands or anointing experienced such intense, palpable sensations, many compared participating in these practices to undergoing a kind of ritual cleansing, through which God's spirit flushed out sin from the soul, skepticism from the mind, and sickness from the flesh. As one advocate described it, anointing was "the outward representation of the inflow of a mighty supernatural power, penetrating through every muscle, nerve, bone and organ of the human system, and the soul itself." Although they stopped short of designating them sacraments, preferring the term ordinance, leaders of the divine healing movement frequently applied the classic language of sacramental theology to the ritual practices of healing. Like baptism and communion, laying-on of hands and anointing were outward, visible symbols that signified an internal, and therefore unseen, transformation. In his well-circulated work *Inquiries and Answers on Divine*

Healing, A. B. Simpson affirmed that anointing "signifies His personal coming into the body" and "sustains to the matter of healing a similar relation to that held by baptism and the Lord's Supper in connection with our professions of Christ as a Saviour, and our deeper communion with Him spiritually."[35]

Simpson's comments suggest that, like the sacraments, united prayer, laying-on of hands, and especially anointing also served a confessional purpose. Through these practices, individuals enacted their separation from sin and sensuality and acknowledged their consecration to God. A. J. Gordon, in his influential treatise *The Ministry of Healing*, affirmed, "As in Baptism the disciple confesses his faith in the cleansing power of Christ's atonement, by the use of water; or, as in Communion he declares his dependence on Christ for spiritual sustenance, by the use of bread so [in anointing] he avows his faith in the saving health of the Spirit by the use of oil." "In other words," Gordon continued, "this whole ceremony is a kind of sacramental profession of faith in Jesus Christ as the Divine Physician acting through the Holy Ghost." Anointing was both a rite of passage, through which an infusion of divine power transformed a sickly sinner into a strong and vigorous servant, and a public declaration on the part of the individual that she belonged, body and soul, not to herself or to her family or to her culture, but to the community of believers who acknowledged Christ as healer, and, indeed, to Christ himself. As the Methodist minister John Cookman put it, being anointed with oil served as "a seal that I had given myself over wholly to the Lord."[36]

Within the context of late-nineteenth-century divine healing, practices such as prayer, laying-on of hands, and anointing served as rites of separation and rituals of spiritual formation. By obeying the directives given in the Bible, Christians who participated in this movement attempted to regulate the influence of rationalism and materialism upon their minds so that they could resist the effects of illness and pain upon their flesh. Through the practice of prayer and sacred touch, suffering individuals opened themselves to receive the "vital energy of the Holy Ghost," a power that promised to renew their minds, heal their bodies, and redeem their souls. Only this "indwelling *life*," Carrie Judd explained, would enable them to "realize with wondering joy, that mystery which fleshly sense can never perceive, that 'we are members of His body, of His flesh and of His bones.'"[37]

"Resting in God": Healing and the Priority of Divine Power

Paradoxically, while leaders of the divine healing movement asserted that engaging in ritual practices and acting faith were integral parts of the healing process, they also cautioned that petitioners who placed too much credence in their own efforts to overcome illness would surely stumble. Although they commended practices such as anointing as aids to spiritual transformation and "means" through which God channeled healing power, apologists like Simpson and Judd insisted that these rites were not efficacious in and of themselves and warned participants not to attribute unwarranted potency to mere rituals. Similarly, faith cure advocates advised sufferers who sought healing not to put undue emphasis on the role of personal volition in the practice of acting faith. Reflecting upon his own initial encounter with divine healing, for example, Simpson recalled that his first efforts to step out upon God's promises failed miserably because, as he put it, "I was trusting in myself, in my own heart, in my own faith." Only when he recognized that faith itself was a gift of God, rather than a work of the human will, was he able to obey the command to arise and walk without faltering. "Our very faith is but the grace of Christ Himself within us," he wrote. "We can exercise it, and thus far our responsibility extends; but He must impart it." Elizabeth Baxter made an analogous argument in a sermon preached at Bethshan, the faith home she founded in London. Rather than looking to themselves—for faith or for the strength to act it out—Baxter urged her audience to allow their bodies to become "a theatre for God's acting." This was possible, she explained, because God, "the source of all strength," was alive within them. "I am crucified with Christ," she proclaimed, citing Galatians 2:20, "nevertheless I live; yet not I, but Christ liveth in me.'"[38]

According to these evangelical Protestants, then, acting faith was a performance accomplished not by individual agency but by an incursion of divine energy. Like spiritual salvation, they insisted, bodily redemption involved renouncing one's own will, ceasing "all self-effort" and "yielding to God." In surrendering the self to God, Judd explained, an individual entered into "complete harmony with His blessed will" and became one with Christ: "We are no longer separate beings, with different wills and designs, but His life in me, I have 'the mind of Christ,' . . . and, moreover, I am 'flesh of His flesh and bone of His bones.'" Union with Christ meant letting go and losing oneself in God. Within this theological framework, acting faith involved not an exertion of the will in order to bring behavior into conformity with belief but rather a setting aside of the self in order to make way for the transforming influence of the Holy Spirit, who stood ready to invigorate both body and soul.[39]

This rather complicated understanding of the relationship among personal agency, divine sovereignty, and healing served several purposes for the people who espoused it. On the one hand, instructing invalids to act faith but not in their own strength had the effect of lowering the bar, making a daunting directive seem feasible. Sufferers who were intimidated by the command to rise and walk needed only to recognize the power they possessed—or, the power that possessed them—in order to carry out this instruction. "The body of Christ is the living fountain of all our vital strength," Simpson wrote. "The healing which Christ gives us is nothing less than His own new physical life infused into our body. . . . It is the very life of Jesus manifested in our mortal flesh." If an individual could grasp this notion, acting faith would become effortless: "This principle is of immense importance in the practical experience of healing. . . . When we cease to put confidence in the flesh, and look only to Christ and His supernatural life in us for our strength of body as well as spirit, we shall find that we can do all things through Christ that strengtheneth us."[40]

Insisting that healing involved acting faith without expending effort also enabled advocates of divine healing to counter the allegation that faith cures were the product of will power. In the latter half of the nineteenth century, a growing recognition of the "intimate relation between the mind and body" lent credence to the notion that "marvelous effects" could be "produced upon disease by various kinds of mental excitement." Throughout the nineteenth century, in fact, various forms of "mind cure" made headway on both sides of the Atlantic, as popular audiences and eventually even some medical professionals gave credence to the notion that mental suggestion represented a potent means of bringing about bodily healing. According to proponents of what eventually came to be known as mental therapeutics, a physician's role was to prescribe not only treatments designed to call forth a response from the patient's body, such as the "drastic purge," but, also, or even instead, to enjoin "cheerfulness, hope, pleasant occupation of the mind" and "kindly dispositions of heart" upon the patient in order to "call forth the energies of his will on the side of recovery."[41]

For skeptics, theories of "mental physiology," "psychological researches," and experiments in "suggestive medicine" offered ammunition for discrediting the claims of divine healing. According to critics like Methodist minister James M. Buckley, editor of the influential denominational newspaper *The Christian Advocate,* the cures brought about through "faith-healing" were "a natural result of mental or emotional states." In an essay entitled "Faith-Healing and Kindred Phenomena," published in the June 1886 edition of *The Century Illustrated Monthly Magazine,* Buckley highlighted the similarities between divine healing and various forms of what he called "mind-cure," including animal magnetism, mesmerism, Spiritualism, Christian Science, and even quack medicine. All of these movements, Buckley asserted, succeeded in curing certain nervous ailments and sometimes even acute diseases, but they did so not through any religious or supernatural force but through the purely natural power of suggestion.[42]

Loath to have divine healing conflated with quackery or, worse, with what they considered to be the false teachings of rival movements such as Spiritualism and Christian Science, faith healing leaders such as A. J. Gordon insisted that "faith cures" were "the result of God's direct and supernatural action upon the body of the sufferer."

No one who believed in the scriptural promise that the prayer of faith would save the sick, Gordon wrote, had ever, "so far as we know, considered that its fulfillment depends on the action of mind upon mind." Interpreting miraculous healings as "natural" events, evangelicals like Gordon warned, was insulting to bedridden invalids who "had willed again and again, and fallen back fainting in weariness and despair," as well as to the God who finally enabled them to get up. "Is it not fearful sin," one advocate of faith cure asked, "to ascribe the direct power of the Lord Jesus in healing to any other source, as so many presume to do, such as the will, imagination, or nervous excitement?"[43]

While debates about the role of human volition in the process of healing expose evangelical efforts to erect and police boundaries between faith cure and other healing movements, they also reveal the extent to which advocates of divine healing participated in the complex and contentious gender politics that characterized late-nineteenth-century culture. During this period, conversations concerning the relationship among will, mind, and body were inextricably bound up with contests over the proper interpretation and enactment of healthy womanhood and manhood, especially amid mounting anxieties over the future of the Anglo-Saxon race. This broader context provides an essential framework for understanding the idiom of acting faith, and particularly the emphasis its proponents placed upon the complicated relationship between divine power and personal agency in the process of healing.

Although an array of economic, political, and cultural forces worked to destabilize associations between true womanhood and self-sacrifice during the latter half of the nineteenth century, certain aspects of the domestic ideology remained remarkably influential. While many health and physical education reformers challenged the notion that women were inherently frail and delicate, prominent medical theorists continued to champion the idea that the vagaries of the female reproductive system wreaked havoc upon women's physical, mental, and emotional well-being. Specialists in the nascent fields of gynecology, neurology, and psychology contributed to a burgeoning corpus of "scientific" literature that associated a woman's health primarily with the maintenance of menstrual regularity, a feat that required careful and vigilant conservation of energy, especially during the critical phase of puberty. In order to navigate safely and successfully the passage from adolescence to womanhood, certain leading physicians argued, a young girl approaching puberty ought to avoid rigorous mental activity or emotional excitement and engage only in domestic tasks that would facilitate the proper development of her maternal organs. In his controversial text *Sex in Education: or, A Fair Chance for the Girls* (1870), for example, Harvard's Edward Clarke insisted that young women ought to dress sensibly, eat moderately, and refrain from both "muscular and brain labor" during adolescence in order to "yield enough force for the work" of establishing regular menstrual periods. Translating the domestic ideology into the discourse of medical science, Clarke argued that a woman who overstepped the boundaries of her appropriate sphere by pursuing educational or other so-called unwomanly activities drew her limited vital energies away from the crucial task of regulating her monthly cycle. Women who pursued such a course at any age ran the risk of ruining their reproductive systems and therefore of failing to fulfill their proper roles as moral guardians of their households and progenitors of healthy children who would carry forward the advancement of civilization.[44]

The remedies physicians prescribed when women did fall ill closely resembled the therapies they recommended for developing adolescents. Treatments were often premised upon the supposition that the patient's ailment must be related to the malfunction of her menstrual rhythm or to some sort of inappropriate exertion that had overtaxed her innately delicate physical and emotional constitution. Either way, doctors frequently suggested that a sick woman needed to assume a retiring posture, avoid all endeavors that might excite her nervous system, and undertake only those activities that reinforced the maternal role, in order to replenish her vital energy and regain her health. As the century progressed, orthodox physicians, in particular, increasingly emphasized the importance of rest as a cure for women's diseases. S. Weir Mitchell, a renowned Philadelphia neurologist, first recommended the "rest cure" in 1872, as a treatment for battle weary Civil War soldiers. The rest cure became an extremely popular prescription for women suffering from nervous disorders as well as organic diseases such as cardiac and kidney ailments in the latter decades of the nineteenth century.[45]

Under the rest cure, potentially stimulating behavior of any kind, often including reading, writing, and visiting with family or friends, was prohibited, in order to assure that the patient's mental and emotional energies could rest. When L. Etta Avery, who suffered from neurasthenia and spinal trouble, was admitted to the Adams Nervine Asylum just outside Boston, for example, she "was under the perfect rest treatment, not being allowed to raise my hand to my head, or do anything for myself."[46] As Avery's comment suggests, the rest cure also compelled an individual to cede control of her treatment to her physician, submitting to his instructions without comment, question, or complaint. After straining the nerves of her spinal cord while practicing gymnastics in a ladies seminary, Almena J. Cowles of Amherst, Massachusetts, struggled to regain her health for several years until her nervous system became so taxed that, as she put it, "my brain was nearly worn out." Her physicians told her that her "indomitable courage and will-power" alone had been keeping her up, but that she would never recover her strength if she continued to pursue this active course. Instead "she must have rest." Accordingly, on 1 January 1881, Cowles was admitted to the Adams Nervine Asylum, where she was "confined to bed" for eight months and placed "under the care of the most skillful physicians in New England," who did everything "in their power" to help her. In August, after reading Judd's *The Prayer of Faith*, Cowles wrote to Sarah Mix, expressing some concern about carrying out the directives she found there: "About *acting faith*," she wrote, "I would not be allowed to do more than at present, unless I say my pain is gone or greatly relieved."[47]

For Avery, Cowles, and countless other women, submission remained an integral element of the experience of illness and recovery, despite efforts by reformers to link the achievement of physical health with personal agency and voluntary activity. Obedience to an authority other than "self-will" was required, it seemed, in order to successfully overcome, or at least to endure, troubling physical ailments. With the growing popularity of "mind-cure" in the 1880s, submitting oneself to the will of a more powerful other took on added resonance, as respected physicians like Mitchell and George Beard began to experiment with this increasingly acceptable form of treatment. The theory of mind cure was especially applicable, its adherents argued, in cases that involved "nervous conditions" like hysteria which were peculiarly, if not exclusively, associated with women.[48] In situations such as these, went the claim, "the stimulus of sudden command from a stronger will" provided the necessary catalyst that enabled bedridden invalids to arise. "By the direct influence of a strong will over a weaker one," an author explained, "an invalid may be controlled and raised from his debilitated and diseased condition to soundness of mind and body."[49]

Given this context, the reasons for Cowles's reluctance about acting faith become clear. If she were to "get right out of bed and begin to walk," as Mix had instructed, she would be disobeying doctors' orders by exercising both her body and her will in ways that they had prohibited, and thus, she feared, potentially undermining her bid for health. When Cowles failed to respond to prescribed treatments, however, her physicians eventually discharged her from the Nervine Institute and made arrangements for her transfer to the Home for Incurables in Brooklyn, New York. At that point, Cowles decided to give divine healing a try. She sent for "some faith people" to come pray with her. After she had been anointed according to the command in James 5, Cowles finally found herself able to act faith. "God gave me the strength to rise," she recalled, "and I walked the length of the room without pain, then knelt and praised the Lord for His wonderful goodness, rose and dressed and walked downstairs wholly healed of my diseases." Over the next six months, Cowles returned to her home in Amherst and took on many duties "by simply trusting in the healing power and sustaining grace of Him who said, 'My strength is made perfect in weakness.'" Her newfound potency was not, Cowles adamantly insisted, the product of self-assertion. "I am not allowed to use any will-power," she wrote, "but rest in God's love and receive strength from Him moment by moment."[50] Healing, for Cowles, still involved obedience to a will other than her own. But by submitting to God, paradoxically, she received the power to perform actions that disproved her doctors' diagnoses. Cowles was not incurable, she merely needed the right prescription. Where the rest cure had failed, resting in God had succeeded, empowering Cowles to arise and walk without overstepping the medical theories and gender norms that required her to remain passive in the curative process.

If acting faith without effort offered women like Cowles a way of consenting to the rhetoric of passivity while at the same time enabling them to transcend some of its implications, this same strategy posed distinctive problems for men. In the late nineteenth century, submissiveness and weakness were not male virtues. Even the Victorian ideal of manly self-restraint was becoming suspect in a climate of cultural and economic changes. Mounting anxieties over an apparent epidemic of nervous exhaustion among white upper- and middle-class businessmen, in particular, contributed to the reevaluation of self-denial as a characteristic of true manhood. According to neurologists such as George Beard, who coined the term "neurasthenia" in his classic text on the subject, *American Nervousness*, overexposure to books, "brain work," and other pressures of modern civilization had depleted many men of their vital energy. Within this context, virility, strength, and forcefulness became increasingly important markers of healthy Anglo-Saxon masculinity. Consequently, when men did suffer from "nerve weakness" or other sorts of illness, doctors rarely ordered them to adopt a recumbent pose and remain utterly immobile for weeks in order to regain their equilibrium. Although physicians did sometimes recommend the remedy of rest for men, especially for those suffering from neurasthenia, they usually combined this prescription with other forms of treatment, such as vigorous physical activity designed to help replenish their "natural" strength and "nerve-force."[51]

Given the close association between masculinity and virility, any therapy that required men to admit their weakness and assume a submissive posture in order to receive healing was bound to arouse the ire of critics, and faith cure did. Opponents like the vociferous James Buckley, were quick to point out the threats that the divine healing movement posed to prevailing gender norms. "Faith-cure . . . is a pitiable superstition, dangerous in its final effects," Buckley charged. "Its tendency is to produce an effeminate type of character. . . . It destroys the ascendancy of reason in the soul."[52] Framed in this manner, acting faith might restore a man to health, but it would emasculate him in the process.

Defenders of divine healing countered that Buckley and other naysayers misunderstood the complex relationship between the divine will and human agency in the therapeutic process. Submission to God, they argued, did not result in quietism or "mere passivity," nor did it turn a willing individual into "an enervated, mindless be-ing" or a "weak creature, without backbone." According to the Reverend A. P. Moore, for example, "the rest of faith" was not inconsistent with "those accounts of Christian living which describe it as a race, as a warfare, as involving toil, and earnestness and exertion." Indeed, it was only by resting in faith, by yielding to God, that an individ-ual had any chance of vanquishing disease and living a truly victorious Christian life, for only by submission could a person receive what Moore called "the nerve-power of the soul." Through this indwelling force, Moore wrote, "the mighty life of our Risen Glorified Head flows through our every fibre, and with God in us, through faith, we attempt and achieve a life and service beyond our utmost dreams before." As A. B. Simpson put it, human beings in their natural state "wanted a positive fountain of vi-tal energy," which Jesus supplied. By acting faith, individuals gained access to this es-sential force. "His bodily energy vitalizes your body, and you can take it, you have a right to take it to-day," Simpson proclaimed. "I take it afresh to-day from the living Christ—His nerves, and heart, and brain, and bodily strength for my own life." Fur-thermore, Simpson suggested, sick people were not the only ones who needed this in-fusion of divine strength. Everyone would be better off if they learned to partake of this power "every morning," as Simpson himself was in the habit of doing. In this view, the indwelling power of God trumped all individual efforts. "It is a better kind of health," Simpson insisted, "and it has given me many times the strength of my own natural energy."[53]

By focusing on the vitality, power, and vigor that infused a person once he sub-mitted his own will to God, men like Simpson and Moore attempted to accommo-date the idiom of acting faith to their culture's notion of true masculinity. Rather than emphasizing the need for passivity in the healing process, they shifted attention to the empowering outcome, even going so far as to suggest that men who drew strength from the "Christ-life within" were, in fact, more vigorous and manly than those who relied upon their own will power. For the many clerical and lay men who participated in divine healing, this argument seems to have been convincing. When the Reverend T. C. Easton, pastor of a Reformed Church in New Brunswick, New Jersey, recognized that healing involved not only "a full and unreserved surrender of my entire being to God" but also "the risen life of Jesus as my life," he was able to overcome his impres-sion that "faith-cure may be all well enough for weak, nervous women, and hysterics" and to trust the Great Physician rather than the surgeon's knife to mend the metatarsal bones in his lame foot. Similarly, in his testimony of healing, George P. Pardington in-sisted that the "power of the Lord" in his body enabled him "always to conquer in his strength." Through this indwelling force, Pardington wrote, "I am no more the help-less boy, but the strong, firm, vigorous young man."[54]

Accounts such as these demonstrate that the rhetoric of vigor and power helped make divine healing appealing to men of both ministerial and lay status. Indeed, many champions of faith cure were male theologians, and lay men did actively participate in all aspects of the movement. The fact remains, however, that women outnumbered men in the ranks and also achieved remarkable status as leaders. Despite their efforts to mask passivity, or at least to make it palatable to the male population, proponents of faith cure found a more willing audience among women, who could acquire the blessings of health by acting faith without losing too much of their cultural capital.[55]

Conclusion

The primacy of God's sovereignty, the power of ritual practice, the imperative of human agency—these were the key variables in the calculus of late-nineteenth-century divine healing. By configuring these factors in a paradoxical fashion, partisans of divine healing sought to solve several problems in the practice of Protestant Christianity. First, for those who embraced an enigmatic understanding of the relationship among personal volition, religious ritual, and divine supremacy, this formula offered a method for recasting their own experience of physical suffering. Medical anthropologists have asserted that pain is more than a physiological phenomenon; they maintain that, while physical discomfort itself is rooted in bodily processes, the ways in which human beings interpret, respond to, and experience pain are shaped by the interaction of personal convictions and broader cultural, social, and historical forces. Advocates of divine healing recognized what theorists have called the "psychosocial" or "culturogenic" nature of pain; they also espoused the corollary conviction, expressed by certain contemporary pain specialists, that by altering their beliefs about affliction, as well as their behavioral responses to it, human beings can "completely reconstruct" their experiences of illness, pain, and recovery. "Change the mind (powerfully enough) and it may well be that pain too changes," scholar David Morris has asserted. "When we recognize that the experience of pain is not timeless but changing, we may also recognize we can *act* to change or influence our own futures." Sarah Mix, Carrie Judd, A. B. Simpson, and other devotees of divine healing would have agreed with Morris's reflections. By acting faith, engaging in healing rituals, and resting in God, these evangelical Protestants were attempting to modify the present experience and future implications of pain for themselves and for the wider community of Christian saints of which they counted themselves a part.[56]

Participating in divine healing thus offered individuals means for pursuing both personal transformation and broader cultural reform. In addition to enabling believers to conquer illness and counteract its effects upon their own flesh, the doctrines and rites of divine healing supplied strategies for navigating, and sometimes resisting or modifying, the complicated religious, cultural, historical, economic, and social circumstances that influenced the ways in which pain and suffering, illness and healing, were understood and performed. To act faith was to defy a central premise of Reformation theology and to reject the authority of medical experts; to receive the laying-on of hands was to close one's mind to rationalism and materialism while opening one's body to the incursion of supernatural power; to abandon one's self to God was to stretch certain normative constructions of gender without transgressing their limits.

The practitioners of divine healing formulated their theology and practices within a historically and culturally contingent constellation of issues, but the solution they posed to the predicament of late-nineteenth-century illness and suffering was applicable, they claimed, to a perennial problem in the history of Christian practice. In declaring that healing was entirely the work of God while at the same time instructing invalids to rise up and walk, ministers of divine healing were negotiating one of the thorniest dilemmas in Christian theology, that is, deciphering the relationship among divine sovereignty, ritual practice, and human volition in the processes of salvation and sanctification. For the Protestants who participated in the faith cure movement of the late nineteenth century, grace and faith, God's power and personal agency, religious practices and the healing of body, mind, and soul were inextricably, if inexplicably intertwined.

CHAPTER EIGHT

Observing the Lives of the Saints

Sanctification as Practice in the Church of God in Christ

ANTHEA D. BUTLER

In the first half of the twentieth century, African American churches in the Holiness and Pentecostal traditions fascinated anthropologists and sociologists. These "Sanctified" churches, as Zora Neale Hurston termed them, embraced traditional religious practices such as fasting, prayer, and modest dress as a major part of their spiritual discipline.[1] In studies of these churches, however, these disciplinary practices are usually glossed over and greater attention is given to chronicling "power practices" such as dancing, shouting, glossolalia, and trance. The latter were the practices most often depicted in early accounts of the Sanctified churches, and much of what scholars know today about the practices of these churches is in large part based on these accounts.

Early anthropologists and sociologists who described worship practices of the Sanctified churches often overlooked the human body as a producer of spiritual power. By focusing on performances and manifestations, they misinterpreted the Sanctified church, seeing its practices only through the lens of its music and believing that ecstatic spiritual practices were the consequence of the emotional music or of spirit possession.[2] Consequently, the picture of what sanctification meant in the religious rituals and practices of Sanctified churches, and of how the everyday lives of church members were both liberated and restrained by those practices, remains obscure. Focusing on the importance of the disciplinary practices and exploring their relationship to the ecstatic, bodily practices illuminates the historical discourse about the religious practices of Sanctified churches. Disciplinary and power practices were both important in these churches, but disciplinary practices governed the sanctified life, while practices of shouting and dancing acted as proof of sanctification. Disciplinary practices were the primary practices; they facilitated ecstatic practices, which were by-products and evidence of sanctification.

The priority of discipline can be seen in the Church of God in Christ (COGIC), a Sanctified church which was founded in 1895 by Charles Harrison Mason and C. P. Jones and then embraced Pentecostal beliefs in 1906.[3] COGIC espoused doctrines of sanctification (also referred to as Holiness) and Pentecostalism, which claimed that the proof of sanctification was speaking in tongues.[4] For COGIC members, who called themselves the Saints, sanctification was "a way of thinking about life," as Dorothy Bass described it in her book *Practicing Our Faith* (1997).[5] To an outsider, like sociologist William A. Clark, "the mode of life required by Sanctification" seemed "too unreal for the social-minded being."[6] But COGIC members created a social world in which the practices of sanctification regulated one's participation or exclusion, and to the sanctified this world was real indeed. COGIC practitioners used the disciplinary practices of the church to regulate their religious and social worlds. The ecstatic practices were used to lure those outside the social world of COGIC and as a way to distinguish between those who were attracted to the ecstatic practices and those who were repulsed by them. Michel de Certeau's discourse on "tactics and practices" in *The Practice of Everyday Life* helps illuminate the manner in which the ritualized dances and possession manifestations of sanctification compelled and repelled outsiders while validating the worth of these practices for those inside the social world of sanctification.[7] By using ecstatic practices tactically, worshipers were able at times to control services, observers, and situations that otherwise would have been out of their purview.

Perhaps in this sense, Zora Neale Hurston's assessment of sanctification as "a protest against the high brow Negro tendencies" of outsiders was correct. COGIC members used the practices of sanctification to reject the appeal of the "high brow" in favor of practices that seemed to be imbued with a type of power that was not just temporal, but spiritual. Investigating how this spiritual power was made manifest through disciplinary and ecstatic religious practices reveals a complex picture of the benefits and drawbacks of the Sanctified life.

It is necessary first to consider the theological meaning of *sanctification* as used in reference to COGIC and other Sanctified churches. Within the nineteenth-century Holiness movement, "sanctification" provided healing, power for service, and, most importantly, cleansing from sin.[8] Sin encompassed not only wrongs against one's neighbor or God but also partaking in things that were harmful to the body, such as alcohol, cigarettes, and sexual activity outside of marriage. For some Holiness adherents, the cleansing of sanctification removed the desire to sin from a person's life. Proponents of the Holiness movement debated the nature of sanctification as they tried to discern who was sanctified and who was not. Out of this discussion came the Pentecostal movement, which claimed that glossolalia, or "Spirit baptism," was a sign of sanctification. Glossolalia became the defining experience of sanctification for many who moved into Pentecostalism, and some Pentecostals even went so far as to claim that glossolalia was the only experience of sanctification, rather than a sign that sanctification had already occurred.[9] Those churches that rejected this innovation and kept sanctification as the primary focus of their practices were termed Sanctified or Holiness churches. Outward manifestations such as shouting, holy dance, prophetic utterances, and trances were not validated as signs of sanctification in these churches unless a person had already undergone the sanctification process.

Making the spiritual physical, the process of pursuing what I term "the Sanctified life," included a variety of physical practices. Those who embraced sanctification, unlike their Protestant forebears and contemporaries, exhibited a great "love of the body" as a tool of worship and empowerment. As a tool for the regulation of life and production of sanctification, the body became an important and contested space for Sanctified church members; at a time when black bodies were being regulated and restrained by whites and blacks alike, the power to deny one's body and at the same time free it in sanctified dance and song was a heady power.

How should ecstatic worship practices be understood in light of the worshipers' belief in sanctification? In examining the daily lives of those seeking sanctification, a better understanding of how the principles and practices of the Sanctified churches worked individually and communally emerges. What was it like for those who lived the Sanctified life? What was expected, and what practices invigorated and constrained individuals in their daily lives? The actual practices of sanctification, these manifestations, and the attendant presentation of the practices in the worship service provide a map of the "body"—both the sanctified bodies that engaged in these practices and the body of persons engaged in pursuing their faith in ways that met at times with disapproval from outsiders.

Sanctification and Bodily Practices

The official manual of the Church of God in Christ refers to sanctification as "that gracious and continuous operation of the Holy Ghost, by which he delivers the justified sinner from the pollution of sin, renews his whole nature in the image of God and enables him to perform good works."[10] This doctrinal statement outlines the pattern of practices that encompasses sanctified living. First, the pollution of sin and the practices that cause one to sin were singled out for cleansing. It was not enough to have made a profession of belief in Jesus Christ; one also had to want to be cleansed of sin and remade anew. For those living in urban areas during the 1920s and 1930s, the city contained many pollutants. Sanctified church practices helped believers control carnal desires that prevented them from attaining holiness. Smoking, snuff dipping, and the use of alcohol were forbidden and were ridiculed as improper behavior in sermon and song.[11] Following the examples of the health and temperance movements of the latter part of the nineteenth century, policies limiting the introduction of these substances into the body were referred to as "intake practices," and they were usually the first religious practices adopted by members of the Sanctified church. Such cleansing practices drove out the unclean elements from the body, so that the Holy Spirit could reside within the individual, and initiated a spiritual discipline. A list of COGIC's doctrinal beliefs published in 1926 links holiness of the body to sanctification and provides a scriptural basis for each:

> God's will is to sanctify to keep from fornication—I. Thess. 4:3
> Holiness of the Body—Romans 12:1
> Temple of the Holy Ghost is holy—1 Cor. 3:16–17
> What we eat is sanctified by the word and prayer—Tim 4:4–5
> Without Holiness no man shall see the Lord—Heb 12:14[12]

The scriptural references reinforced the bodily nature of sanctified discipline.

If the intake practices were insufficient to cleanse a person of the desire to sin, fasting could cure it. A crucial element of the cleansing phase, fasting helped participants to deny themselves, proving that readiness for the flow of the Holy Spirit into the worshiper would not be hampered by substances in the body. In a pamphlet about fasting, Dr. Sister Pearl Page Brown wrote:

> Fasting is another powerful offensive spiritual weapon. Without this weapon you are not fully equipped for battle. Just as we have been equipped with the weapon of prayer, God wants us to be equipped with the weapon of fasting. Prayer and fasting go together to penetrate and to break through every resistance that the enemy has built. Fasting strengthens and intensifies our prayers. As you begin to use your spiritual weapon of fasting, as you humble yourself through fasting and prayer before God, you will break through enemy territories and claim victory in every circumstance. God is calling all of His people saints to "Blow the trumpet in Zion, sanctify a fast, call a solemn assembly." To sanctify means to set apart for God a fast to consecrate ourselves for the work He has given us to do, to humble ourselves before God, and to repent of all sin and disobedience in our lives. Joel 2;15; Exodus 34:38, Leviticus 23:27; Deut. 9:9; Samuel 7:6.[13]

Fasting was one of the foremost individual and corporate practices of the COGIC branch of Sanctified churches. COGIC members usually fasted by refusing food or water for whatever period of time an individual felt that God required. Leaders held fasting in such esteem that the annual convocation of that church started out with a corporate fast of three days for all participants. This was intended to purge the body and prepare it for the eventual power of the Spirit. It also assured participants that any forces preventing a person from fully embracing the Spirit would be purged through denial of the bodily comfort of food; the discipline of fasting removes "bondages" from a person's life. Fasting was to be used as a weapon against the Devil in order to free believers from sin and, at times, to intercede for healing. Founder C. H. Mason's own personal practice of dietary restrictions prompted him to add a dietitian to his staff in the 1930s, and his constant emphasis on eating "proper" foods, like fruits, vegetables, and nuts, perhaps signaled a preoccupation not only with digestion but with the effects of food on his spiritual state.[14]

What was on the body was as important as what was in it. Dress was crucial to the practices surrounding the presentation of the body in COGIC. The leader of the Women's Department of COGIC, Lizzie Robinson, instructed women to "Dress As Becometh Holiness." Dressing for holiness meant that the body would remain covered, even in warm weather. Rules for dress, like rules for the consumption of substances, were reinforced by means of scriptural admonitions. The first rules for COGIC women's work covered the basics of sanctified dress:

> Rule #4. All members and missionaries must not wear hats with flowers or feathers nor Short Dresses, Split Skirts or Short Sleeves. . . . Rule #5. All members and missionaries must dress in modest apparel as becometh holiness, professing Godliness with good work.[15]

The dress code, first appearing in the 1920s, was a response to the fashions women were wearing in the speakeasies, or jook joints, where blues music and liquor were readily available. Women were the primary focus of the COGIC dress code, but men were admonished not to wear ties with their shirts. The dress code acted as a disciplinary practice, setting boundaries for sanctified behavior. Dress styles were one of the practices that posed problems for those who wished to become members of Sanctified churches. As the following excerpt makes clear, some women's desire to dress "sinfully" kept them from attaining holiness:

> I was wretched and undone, and was very sinful. My hair was cut in a boyish bob, and my skirts knee high, most of my blouses were without sleeves, and really, after hearing the gospel preached, I became a penitent. One day I decided to alter a garment so that I would not be ashamed to go to the Altar. But before I finished the garment, time came to prepare dinner, and I went to pick green peas. Oh, what a glorious day for me. While in the pea patch, I believed, and my sins were washed away. Then I began to glorify God. The Holy Ghost came upon me and I fell to the ground. I glorified the name of Jesus,

and the spirit took full control of my tongue for a time. I spoke with other tongues as the spirit gave me utterance. Oh my, how happy I was for I knew that I was saved, and Baptized with the Holy Ghost and fire, and ever since that glorious day my desire has been to walk with god in the beauty of holiness, and to be of some help, and to assist in some way to improve the character of young women and girls.[16]

Sister Minnie Carter, the woman who gave the above testimony, linked her subsequent experience of speaking in tongues to her obedience in adopting appropriate Holiness dress. She felt that only when she could submit herself to the discipline of modest dressing, rather than wearing sleeveless blouses and knee-high skirts, could she hope to be filled with the Holy Spirit. Testimonies like these, as well as admonitions, especially by the women of the church, were reinforced in meetings and addresses. Women who joined the church were required to turn their pants into dress skirts, and "fixing" the splits in their skirts occupied a good deal of new converts' time in the church. A sewing circle publication designed to help women learn to sew and produce household goods devoted a small section to how to sew up a split skirt and to change a pair of pants into a skirt.[17]

Dress was employed as a tool in the promotion of the sanctified life, and it helped identify members, giving them another level of distinctiveness in addition to the worship practices they engaged in. Dress codes, more than the fasting and abstinence regulations, were an effective way to display community: the modest dress was often commented upon by observers. The major purpose of dress, however, was to prevent any sexual connotations from being associated with the free worship practices. In short, dress codes regulated sexuality.

Abstinence from any type of sexual activity was expected of unmarried members of COGIC. The prohibition against sexual activities was inculcated in young members through dress and through the "purity class," which was founded in 1926. The most recent purity class book describes its history as follows: "In 1926 the late Mother (Elnora) C.J. Johnson of Michigan had a vision to create an organization designed for the purpose of preserving in Christian youth a high moral standard of living. The moral decay of the 1920's was destroying the basic principles of Christian Living the church had been upholding. This predicament necessitated the purity class."[18] Regulating speech, dress, and sexuality, the purity class was another way to instill the practices of sexual abstinence in unmarried, young saints. Given the date of its inception, it may have been created partly in response to blues music, which also permeated the storefronts of the urban areas where COGIC thrived.

Those who were married were expected and encouraged to take part in their marital duties with their spouses except during times of fasting and prayer, when COGIC members were to refrain from sexual activity.[19] In any case, sex outside of the marriage bed was forbidden. Sex with members of the same sex was also prohibited. COGIC members were expected to put away the sin, not indulge in it and then perform a symbolic act to clean it up. Sanctification and the process of cleansing oneself from sin was just as important, perhaps even more so, as engaging in a sacramental practice like baptism. Those who came into COGIC with the sin of adultery or other prohibited practices could not expect that the mere fact of being baptized would sanctify them:

> It is the spirit of the Antichrist that would make one say that those who have other women's husbands by being baptized in water (prayed over and anointed) would make it all right. Nowhere did Jesus nor the disciples pray anointing on water. Now, if the man can stay with the other man's wife then it won't be any need of the man who abuses himself with another man. I Cor 6:9.[20]

This is not to say that baptism did not matter in COGIC—it did, and Mason baptized many COGIC members in the Mississippi River during convocation times.[21] But only the crisis experience and the mortification of the flesh that prepared the body for sanctification could free COGIC members from the desire to sin. Repudiation of the sinful act had to accompany the cleansing ritual.

The practices of self-denial and fasting and the regulation of dress and of sexual activity were only the tip of the iceberg. Movie watching, secular music, chewing gum, sports, and jewelry wearing were all forbidden to those who sought to live the sanctified life. Each of the five senses was monitored by the invisible gatekeeper of sanctification, and only by ordering bodily functions would individuals be able to monitor their progress toward God's presence. While they regulated the community, these routinized practices also became part of individual lived experiences. Even individuals' mode of address changed in the Church of God in Christ. Those who embraced sanctified beliefs and practices in the COGIC tradition called each other "Saints," a method of address that denoted those who were inside the community of the sanctified. The designation reflected the ability of the community of the sanctified to enforce the importance of the practices they engaged in. It also upended traditional methods of address in most of the churches of this period, and thus it became a method of challenging the status quo. Finally, it helped to knit together a community whose members had migrated far from their southern homes to the cities of the North. The strictness of the bodily practices of COGIC helped to set boundaries that provided comfort for the members of the church, not an onerous lifestyle.[22] Even to those who were not sanctified, the practices of COGIC were clear, though daunting. One woman interviewed by a sociologist in the 1930s remarked: "I like to go there, but I'm not sanctified. I like to play ball, they don't want you to do that or smoke, drink, dance, or play cards."[23]

Reinforcing Sanctified Practices

There was a gendered element to the practices that assisted the quest for sanctification in COGIC. Although all of the Saints were expected to fast and to keep from drinking, smoking, and chewing, women were encouraged to model sanctification within the COGIC community. While the pastor held sway in the Sunday morning and evening services, women of COGIC were able to take a preeminent place as the enforcers of sanctification practices because of the structural agency afforded to them in the Women's Department. Founded in 1911 by Bishop Mason, the Women's Department, under its first leader, Lizzie Robinson, reinforced the tenets and practices of sanctification outside the Sunday meeting.[24] Robinson, called "Mother Robinson" by her charges, had been involved in the Holiness movement prior to becoming a Pentecostal. She dressed herself in a strict Holiness manner, habitually wearing a uniform of a long black skirt and a crisply starched white blouse. Stern and directive, she made her presence felt throughout the COGIC membership in both rural and urban areas. It was the Women's Department that turned practices of sanctification into the habits of the church members.

Under Robinson's leadership, the Women's Department put together prayer and Bible bands. Within these groups, the principles—or what was often referred to in COGIC as the "doctrine"—of sanctification were reinforced.[25] Women, as modelers and enforcers of sanctification, reordered a world that was seemingly male dominated, placing themselves at the center of holiness life. One writer expressed the role of women's sanctified behavior succinctly: "The purpose of Holy Women is to LURE men into the body of Christ by lifting him up, and not to LURE them to their own bodies by lifting IT up."[26] If their attire and manner were in keeping with holiness, women could bring men into sanctified living by their very demeanor and dress. Perhaps the holiness dress was alluring as well, keeping the frame of women's bodies safely secreted from the wandering eyes of men.

The major practice of women that facilitated sanctification was prayer, which men also participated in. Prayer meetings were a natural outgrowth of the fasting practices and were coupled with fasting as a way to cleanse the body and at the same time to seek God for spiritual breakthroughs. For Mother Robinson, consecration through prayer began with the Scripture passage she used as her consideration in founding the Women's Department, Jeremiah chapter 9, verses 17 through 20, from the King James Bible, her quotation of which reads:

Thus saith the Lord of Hosts, consider ye, and call for the mourning women, that they may come, and call for the cunning women, that they may come. And let them make haste to take up a wailing for us, that our eyes may run with tears, and out eyelids gush out with waters. For a voice of wailing is heard out of Zion, how we are spoiled! We are greatly confounded because we have forsaken the land, because our dwellings have cast us out. Yet we have heard the word of the Lord, O ye women and let our ears receive the words of His Mouth, and teach your daughters wailing and everyone her neighbor lamentation.

The passage highlights the professional mourning women, who take their place to pray and wail for Israel. Influenced by this text, Mother Robinson encouraged women to set aside time for intense prayer and consecration, in sessions which they called "shut-ins." Typical early methods of consecration included these overnight prayer meetings, fasting, and intensive Bible studies. The overnight prayer meetings started at dusk and broke up the next morning. These communal practices of prayer intensified solidarity and quickly identified those who were unwilling to consecrate themselves. Participants spent all night in prayer, often crying out in loud voices and weeping. Moaning or groaning in the Spirit accompanied the prayer time, which was unstructured and involved prostration before God, walking, reading Scripture, and kneeling in reverence. Fasting usually began prior to the prayer meeting and commonly lasted three days. Mother E. J. Dabney, a COGIC woman revered among the denomination for her prayer meetings, described one shut-in: "We were unable to buy fuel enough to heat the building for the evening services, and make it comfortable for those who prayed with me when we fasted seventy two hours, therefore, we wrapped ourselves in blankets and quilts to keep warm, Sometimes I was so cold my whole body was numb, but those faithful praying church mothers and daughters of mine drew near to me."[27]

Mother Dabney's account illustrates another way in which the women and men of COGIC communally reinforced the practices of sanctification. Addressing other church members in familial terms like Brother, Sister, and Mother, a practice that COGIC took from the Holiness movement, created a family aspect in the churches and fostered a strong bond between practices and community. It would be much harder to leave E. J. Dabney alone in a night of strenuous prayer if you thought of her as "Mother Dabney." In the passage above, Dabney as spiritual mother takes on an even greater importance as she gathers her "daughters" around her. Even Bishop Mason was referred to as "Dad" Mason. Such fictive familial relations helped to bring together the community and set up a system in which one's sanctification was reinforced not only by the fear of the Lord but also by the fear of disappointing one's family in the Lord. Familial modes of address served as a reminder to the Saints that the family was sanctified, and thus even if the members of their biological family were not, there was a place where they belonged.

The Effects and Affects of Sanctified Practices

The practices that validated sanctification of COGIC members held in tension release and ridicule. The practices that paved the way for sanctification were mild compared to the proof that one was sanctified. The body, normally rigidly controlled, became uncontrolled as the experiential and spiritual aspects of sanctification presented themselves. Glossolalia, shouting, dancing, and trances all seemed to have a sense of uncontrolledness about them, but it was the "yieldedness," or consecration, that the Saints experienced that allowed the Holy Ghost to move through them.[28] "Bodily possession," as historian Ann Taves referred to Pentecostal possession, encompassed all of the ecstatic practices, and its appearance was contingent upon how much the body had been prepared by means of sanctified living. By submitting their bodies to the rigors of fasting, consecration, and prayer, the Saints became prepared to receive the power of the Holy Spirit within them. At times, this submission was a rigor, but expectations of the power to come were a compensation. New converts to COGIC could not expect ecstatic experiences to occur right away; the experiences had to be won through the process that others had gone through. The body work that had been done through fasting, prayer, and abstinence was manifest in the Holy Spirit's subsequent control over the body.

Speaking in tongues, or glossolalia, and its subset, spiritual singing and "trembling," were the outgrowth of sanctified living and were in public view at worship services. The practice of tongues speaking was the most foreign to the outsider, and the bodily manifestations that attended speaking in tongues at times both compelled and repelled the observers of them.[29] For adherents, the theology of tongues speech and the mandate for the practice can be found in Acts chapter 2, verses 1 through 5: "And when the day of Pentecost was fully come, they were all with one accord in one place. Suddenly there came a sound from heaven, as of rushing, mighty wind, and it filled all the house where they were like as of fire, and it sat upon each of them: and they were all filled with the Holy Ghost and began to speak with new tongues as the spirit gave them utterance."[30] Speaking in tongues, for the Saints, manifested the Holy Spirit's work within their lives and the fulfillment of sanctification's purpose: to cleanse their lives so that the Holy Spirit could move through them and use them for service. The appearance of tongues also signaled the connection to Scripture and to the first Christians, who had experienced the day of Pentecost. Saints employed tongues speech in a variety of ways: as a personal prayer language, in spiritual singing, in worship, and as a prophetic gift. Scriptural admonitions about the efficacy of speaking in tongues pointed, they felt, both to the benefits of the practice and to the mandate to engage in it. As Mary Mason put it:

> Our Lord Jesus did not say that some of them that believe should speak with new tongues, but them that believe shall speak new tongues. When did this great work begin? On the day of Pentecost Acts 2:1–5. . . . Did God intend the speaking of tongues to be in the church? And Good [*sic*] hath sent some in the Church first Apostles, secondly, prophets, thirdly teachers. After that miracles, then gifts of healing, and helps [*sic*] governments, diversity of tongues I Cor. 12–28. For he that speaketh in an unknown tongue speaks not to men, but unto God, for no man understandeth him, how be it that the [*sic*] in the spirit he speaketh mysteries I Cor. 14.[31]

In COGIC, tongues speech empowered individuals, giving them access to the power of the early church for prophecy, healing, and miracles. Tongues speech was a conduit, a means by which the Holy Sprit could speak through a person for prophecy, perhaps in a language that listeners would understand. For COGIC members and Pentecostals, speaking in tongues was the sign that sanctification had taken hold in an individual's life. It was a sign to the believer of God's work through him or her and a sign to the unbeliever of the power of the Holy Sprit to cleanse and renew. The goal of all the practices, which also separated the Saints from the outside world, was to have the Holy Spirit flow through their bodies.

Yet for outsiders speaking in tongues resembled a state of possession:

> Ardor Increases, actions of hands and feet grow more vigorous until a stage of ecstasy is reached that requires a more thorough release of the spiritual forces acting within. One begins to speak in tongues "me, me, me," then another "tut, tut, tut." So it goes. Speaking in tongues is contagious. The worshipers seem to feel that they are closely approaching the sacred realm of the Holy Spirit. . . . The worshiper who first began to speak in tongues is seized with an urge to dance. She dances with great vigor, a dance which she executes with a degree of gracefulness that indicates she has put a great deal of time practicing it.[32]

While to outsiders tongues speech and other possession states seemed to be out of the believers' control, for the Saints, tongues speech did not occur randomly. It was to be done "decently and in order," which meant that it was reserved for the musical part of the worship service or for individual prayer times.

Bishop Mason's explanation of tongues speech in an excerpt from one of his early sermons shows how the locus of power is shifted in the service.

Speaking in tongues is the wonderful work of God. All that did not have this work in them on that day were amazed and in doubt about that wonderful work of God, and so it is today with all that have not this blessed work going on in them, they cannot understand it; they will say everything about it. Sinners, converted ones and sanctified ones and all wonder and will wonder when they hear or see this movement of the Holy Ghost going on in the Saints of God. If the Holy Ghost does not speak in them, they can't understand his speaking the wonderful works of God in other tongues.[33]

Sinners who converted, and even some of the sanctified, he argued, could not understand the Holy Ghost if they did not allow the Spirit to speak through them. Mason's explication suggests that community boundaries around practices conveyed their power over the sacred space and over the outsiders within their churches.

At times, however, the boundaries between sinners and Saints were breached, and the Spirit reached out to those who were "on the wrong side of the pew." In an article in *Ebony* magazine commemorating the fiftieth anniversary of COGIC, a woman reminisced about her conversion from skepticism to belief: "I went crosstown so that I could laugh at the sanctified folks. Hah! I'm here so they can laugh at me now. I'll be glad if they do [laugh] when I'm rejoicing."[34] Willie Mae Ford, a popular gospel singer who in the 1930s became Pentecostal, described her experience of being filled with the Holy Ghost:

I was in Ohio singing and Mrs. Artelia Hutchings was singing, Let It breathe on me, let the Holy Ghost Breathe on me. When the Holy Ghost hit me, I hit the floor. On the Train coming back to St. Louis, I kept everybody up all night long, trying to talk, speaking in tongues. Honey, this child got soused good. The Lord had to fix me up, because you see I was a wild person, just like a wild buck. I made fun of holiness people. I laughed at 'em and tried to do the holy dance. I would just cut up.[35]

Ford's testimony mentions her previous mockery of Holiness people. Having frequented Sanctified services as a visiting Baptist gospel singer, she had been both intrigued and repelled by the practices in the Sanctified church until she experienced glossolalia. From that point forward, it is said, she exhibited a new "anointed" style of singing and preaching that led her later to pursue ordination in the African Methodist Episcopal Zion Church.[36] Ford's use of her body to accentuate the songs she sang as a sanctified woman points to both the use of the body in sanctified singing and practice and the importance of women who modeled sanctification.

Tongues speech was also combined with music to create "spiritual singing," also called "singing in the spirit." Spiritual singing was the practice of singing along with the music of the service but in tongues rather than English. Singing in the spirit required a person to allow the Holy Spirit to flow through her or him in a song, and that song, coupled with sanctified music, brought the presence and power of God into the Saints' services. Mary Mason wrote: "Spiritual singing is another manner in which God expresses Himself [t]hrough him [Bishop Mason]. By it evil spirits are driven away and souls are called to repentance. . . . Very often the power of God is so gloriously manifested through the singing that the assemblies of saints are aroused with the same fire of enthusiasm and take up the theme and sing together with him till they are carried to heights unknown with the natural mind."[37]

Spiritual singing in tongues seems to have the closest relationship to what was termed "sanctified music." Sometimes spiritual singing would begin as a "jumped-up song," a song that was created on the spot to fit the particular moment in the service. One interviewee described the jumped-up song: "It is when you feel the Spirit of the Lord [acting] on your soul, and you jus' gets up and sings whatever comes to mind."[38] Most songs that began as jumped-up songs became spiritual singing in the unknown tongues that only God would be able to understand. For both the observed and the observer, the singing had the effect of drawing all church members into the practice, creating a cohesiveness in the congregation that was difficult for outsiders to follow.

More often than not, observers looked upon the display of speaking in tongues as a contagious, learned, and ecstatic practice of possession. It was usually accompanied by the dance or shout. C. H. Mason's understanding of shouting in the Sanctified church was threefold: it was a biblical act of worship, an emulation of other religious dancers like King David, and an act of victory.[39] For Mason, shouting was biblically based and related closely to the dance, in which one would both shout and dance to the Lord. In his text, "Is It Right for the Saints of God to Dance?" Mason introduced the Scripture passages that justified his threefold understanding of shouting: "The children of God dance of God, for God, and to the praise and glory of his name. They have the joy of the spirit of the Lord in them, they are joyful in their King—the Christ. At times they may be dancing Christ is all, or none but Christ. How sweet it is to dance in Him and about Him, for he is all. So to dance in the Spirit of the Lord expresses joy and victory."[40] The dance for Mason was also the ring shout, which African Americans participated in as a worship practice in slavery. The ring shout was usually begun in worship as an act of volition, that is, it did not begin as a direct response to the Spirit but as a way to call the Spirit down into the service. Dance had two main purposes: to demonstrate worship of God and to show that God (the Holy Spirit) inhabited the dancers. The shouting/dancing was engaged in as a voluntary act, an act that would show deference and reverence for God's work in the believer's life. Like the ring shout, the dance was to be entered into deliberately, the impetus being the scriptural admonitions to worship.

In descriptions by Works Progress Administration workers and in other anthropological and sociological accounts, the worship of the shout was attributed solely to possession by the Spirit, which missed the intentionality of the shouting and its purpose as a practice within the church. For example, Hurston explained shouting in the Sanctified church of the COGIC service as follows:

> There are two main types of shouters 1. Silent. 2. Vocal. There is a sort of intermediary type where one stage is silent and the other vocal. The silent type takes with violent Retching and twitching motions. Sometimes they remain seated; sometimes they jump up and down and fling the body about with great violence. Lips tightly pursed, eyes closed. The seizure ends by collapse. The vocal type is more frequent. There are all gradations from quiet weeping while seated, to the unrestrained screaming while leaping pews and running up and down the aisle. Some, unless restrained, run up into the pulpit and embrace the preacher. Some are taken with hysterical laughing spells.[41]

For Hurston, shouting was a practice that was a survival of "African Possession by the Gods."[42] Her descriptions, therefore, all conformed to a template of spirit possession. Focusing on the motor functions of the body, she described the shouting as "being in the ecstasy." Other sociologists, like William Clark, described the worship and shouting of the Saints in similar fashion.

> As this part of the service processes [*sic*] the more sensitive and susceptible communicants can be observed to become more physically active. Muscular twitching becomes observable, and automatic motions of limbs become more frequent in some. Others demonstrate changes in the form of facial tics and distortions. Another type of cataleptic manifestation is the communicant whose body, on being permeated with the Holy Ghost, slowly straightens up and becomes rigid. It was these types that brought the Holiness groups into disrepute in the early days and earned for them the name "holy rollers."[43]

The manifestation of motor practices, to outside observers, was caused by possession and did not seem to have a focal point. The possession was induced primarily by music but also at times by the preaching of the pastor. It was, however, always described as "getting the Spirit," which the Saints would have argued they already had. For the Saints, shouting represented both a move of the Spirit and a mode of worship that did not have to be influenced by the Holy Spirit to be engaged in. Mason believed that the shout could be engaged in with or without Holy Spirit possession but that it was not done involuntarily, as Hurston believed. Mason took great care to validate the practices of dancing and shouting with scriptural references:

The word of the Lord Says: let them praise Him in the Dance: Psa. 149:3, also 150:4; Then shall the virgin rejoice in the dance, both young men and old together Jer 31:13. When Israel's joy ceased her dance was turned into mourning, Lam 5:15, Judges 21:21. There is a time of dance or a time of dancing—Eccl. 3:4.

Dancing shows that we have victory I Sam 18:16; Dancing is mentioned four times in the New Testament. Christ himself makes mention of it Matt 11:17, Luke 7:32. In the 15th chapter 25th verse of Luke, in his parable of the Prodigal son, says he was received with music and dancing.[44]

The practice of trembling occurred when tongues speech "spilled over" into a bodily tremor or dance. The presence of the Spirit could cause the body to tremble, and a person could even experience a type of fainting, or being "slain in the spirit." This, too, was justified by Mason with scriptural references:

Do People tremble when they are under the power of God, and so is it right? Yes. Please read now in this subject Psa. 2:11, which says, serve the lord with fear and rejoice with trembling Eph. 6:5. . . . If the church is praying to God and some fall on their faces are they hypnotized? No. It shows that God is in the people of God Of Truth. 1 Cor. 14:24– 25. Men fell when Jesus owned he was the Christ. John 18:6. Also when he arose from the dead, the keepers did shake and became as dead men. Matt. 24:4.[45]

The right to "discern" the Spirit in the one speaking in tongues or trembling was the prerogative of the other Saints. If other members of the congregation had not observed a Saint's adequate engagement in fasting, prayer, and sanctified living, any trembling or speaking in tongues was subject to censure. It was also important for the Saints to delineate the difference between their motor practices and the similar manifestations in spiritualist churches, which often were located nearby. Special care was taken to differentiate between another spirit and the Holy Spirit as the agent that caused the manifestation.[46]

For the Saints, of course, speaking in tongues, trance, dancing, and shouting were the natural outgrowths and evidence of all the practices that made up the sanctified life. Yet, for all of their peculiarities, speaking in tongues was the practice that gained the most attention from the public. Even *Ebony* magazine, in a fiftieth anniversary article describing the COGIC convocation, led off by mentioning the controversial practice: "Because they 'spoke in tongues,' danced in religious joy and believed that men cannot be saved without holiness, a small band of Baptists was ejected from its little Arkansas church in 1895. Today their critics still look askance at the holy dance and turn deaf ears to 'speaking in tongues.' But even the harshest of their well-informed critics concede that the Church of God in Christ has arrived in numbers and prominence."[47] Later, the article described the church as having "the true spirit of the Ne-gro." For many observers, that spirit caused the rebirth of "song making," as Zora Neale Hurston described it.

Yet, it was the disciplinary practices of COGIC that inspired sanctified music, and, for those who both practiced sanctification and performed sanctified music, the tensions between the practices of sanctification and musical performance increasingly became acute. Sister Rosetta Tharpe (née Thorpe), gospel singer and guitarist, struggled with these tensions. Tharpe, who began singing in the church at the age of six, traveled with COGIC preacher F. W. McGee and her evangelist mother from an early age, and her proficient and inspired guitar playing attracted the attention of those within and without the Sanctified church.[48] When she moved from the South to Chicago in the 1930s, the blues and other musical styles began to heavily influence her, yet she continued her performances in COGIC and other Holiness churches until moving to New York. That move opened up another world to her. She began to play with big bands under leaders like Cab Calloway and Lucky Millander at the Cotton Club, but COGIC members frowned upon her taking sanctified music into unsanctified places. The clothing she wore in the clubs was brightly colored and stylish, and that also attracted the ire of Saints. Church members began to murmur about whether she was still sanctified or not, and her base of support within the church slowly eroded.[49] For the Saints, consorting in clubs and the like was tantamount to repudiating practices of sanctification, even if Tharpe protested that she still continued to live a holy life. She managed to hold the two worlds in tension until the early 1950s, when she recorded a few blues tracks with another Sanctified church singer, Madame Marie Knight, who also performed at the Cotton Club. The foray into the blues caused Tharpe to lose a significant portion of her fan base, and as a result her singing engagements trailed off. She died in the early 1970s.[50]

Another unforeseen problem arose when unsanctified musicians started singing in the sanctified music style. Mahalia Jackson, a famous gospel singer, learned how to sing in the sanctified way by listening to the singing at a Holiness church near her home when she was growing up. When she moved to Chicago, she had her first voice lesson, during which the teacher chastised her severely for her singing style. "You've got to learn to stop hollering. It will take time to build up your voice. The way you sing is not a credit to the Negro race. You've got to sing songs so that white people can understand them."[51] During the 1930s and 1940s, the sanctified style of singing, which sounded like hollering to some, was emulated by many in the gospel music field, causing consternation to those who were trying to support the "true saints" as opposed to the performers. For those who observed this style of singing being offered as an art form and entertainment, the true meaning of practices that COGIC members valued as reflections of sanctification was even more blurred and obscured. In some sense, these imitators may also have served COGIC members by the representation of their practices, even though the performers themselves were merely avid imitators.

COGIC would later go on to export sanctified music to the world through other musicians, but when sanctified music first moved out of the sanctuary, the disciplinary practices surrounding its performance and creation were obscured and their meaning distorted. The relationship of sanctification, music, and its practitioners was always lodged in admonitions and literal interpretations of Scripture and was crucial to preserving both the practices and the theological foundations of the Sanctified church. Without music to "stir up" the practices in the Sanctified church, sanctified living would reside only in individual actions of piety that did not draw others into the circle. The markers of the sanctified—their dress, their music, their dancing, their preaching styles—all combined in the worship service to serve both to bind the church family together and as boundary between the sanctified and the world. Sanctified music acted as one catalyst that allowed the sanctified to express both the power and the efficacy of sanctification through their bodies, and it also provided a boundary that separated the sanctified from the unsanctified.

The Unreal Life: The World of the Sanctified

Most academics and cultural critics of the early part of the twentieth century had inaccurate views of the practices of the Sanctified churches. William Clark's assessment that "the mode of life required by Sanctification" is "too unreal for the social-minded being" perhaps indicated only that the sanctified life was too unreal for his understanding. The mode of life of the sanctified, with its regulations, its corporeality, and its totality, ordered the lives of the Saints. This unreal mode of life provided access to a real world of spirituality and provided its followers with a social outlet for expressing their sanctification. For women in COGIC, the sanctified life helped reverse patriarchal structures, at times assisting women in wresting away power from dominant males. The disciplinary practices ordered the lives of Saints, who had migrated to urban areas from rural ones, and helped them keep the rhythm of the sacred lives they had pursued in rural climes, refocusing their lives around the church. By setting up habits of life and worship centered on the doctrine of sanctification, the Saints created a protective identity that counteracted the ridicule of those who depicted their practices as mere spirit possession and backward behavior.

The world of the Sanctified churches also prohibited its members from having freedoms that others experienced in the urban world. The demands of sanctified living in the face of modernity challenged the younger members of the church. Even today, the rhetoric of church leaders hearkens back to the "old landmarks" of sanctified living. It is difficult now in COGIC to ask women to wear only dresses. The rigors of everyday life preclude practices like protracted prayer and fasting. Consequently, older members of congregations have become the repositories of practices that the young have long since modified or abandoned. Practices not readily understood in the past by outsiders are perhaps even less understood by those who are present in Sanctified churches today. Keeping their bodies in subjection to worldly desires may, in a strange way, have frozen out attempts at changes that would have made the sanctified life in COGIC more palatable to a new generation of members. Sanctified music lives on in the strains of contemporary Christian Gospel music, but many who perform it have forgotten the roots of sanctification disciplines that allowed those in the Sanctified churches to play the world's music in the church. Perhaps for the Church of God in Christ, sanctified music worked like a siren, luring its hearers away from its real meaning: disciplined spiritual living that would find a release in music consecrated in holiness.

CHAPTER NINE

The Practice of Prayer in a Modern Age

Liberals, Fundamentalists, and Prayer in the Early Twentieth Century

RICK OSTRANDER

During the first quarter of the twentieth century, as the battle between self-described fundamentalists and modernists among American Protestants intensified, a Kansas pastor penned an article for the conservative publication *Moody Bible Institute Monthly* entitled "Flattening the Spiritual Life." The danger of liberalism, this pastor warned, was that liberal theology produced a deadened spiritual life: "They do not believe that God specifically answers prayer; they do not believe in individual conversion and salvation. . . . These are the things that deepen the spiritual life of the believer. If you fill the well with rocks, of what use is it to come there to draw water?" The end result of tolerating liberalism in the Protestant churches, he cautioned, would be a flattening of the spiritual life of the Christian. By contrast, fundamentalists portrayed themselves as leaders of a religious movement that would revive the dormant piety of the mainline churches. Moody Bible Institute president, James Gray, proclaimed, "fundamentalism represents a revival of our holy religion," and he went on to place fundamentalism in historic succession to seventeenth-century Pietism and eighteenth-century Methodism, movements that spiritually revived the dead orthodoxy of the day.[1]

Liberal Protestants reversed the characters in this story. In their version, fundamentalism represented the cold legalism of the past, while the liberals brought a spiritual breath of fresh air to America's churches. According to New York pastor Harry Emerson Fosdick, an embodiment of classic liberalism, the liberal "has come into his new attitudes and ways of thinking . . . through the deepening of his spiritual life. He is a liberal because he is more religious, not because he is less." Recalling his own migration to liberalism, Fosdick cited the influence of men such as William Newton Clarke: "Their revolt, like that of Jesus against the orthodoxy of his time, was in the interest of a deeper, more vital, more transforming Christian experience than literalism, legalism, and authoritarianism could supply. The result for many of us was not alone a new theology but a new spiritual life."[2]

The dispute between fundamentalists and liberals of the early twentieth century, therefore, was to some extent a dispute over the nature of Christian piety. Both groups claimed to be the proper vehicle for recovering vital Christian practices that they believed were in peril in the modern age. Such concern over the persistence of practice is not uncommon, as theorists of religious practice can attest. Practice is deeply intertwined with historical change, a process in which, in the words of Catherine Bell, "past patterns are reproduced but also reinterpreted or transformed." According to Marshall Sahlins, rituals allow a community to "subdue" a new situation, and they thereby enable the traditional structures to continue to thrive in legitimate and relatively unaltered ways. The practice of prayer in the early twentieth century provides a rich arena for observing such dynamics at work.[3] For early-twentieth-century Christians, maintaining (and in some ways altering) the practice of prayer in the modern world enabled them to make sense of a hectic modern world—symbolized by commuter trains in fundamentalist leader Charles Blanchard's introductory quote— while retaining the traditional faith. As Catherine Brekus notes in Chapter 1 of this volume, religious practices serve to mediate cultural changes, because their timelessness gives the practitioner a sense of continuity with the past even though the practices may be modified in significant ways. Clearly the practice of prayer served such a purpose for early-twentieth-century Protestants.[4]

At the same time, in the midst of cultural change, practice can have a conserving influence on belief. Modern church commentators such as Dorothy Bass remind us that, as the Church Fathers put it, *lex orandi, lex credendi*—prayer shapes faith. Bass and others have called for renewed attention to Christian practice for this very reason. They believe that reviving Christian practice can be a way to strengthen Christian faith at a time when traditional beliefs seem to be waning. As Bass asserts, "we can believe more fully as we act more boldly." In the early years of the twentieth century, the practice of prayer seems to have kept liberal Protestants believing and practicing things about a personal God that their intellectual framework would not have led them to retain. In all, the study of fundamentalist and liberal practices of prayer provides rich material for contemplating the complex intermingling of belief, practice, and cultural change in the modern world.[5]

Christians historically have emphasized the importance of maintaining a personal devotional life. Twentieth-century Protestants, however, feared that the regular, faithful practice of prayer was endangered in the modern world. William Adams Brown, professor of systematic theology at Union Theological Seminary in New York and a leading liberal spokesperson, began his 1927 book on prayer by claiming, "One of the outstanding facts in the religious life of our generation has been the decline in the practice of prayer." Specifically, the practice of prayer was under attack on both philosophical and practical levels. Philosophically, the efficacy of prayer was seen as problematic in the more secular society of the early twentieth century. The "critical temper," in Brown's words, of modern science made traditional understandings of prayer seem irrational. Petitionary prayer, with its vision of a God rushing to the rescue of his children, did not seem reasonable in a culture in which science had seemingly ruled out supernatural intervention. Thus, the religious and popular literature of the period was peppered with remarks similar to one made by Frederick Spurr in 1924 in the denominational journal *The Baptist:* "A chill has fallen on the hearts of many. Doubts concerning the efficacy of prayer are far more common than some of us imagine."[6]

Christian prayer was beset by a more practical problem as well, as the following lament by the Protestant writer Charles Blanchard indicates.

> There is probably no one fact in modern life which has more seriously interfered with family prayer than the early and late trains which have become necessary in view of the complexity of modern life. When men lived and worked in their homes, for themselves, conditions were radically different from those which at this time exist. Men are now cogs in wheels and the wheel cannot turn if cogs are absent or broken. The result is that in every great city in the world, thousands of people, young, middle-aged and old, hasten from their homes in the morning and return to them late at night. How shall these persons share in the home prayer which used to characterize every Christian household? How shall they even have the time required for deliberate and effective personal prayer?[7]

Cultural observers claimed that traditional devotional practices were being threatened by the changes associated with modern economic and social life. With the emergence of the middle class and a consumer culture, Americans were seen as too busy pursuing the good life to devote much time to the cultivation of Christian spirituality. "Protestants," observed historian Donald Meyer, "were learning how to spend and consume, having produced and saved as Calvin and Wesley had urged." Sinclair Lewis's depiction of the fictional George F. Babbitt, the quintessential American businessman, summed up for many the spirit of 1920s middle-class culture. Lewis walks the reader through a typical day in Babbitt's life full of business calls, lunches at the club, and booster meetings. Except for an obligatory Sunday morning church service, religion is conspicuously absent from Babbitt's life.[8]

In 1924, sociologists Robert and Helen Lynd conducted a study of Muncie, Indiana—dubbed "Middletown" in their book. Their goal was to assess how American society had changed since 1890, using a typical American community as their test case.

Among other things, the Lynds studied Middletown's religious institutions and practices, which, they claimed, were in a state of crisis. Christian belief was still common and church attendance a community expectation, but, they wrote, "one infers that doubts and uneasiness among individuals may be greater than a generation ago."[9]

The Lynds focused on two areas where, they claimed, traditional Christian practices were in decline—family devotions and Wednesday evening prayer meeting. According to the ministers that the Lynds interviewed, the observance of regular family prayer had become almost extinct in the 1920s. In most churches, they claimed, only about 5 percent of the people actually practiced family prayers. Such rituals survived primarily among the working class, they believed. Concluded the Lynds, "it is generally acknowledged that the family altar is disappearing."[10]

The midweek prayer meeting, a tradition among American Protestants, was in an equally moribund state, the Lynds believed. The meeting was being crowded out by other events, they claimed: "Despite the efforts of the Ministerial Association to keep Wednesday evening free from other community activities for prayer meetings, the community no longer makes any effort, even outwardly, to observe this former custom; instead, the prayer meeting occasionally alters the hour or even the day of its meeting to give place to other events." The prayer meeting itself, one Middletown pastor remarked, was "a modern minister's nightmare." Only a small handful of faithful churchgoers bothered to attend, and those who did attend were reluctant to pray out loud or present requests for prayer. Thus, another minister noted, prayer meetings often ended up with the pastor "talking the prayer meeting to death." Some churches had temporarily increased attendance by introducing practical topics into the meetings, but in general, the Lynds concluded, the prayer meeting was joining the "family altar" on the road to extinction.[11]

Protestant writers across the theological spectrum shared the Lynds' pessimistic assessment of the state of Christian devotional practice in the 1920s. A century earlier, the New England Tract Society had issued a pamphlet of instructions for private devotions. Concerning the duration of such exercises, the author counseled, "perhaps the medium, most generally suitable, is an hour at morning and evening." One may question how many early-nineteenth-century readers followed such advice, but certainly by the twentieth century such strictures seemed unreasonable. The bustling middle-class urban culture that science had helped create apparently left little room for traditional Protestant devotional rigors. "We do not live in a praying age," lamented fundamentalist leader Reuben Torrey. "We live in an age of hustle and bustle, . . . an age of human organization and machinery, of human push, and human scheming, and human achievement; which in the things of God mean no real achievement at all." Harris Hale, a Baptist, expressed the concerns of many church leaders when he exclaimed in 1923: "There is no time to pray. The morning is so hurried. The evening is so crowded. It is impossible to get the family together for five minutes for the great act of worship. And so an institution which was the buttress of society is going to pieces: *there is no time to pray.*"[12]

Of course, such statements must be regarded with some skepticism. From the Puritans to the present day, American religious leaders have often bemoaned their generation's spiritual laxity in comparison with that of previous Christians. Indeed, the notion that Christian practice is endangered in "modern" life is hardly unique to this generation. Benjamin Trumbull, for example, writing in 1805 (a period we now call the "Second Great Awakening"), claimed, "it is lamentably evident, that prayer and family religion are exceedingly neglected, and rapidly on the decline." W. S. Tyler, writing a generation later, perceived much the same thing: "The house of God, prayer-meeting, the closets, and the consciences of Christians, do they not all bear witness to a sad dereliction of duty in this respect?" However, the frequency of declension rhetoric in early-twentieth-century religious literature, combined with the significant social and economic changes that were occurring, lends credence to the notion that this was a justifiably salient issue for Christians of that era. Whether prayer was actually in decline or not, Protestant writers *perceived* the recovery of prayer to be one of the main challenges of their day.[13]

Fundamentalism and Prayer

Fundamentalists, for their part, adamantly resisted the notion of accommodating traditional practices to modern constraints. Conservative leaders were adamant about the need for an intense, consistent, time-consuming individual prayer life despite the pressures of modern life. Such writers asserted without exception that, as one of them put it, "our devotions are not measured by the clock, but time is of their essence." Reuben Torrey pronounced with typical bluntness,

> The Christian who doesn't spend much time in prayer, is disobeying God, just as much as the man who steals, or commits adultery, or murders. The same God who said: 'Thou shalt not commit adultery, thou shalt not steal' also said: 'Continue steadfastly in prayer.' One is a commandment just as much as the other; and you are a sinner if you don't keep the commandment; you are disobeying God; you are a rebel against God if you don't spend much time in prayer.

Such writers were reluctant to specify just how much time one should spend in prayer, but in general these writers seem to have regarded one half-hour a day as an appropriate minimum for the Christian, with another half-hour spent in Bible reading.[14]

Moreover, individual prayer was to be done in private—in the "prayer closet," as they called it—and in the morning. S. D. Gordon, an itinerant speaker and prolific writer on devotional themes, remarked concerning those who would attempt to pray in the midst of the day's activities: "You can pray anywhere, on a train, walking down the street, measuring calico, chopping a typewriter, dictating a letter, in kitchen or parlour or shop. But you're not likely to, unless you've been off in some quiet place, with the door shut." Though prayer in the evening was expected as well, devotions ought to be done in the morning, according to fundamentalist writers. "Every child of God," Reuben Torrey declared, "should set apart the first part of the day to meeting God in the study of His Word and in prayer." To those who would protest that they felt more like praying in the evening than in the morning, Torrey replied, "when we feel least like praying is the time when we most need to pray."[15]

The lives of fundamentalists seemed to bear out this intense devotional ethic, as the example of Torrey illustrates. Rueben Torrey was one of the most influential fundamentalists of the early twentieth century. A graduate of Yale and a disciple of the Gilded Age revivalist Dwight L. Moody, Torrey served as superintendent of Moody Bible Institute from 1889 to 1908 while also conducting evangelistic campaigns in the United States, Australia, and the United Kingdom. In 1912, he accepted the position of dean of the Bible Institute of Los Angeles (later Biola University). Before his return to itinerant evangelism in 1924, Torrey served simultaneously at Biola and as pastor of the Church of the Open Door in Los Angeles. Although he is often remembered as an exemplar of rigid, polemical fundamentalism, prayer life lay at the heart of Torrey's concerns. His biographer recalls, "Frequent prayer was a necessity for Dr. Torrey. He referred every detail of his life, temporal and spiritual, to God." Even during Torrey's revival campaigns, much time was set aside for individual prayer: "There was no time limit to his prayer life. . . . He spent considerable time in secret prayer for God's blessing on the city in which he labored." Torrey approached the prayer life in an orderly manner. Because, he believed, God was revealed most fully in the Bible, Torrey used "biblical formulas" in constructing his prayers. Such a habit was consistent with the instructions given by the popular devotional writer Andrew Murray and others. Fundamentalists were instructed to use the text of Scripture as the "raw material" of prayer, praying back to God the words through which God revealed himself to them. Torrey's avid interest in prayer continued amid the religious controversies of the 1920s. He once remarked, "I think if God has given me any special message it has been to call people to prayer." His two books and numerous sermons on the subject did just that.[16]

Another fundamentalist, Richard Oliver, represents the fundamentalist ideal at the grassroots level. Oliver, a gospel musician and songwriter, attained martyr status among fundamentalists when he died in an automobile accident in 1930 at the age of thirty. As an adolescent, Richard Oliver committed himself to the Christian life. He did this, he noted in his diary, "by not neglecting to pray evenings, by reading a chapter in my Bible every day, by thinking holy thoughts and not debasing ones." Oliver spent his summers playing piano at the Cedar Lake Bible Conference in northwest Indiana, a summer conference that was run by members of the Moody Memorial Church in Chicago and its charismatic pastor, Paul Rader. At Cedar Lake, Oliver organized a prayer meeting for four students who, while other workers were playing games or swimming during recreation time, would meet under a tree for prayer and Bible study. Later, while a student at Northwestern University in Evanston, Illinois, he would memorize passages from the book of Romans while walking from his apartment to the campus.[17]

After graduating from Northwestern, Oliver served as an itinerant musician for evangelistic campaigns and took a faculty position at the fledgling Dudley Bible Institute in Massachusetts. At Dudley, Oliver's "trysting place" for his morning devotions was a grove of oak trees high on a hill. "I love to sit there to read and meditate," he wrote. "It is so still, and the Lord seems so near, so real." For Oliver, just about any situation could evolve into a prayer meeting. One example recorded in his diary occurred on a Sunday night. Upon returning from a church service, the car that Oliver and his Dudley Bible Institute students were traveling in broke down. Since they were in an isolated rural area, they held an impromptu campout: "We found a can of waste paper and a lot of firewood, and before long the eight stranded Carollers sat about a 'rip snorting fire' and were much cheered by its warmth and light. It was much like Scout camp over again. We told stories of camp life, sang choruses, and had a prayer meeting." The next morning the men combined a hike back to the school with impromptu Bible study. Oliver recalled, "we hiked for about four miles, then sat down by the roadside and read a chapter. All were happy." In all, Richard Oliver's diary reads as a log of intense spirituality suffused with episodes of prayer.[18]

Fundamentalist church congregations often displayed active corporate prayer lives that paralleled the the models commended to individual Christians, as the example of Moody Memorial Church in Chicago illustrates. Moody Memorial Church was not officially connected to Moody Bible Institute, but significant overlap existed between the two institutions. Founded in 1864 by the famous late-nineteenth-century evangelist, Moody Church came to be a bastion of fundamentalism. Its four thousand–seat auditorium, completed in 1925, was one of the most impressive church structures in the nation at the time. Its pastor, the colorful, charismatic evangelist Paul Rader, gave the church visibility that stretched far beyond the congregation's near north side neighborhood.

Moody Church approached corporate prayer in the same way that individual fundamentalists practiced personal prayer—with zeal and systematic thoroughness. Requests for prayer from missionaries in the field often graced the front page of the Moody Church weekly bulletin. Prayer cards containing the names of the church's dozens of missionaries and their locations were distributed to church members with the instructions, "please take this prayer card before the Lord daily and talk to Him about each one." The church displayed the same intensity concerning family prayer. Members were warned that, "a home without the reading of the Bible and prayer cannot have the blessing of God." The practice of family prayer was a requirement for those who desired to become a church deacon or elder. In a written application form, candidates for leadership roles were asked, "Do you maintain the daily family altar?" In a survey conducted in 1927, 60 percent of Moody Church members claimed to practice regular family prayer in their homes. While such a figure is not overwhelming, it far exceeds the 5 percent that Robert and Helen Lynd estimated for residents of Middletown.[19]

Moody Church in the 1920s was an avid sponsor of prayer meetings. In 1920, for example, the church calendar included a Young Women's Bible Class Prayer Meeting every Saturday evening at 7:15, in addition to the regular Midweek Prayer Service on Wednesday. Three prayer meetings occurred on Sunday: at 9:00 a.m. the Tabernacle Ushers' Band met for prayer; at 1:30 a Revival Prayer Meeting was held; and at 2:30 the Sunday School teachers met for their separate prayer meeting. A year later, a Friendly Bible Class prayer meeting was inaugurated each Sunday at 2:30, concurrent with the Sunday School Teachers meeting. In 1929, it was reported that the Ushers' Prayer Meetings had been going strong for years each Sunday morning, and that during special evangelistic rallies the ushers met each night of the week from 6:45 to 7:30. It is impossible to know how many church members actually attended such meetings. However, regular attendance was clearly an expectation. Members were instructed: "It is the duty of each member of the church to be present at every prayer meeting so far as possible. There is no obligation on the pastor that is not on every member. . . . Let this duty push aside social functions."[20]

Moody Church's success in supporting the practice of corporate prayer is most evident in that barometer of religious decline spotlighted by Robert and Helen Lynd—the midweek prayer service. The Wednesday evening prayer meeting had long been part of the Moody Church schedule. However, with the onset of the liberal-fundamentalist controversies in the mid-1920s and concerns among Protestants about the decline in Christian piety, the midweek service acquired greater prominence at Moody Church. The *Moody Church News* declared in 1926, "The mid-week prayer and fellowship meetings in the Moody Church have been increasing in interest and attendance for the past several weeks. . . . The prayer meetings are now the best ever held in the Moody Church." Between 700 and 800 people attended each week. In 1927, the church boasted of its Wednesday prayer meeting: "The mid-week service held each Wednesday evening in Sankey auditorium is the marvel of all who attend. Last week the room was filled to capacity."[21]

In the late 1920s, the Wednesday evening prayer meeting was attracting the attention of outsiders. A university professor who took his class to observe the service remarked, "the large attendance at a mid-summer prayer service was indeed astonishing and the interest and helpfulness gripped us all." Unlike the desultory Middletown services reported by the Lynds, the Moody Church meeting was highly participatory. A visitor from Texas described the meeting as characterized by "simplicity and democracy." After a time of congregational singing and announcements of prayer requests from the pulpit, a number of voluntary prayers were voiced by the members of congregation. This was followed by testimony and more prayer requests, in which about one hundred people—many of them visitors from others states and nations, "more young than old"—participated. These were interspersed with songs and more prayers. In all, the success of the Wednesday prayer meeting at Moody Church demonstrated the application of the fundamentalist propensity for organization and promotion to corporate prayer.[22]

The fundamentalist concern for maintaining fervent practices of prayer in the modern world stemmed from a theology that emphasized God's transcendence. Because fundamentalists generally viewed God as separate from creation, spiritual activities were basically *super*-natural; they were seen as a way to get beyond the mundane, visible world and experience God directly. In a remark that spoke volumes about conservative Protestant theology, D. L. Moody once claimed that the person who prays daily "cannot be more than twenty-four hours away from God." Hence the importance of specific acts of prayer both individually and corporately. Prayer enabled the individual to leave the world and enter God's presence, where he or she would be infused with spiritual energy to withstand the onslaughts of a godless world. The visible world thus served as merely a backdrop to specific acts of prayer for fundamentalists—an inspiring setting, perhaps, but ultimately just a jumping-off point into the realm of spiritual practices.[23]

This approach to the spiritual life is demonstrated most vividly by fundamentalist Bible conferences such as the Winona Lake Bible Conference. Established in the late nineteenth century by Indiana Presbyterians as a summer resort, Winona Lake Conference Center began moving toward conservative Protestantism after 1910. In that year, evangelist Billy Sunday built his summer home on the conference grounds. When William Jennings Bryan became president of the board in 1912, Winona Lake's status as the premier Bible conference in the country was assured. In the 1920s, fundamentalist evangelist William Biederwolf assumed leadership of the conference and pushed it in a decidedly fundamentalist direction. A host of fundamentalist leaders frequented the conference meetings, including Bob Jones, Sr., Bob Shuler, James Gray, and even the Princeton theologian J. Gresham Machen (though he complained about the "rough house" atmosphere that prevailed in the meetings).[24]

As Winona Lake evolved from a nineteenth-century middle-class vacation resort to a fundamentalist Bible conference, the spiritual tenor of the conference changed. Earlier descriptions of the conference emphasized the natural beauty of the grounds and the spiritual revival that contact with nature could produce. In 1918, a reporter for the Winona *Herald* remarked, "Picturesque spots which abound throughout the park bring additional pleasure to the eye. There are song birds everywhere; playful squirrels frisk in the branches overhead; fountains sending forth purest water murmur musically here and there." In such a setting, the narrator continued, "there arises within the soul a thrill that heightens appreciation, and intensifies a desire for the nobler achievements of life." Educational lectures, classical music concerts, and evening entertainments augmented the natural setting of the grounds to produce a spiritually invigorating environment.[25]

With the ascension of fundamentalism at Winona Lake in the 1920s, prayer meetings and church services began to crowd out other events in the schedule. By the late 1920s, the weekly schedule had solidified into a rigorous regimen that only the most avid practitioner could call "refreshing." The day began with prayer and testimony at 7:30 a.m., followed by three consecutive worship services before lunch. The rest of the day included a 2:00 sacred music concert, a missionary talk at 3:00, a hillside service at 6:30, and the main evening service at 7:30. Thus, for fundamentalism, spiritual rejuvenation became synonymous with participation in prayer meetings and church services. In contrast to the 1918 description, the description of Winona Lake in the late 1920s proclaimed: "Surely this Program, in content and compass, offers to men and women of intensified spiritual sense, of increasing spiritual vision, of breadth in kingdom outreach and possibility, and of deepening surrender to the Holy Spirit, all they can desire in inspiration, in Biblical nourishment, . . . and in enlarged personal equipment for life and life-service." Nowhere is mentioned the natural setting that the earlier program had so effusively promoted. Nature had become, as it were, merely the background slide on which the "text" of the devotional life was superimposed. For Winona Lake fundamentalists, spiritual practices occurred in a supernatural realm of their own.[26]

All of these prayer meetings would seem to indicate a religious movement steadfastly committed to preserving intact a traditional practice in the face of changing cultural conditions. A closer look at fundamentalist practices, however, reveals a more complex picture. For one thing, fundamentalists displayed a surprisingly modern propensity to document and quantify their prayers. Moody Church maintained detailed accounts of its prayers. Its "Great Commission Prayer League" received prayer requests by mail and referred them to church members for prayer. During one six-month period, 1 January 1919 through 1 July 1920, the organization recorded 20,964 answers to prayer and 28,479 conversions to Christianity, purportedly as a result of the league members' prayers. Precise records were also kept concerning prayer requests brought to the platform at worship services, and such requests were catalogued according to type. In November 1921, for example, church records revealed 310 requests for "spiritual blessings for others," fourteen for "temporal blessings," twenty-three for "healing for others," and two for "healing for self." The Moody Bible Institute kept precise records on student prayer meetings. A 1922 report claimed that exactly 1,324 "stated prayer meetings" had occurred. The Winona Lake Bible Conference displayed similar traits. Its scripted schedule of prayer meetings and services was a far cry from the exuberant, spontaneous camp meetings of the previous century, but the conference's busyness and orderliness would have appealed to its largely urban middle-class constituency. If Babbitt had been a praying man, the fundamentalists' "organization man" approach to Christian practice is what one would have expected of him.[27]

Furthermore, the Richard Olivers notwithstanding, most fundamentalists had to negotiate the constraints of modern social and economic life. Lettie Cowman's *Streams in the Desert* provided fundamentalists with a means of practicing a modern prayer life within the comforting traditional vessel of a morning quiet time. The volume contained two-and-a-half minute devotionals with a formula of poems, Scripture, and short passages to comfort Christians in trials. However, the volume was heavy in selections from writers popular among fundamentalists such as A. T. Pierson, F. B. Meyer, Andrew Murray, Charles Trumbull, and A. B. Simpson. Moreover, Cowman's devotionals cited a Scripture text to be read but did not print the passage. Thus, practitioners were required to break open their tattered Bibles just as earlier Christians had purportedly done—but without the expectation of a thirty-minute devotional session. The overall form of the devotional was adapted to modern life, but the practice of flipping through the pages of one's Bible provided continuity with past practices. It is no wonder that *Streams in the Desert* became, according to its publisher, "a daily devotional classic, a leader in its field." It made the biblicist content of traditional devotions digestible in the time constraints acceptable to 1920s rank-and-file fundamentalists. As in the case of eighteenth-century evangelical devotional writers, fundamentalist practices of prayer helped to mediate cultural change by providing the appearance of continuity while at the same time displaying distinctively modern traits.[28]

Liberalism and Prayer

While fundamentalist practices of prayer displayed few and subtle signs of accommodation to the modern world, liberal practices by contrast displayed a spirit of cheerful, thorough adaptation to it. *Christian Century* editors Herbert Willett and Charles Clayton Morrison prefaced their 1919 devotional volume *The Daily Altar* with the claim: "For the mood of our time the lengthy and more formal exercises of household devotion of former days cannot be revived. Nor need this fact be deplored." Traditional prayer practices—what Willett and Morrison called "obsolete and discarded habits of devotion"—were dead, they believed, and so much the better. Methodist writer James M. Campbell's suggestions for family prayer could not have been further from the fundamentalist outlook:

> The habit of family worship will not be recovered until it is adapted to existing conditions. The long and leisurely and often dreary exercises of our forefathers are no longer suitable. What is needed is something brief and bright; the repeating it may be of a few favorite texts, and the lifting up of the heart in a few words of prayer. . . . In many instances it will be that or nothing. But let no one despise any method that maintains the religious unity of the home.[29]

In contrast to fundamentalists, therefore, liberal Protestants displayed a more relaxed, flexible approach to daily devotions. In 1913, the liberal writer Lyman Abbott advised his readers concerning individual prayer, "take a little time every day to form a habit of communion with the invisible." Harry Emerson Fosdick, the leading public voice of liberal Protestantism in the 1920s, had, during the previous decade, written a series of widely read daily devotional guides that applied Abbott's advice in concrete form. Each volume contained a printed Scripture passage, a one-paragraph comment on the passage, and a short written prayer for each day. These devotions typically could be completed within two or three minutes; also included was a weekly passage by Fosdick that required fifteen minutes to read. Liberal Protestants of the 1920s continued the tradition begun by Abbott and Fosdick. Devotions in Willett and Morrison's *Daily Altar* took about one and a half minutes to complete. William Adams Brown's *The Quiet Hour*, which appeared in 1926, construed the notion of an "hour" quite figuratively for modern readers. It contained meditations and a prayer on a passage of Scripture that might be accomplished in five to ten minutes.[30]

While their fundamentalist counterparts tended to be quite explicit about times and durations, for liberals flexibility in prayer was crucial. "Every man must be allowed to pray in his own way," asserted Fosdick. "There are as many different ways of praying as there are different individuals." Consequently, "the time involved in the deliberate practice of prayer may indeed be brief or long," depending on the person. William Adams Brown echoed Fosdick in *The Life of Prayer in a World of Science*. Christians needed to develop a regular habit of daily prayer, he believed. However, he said, "the time involved will vary greatly for different people. . . . How long we stay is between us and God. It is the quality that counts, not quantity." Moreover, though one should have daily prayer, Brown advised, "the question when to take it, each must decide for himself what his time of prayer shall be—whether it shall be morning or evening, or some time snatched from the pressure of the day's work."[31]

Liberal Protestant churches displayed a similar willingness to adapt habits of corporate prayer to the modern world. One such congregation was Chicago's Fourth Presbyterian Church, a bastion of moderate "evangelical liberalism" that sought to span the divide between progressive and conservative Protestantism. While involved in Social Gospel causes, the church also remained involved in traditional evangelism. It sponsored Billy Sunday's Chicago campaign and counted on its membership role professors from the nearby Moody Bible Institute.[32]

Fourth Presbyterian Church sought to maintain a vibrant Wednesday evening prayer meeting throughout the 1920s. However, concerns about the vitality of the prayer meeting appeared. Promotions of the service and admonishments to attend began to show up in the monthly church newsletter in 1926. In March of that year, for example, the church bulletin proclaimed, "the Midweek Prayer Service is not considered out of date by some of the strong men of the country today." It went on to cite some rather dubious support by a Chicago judge: "It is the duty of every Christian, who is so situated in life that he can do so, to attend regularly the weekly prayer meetings of his church, even though they may be, at times, mighty dull." Perhaps with an eye directed a few blocks north to Moody Church and its prominent prayer meetings, Fourth Presbyterian Church announced in the summer of 1926, "The attendance at the midweek Church Prayer Service through the summer months has been most gratifying. Frequently ministers from other towns and cities have been present." To boost attendance, its popular pastor, Timothy Stone, sometimes preached at the Wednesday night service in addition to his other preaching duties on Sundays.[33]

While Fourth Presbyterian Church represented a moderately liberal church of the 1920s, Hyde Park Baptist Church, located on Chicago's south side, embodied the progressive edge of early-twentieth-century liberal Protestantism. William Raney Harper, the first president of the University of Chicago, was a member of Hyde Park Baptist Church, and the congregation essentially functioned as the chapel for the campus until University Chapel was built in 1928. The membership roll of Hyde Park Baptist Church included such modernist luminaries as Gerald Birney Smith, Shailer Mathews, Shirley Jackson Case, and Henry Nelson Wieman. A church populated primarily by busy urban middle-class professionals, Hyde Park experienced firsthand the difficulties of continuing the traditional midweek prayer meeting in the modern world that the Lynds had observed in Middletown. The decade of the 1920s found this liberal congregation struggling to keep the prayer meeting populated and vibrant. Pastor Charles Gilkey met with church deacons to devise a strategy for boosting the meeting and to find ways to involve the young people of the church in the service. In 1923, the church bulletin admitted, "it is increasingly difficult to secure attendance upon this service. In our church the effort is constantly being made to present such subjects for consideration at the Wednesday evening service as will prove of interest and value. Variety has been sought and with no small measure of success."[34]

Apparently the success was short-lived. Attendance at the midweek prayer meeting lagged, and beginning in 1925 Wednesday evening services were discontinued during the summer months due to lack of attendance. In 1926, a church commission studied the problem of the Wednesday service and reflected, "Many Christians remember with especial gratitude the contribution of the prayer-meeting to their religious life." However, other church interests and activities were crowding out the prayer meeting. The commission regarded this as inevitable and recommended a new policy: Members who were so inclined should form "voluntary circles for the cultivation of the religious life" that would meet regularly in homes or at the church. Wednesday evening would become "Church Night"—"an opportunity for the various groups in the church to express and demonstrate to us all their distinctive ideals and achievements." Its theme was "Social Fellowship in a Christian Atmosphere." Thus did Hyde Park Baptist Church maintain the practice of gathering on Wednesday evening; however, the meeting was devoted not to prayer but to lectures and sermons on various topics, such as "Religious Resources for Living," "World Peace," and even, ironically, "Religious Perplexities—Difficulties About Prayer." As with individual devotions, the traditional ritual of the prayer meeting was reconstituted in modern ways.[35]

Just as fundamentalists' theology of a transcendent God influenced their prayer lives, so too the liberal willingness to adapt their devotional lives stemmed in part from their belief in God's indwelling presence in all of creation. Harry Emerson Fosdick began his book *The Meaning of Prayer* with a chapter entitled "The Naturalness of Prayer." That phrase encapsulates well the basic difference between liberals and fundamentalists as revealed in their practices of prayer. For liberal Protestants, infused with the doctrine of divine immanence, prayer should fit seamlessly into the natural rhythm of life. Whereas D. L. Moody had claimed that the Christian who practiced daily devotions was never more than twenty-four hours away from God, liberals believed that the visible world was itself a vehicle for communion with God. The liberal theologian Borden Bowne claimed, "we shall find God everywhere, not merely in unmediated and miraculous manifestations." Or, as James M. Campbell put it, "the world is a temple, any spot thereon an altar." This contrast between the liberal and fundamentalist approach to prayer is best seen in the notion of spiritual retreat. While fundamentalists often spent their summer vacations attending services at Bible conferences, liberals, finding nature itself their most effective vehicle for the devotional life, typically retreated to summer homes in beautiful settings.[36]

As in so many other ways, William Adams Brown typified liberal Protestantism in this regard. He owned a summer home in Mount Desert, Maine, that served as his family's private spiritual retreat. He described its setting in intimate detail: "A little ravine, opening almost from the door of the living room and bordered by rocks covered with polypods and bunchberries, leads under an arch of trees to a sheltered garden framed on all sides by trees. A little grass plot in the center is bounded on one side by a formal rose garden, on the other by a circle of phlox, peonies, delphiniums and monkshood." For Brown, tending his garden at his summer home was more than recreation; it was the stuff from which spiritual revival proceeded. William Adams Brown's devotional poem from *The Quiet Hour,* perhaps inspired by his summer retreat in Maine, encapsulates the liberal Protestant approach to prayer and spiritual revival:

> Afar I sought thee in the radiant sky,
> > But thou art near.
> In every breeze that sings its lullaby
> > Thy voice I hear
> So let me feel Thy presence day by day
> > In wind and sod,
> That every bush I meet upon my way
> > Shall glow with God.

Brown's experience was typical among liberal Protestants. Fosdick and Gilkey also owned summer homes in Maine, where they spent their days hiking, sailing, and writing. Henry Sloane Coffin, pastor of the Madison Avenue Presbyterian Church in New York City and a leading liberal of the day, fondly described his summer home in Lakeville, Connecticut, with wildflowers lining the long, curving driveway.[37]

Of course, such distinctive approaches to summer vacation reflected to some extent cultural differences in the groups. As social elites, liberal Protestants tended to value places of quiet contemplation and refinement rather than the summer Bible conferences with their jostling crowds and ramshackle facilities. At Hyde Park Baptist Church, it was simply assumed that Pastor Gilkey would be at his summer home in Maine from June until Labor Day. William Adams Brown's Mount Desert community, which included residents such as Harvard president Charles Eliot and Johns Hopkins University president Daniel Coit Gilman, produced this tongue-in-cheek prayer that the locals were fond of reciting:

> We thank the goodness and the grace
> That brought us to this lovely place,
> And now with all our hearts we pray
> That other folks may stay away.[38]

However, one should not push a sociocultural interpretation too far. Even fundamentalist leaders who could afford to seclude themselves in nature for the summer often chose to reside amid the crowds and regimented meetings of Bible conferences. Billy Sunday, no stranger to wealth, could have built an idyllic summer retreat anywhere in the country. However, associating Christian practice with gatherings and religious events, he built his summer home at Winona Lake. Reuben Torrey founded a Bible conference in Montrose, Pennsylvania, while other fundamentalist leaders spent their summers at Bible conferences such as Sandy Cove in Maryland and Mount Hermon in California. More than simply revealing social class distinctions, these contrasts illustrate the different approaches to religious practice taken by fundamentalists and liberals. The fervent prayer lives of fundamentalists were inspired by the belief that God was removed from the world and that praying involved getting out of this world and into the spiritual realm. For liberals, the world was itself the spiritual realm, and direct encounters with the visible world could have a spiritually rejuvenating effect.

Thus, while fundamentalists generally resisted adaptation, liberal Protestants, informed by a doctrine of divine immanence, were more open to accommodating Christian practice to the modern world. As in the case of fundamentalism, however, a closer look reveals more complexity in the relationship between liberal belief and practice. As noted earlier, practice, by its habitual nature, can help sustain the beliefs that generate it. Or, in our context, prayer not only results from faith but helps shape and sustain faith. In the case of liberal Protestantism, one suspects that their practice of prayer kept them doing and believing things that their theological principles may not have supported.

Liberal prayers for physical healing, for example, demonstrate the power of practices to sustain themselves through cultural and intellectual change. Liberal Protestants claimed to accept wholeheartedly the scientific world view of the early twentieth century. And science had seemed to rule out prayer as a causative factor in the workings of the universe. Liberals at the turn of the century had been somewhat ambivalent the relationship between science and petitionary prayer, but by the 1920s liberal Protestant writers were rejecting supernatural intervention in response to prayer. Harry Emerson Fosdick, for instance, bemoaned "the futile and dangerous extension of prayer to realms where it does not belong." Prayer, he said, "is a poor reliance if one is mainly intent on managing the external world."[39] The reason that William Adams Brown titled his 1927 book on prayer *The Life of Prayer in a World of Science* was that he believed the theology and practice of prayer had to be reworked in light of the naturalistic constraints of modern science. Logically, this meant that prayer requests should be confined to spiritual and moral concerns and should not address changes to the natural order, such as physical healing.

Nevertheless, one encounters in liberal church records occasional prayers for physical healing. For example, in a 1924 sermon at Fourth Presbyterian Church, Timothy Stone recounted an episode of prayer for the sick at his church. A man with a sick child prayed, and, Stone recounted, "the boy got well, almost against the judgment of the consulting physicians." What made the difference, he claimed, was "a prayer outside of a little bedroom." Even at the more thoroughly modernist Hyde Park Baptist Church, when long-time church member Charles Marsh was seriously ill, Charles Gilkey and the elders prayed that he would be healed and restored to the congregation. Such prayers for physical healing may seem surprising given the intellectual difficulties concerning prayer that many liberals reported. However, it had been customary in Protestant churches to pray for the sick, and liberal Protestants, it seemed, drew on that traditional practice even if some of them may have personally harbored intellectual doubts about God's ability or willingness to circumvent the natural processes of the physical world. Or perhaps their own experience had conditioned them to maintain faith in practices that their intellectual peers in modern America would have doubted. In a sermon on prayer's effectiveness, Timothy Stone remarked, "from the simple incidents that God gave us as a direct answer to prayer when we were little children many of us learned this lesson." Perhaps childhood experience had provided a foundation for petitionary prayer for some modern Americans that scientific arguments could not erode. Traditional practices, it seemed, could take on a life of their own, even when their intellectual buttresses had been undermined.[40]

Indeed, when one notes the devotional teachings of liberal Protestants on the extreme end of 1920s liberalism, one can appreciate just how traditional the mainstream liberal practices remained. University of Chicago professor Henry Nelson Wieman, for example, wrote a devotional guide in which he avoided using the word *prayer* altogether. Taking the liberal doctrine of divine immanence to its logical extreme, Wieman defined God as "that integrating process which works through all the world . . .

to maintain and develop organic interdependence and mutual support between all parts and aspects of the cosmos." Thus, practicing daily devotions did not require any sort of communion with a personal God, for, Wieman claimed, "a man does not need to believe in God in order to worship." Wieman went on to recommend a daily regimen of personal meditation devoid of any theistic implications. Shailer Mathews, whose book *The Faith of Modernism* was the most widely known manifesto of 1920s liberalism, articulated prayer in similar terms: "You want to get something or do something, and don't know how. You feel there are forces, within or without, that would help you if you could summon them. By conscious effort you make your wishes clear and 'expose yourself' to the forces. You try to 'reach up.' You put your wishes into words, for they are meaningless otherwise. That, as I understand it, is prayer." Such was a far cry from traditional Protestant descriptions of prayer as a conversation with a personal God.[41]

By contrast, the prayer lives of many liberals remained squarely rooted in traditional practice. Lyman Abbott, for example, used biblical content and the mental image of Jesus to buttress a traditional prayer life. In recounting his technique for prayer, Abbott wrote in the third person, "when he kneels to pray, he first reads something from the Gospels, then forms in his mind a picture of Jesus, sits down by the side of the man and talks with him and prayer becomes easy conversation." Henry Sloan Coffin maintained a family altar that seemed vintage nineteenth century. His biographer wrote:

> In the Coffin home each day began with family prayers. Immediately after breakfast the household including the servants and whatever guests might be there at the time gathered in the drawing-room. Coffin read a brief passage from the Bible after which the group knelt while he offered prayer. His spontaneous devotions in this intimate circle had the same deeply moving sincerity and beauty of expression which characterized his conduct of public worship for which he carefully prepared.

Coffin's example was typical among classic liberals. Harry Emerson Fosdick's *The Meaning of Prayer* was conceived from a personal prayer life that had led him out of a time of deep religious doubt in college. Furthermore, his exhaustive knowledge of scripture, gleaned from countless hours of daily Bible reading, was legendary among his peers and successors. It is difficult to resist the conclusion that for such liberals, their continued belief in a personal God was sustained in part by their daily practice of personal prayer.[42]

Nevertheless, liberal belief and practice was quite distinct from that of its fundamentalist counterpart. A pair of vignettes vividly illustrates the alternative ways in which traditional Christian practice could interact with modernity in early-twentieth-century America. At Moody Church's Cedar Lake Bible Conference, a group of women waiting to take the train back to Chicago organized an impromptu prayer meeting and ended up missing their train. As their pastor E. Y. Woolley recounted: "They had been so absorbed in their prayers that shouts, laughter and train whistles failed to move them." Woolley hurriedly procured a conference bus that conveyed the women to another train station, from which they boarded a train that arrived in Chicago ahead of the original Cedar Lake train. Commented Woolley, "Imagine the surprise and consternation of the hard hearted friends who did not go to the prayer meeting in order to catch the excursion train, when they saw their friends standing on the platform waiting to receive them." To the fundamentalist mind, true prayer made one oblivious to the material world. Modern culture, symbolized by the train and the timetable, was simply a distraction to the real business of Christian devotion. These Christians, however, still were required to function in a society that, to them, was inimical to Christian practice. Their frantic attempt to return to Chicago by bus and train so that they could resume their roles in urban society bespoke their obligation to modern culture. Traditional practice and modern life had to coexist, despite the difficulties—or missed trains—that could ensue.[43]

By contrast, William Adams Brown in *The Life of Prayer in a World of Science* advised his readers that amid busy schedules, Christians should be creative in how they went about the practice of daily prayer. One gentleman, Brown recounted, prayed as he rode the New York City commuter train into work each morning. This man would gaze into the faces of the other passengers, trying to imagine how they would appear to the eye of God. Brown recommended such a method as a way to maintain a prayer life in the busy modern world. He concluded, "let us realize that we are in a world of wonderful and ennobling things, and yield ourselves up to the contemplation of them." For Brown, the commuter train itself became a means of continuing devotional practices. Nevertheless, prayer on a train was substantially different—in content, location, and even body position—from devotions in the traditional "prayer closet." In both cases, the fundamentalist and the liberal, Christian practice and cultural change were intertwined in complex and sometimes unpredictable ways.[44]

PART IV

LIBERAL PROTESTANTS AND UNIVERSALIZING PRACTICES, 1850–1965

CHAPTER TEN

Cosmopolitan Piety

Sympathy, Comparative Religions, and Nineteenth-Century Liberalism

LEIGH E. SCHMIDT

In 1871 Thomas Wentworth Higginson (1823–1911)—a fierce abolitionist, a renowned colonel of a black regiment during the Civil War, an activist for women's rights, and a wide-ranging man of letters—published the most influential of his many religious essays, "The Sympathy of Religions." He wrote much of the piece in the winter of 1870 for a lecture in Boston, but he had first focused on the subject during a six-month sojourn in the Azores in 1855–56, intending it as part of a planned book on "the Religious Aspects of the times," which he never completed.[1] The published essay soon began circulating as a tract, distributed by that great New England club of garrulous radicals, the Free Religious Association, and was warmly received. It cropped up in Chicago in the 1880s as an ecumenical tract among religious liberals there, midwestern heirs of William Ellery Channing, Ralph Waldo Emerson, and Theodore Parker. Eventually it was republished as a philosophical standard for the World's Parliament of Religions in 1893, and Higginson himself journeyed to the gathering to give his latest rendition of what was by then a well-traveled manifesto. The essay was published in London in 1872 and translated into French in 1898, giving it international reach. When Higginson met the renowned scholar Max Müller on a trip to England, the latter immediately lit up, delighted to meet the author of "The Sympathy of Religions," and promptly invited him to visit Oxford.[2]

Higginson's basic claim—that the foundation of religious unity and harmony lay in extending the notion of sympathy into the realm of comparative religions—set his essay within long-flowing currents in moral philosophy that ran from Lord Shaftesbury, Francis Hutcheson, David Hume, and Adam Smith forward. In eighteenth-century discussions of the moral sentiments, sympathy was, especially, an ethic of fellow-feeling with those in pain or distress. But, it was more than that. Cultivating sympathy was a way of bridging differences and recognizing commonalities; it provided a basis for overcoming isolation through affective connection, a way of joining people in shared enterprises. Social bonds were formed and sustained through a solidarity of sympathetic emotion—a universal human sentiment more essential to the benign functioning of civic, commercial, and religious life than the particularities of any special revelation.[3] Higginson hoped to turn that moral theorizing into a practical paradigm for dealing with the rapidly growing "knowledge of the religions of the world," to mold sympathy into an instrument for transforming Christian uniqueness into religious openness: "When we fully comprehend the sympathy of religions," he concluded, "we shall deal with other faiths on equal terms." He sought through sympathy to release the liberal religionist into a global field of spiritual appreciation, cosmopolitan rapport, and eclectic insight.[4]

Sympathy, by definition, involved moral practice; it was a way of interacting with others that meant not only feeling compassion toward them but also acting with understanding in relationship to them. It was necessarily a *negotiated practice* that took place within the shifting flow of relational contacts, affinities, and disconnections. As a liberal virtue, it certainly could be habituated, but it was not easily ritualized as a daily practice, set predictably in time and readily repeatable, like morning and evening prayer. Despite its fluidity, sympathy was clearly an embodied virtue and a disposition of practical consequence. As one liberal metaphysician advised those who wanted to do the hard work of overcoming "a mass of personal prejudices" and "to give sympathy to others," "Practice, here as in everything else, is what helps. And the object is well worth working for." The very complexity of this virtue—manifest through unpredictable exchanges and subtle dispositions toward others—illustrates why the formulation of practice as an analytic construct in American religious history needs to be similarly broad and flexible, not confined to the routinely recognized practices of piety.[5]

Higginson and other nineteenth-century liberals saw the "sympathy of religions" as a posture of openness to religious exchange, commonality, and comparison. Such intellectual theorizing about sympathy conditioned liberal encounters across cultures and was, in turn, reshaped by how that theory worked (or failed to work) in practice. Higginson's own sympathies, their expanses and their limits, are one very good measure of how the theorizing fared on the ground. He kept an extensive journal during his trip to the Azores, an excursion that proved to be, among other things, a sustained encounter with religious difference in the form of Portuguese Catholicism. His accounts allow a glimpse into how he negotiated religious variety even as he was initially constructing his theory of religious similarity. Higginson's sympathies were fraught with ambivalences; they were built on a foundation of respect and equality yet were ever entangled with the condescension of the civilized, the genteel, and the enlightened. Even as he looked far and wide for spiritual inspiration and was happily eclectic in rummaging through sacred books, his assumptions about religious essentialism and sameness made his sympathies absorptive and homogenizing. In Higginson it is possible to see how religious liberals imagined a framework for religious inclusion and simultaneously labored to live that ideal in on-the-ground encounters. Sympathy, all agreed, "must reveal itself in living acts rather than loud professions," and Higginson's own experiences suggest that the sympathy of religions actually worked better when conceived as a relational practice than a comparative theory.[6]

Any practical success of Higginson's theory as a religious go-between also had a flipside of unreliability as a marker of a distinct Christian character. The sympathy of religions, in its embrace of an intentionally cosmopolitan piety, invited liberal Protestant identities to be blurred, if not to vanish, into a post-Christian universalism. Sympathy, so conceived, acted as a solvent, eroding the bounds of liberal Christian identities: it proved a constitutive part of a religious culture that invited liturgical experimentation and devotional appropriation; it authorized new hymns and prayers for free churches ready to give witness to the "universal religion"; it invited the compilation of world scriptures and encouraged appreciation of diverse expressions of the human "quest" for God. The liberal embrace of the sympathy of religions in the late nineteenth century helped to create a cultural milieu in which the very particularity of the Christian gospel could be questioned and in which new practices could be imagined, from universalized notions of meditation to interfaith dialogues in which no single religion claimed a monopoly on holiness and truth.

In the current cultural climate, in which many Protestants now hope to reclaim historically grounded Christian practices as a way to strengthen well-differentiated religious identities, reexamining the nineteenth-century liberal delineation of sympathy as a virtue may appear to produce only a cautionary tale of lost solidity. For contemporary constructivists who are especially interested in forming and conserving Protestant ways of living, that loss would seem to make sympathy a hard virtue even to recognize as a Protestant practice, let alone to recover. But, the caution works at least as well in reverse. In a global, pluralistic culture, Protestants certainly still need practices of cosmopolitanism as much as practices of particularity.

The Career of an Essay and a Concept

Sympathy, as historian Elizabeth B. Clark demonstrated, was a bedrock virtue of antebellum abolitionists; it operated as a moral imperative to identify with the sufferings of slaves and then to combat those cruelties. For many religious liberals in the

1840s and 1850s, antislavery activities were an indispensable part—in Unitarian James Freeman Clarke's formulation—of extending "our sympathies beyond 'the little limits of our own State and neighborhood.'" William Lloyd Garrison even turned the chained slave into an iconic emblem of moral guidance and devotional remembrance, placing the image on his mantelpiece and on the masthead of the *Liberator* in order "to keep my sympathies from flagging." In these circles, Elizabeth Clark concluded, the moral sentiment of sympathy served as a compelling disposition toward benevolent action and was cultivated as a conscientious religious practice.[7] Abolitionist sympathies would be Thomas Wentworth Higginson's primary compass in the 1850s, and so, when he moved into the realm of overcoming religious conflicts and achieving spiritual unity, he naturally carried such ethical preoccupations with him.

In 1847 Higginson graduated from Harvard Divinity School, the leading training ground for religious liberals, and then took a Unitarian charge in Newburyport, Massachusetts. As a second-generation transcendentalist and a political radical, not only on questions of slavery, but also on those of factory labor and women's rights, he proved too outspoken for his congregants and was soon removed from that pulpit. Eventually finding a religious society in Worcester more receptive to his abolitionism and his tactless zeal, he moved to the Free Church there in 1852. From that venue, "a seething centre of all the reforms," as Higginson described it in his autobiography, he expanded his agitation and became "almost in fashion, at least with the unfashionable."[8] By 1854, he had taken still more direct action, leading a riotous assault on the Boston courthouse, where Anthony Burns, a captured fugitive slave, was under guard. Even after being clubbed by police and arrested in this failed rescue mission, his ardor did not cool. He recruited antislavery settlers for armed struggle with proslavery forces in Kansas, was among the "Secret Six" who helped fund John Brown's insurrection at Harpers Ferry, consistently kept up his ties with Garrison and the *Liberator*, and was appointed in 1862 to lead the First South Carolina Volunteers, an African-American regiment that he commanded until a war wound and disease forced him out of the army in 1864.[9]

Though remembered far less for it, Higginson was equally radical in theology. He was midstream in his efforts at a first book when he departed the Azores in 1856 to take up the Kansas struggle full-time, shelving his fragmentary manuscript on religion, "The Return of Faith and the Decline of the Churches." The abandoned book contained the seeds of his sympathy essay, though his ideas on the subject were developing within more immediate theological frays, radical sticking points such as the rejection of the Lord's Supper and Jesus's messianism. The outlines of his larger argument were apparent in the chapter drafts he did finish: Protestantism, in its sectarianism and half-baked revolt, was an embarrassing failure; Catholicism, while more attractive in its comprehensiveness and consistency than Protestantism, offered finally a faux universalism; and the alternative was "a Catholicism which is more than Roman," a universal religion in which Buddhism, Islam, Hinduism, and Christianity, among other traditions, "will disappear, . . . absorbed into something larger and grander." Higginson already discerned an equivalence of insight among sacred books, a shared profundity and ethical awareness across religions. Jesus and Buddha, for instance, were equal exemplars of noble and beautiful lives of "self-consecration." He saw New England's churches as being in grave decline; the ministerial ranks were made up of all too many men who lived wretched lives of intellectual dishonesty and who failed to face squarely the new knowledge about the religions of the world and about Jesus and the Scriptures. For the return of faith, a momentous transition would be required, a shift from the outworn doctrines of Christianity to the "sublime sympathy of Universal Religion."[10]

Making that transition would require a reinterpretation of religious authority. Higginson had published an initial discourse in 1854 on the problem of Protestant biblicism, a sixteen-page tract called "Scripture Idolatry," which he planned to turn into a central chapter in his book. In that piece, he sought to dismantle the Bible as a foundation of authority: "Of all the uncertain tribunals ever adopted by fallible mortals, the Bible appears to me the most uncertain," he wrote. On the crucial moral issues of the day—slavery, total abstinence from alcohol, capital punishment, and polygamy, to name four—Higginson saw the Bible as akin to the Florida Everglades, a "wilderness of texts," a tangle that made sorting out the scriptural from the unscriptural fruitless, if not impossible. Higginson read Scripture, in part, as a man of reason, a latter-day Tom Paine who wanted to hack his way through the "utter indelicacy," "terrible cruelty," "entire improbability," and "strange miscellany" of the Bible in order to create a clearing for the light of "simple Natural Religion."[11]

His radicalism was not merely deism dressed up in transcendentalist garb. In the place of biblical revelation, Higginson, like other liberals, turned inward to a domain of universal moral conscience and spiritual illumination more complexly experiential than the streamlined common notions of English deists. As the Bible's authority ostensibly tottered and crumbled under his scrutiny, Higginson, like Emerson and Parker, strode in among the ruins to offer hope:

> The soul needs some other support also; it must find this within;—in the cultivation of the Inward Light; in personal experience of Religion; in the life of God in the human soul; in faith in God and love to man; in the reverent study of the vast and simple laws of Nature. . . . [I]n these, and nowhere else, lies the real foundation of all authority; build your faith here, and churches and Bibles may come or go, and leave it undisturbed.

The location of authority shifted to personal religious experience, but certainly not as evangelicals understood it. Higginson's radical turn to experience as authoritative—a move characteristic of nineteenth-century liberal theology—was at once hyper-Protestant and post-Christian. Or, in a distinction of his own devising, he was not "anti-Christian," but "extra-Christian," ultimately operating from a position "outside the Christian Church and name."[12]

The transformation of devotional emphases that this reorientation of authority entailed was very much evident in "My Creed So Far as I Have One," another of Higginson's unpublished manuscripts. In its formulation of religion as solitary moments of epiphany it offered a portal that led directly from Emerson to William James.

> When the devout emotions come, says Emerson in substance—I have not the passage at hand—"yield to them; no matter what your theory, leave it as Joseph left his coat in the hands of the harlot, and flee." In the life of every thoughtful man, . . . there are moments of care, sorrow, depression, perplexity when neither study nor action nor friends will clear the horizon: the tenderest love, the most heroic self-devotion leave the cloud still resting, the perplexity still there. It is at such times that the thought of an Unseen Power comes to help him; by no tradition of the churches, with no apparatus of mythology; but simply in the form that the mystics call "the flight of the Alone, to the Alone." It may be by the art of a prayerbook; it may equally well be in the depth of a personal experience to which all prayerbooks seem an intrusion. It may be in a church; it may equally well be in a solitary room or on a mountain's height. . . . The test of such an experience; call it prayer or reverie or what you please is as substantial as anything that can come to us. . . . I am not so sure of what I see with my eyes—not so sure that two and two make four—not so sure of any of the forms of the logical syllogism as I am of the genuineness and value of these occasional moments.[13]

In the handwritten text, Higginson had actually crossed out *God* and replaced it with *Unseen Power*, a fittingly amorphous and unbounded designation for the object of transcendental reverie.

Striking out the reference to God was also perhaps the right shift for someone who was deeply interested in spiritualism throughout much of the 1850s. Higginson, who after abandoning "The Return of Faith" found time to write two measured pamphlets in spiritualism's defense, regularly sang its praises as a gospel of gladness and progress versus a Calvinist theology of terror and gloom. By 1859 he was ready to pin many of his hopes for a mighty religious transition on this movement, "destined to utterly transform religious denominations" through its expansive anti-creedalism and experiential openness.[14] In the years when Higginson made his initial forays into the sympathy of religions, his theological interests were appropriately eclectic: by turns, transcendentalist in his emphasis on soulful experiences, spiritualist in his curiosity about mediums and the evidences of immortality, radical Unitarian in his doctrinal rejections and ethical commitments, and cosmopolitan universalist in his views of the religions of the world.

According to his diary, Higginson "began on Sympathy of Religions" on 24 January 1870 and finished a thirty-page manuscript on 4 February 1870, having devoted at least nine of those days to working on it. Whether he drew directly on his earlier chapter drafts from the mid-1850s or simply started over with those ideas in the background is unclear. Certainly, the project was by then substantially different; it was no longer part of a book but was being prepared as a lecture to be given at Horticultural Hall in Boston, on 6 February 1870. Of the event, Higginson noted simply in his diary: "Read my lecture 'Sympathy of Religions' which seemed to please people very much."[15] The event went well enough that he did immediately set out to revise the discourse for publication. It appeared early the next year in the *Radical,* an important nexus of liberal communications, clubs, and associations. The essay received favorable notice from several second-generation transcendentalists and freethinking titans, including Octavius Brooks Frothingham, and from reform-minded media such as the spiritualist newspaper *Banner of Light.*[16] Though he dwelled often on religious topics, including a range of discourses on everything from "The Character of the Buddha" to "Greek Goddesses," Higginson always took special pride in the piece on sympathy as his "most learned" achievement. Late in life, when annotating a copy of his seven-volume collected works for his secretary, he placed this essay among "the very best things I ever wrote," "the most varied & labored piece of scholarship I ever produced."[17]

The essay's real home was with the Free Religious Association (FRA), founded in 1867 as a loose organization of religious liberals through which they intended both to further an incipient scientific study of religion and to explore the basis of a universal spirituality. Higginson, extremely active in this group for the remainder of his life, served as a vice president and then president of the association. By one in-house tabulation, he attended "more of its councils," presided over more of its social gatherings, and "delivered more addresses from its platform than any other person."[18] Along with Emerson, Frothingham, Lucretia Mott, Lydia Maria Child, William Potter, Francis Abbot, and Felix Adler, Higginson was a guiding presence in the association and among its leading literary figures, notably through his frequent contributions to the *Atlantic Monthly* and his *Army Life in a Black Regiment* (1870). The FRA made the sympathy essay its own, turning it into one of the charter documents of the organization and publishing it in 1876 as a tract—100 copies for $3.00. From there, it became a commonplace of "our Liberal Faith" and an intellectual prologue to the World's Parliament of Religions.[19]

The essay opened at sea, passing "from island on to island," perhaps an imagistic legacy of the excursion to the Azores. "The human soul, like any other noble vessel, was not built," Higginson emoted, "to be anchored, but to sail." The global web of commercial shipping, which so much facilitated the accumulation of knowledge that made Higginson's religious comparisons possible, was also present from the opening lines: "It would be a tragedy," he averred, "to see the shipping of the world whitening the seas no more, and idly riding at anchor in Atlantic ports; but it would be more tragic to see a world of souls fascinated into a fatal repose and renouncing their destiny of motion." It was an instructive image in which the market's unceasing transport of cargo paralleled the movement of religions from "stranded hulks" into the flux of endless exchange. In all that sparkling motion of ships and souls, in the twinned fluidity of religion and the market, Christian devotions were no "more holy or more beautiful" than "one cry from a minaret" or the soft murmuring of "Oh! the gem in the lotus—oh! the gem in the lotus." All were equally symbols of spiritual aspiration.[20]

Higginson's essay was filled to bursting with optimism. The fast-growing knowledge of the religions of the world was not threatening or dispiriting but productive of progress, freedom, and concord: "There is a sympathy in religions. . . . [E]very step in knowledge brings out the sympathy between them. They all show the same aim, the same symbols, the same forms, the same weaknesses, the same aspirations." Certainly, Higginson acknowledged, there were "shades of difference" that emerged upon "closer analysis," but even those differences worked in symphonic harmony. And finally such nuances hardly mattered, for once the inquirer was alert to all "the startling points of similarity, where is the difference?" Religions took on the same forms from place to place, and it was the commonality of patterns (symbols, rituals, ethical precepts, holy days, sacred places, saints, saviors) and not sectarian "subdivisions" that mattered. Religion was not something to put under a microscope; it required instead a macroscopic vision in which all religions could be seen as facsimiles of one another. If difference continued to crowd into view, if particularity persisted, that was where religion failed, where it lapsed into creedal precision and lost sight of the universal, where it became a constraint rather than an inspiration for wayfaring souls.[21]

These points of unity, these universal sympathies, set the spirit free of any single institution, scripture, or tradition. From all religions and sacred books, from the Vedas and the Bible, from Chinese Buddhists and "Galla Negroes" will be "gathered hymns and prayers and maxims in which every soul may unite—the magnificent liturgy of the human race." The implications of such sympathies for liberal spirituality were manifest: The seeker of truth was not merely invited but enjoined to explore widely, to create a new scripture out of selected sheaves from the vast storehouse of religious inspiration. That might mean gathering the moral gems of Jesus or stringing together luminous passages from Emerson and Thoreau or pulling them all into the company of the Buddha. Higginson grandly proclaimed, "I do not wish to belong to a religion only, but to *the* religion; it must not include less than the piety of the world."[22]

That vast expansion of piety was, to Higginson, spirit-enlarging and spelled the ultimate undoing of religious exclusion, partiality, and rivalry. No single faith could claim a monopoly on love, truth, devotion, forgiveness, prayer, equality, honesty, or mystical illumination; "all do something to exemplify, something to dishonor them"; "all show the same disparity between belief and practice, and each is safe till it tries to exclude the rest." Though Higginson still threw the occasional bone to Anglo-American Protestantism—in its production of "manners," "arts," and "energy"—that hardly made his argument more palatable to his orthodox brethren. Christian claims to uniqueness and superiority and the whole missionary enterprise would have to yield the platform to the sympathy of religions, to meeting those of other faiths on common ground. As Higginson concluded bluntly of the exclusion of exclusion at the heart of liberal inclusion, "The one unpardonable sin is exclusiveness."[23]

Higginson's essay launched the idea of the sympathy of religions into prominence, and the theory became a commonplace in liberal theological discussions from the 1870s through the 1890s. Heir to the learned cosmopolitanism of Europe's republic of letters, Higginson's speculations had visible roots reaching back into the seventeenth and eighteenth centuries to Lord Herbert of Cherbury, Ralph Cudworth, and David Hume. Still, the more immediate and important intellectual company he kept was found a lot closer to home: Emerson, Parker, Frothingham, Lydia Maria Child, Samuel Johnson, Samuel Longfellow, David Wasson, Cyrus A. Bartol, Ednah Dow Cheney, John W. Chadwick, and Minot Savage, all of whom participated in this imagining of a cosmopolitan religion of shared ethical principles and spiritual aspirations. By 1870 Higginson and the other members of the FRA certainly knew of the European work on the emerging science of religion, especially Max Müller's, but the debate about the sympathy of religions still retained a provincial New England feel. A clubby band of radicals was trying to negotiate a religious multiplicity that they knew was far larger than Unitarian and Congregationalist polemics against Calvinism. Higginson, Longfellow, Johnson, and company cast aside even moderate Unitarian compromises such as those of James Freeman Clarke, who was valiantly surveying the religions of the world while doggedly retaining the ultimacy of Christianity.[24]

Higginson's conceptualization of the sympathy of religions achieved a proverbial quality in these liberal circles: Bartol, Chadwick, Cheney, Child, and Savage all echoed it in their writings. The "Universal Religion" to come, Chadwick prophesied in 1894, would be "that Sympathy of Religions which already has possessed the mind and heart of many an individual thinker and explorer."[25] Such liberal assent did not mean that the construct went unchallenged among Higginson's compeers. Some sought to refine it, and others were ready to question its basic premises. Francis Ellingwood Abbot and William J. Potter, leading participants in the FRA, found Higginson's formulations wanting and offered especially pithy critiques at the time of the essay's initial appearance. The sympathy of religions, both claimed, was at best a partial account, and it required "a companion-picture" of "the 'Antagonisms of Religions.'" Potter insisted, "[W]hat makes the special religions is not so much the things in which they agree as the things in which they differ—that is, the claims which are peculiar to each religion." Abbot and Potter matched Higginson's optimism about "a common groundwork of ethical and spiritual intelligence" with a frank emphasis on the conflicts that were constitutive of divergent religious cultures. Later, another arch liberal, Joseph Henry Allen, offered a more pointed critique along the same lines. Noting the religious animosities that circled the globe in the 1890s—from pogroms in eastern Europe to Muslim-Hindu bloodshed in India—Allen deemed Higginson's concept to be naïve and colorless: "We have not much encouragement . . . for any signs of the 'sympathy of religions.' Each of them, so far as we can see, while it is a living force is far from sympathetic. Nay, it is antagonistic and aggressive." By 1897, William Wallace Fenn, a liberal who enjoyed dousing liberalism's *ignes fatui,* announced that the "idea of the sympathy of religions" had often produced little more than "a huge cloud of thin but amiable sentiment."[26]

If Allen's critique, along with Fenn's, edged toward outright rejection of the "alleged" sympathy of religions, Potter and Abbot maintained a clear affinity with the idea. While they cautioned that Higginson's construct was too much about the unity of religious precepts and ideas, they continued to affirm it as a stepping-stone to a still greater spiritual unity—that is, to a "sympathy of souls." In this view, Higginson sought the essential sameness of religions but provided an inadequate grounding for "real fellowship" or "an embrace of souls." The cautions of Potter and Abbot were revealing: Higginson was clearer in his essay about the supposed sympathy that inhered between religions as discrete objects of comparison rather than the sympathy that needed to be cultivated as a relational dynamic among people of different cultures. Both Abbot and Potter suggested that the "sympathy of souls" was closer to the heart of liberal universalism, to "the spirit of the idea" of religious unity, than was Higginson's distillation of commonalities. In other words, Higginson's essay was doing "great service" as an intellectual exercise in abstracted comparisons, but would it produce a spiritual practice of sympathy? Would souls be bound together through empathic communication and understanding? Would, in Abbot's phrase, "cosmopolitan relationships" be realized?[27]

The Azores and Beyond

Higginson's essay, having begun with the motion of the sea, ended with the sudden illumination of a "foreign cathedral" on an island in the Azores two thousand miles from Boston. That in his essay Higginson should return, fifteen years later, to his experience of Portuguese Catholicism as the culminating episode for his lecture suggests that this excursion remained formative in shaping his thoughts on the sympathy of religions. When he and his wife Mary sailed for the Azores in October 1855, they did so mostly in hopes of improving her chronically poor health. For himself, Higginson looked forward to the trip as a break from the intense pressures of his reform efforts, even though he had a hard time parting with Worcester's "moral electricity" and could not let go of his habits of self-discipline. ("The disease of my life—the need of a few more hours in the 24, still haunts me here," he noted in his journal.) The islands, especially Fayal, were becoming, by the 1840s and 1850s, an increasingly popular place of resort for well-heeled New Englanders who were seeking a salubrious climate in which to convalesce and calm their nerves. Among Higginson's many causes was health reform, so his own report on his trip to Fayal, published in the *Atlantic Monthly* in 1860, underlined these associations. He emphasized flowers blooming all through the winter and songbirds that sang "without ceasing"—a climate so favorable to health and an "out-door life" that it made Boston feel like "a hospital for consumptives."[28]

Over the next three decades, this Anglo-American fantasy of the Azores as "the sanitarium of the world," as "a perfect heaven for a neurasthenic," was established as a truism of the burgeoning tourist industry. As New Englander Alice Baker noted in her guidebook to the islands in 1882, "The tired teacher finds here enforced rest with continual diversion; the nervous invalid, an engrossing change of scene, with absolute quiet, no temptation to hurry, and no excuse for worry." The languor of the islands was, of course, a kind of self-deception to which tourists were especially prone. Horta actually bustled as a commercial port and served as an important outpost for American whalers from New Bedford and Nantucket. New Englanders were a significant commercial presence on Fayal, and the Charles Dabney family, with their commanding mansion and gardens overlooking Horta, served as the hub of American enterprises in the islands.[29]

"There seem plenty of entertainments there," Higginson wrote in anticipation of the journey, "oranges, music, whaleships, Catholic priests, and a steep mountain 'Pico' half as high again as Mount Washington." As his inclusion of Catholic clergy in this list suggests, integral to his expectations was the possibility of witnessing the "Moorish" Catholicism of Portugal.[30] The arrival at Fayal on 9 November far exceeded his dreams of exoticism. "O wonderful, wonderful, & most wonderful, & again past all whooping!" he exclaimed:

> Nobody ever told us, nobody ever prepared us, we knew nothing of it! They told us of the views & the mountains & the ocean, but that we should step suddenly into all the South of Europe at once, set our feet into Lisbon & Madrid & Naples all in one, a place where not a person looks as any person ever looked in America, not a sound but is new, not a square inch of surface that is like anything we ever saw before;—nobody ever prepared us for this. We have had the day that comes but once in a life—the first day in a foreign country. At Singapore or Batavia we should feel no farther from home.

He felt under "a bewildered spell" of the "picturesque and strange." At first, he seemed to do little more than stand agape at the window of his lodgings in Horta, transfixed by everything from caps to capes, from fruits to palm trees, from red-tiled roofs to basketwork, from robust and vigorous women to sun-basking children. He was a tee-totaler, but he described his experience as one of utter intoxication.[31]

If Higginson was initially bedazzled with surprise in encountering the Azores, it was not for lack of Anglo-American travel accounts and guidebooks. As early as 1769, Thomas Hickling, a Boston merchant, deserted his wife and children and landed in the Azores, or Western Islands, a commercial meeting point between Europe and the Americas of calculable consequence in Atlantic trade. Hickling rose to wealth on Sao Miguel through citrus exports, a business he came to dominate by 1800. When his children discovered his whereabouts, they journeyed to the islands to restore the broken bonds of "parental affection." His daughter Catherine kept an extensive journal about her visit in 1786–87, and it offers an early glimpse of the encounter between New England Protestant travelers and the Catholic populace of the islands. The young woman especially "felt a great pity" for the nuns she met; "tho' they appeared happy, yet such a state of confinement must be repugnant." Her pity was akin to Higginson's sympathy in its compassion for those denied liberty, but at a religious level their conceptions were far apart: "I wish my God to be their God, but I can not let their God, b[e] my God, I can not worship Idols," Hickling concluded. "[B]less God, I was born of Christian Parents in a more enlightened land. . . . I rejoice every day, that I was not educated in the Catholic faith," she exulted, with a thankfulness that held steady over her nearly two-year stay in the islands.[32]

The American account most contemporaneous with Higginson's was Silas Weston's *Visit to a Volcano; Or, What I Saw at the Western Islands* (1856). Weston, who spent only eleven days touring the Azores, undertook the same two major hikes that Higginson did—one to Caldeira, a volcanic crater on Fayal, and the other to the top of

Pico, the great peak across the harbor from Horta. There the similarities of these New England travelers ended. Weston, an adventurer who loved a tall tale, made unceasing fun of the locals, including a hearty round of mimicry of some beggars who annoyed him with their entreaties. The poor were turned into confidence men and rogues who elicited not sympathy but contempt: "The people beg for profit rather than from necessity," Weston quickly concluded. He and some of his traveling companions amused themselves "a short time by purchasing fruit and throwing it into the centre of the square, to see the beggars run and scramble for it." Difference—whether of architecture, conveyance, or farming—held his attention only as a matter of derision, not wonder and whooping. Of the way a boatman transported a local woman ashore atop his shoulders, Weston commented that the pair "much resembled a monkey perched upon a baboon."[33]

British travel accounts showed little more sympathy than those of Hickling and Weston and often more bellicosity. In 1810 Robert Steele, a lieutenant in the Royal Marines, experienced "a sensation of disgust" in encountering Catholic "ignorance and superstition" and felt keenly the superiority of British civil liberty to an absolutism in church and state. Such sentiments convinced him that the archipelago should be seized and placed under British rule. Another observer, in 1834, also far more interested in maximizing the economic and strategic utility of the islands for England, simply dismissed the religious practices of the people as vulgar, bigoted, priest-ridden, and immoral; the convents were "little better than public brothels." While the funeral procession of an infant riveted one British traveler in 1831, he was still at a loss to express his sense of how the ludicrous mixed with the solemn in these rites: "I am too much a friend to liberty of conscience, and universal toleration, to wish to treat them with levity and disrespect, and willingly forego those comments that I might otherwise be tempted to indulge in, though I could not avoid asking myself again and again, during the day, *Is this really the nineteenth century, and can such things be?*" Toleration did not mean acceptance but forbearance; clearly, sympathy would demand much more of the liberal soul.[34]

Before Higginson's visit, Fayal had already become the occasional haunt of transcendentalists and Unitarians: the United States consul, Charles Dabney, was noted for "his sympathy with free thought in religion," and he and his extended family helped make the island especially hospitable for Boston liberals in the mid-nineteenth century. In 1843, for example, the Dabneys hired Samuel Longfellow as a tutor for their children. Longfellow, who had fallen under the sway of the transcendentalist movement the year before as a student at Harvard Divinity School, enjoyed the stint; it improved his impaired health, and it afforded him time for pleasant rambles of isolated self-reflection. Reclusive and spiritually restless, he resorted to the natural beauty of the Azores as Thoreau soon would to Walden Pond. "I have lived some beautiful hours and had some revelations from the world around me," Longfellow reported in a letter to his close friend Samuel Johnson, "revelations which have given peace to my soul and which I hope may prove nourishing dews to the germs of spiritual life within me." Through his "solitary walks" he was lifted out of his moods of despondency and harsh self-criticism. At such times, "nature whispered" to him words of inner peace:

> Vex not thyself because thou art not as others! Be content to be that which thou art; manifest thyself according to the laws of thy individual being. The flower at thy feet hopes not to be a star, nor strives to be aught but a flower. Be calm, and fear not but thou wilt find thy place. . . . Such lessons did the trees and rocks and waters, the green hills and that calm, majestic mountain breathe into my heart. Nor were words of man wanting, and in the pages of Emerson I found strength and reassurance. I am content now to be silent when I have nothing to say. Indeed, I begin to think silence better than words.

Following Longfellow to Fayal were such leading liberal ministers as Thomas Starr King (1848), John Weiss (1851), and Cyrus Bartol (1868).[35]

Most New England visitors not only immersed themselves in the sunlit landscape but also displayed considerable curiosity in witnessing Catholic processions and devotions. Longfellow noted that he attended "Catholic mummeries with poetic faith." "There is," he wrote to a friend back home, "a sentiment of the poetic and a sentiment of the past hanging about them which appeals to my ideality and reverence." Still, he could not shake the predictable Protestant sadness at "how dead and lifeless a shell these forms have become." Woeful, yet rapt gazing at Catholic ceremonies was a common practice of Protestant travelers, but Higginson took this staring to a new level of absorption, duly attending "all ecclesiastical festivals, grave or gay." In one paragraph alone in his *Atlantic Monthly* piece, he mentioned seven distinct solemnities from Carnival through Holy Week to Pentecost that he had ardently observed.[36]

Higginson recounted his experiences of Portuguese Catholicism in three places over a fifteen-year period: first in his journals and letters at the time, then in the *Atlantic Monthly* in 1860, and finally as the concluding episode in "The Sympathy of Religions" in 1871. During his travels in 1855 and 1856, he delighted in almost all aspects of Portuguese life, even as he kept his provincial love of New England safely intact: "They are indeed an attractive people," he remarked of the locals he met, "though I never for an instant prefer them to my earnest & resolute Yankees." Still, he threw himself into learning the language and was fearless in his pursuit of fluency; this helped earn him the respect of the people. "The Dabneys say that I am quite popular," Higginson noted with pride in his journal, "because of the pains I have taken to adapt myself to their ways." He styled himself a connoisseur of oranges and tangerines, participated in local dances, and laughed with Catholic acquaintances about the oddities of his identity as a Protestant "padre" (his being married and being a teetotaler were particularly puzzling, as was his lack of clerical garb and his inability to perform the Mass). Time and again, he commented on the beauty of a church service or the allure of a crowded procession. On Palm Sunday, he became a delighted souvenir seeker intent on locating one of the ornaments used in the festival, ears of corn decorated with ribbons and flowers, to bring home as a memento. The bells, the fireworks, the church decorations, the music, the candles, and the Carnival scenes all impressed him; his only disappointment was that Mardi Gras had not been even livelier and more mischievous.[37]

Throughout his journal, his chief impressions were favorable. Of the solemnities on Good Friday, he summarily remarked that these "were the most impressive we have seen." Of the rites of Hallelujah Saturday, "the best of Holy Week," he declared that "all was breathless anticipation," "all was joy." Again he became a devout souvenir seeker, and to his delight a Portuguese woman gave "Senor Padre Thomas" one of the three flower-bedecked candlesticks that had blazed on the central altar and in procession. This he planned, in turn, to pass on as a treasure to his sister Louisa as "her private candlestick." Though he did occasionally express anticlerical sentiments, even then he was mostly reassured that the Portuguese people themselves were every bit as suspicious of overbearing priests as he was. When he saw the laity in one church rise up against a cleric whom they charged with thievery, Higginson rejoiced that this "comes very near being a *Free Church,* after all!" At the time, on the ground, Portuguese Catholicism with its sundry "Orientalisms" occasioned in Higginson no revulsion or fear, no impulse to reform or purify; instead, it produced moments of curiosity, recognition, and gift giving.[38]

Still, the empathic sentiments that Higginson mustered were hardly uncomplicated. He admitted that attending these festivals did not feel to him like a religious act but remained instead a matter of aesthetic appreciation or artistic inspiration: "I suspect," he observed with a tinge of regret, "that I am beyond finding anything but *beauty* in any procession."[39] At times, Higginson seemed more a poet, voyeur, collector, and curiosity seeker than a sympathetic soul. In a series of emotion-laden experiences, each suggesting a tangle of observational relationships, sympathy was inevitably interlaced with other feelings. His ideas about the sympathy of religions were just emerging in "The Return of Faith" during this sojourn abroad, and in his everyday encounters that sentiment remained uneven and inconsistent. The realization of moral feeling in lived practice required improvisation and negotiation; travel, especially in Catholic climes, put liberal sympathy to the test in a current of cultural translations and mistranslations.

In working back through his journals and turning them into publications, Higginson further compromised his sympathetic sentiments; the tone of his observations lurched toward critical disengagement. Four years after leaving the Azores, in "Fayal and the Portuguese," he sniffed at the rituals as "acted charades" and at the churches as "vast baby-houses." "It must be owned," Higginson claimed in retrospect, "that these things, so unspeakably interesting at first, became a little threadbare before the end of winter; we grew tired of the tawdriness and shabbiness which pervaded them all, of the coarse faces of the priests, and the rank odor of the incense." Now, as a litterateur, he played openly to Protestant prejudices and made the religion of nature the singular source of inspiration that this land of health offered. With his proclivities to imitate Thoreau (he made a pilgrimage to Walden Pond, "that storied spot," shortly before embarking on his trip in 1855), Higginson held up immersion in the outdoors as the genuine spirituality that the Azores fostered. "The vapor in the atmosphere makes it the chosen land of rainbows," Higginson gushed about Fayal in December 1855; "we have seen a great many, & one perfect one by moonlight." By 1860, that was the only piety he offered his readers in the *Atlantic Monthly*: "When over all this luxuriant exotic beauty the soft clouds furled away and the sun showed us Pico, we had no more to ask. And the soft, beautiful blue cone became an altar for our gratitude, and the thin mist of hot volcanic air that flickered above it seemed the rising incense of the world." The pungent incense of the churches had given way to the purer and more authentic smells of nature.[40]

Still more problematic for Higginson's account of sympathy was the way he rescripted his experience of the culminating rites of Holy Week, a rewriting evident already in 1860 and then made a capstone of his essay in 1871. (It was this last version of the story that he would reiterate as the conclusion to his speech before the World's Parliament of Religions in 1893.) Between 1856 and 1871, he moved from an engaged and glowing account of Hallelujah Saturday to an increasingly distant, judgmental perspective. He wrote in the last paragraph of "The Sympathy of Religions," that the Portuguese church

> looked dim and sad, with the innumerable windows closely curtained, since the moment when the symbolical bier of Jesus was borne to its symbolical tomb beneath the High Altar, while the three mystic candles blazed above it. There had been agony and beating of cheeks in the darkness, while ghostly processions moved through the aisles, and fearful transparencies were unrolled from the pulpit. The priests knelt in gorgeous robes, chanting, with their heads resting on the altar steps; the multitude hung expectant on their words. Suddenly burst forth a new chant, "Gloria in Excelsis!" In that instant every curtain was rolled aside, the cathedral was bathed in glory, the organs clashed, the bells

chimed, flowers were thrown from the galleries, little birds were let loose, friends embraced and greeted one another, and we looked down upon the tumultuous sea of faces, all floating in a sunlit haze.[41]

At various points in this essay, Higginson's reinsertion of dissimilarity and critical distance at the expense of sympathy introduced contradiction. The tensions inherent in his construction were at no point more apparent than in this concluding passage as he "looked down" upon the festive throng.

His theory of sympathy as a comparative technique failed him in this closing scene in the Portuguese church. In the essay, he now placed himself in a space grandly reconfigured as a "tumultuous sea" of Catholic otherness—dark, mystical, flagellating, ghostly. By what alchemy would he transform such feelings back into an expression of engagement? How would he move from distance to common ground, from difference to similarity? Suddenly, he claimed, his own illumination came: "The whole of this sublime transformation consisted in letting in the light of day! These priests and attendants, each stationed at his post, had only removed the darkness they themselves had made." If "this thought smote" him at the moment of his initial observation, as he subsequently maintained in redescribing the experience, that epiphany went unrecorded in his journal. Apparently, only upon further reflection did he take refuge in a simple natural religion that expunged his earlier feelings of attraction and connection. "Unveil these darkened windows, but remove also the darkening walls; the temple itself is but a lingering shadow of that gloom. Instead of its coarse and stifling incense, give us God's pure air, and teach us that the broadest religion is the best."[42] In closing with this image, Higginson's liberal sympathy seemed not about bridging differences but about demolishing them. Now configured as a comparative theory, Higginson's construct failed as a relational practice. The sympathy of religions, in effect, cancelled the sympathy of souls.

Higginson always had a lot of irons in the fire, and so it would be tempting to consider this revision as a memory lapse of a writer who roamed widely and whose strength was never in making a sustained argument. Yet, he had many opportunities to emend this essay, and he never tampered with this concluding illustration of the pure universal religion rubbing out the particularities of local religious practices. In the moment of direct encounter in 1855–1856, Higginson was often able to practice a respectful understanding, but the more he actually speculated about the sympathy of religions, the less connected he became to the Portuguese Catholicism that had helped spark his initial reflections. Was the immediate journal somehow the "more real" or authentic account? As Higginson noted at one point in his *Army Life in a Black Regiment,* "I must resort to a scrap from the diary. Perhaps diaries are apt to be thought tedious; but I would rather read a page of one, whatever the events described, than any more deliberate narrative,—it gives glimpses so much more real and vivid." Or, were the comparative abstractions of 1871 the better measure of liberal sympathy? Through the theoretical pursuit of sameness, Higginson actually managed to obscure, rather than highlight, the makeshift sympathy that he had unevenly improvised in 1855–1856.[43]

In the end, it was not Higginson's ideas about the sympathy of religions that mattered most, except perhaps as liberal exhortation. Rather, just as he had put his body on the line in the fight against slavery, it was his living example that offered the more complex testimony. After his trips to the Azores and through Kansas, he went on to become a vociferous witness to African American valor during the Civil War and remained an insistent champion of black soldiers and civil equality. From his days as a colonel, he also gained a sympathetic ear for slave spirituals and became an amateur folklorist of "negro-Methodist chants" and prayers. As with Portuguese Catholicism, he tended to turn religious expression into art: that is, to treat spirituals as folk ballads of great poetic beauty, relics in need of collecting and preservation. Still, there was no more influential transcriber of the spirituals in this period than Higginson, who described his feelings toward his "Gospel army" as that of "sympathetic admiration."[44]

Higginson, also a fervent champion of Emily Dickinson's deeply meditative verse, recognized the poetry of the spirituals as a source of courage and "tie to heaven" so sublime in expression that "history cannot afford to lose this portion of its record." Moved by the "religious spirit" of the soldiers in his command, he observed, "[their piety] grows more beautiful to me in living longer with them." He even developed an appreciative understanding of the clapping, drumming, dancing, and ecstasy of the ring-shout tradition, insisting that such rites were "thoroughly identified" with the "most genuine religious emotions" of the soldiers. "The extremes of religious enthusiasm I did not venture to encourage, for I could not do it honestly," Higginson related; "neither did I discourage them, but simply treated them with respect, and let them have their way." In turning his Civil War journals into his famed book, he paid the black soldiers the supreme compliment of liberal religion as he added two telling comparisons: "Their philosophizing is often the highest form of mysticism; and our dear surgeon declares that they are all natural transcendentalists." Again, on the ground, his liberal sympathies served him better than his studied modes of comparison, which, in this case, turned the religious experiences of African Americans into one more example of Emersonian spirituality. The relational practice of sympathy remained more dynamic than the comparative theory of underlying sameness to which it was joined. "True sympathy teaches true largeness of soul," Higginson averred, making one as open to Gullah prayers and songs as to Buddhist chants or sutras.[45]

After the war, Higginson ceased any formal ministry and turned his religious energies to the FRA and its platform of religious inclusion and universality. He described that organization as "no place for patronizing, nor even for toleration; it is a place of simple religious equality." If its successes seem rather modest in retrospect—for example, the alliance it formed among certain Unitarians, freethinkers, liberal Jews, progressive Friends, Universalists, spiritualists, transcendentalists, and Vedantists—its inclusive platform was seen as anything but tame at the time. To be sure, the FRA shared the larger liberal dilemma of whether to exclude the exclusive: "Into our kingdom of heaven no sectarian may enter," announced Octavius Brooks Frothingham, the society's first president. "Drop the polemic, the controversialist, the apologist, and be a seeker, willing to stay or to go, whithersoever the spirit of truth leads. Hold all opinions soluble, and you are one of us." That pluralistic dilemma hardly slowed them down in their desire to wake Americans from "the dream of exclusive revelation," and Higginson, like the rest, delighted in the challenge of this emancipation, the latest "war of liberalism." Samuel Johnson rallied the gathering in May 1870: "I found myself democratic in my religious thought in the selfsame hour and from the same conviction that made me radical in my politics. A privileged race or sex cannot be more unnatural in the political order than the asserted absolutism of Christianity among religions is in the divine."[46]

With the sympathy essay in a kind of national syndication through the FRA, Higginson pressed on. He prodded Americans to cultivate more appreciative views of Buddhism and Islam and weighed in against sectarianism and creedalism at every opportunity. In 1877 he even chided his beloved FRA for its practice of tolerating "all but intolerance" and pressed now for ways to include the voices of those who otherwise spurned liberal principles. "Are we as large as our theory?" he asked. "Are we as ready to tolerate . . . the Evangelical man as the Mohammedan?" Unlike the position he took in his piece on sympathy, he now recognized the exclusion of those with exclusive claims as its own form of narrowness and a formidable "internal danger" to any liberal organization. Not that he ever resolved this issue to his satisfaction; he, like the rest of the FRA, remained terribly alienated from evangelicals and the old-time religion, and the more orthodox liberal Protestants (such as the Episcopal priest Phillips Brooks) invariably responded negatively to invitations to participate in the organization.[47]

Three months shy of his seventieth birthday in 1893, Higginson headed to Chicago for the World's Parliament of Religions and an auxiliary meeting of the FRA, the first meeting of the organization held outside New England. As *eminence grise* among religious representatives there, he participated in these events with characteristic aplomb and saw the parliament as a grand fulfillment of the FRA's original platform.

Though he made highly favorable remarks about the Roman Catholic delegation at the gathering, Higginson's voice lacked the transcendental newness and prophetic edge that it had possessed in the late 1840s and 1850s. His public remarks offered no critique of the circus of Anglo-American condescension toward "primitive" religions then on display at the concurrent Chicago World's Fair, and he left unnoticed the holes that remained in the parliament's representation of the "great religions." In lecturing one more time on the sympathy of religions, Higginson gestured backwards toward the radical Unitarian ferment of the mid-nineteenth century more than he did forward into twentieth-century developments in ecumenism or the history of religions. At this point, he chose to celebrate the distance already traveled rather than to emphasize the distance yet to go toward his version of a cosmopolitan piety.[48]

By the turn of the century, the mantle of spokesman for cosmopolitan piety had been passed from Higginson to others. In 1899 the scholar Lewis G. Janes succeeded Higginson as president of the FRA and made the advancement of the "noble principles and sentiments" of "The Sympathy of Religions" a major part of his own agenda. At that time Janes was already directing the Monsalvat School for the Comparative Study of Religion as part of an annual summer retreat at Eliot, Maine. Known as the Greenacre community, these gatherings had first been organized by Sarah J. Farmer in 1894 as an embodiment of the ideals of the World's Parliament. With the Monsalvat School and the wider programs of Greenacre, Janes and Farmer opened up an influential forum for the exploration of comparative religions and created a highly visible public space for the enactment of liberal sympathies and eclectic affinities. Representatives came from Buddhism, Vedanta, Zoroastrianism, Jainism, liberal Protestantism, reform Judaism, transcendentalism, New Thought, and theosophy; from Annie Besant to Paul Carus, from Swami Vivekananda to D. T. Suzuki, all converged there with a shared optimism about the realization of a new day in religious cosmopolitanism. "All religions are true," so an epigraph on the program book for 1897 declared; "they are like so many rivers, flowing towards the one ocean of Light and Love infinite." Sectarianism was finally to give way to a liberal millennium of universal peace, harmony, and reconciliation.[49]

The grander dreams of Greenacre, needless to say, went unfulfilled. Tensions first between Janes and Farmer and then among transcendentalist philosophers, New Thought metaphysicians, Vedantists, and Bahá'ís corroded the Monsalvat School. Also, Farmer's nonchalance toward fund raising plagued the community from the start. Even with financial support rolling in from Phoebe Hearst, Farmer was hard pressed to keep the summer programs solvent. By 1905, the pressures to maintain a full-orbed liberal eclecticism were openly colliding with specific Bahá'í claims to being the ultimate basis for religious universalism, and Farmer herself got caught in the crossfire. She began suffering recurrent bouts of nervous instability and in the last years of her life sought refuge from the summer community's quarreling factions in a sanitarium. Still, Greenacre's flowering between 1893 and 1910 revealed the staying power of the sympathy of religions as an ideal as well as a contentious practice in liberal circles.

The example of two attendees at Greenacre, Vedantist Swami Sârâdananda and radical Unitarian Alfred W. Martin, suffices to demonstrate those ongoing allegiances. Sârâdananda, showing his familiarity with liberalism's theological vernacular, set the stage in May 1897 for his summer participation at Greenacre with a discourse expressly on "The Sympathy of Religions" before the FRA. (In return, one of Greenacre's New Thought leaders, Horatio Dresser, published the paper in his *Journal of Practical Metaphysics*.) "By sympathy," Sârâdananda related, "the Vedantist does not mean a kind of dull indifference, or haughty toleration, which seems to say, 'I know you are wrong and my religion is the only true one, yet I will let you follow it, and perhaps one day your eyes will be opened.' His sympathy is not a negative one, but it is of a direct, positive nature, which knows that all religions are true, they have the same goal." The Vedantist, Sârâdananda insisted, did not reduce the "religious orchestra of the universe" to mere "monotones." The sympathy of religions (Sârâdananda was much clearer than Higginson on this point) would not be purchased at the price of particularity and variation: "The mission of Vedanta to the West is not to make Christians Hindus, but to make the Christian a better Christian, a Hindu a better Hindu, and a Mohammedan a better Mohammedan." Reaching God required specific paths, not a uniform one "in the place of the many."[50]

Alfred W. Martin, a Harvard-educated minister who went west to Tacoma to lead a Free Church society, made the trek back to Greenacre in 1897 to offer the season's closing lecture, "Universal Religion and the World's Religions." That topic became his life work. In one book after another, he strove to make people "more cosmopolitan" in their "sympathies" and "more responsive" to diverse scriptures. From *Great Religious Teachers of the East* (1911) to *Seven Great Bibles* (1930), Martin charted the progress of liberalism from mere toleration to the "cultivation of that modern virtue, appreciation." "Toward the Bibles of the great religions," he related, "appreciation takes the eclectic attitude, asking of each: What have you to offer? What can we borrow from your moral and spiritual thesaurus to increase our own sources of inspiration?" Martin's appreciation still echoed Higginson's sympathy at many points, but it also revealed how liberal theorists of pluralism were consolidating the shift of ground from "resemblances" to "differences." Sectarian narrowness was still the bugbear, but the peculiar teachings of distinct religions were to be "recognized" and "respected," not effaced. The acknowledgment of difference was now "the indispensable condition upon which the only unity in religion worth having is to be attained—*unity in diversity.*" As Martin declared, his vision of a "fellowship of faiths" was in service of "the mutual enhancement of diversities."[51]

In the half-century after Higginson's formative exposition, sympathy and appreciation became bedrock virtues of the liberal character. No doubt those virtues were unevenly and inconsistently applied, but the emphasis on cultivating those sentiments in relationship to people of other faiths remained momentous. Those ideals supported spiritual seeking across religious expanses hitherto little explored and helped create a liberal religious culture that embraced a multiplicitous spirituality. Entering affectionately into that global religious exchange ultimately transformed liberal Christian identities, but to what end? Certainly, liberals deepened their understanding of pluralism and difference, yet they also ransacked other cultures for spiritual treasures (it was always a fine line between creative appropriation and thievery). They staked their identity on cosmopolitanism, but did breadth come at the expense of depth? Religious universalism could be thin, placeless, and vaporous. It was no wonder that some at Greenacre ended up preferring the specificity of Bahá'í teachings and practices over free-floating transcendentalist reveries about beauty and the infinite. Cultivating the sympathy of religions made for a restive, not restful, posture; fluid and relational in practice, the virtue of sympathy suited the modern flux of liberal religious identities. It was the métier of all those aspiring, audacious souls who had declared themselves free to embrace the piety of the world.

Pursuing the sympathy of religions created intractable puzzles about the solidity of Christian identity or any religious identity in a modern, pluralistic society. Yet, it also provided answers to what a vital, mediating spirituality might look like amid that very diversity. William Norman Guthrie, an Episcopal priest in New York City and a participant in the Whitman Fellowship and the Greenacre community, serves as a final exemplar of the possibilities and perils of that new piety. As Tisa Wenger shows in the next chapter in this volume, Guthrie was a liturgical innovator, especially open to the arts, including theater and dance. He cut his literary teeth in the 1890s by offering generous readings of Walt Whitman as "a religious teacher," a bearer of the "vital core" of Quakerism's Inner Light, and a poet-prophet who revealed "the mystic secret of religion." Always on the lookout for ways to relieve the vast "religious boredom" that too many Americans experienced at church, Guthrie took his cue from Whitman's embrace of "companions from lands and literatures strange to Christendom." In 1917 he published *Leaves of the Greater Bible: A Spiritual Anthology,* in which he sought to represent diverse "sources of perpetual refreshment and perpetual inspiration." In his collection he drew on Native American religions, Egyptian sun worship, Zoroastrian prayers, Buddhist writings, as well as Jewish and Christian sources.[52]

To his critics, Guthrie looked like the worst kind of modernist dabbler and crack-pot, and yet, unlike Higginson, he insisted that he remained very much a member in good standing of the Christian church. "We are Christians, and what is more, Angli-cans. Very well, let us start with the Prayer Book, and the Scriptures," Guthrie enjoined at the outset of his *Offices of Mystical Religion* (1927). Unwilling to stop there, how-ever, he kept pressing on the outer bounds of liberal sympathies: "A good God must needs everywhere and in all times have answered His children's prayer for guidance and comfort. There cannot have been any exclusive monopoly granted to any race." Guthrie stumbled time and again in his codification of universalized "ethnic" scrip-tures, inclusive worship services, and fanciful pageants of comparative religion. What kind of leap was it to think that through an act of imaginative identification Chris-tians could come to understand what it meant to be "a true Taoist" or "a true Bud-dhist"? How could Guthrie's wildly resilient faith in shared religious truths justify the collection of "separable lyrics" and "detachable ritual morsels" as if other cultures were curio shops at his artistic disposal? Guthrie wanted Americans to be open and teach-able, filled with Whitman's democratic and pluralistic sympathies and imbued with a sense that the best in Christianity transcended the confines of exclusive creeds. The effort of liberal figures from Higginson to Guthrie to put the sympathy of religions into practice was a titanic endeavor. It represented, in the end, both the sinking and the rescue of Protestant identities in a world of profound religious diversity.[53]

CHAPTER ELEVEN

The Practice of Dance for the Future of Christianity

"Eurythmic Worship" in New York's Roaring Twenties

TISA J. WENGER

In the spring of 1924, the Reverend William Norman Guthrie, rector of St. Mark's-in-the-Bouwerie Episcopal Church in New York City, faced a serious showdown with his bishop. William Thomas Manning, the Bishop of the Diocese of New York, was outraged at reports of "pagan dances" and other "non-Christian forms of worship" at St. Mark's. He ordered Guthrie and his vestry to stop any such activities immediately, describing them as a violation of Episcopal propriety and indeed of Christianity itself. While morning services at St. Mark's had continued to follow the Episcopal Book of Common Prayer, Guthrie had in recent years been experimenting with other styles of worship in special Sunday afternoon services. These services drew liturgical inspiration from a wide variety of sources, including biblical narratives, classical mythology, Native American religions, and other world religions, as well as from contemporary cultural trends such as modern dance and the American pageantry movement. The rector argued that these innovations, religious dance in particular, were crucial to the survival of St. Mark's—and perhaps even for the revitalization of Christianity in the modern world. Defying their bishop, Guthrie and his vestry refused to stop or significantly alter their special services. As a penalty, Bishop Manning refused to make official visits to St. Mark's until all such performances ceased, meaning that St. Mark's would have no access to the bishop's services of consecrating and receiving new members into the church. The standoff continued for eight years, until—much to Guthrie's disappointment—budget constraints and internal parish conflicts essentially forced St. Mark's to discontinue its "special forms of service."[1] Guthrie later resumed a more limited schedule of toned-down liturgical experiments, including some dancing. But the reinstituted special services never received the level of publicity Guthrie had courted in the 1920s, and all such experiments at St. Mark's ended at the rector's retirement in 1937.

Guthrie's experiments with religious dance were in no way representative of contemporary Episcopal liturgical practice or of most American Christian worship. Like Manning, many Christians explicitly rejected dance in worship, and some went so far as to condemn all dance as unsuited to the faithful Christian life both inside and outside the church.[2] Others, however, such as the nineteenth-century Shakers and some twentieth-century Pentecostalists, made dance a central part of worship. Guthrie's experiment with dance at St. Mark's became a forerunner to the later-twentieth-century liturgical dance movement, a widespread effort to incorporate dance into Christian worship. His liturgical experiments provide an illuminating example of the challenges of making innovations in Christian worship. As Guthrie's "eurythmic worship," the practice of dance was a part of the larger Christian practice of worship. His innovations challenged the received—and quite formal—patterns of Episcopal liturgy. His efforts to justify the inclusion of dance in worship required artfully constructed appeals to theology and historical tradition. But even the most artful rationale could not convince the more conservative guardians of Episcopal liturgical practice that Guthrie's innovations fell within the bounds of that tradition, and it is not surprising that he faced stiff opposition. The events at St. Mark's are one example of an ongoing tension in Episcopal practice over the degree of flexibility permitted within the guidelines of the Book of Common Prayer.[3]

This essay places Guthrie and the liturgical practices he innovated within a particular historical moment. Like all religious practices, eurythmic worship at St. Mark's grew out of a particular social context and helped to negotiate and reinforce relations of power within that setting. Despite Guthrie's own best intentions, his use of eurythmic worship in many ways reproduced contemporary inequalities of gender, race, class, and empire. At the same time, the practice of dance at St. Mark's was an intentional effort to bring new life to Christianity through variations in worship. Like theologians today who seek to renew Christian life by recovering an apparently lost integrity of Christian practice, Guthrie intended for his liturgical innovations to revitalize Christianity so that it could better meet the real human needs of his day. And for many who worshiped at St. Mark's, the eurythmic rituals practiced there offered a positive option for the ongoing effort to make Christian tradition speak to modern America.

The Rector, the Church, and the City

William Norman Guthrie's liturgical experiments must first of all be understood in the context of the politics of class and race in early-twentieth-century New York.

Fig. 11.1. St. Mark's Church-in-the-Bouwerie in 1936. Library of Congress, Prints and Photographs Division, Historic American Buildings Survey (HABS, NY, 31-NEYO, 3-1).

St. Mark's Church-in-the-Bouwerie had a venerable history, but by the 1920s the church faced declining membership. In the Dutch colonial period of Nieuw Amsterdam, its location had been the site of a Dutch Reformed chapel on the estate, or "Bouwerie," of Governor Peter Stuyvesant. Under British rule in the eighteenth century, the Stuyvesant family became Anglicans, and they donated the old chapel grounds to the Episcopal Church to become the second parish in Manhattan. St. Mark's Church was completed in 1799. As evidenced by the graveyard that still surrounds the church, it became the home parish for many prominent nineteenth-century New York families. The parish acquired a small chapel nearby, along with a great deal of other real estate on the Lower East Side. But fashionable New York society gradually moved north, and by the twentieth century the neighborhood of St. Mark's was home to many Italian, Russian, and other European immigrants whose religious commitments were primarily Catholic, Orthodox, or Jewish. Around this time, the Bowery district, which like St. Mark's-in-the-Bouwerie was named after the original Stuyvesant estate, began to earn its twentieth-century reputation for poverty, seediness, and alcohol abuse. St. Mark's was a white middle- and upper-class church struggling to survive in a neighborhood undergoing ethnic, class, and religious change. Guthrie interpreted the situation as a spiritual challenge. He wrote, "In a spiritual account of this downtown parish one should not forget the constant pressure exerted by a neighborhood wholly alien."[4] Thus, the events at St. Mark's contribute to our understanding of twentieth-century mainline Protestant efforts to cope with the cultural and demographic changes that were a reality in so many urban settings.

In 1911, when the vestry of St. Mark's invited William Norman Guthrie to become their new rector, they expressed high hopes for his potential to revitalize the parish. Guthrie was by all accounts a dynamic preacher with longstanding interests in linking theology to literature and the arts. He was born in Scotland in 1868 to a Scottish mother and a French father, both of whom became naturalized American citizens; they raised their sons in the Episcopal Church. His maternal grandmother was Frances (Fanny) Wright, the Scottish freethinker, women's rights activist, and abolitionist who founded the anti-slavery colony of Nashoba in antebellum Tennessee. William and his brother Kenneth attended a series of boarding schools throughout Europe. In 1886, at eighteen, William enrolled at the University of the South, an Episcopal college and seminary in Sewanee, Tennessee. There he edited the undergraduate literary magazine and studied classics, poetry, modern languages, and theology. He remained at Sewanee to complete a master's degree in 1891. In 1893 he was ordained to the priesthood and married fellow Sewanee student Anna Stuart. The Guthries would have two daughters, Sylvia and Phoebe Anna; the latter became instrumental in developing many of her father's liturgical experiments at St. Mark's. William Guthrie taught comparative literature for several years at Sewanee, Kenyon College, the University of Cincinnati, and the University of Chicago. He served as assistant rector for short periods of time at several Ohio churches, and was rector of a church in Alameda, California, from 1903 to 1908. He published books of poetry along with studies of comparative literature and theology, and for these and his other accomplishments the University of the South granted him an honorary doctorate in 1915.[5]

As St. Mark's new rector, Guthrie proposed a creative solution to the demographic crisis facing the parish. Because St. Mark's "natural constituency" had been replaced by "a population practically unassimilable to the Episcopal Church," he wrote in a planning statement, the only solution was to appeal to those who were otherwise uninterested in church. He selected as his target audience the artists and intellectuals who frequented Lower Manhattan. Many artistic and literary types, Guthrie wrote, "had become sceptics or agnostics, because they could not see their way to reconcile their general point of view with traditional Christianity," and he argued that by developing services that appealed to them he could make Christianity more meaningful to modern Americans in general. Guthrie criticized conventional Christianity as boring, dogmatic, and irrelevant to modern life. Shortly after his arrival at St. Mark's, he introduced special afternoon forums devoted to lectures on great literature, "sacred books other than the bible," and important historical figures, including poets, classical composers, and national heroes. An assistant rector developed an evening "service of symbolic worship," which Guthrie also described as "a 'Quaker meeting' with artistic support." After this service, the congregation held either a "discussion of spiritual healing" or a "social song service" featuring folk songs from around the world.[6] By all accounts, attendance at St. Mark's services (though not church membership) increased substantially as a result of Guthrie's innovations and his dynamic preaching.[7] His liturgical experiments may have reaped more notoriety than contributing members for St. Mark's, but surely they represent one mainline Protestant variety of "urban religion" formed in encounter with its environs, what Robert Orsi has described as the "religious imagination at work in the city."[8] Guthrie's innovations may therefore be understood in part as a creative religious response to life in the New York City of the 1920s.

The liturgical experiments made Guthrie one of the public faces of Episcopal modernism in the 1920s, and as such he illustrates a side of modernism that historians have not adequately understood. His prominence, at least in New York, is well illustrated in the *New York Times* of December 17, 1923, whose front page featured Guthrie's conflict with Bishop Manning along with three other controversies going on in the Episcopal Church over modernist theology.[9] Guthrie clearly placed himself among the religious modernists of the day, mapping the contemporary religious scene when he expressed relief that conservative Protestants and Roman Catholics were too different to cooperate with each other. If they could work together, he wrote, "they would certainly smash us." However, for Guthrie modernism was not only an intellectual system. He had an abiding interest in religious practice, and condemned modernists who reduced their position to mere rationalism.

> A distinction needs to be drawn between those who are merely rationalists, and those
> who are religionists. My own personal interest lies with the religionists, even if they are

Conservatives, Fundamentalists, legalists, and every other devil of a thing,—provided only they are sufficiently religious for all these objectionable elements to be put relatively in the second plane. I personally get more religious comfort out of the religious offices of a bigot than from the exegeses of even a rationalistic irreligionist.[10]

Liturgical practice is a side of modernism not often attended to in standard accounts of Protestant modernism, most of which have focused exclusively on theology and intellectual history.[11]

The Practice of Eurythmic Worship at St. Mark's

Around 1920, Guthrie began to include dance along with chanted poetry and the fine arts in his special afternoon services, and some of the performances became a regular part of the church's liturgical cycle. "The Pageant in Honor of the Blessed Virgin Mary," first staged in 1921 and performed every year for over a decade, was probably the most long-lived of these services. To celebrate the March 25 Feast of the Annunciation, this liturgy dramatized the angel Gabriel's announcement to Mary that she was to become the mother of Christ. The 1922 version of the service began with hymns, Guthrie's recitation of a poem by Henry Adams titled the "Prayer to the Virgin of Chartres," and a choir performance of an "anthem on the Annunciation," composed by the rector himself. The danced portion of the service was titled "Ritual Dance of the Della Robbia Annunciation." It featured five Barnard College dance students, young women draped in flowing white robes and illuminated by blue spotlights. Their performance concluded with a pose drawn from the fifteenth-century Italian sculptor Andrea della Robbia's rendition of the Annunciation, depicted on a plaque hanging behind the dancers (Fig. 11.2).[12] The spotlights illustrate Guthrie's concern with all aspects of the experience and the environment of worship. Installed in 1921, his state-of-the-art lighting system was intended "to create an essentially religious atmosphere." It featured green, blue, rose red, and amber lights projected from "enclosed chandeliers" installed in the church ceiling.[13] A new ritual introduced in November 1923, titled the "Birth and Progress of the Human Soul," provides a second example of Guthrie's special services. Here, in a ceremony in three movements, the rector provided poetic narration while slides of famous works of sculpture were projected onto a screen in the chancel of the church. Each movement concluded with a dance by four young women, once again dressed in flowing white robes.[14]

Guthrie's efforts at eurythmic worship had close affinities with the burgeoning world of modern dance. Indeed, he and his daughter Phoebe Guthrie developed direct contacts with some of the leading figures of that movement, many of whom

Fig. 11.2. Scene from Ritual Dance of the Della Robbia Annunciation, part of the Pageant in Honor of the Blessed Virgin Mary, a liturgical performance designed by the Reverend William Norman Guthrie. Courtesy of St. Mark's Church-in-the-Bouwerie.

shared his interests in bringing religion and dance together. Guthrie invited Isadora Duncan, the modern dance sensation and social free thinker, to speak at St. Mark's in 1922, although Bishop Manning's opposition forced the cancellation of the event. The rector, his admiration undiminished, held a memorial service after Duncan's death in 1927 in which he praised the dancer's "genius" in recreating "the earliest form of the arts, the Dance."[15] In 1930, the leading modern dancer in the country, Martha Graham, performed at St. Mark's the "Adoration Scene" from the *Chester Mysteries,* a set of fifteenth-century British miracle plays.[16] William and Phoebe Guthrie both corresponded about their experiments at St. Mark's with Ruth St. Denis, who with her husband Ted Shawn had founded the Denishawn Dance Studio and trained a generation of leading American dancers (including Graham).[17] In 1917, Shawn and St. Denis had given the first known modern dance performance during a church service, at San

Francisco's Interdenominational Church.[18] Shawn, a former divinity student, wrote of his relationship with St. Denis, "She, pursuing the dance upstream to its source, found there religion, and I, pursuing religion upstream, found the dance was the first and finest means of religious expression."[19] Such affinities make it easy to understand Guthrie's efforts to incorporate modern dance—and the world of modern culture more generally—into Episcopal practice.

Guthrie also found inspiration in the American pageantry movement, which flourished between 1905 and 1925. The pageantry movement was born out of the Progressive-era emphasis on social reform, and its advocates presented pageants as a way to bring art and democracy together—creating vibrant and progressive communities by uniting citizens in public dramatizations of American ideals. Pageants typically featured vignettes from American history and were usually staged by towns, universities, and civic organizations. As we will see, Guthrie shared the pageantry movement's nationalism and its conviction that good art could inspire—indeed, was essential to—transformation in a community. Guthrie often used the term *pageant* to name his special services, as in "The Pageant in Honor of the Blessed Virgin Mary." His direct connections to the pageantry movement included the choreographer for his early eurythmic rituals, the Barnard College dance teacher Bird Larson, who had taken a course in pageantry at Columbia University Teachers' College (the first such course in the country) and was active in the pageantry movement at Barnard. Both Ruth St. Denis and Isadora Duncan danced in pageants; St. Denis in particular was involved in judging and creating pageants at the height of the movement. This correspondence between modern dance and pageantry should not be surprising; one historian has noted that the pageantry movement and modern dance shared interests in "democratic expression," "native American forms," and a "search for spiritual truth."[20] Guthrie shared these interests as well.

By the 1920s, the pageantry movement had inspired a widespread interest among American church leaders in drama and pageantry as a means of religious education. In that decade, denominational and interdenominational committees, including the YWCA Bureau of Pageantry and Drama, the Church of Christ Committee on Religious Drama, and the Episcopal Church Commission on Church Pageantry and Drama, produced guides to and collections of religious pageants and dramas. Methodist, Baptist, and Presbyterian presses published books about the value of religious pageantry, along with dramas for specific church occasions.[21] Guthrie saw his own work as quite distinct from this general run of church pageants. He wrote to a British clergyman interested in the work at St. Mark's that most of the clergy had "no constructive suggestion" for remedying "the diminished attendance and the listlessness of spirit of the congregations . . . beyond perhaps 'mission' preaching, sermonettes,

[and] sometimes what they disastrously think are religious pageants, and really are silly rompings about the Altar." What was really needed and he believed he offered was a way to integrate art into worship—to create worship that was truly "a-thrill and a-throb with spiritual conviction."[22] Whatever the relative artistic and spiritual merits of his work, Guthrie's inclusion of dance and of non-Christian materials was not characteristic of other church pageants of the period, and this made his version of pageantry controversial. Nevertheless, he was one among many American ministers and church leaders who were experimenting with drama and pageantry in the 1920s.

As Guthrie pointed out, eurythmic worship at St. Mark's was unlike most modern dance and pageant performances in that it was presented as an act of worship, intended as an integral part of the worship experience. Guthrie himself did not dance, but he took a very public role in the special services he directed. Often, spotlights illuminated his figure in the pulpit, and his dramatic poetry recitations and sermonic interpretations of the dance served as very much a part of the overall practice of eurythmic worship. Guthrie cast himself as both director and interpreter of his experimental liturgies. He was over six feet tall and a charismatic speaker, and his imposing physical presence was surely of great significance for the congregation's experience of these services. Available sources give us only limited insight into how the dancers themselves experienced these services. It is clear that Phoebe Guthrie shared many of her father's views of the religious value of dance. She wrote to Ruth St. Denis that the St. Mark's Choreographic Group, which she directed and took on tour during the 1930s, effectively communicated "a real sense of religious worship" to audiences, and presumably she shared in this experience.[23] The dances at St. Mark's never directly included the congregation, who remained in their seats throughout these performances. Yet, to the extent that they entered into the liturgy and found it meaningful, they too were practitioners of eurythmic worship, and indeed were its primary intended beneficiaries.

The Dancing Body

Guthrie's artistic and religious vision notwithstanding, his critics were quite predictably concerned with the specter of young women's dancing bodies in church. After some of the earliest performances of the Annunciation ritual and other dance dramas at St. Mark's, local newspapers in search of a sensational story ran headlines such as "Girls Dance under Spotlight at Church," and "Women Faint in Jam in Mystic Service."[24] In late 1923, Bishop Manning wrote to Guthrie that he was "shocked and scandalized" by these newspaper accounts, and he summoned St. Mark's rector and vestry to meet with him at the diocesan headquarters. There, he informed them that they must stop all objectionable services at St. Mark's immediately.[25] William Guthrie's brother Kenneth Guthrie, an Episcopal priest in suburban New York, reportedly commented that although he supported "religious pageants as a means of instruction and entertainment," dancing was a different matter. Despite the dancers' full-length robes, he invoked an image of nearly naked dancing girls in church. "There is nothing in bare legs, bare knees, and bare hips except notoriety," he wrote. "I think my brother ought not to defy Bishop Manning by permitting such dances."[26] To forestall such criticisms, Guthrie promised the bishop that he would personally ensure that all dancers in future performances were fully clothed and not barefoot, in order to avoid the appearance of impropriety, but he insisted that he could "not abandon his programme of artistic interpretation of religion."[27]

Guthrie's efforts did very little to stop the opposition from many who were embarrassed by what they saw as scandalous displays of female sexuality, and who in any case would not have supported any form of dancing in church. Indeed, the dances at St. Mark's and the controversy over them also reflect the fearful response that popular and modern dance in the 1920s received from many religious Americans. As the "dance craze" of the first two decades of the century swept the nation, sexually charged dances were increasingly popular with the white middle class, increasing many Christians' anxieties about dancing. Many Christian reformers in the period crusaded against any sexually explicit material in modern dance, theater, and popular dance halls, as they did against prostitution, alcohol, and other perceived immoralities.[28] One paper reported that the dancing "girls" displayed "shapely limbs, so little clad that they might have evoked the protests of clergymen who lately have been objecting to the frankness of certain New York plays."[29] No matter how elaborate Guthrie's theological rationale for eurythmic worship, many Christians, including most Episcopalians, would inevitably associate any kind of modern dance with sex and sin rather than with worship.

For his critics, Guthrie's liturgical innovations raised the further specter of religious enthusiasm. Many American Christians identified religious dance with the ecstatic religious practices of Pentecostalism, and they linked Pentecostals to a lineage of sects, particularly the Shakers, whose religious dancing also seemed out of control (despite the controlled formality of nineteenth- and twentieth-century Shaker dance). Recognizing these fears, the rector reassured his audiences that what he had in mind was not "crude and inartistic" like the "phenomena of Shakerism," or like the current "dancing manias" which critics associated with Pentecostalism.[30] As Anthea Butler describes in Chapter 8 of this volume, the Pentecostal saints of the Church of God in Christ certainly would not have endorsed such derogatory caricatures of their religious dancing, which they regarded as a sign of sanctification—something that could only be attained through intensive bodily disciplines. Blinded by racial and class biases, both Guthrie and his critics missed the disciplined practices of sanctification that characterized Pentecostal groups. Indeed, they couched their condemnations of such movements in language associated with women, blacks, and the lower classes generally.[31] A 1923 *New York Times* report on one of Guthrie's dance rituals provides a good example of how gendered fears of religious ecstasy were applied to St. Mark's. The article described "crowds of women" surging at the church doors in vain attempts to reach a dimly lit interior "pervaded with the odors of incense." Once inside, according to the reporter, several women had to be carried out "half-fainting," presumably overcome "by religious ecstasy provoked by the service."[32] Despite the formality and abstraction of the dances at St. Mark's, the *Times* reporter—like those who criticized Pentecostals and Shakers—associated dance with sexualized women's bodies and with an explicitly feminized ecstatic religious experience.

It was not only Protestants who made this association between religious dance and ecstatic religious experience. Guthrie's experiments with eurythmic worship also provided an opening for a Catholic critique of Protestant enthusiasms. One writer for a Catholic news service condemned the "semi-vaudeville" spectacle of "barefoot girls" dancing at St. Mark's, along with other Protestant follies among groups that he labeled the "Church of Rhythmic Activity," the "Holy Rollers," "Holy Jumpers," and "Flying Rollers." The article was framed as a condemnation of Protestant modernists who sought "not only to deny the teachings of Christianity," but also a "modern touch," to replace Christian worship with "entertainment features" and other non-Christian activities. The implication was that the basic Protestant movement away from the reliability of Catholic tradition had led almost inevitably to such varieties of "iniquitous heresy" as dancing in church. In fact, the author claimed that at least one prominent Protestant leader was calling for Catholic help to defeat the "monstrousness" that was growing so rampant in Protestant circles. This Catholic critic associated Protestant fallacies with a ludicrous and even heretical focus on the body, in sharp contrast to the "plain doctrine" of Catholicism. By linking Protestantism with the excesses of the body, he cleverly reversed the common Protestant tendency to place Catholic ritual on the body side of a mind/body dualism in which mind, and therefore Protestantism, was normally favored.[33]

Guthrie left no doubt that he shared the general mainline Christian distaste for ecstatic religious experience, but he argued that the crudeness he saw in such physical movements was an unfortunate result of the historic suppression of religious dance. However misguided ecstatic religious movements might be, their recurrence in Christian history demonstrated the natural "religious impulse" of "bodily expression," which he hoped to revive in a more appropriate manner.[34] He took great pains to emphasize that religious dance at St. Mark's was tasteful and reverent, with no elements of ecstasy or uncontrolled frenzy. Indeed, despite his evident dissatisfactions with the Book of Common Prayer, Guthrie praised its supreme good taste and commended it as the source for his own aesthetics. He praised it as an "incomparable" guide to "right reverence and liturgical taste," albeit one that sometimes inhibited experimentation. He was always careful to praise the Prayer Book's spiritual value and to follow its liturgy in the 11 o'clock service each Sunday morning at St. Mark's, although he admitted that he varied the morning liturgy slightly "so as to increase the spiritual intensity and effectiveness of the service."[35] The more experimental services in the afternoon, he argued, helped to lure an audience who would gradually begin attending the morning services as well. Guthrie was a committed Episcopalian despite his unorthodoxies, and he believed that the Prayer Book provided schooling in liturgical beauty that made Episcopalians—once they were freed from prohibitive restrictions—ideally suited to bring beauty, vitality, and relevancy back into Christian worship in tasteful and appropriate ways.[36]

In keeping with this emphasis on proper taste, Guthrie's approach to religious dance carefully emphasized the virtues of graceful, slow, and "artistic" bodily movements. One of his letters to Bishop Manning, reprinted in a pamphlet on the Annunciation dance, described that performance this way:

> What followed did not resemble in the least a dance but the performance of the Roman Catholic mass raised to an ideal perfection—the reverential attitudes, the changing of the vestments—here it was the Virgin who was glorified by assisting angels. The impression in review falls naturally under the title of some old religious painting for it was as if some masterpiece imbued with that spirit of religion and beauty characteristic of the ages of faith had come to life. The movements of the participants only faintly suggested flesh beneath the long white silken flowing robes—that same suggestion which one receives from Fra Angelico angels moving in the fields of God.[37]

Here—in part for Manning's sake—Guthrie distanced the Annunciation ritual from the literal body and even from the term *dance*. Instead, he emphasized the gracefulness and reverence of the performers' movements, comparing them to the Catholic mass and to the great art of the Italian Renaissance. Guthrie's statements may be read as a veiled articulation of his need to distance his experiments with dance from the ecstatic religious experience associated with Pentecostalism and the Shakers. His discussions of church music reveal a similar class-based aesthetic. Guthrie dismissed most church hymnody as "nothing more or less than jig music" that "actually pain[s] people with sensitive tastes," and he substituted for them the works of classical composers such as Grieg, Schumann, Chopin, Liszt, and Beethoven. Guthrie's constant emphases on tasteful liturgy and the "high arts" suggest significant class distinctions in his vision for the Christian practice of dance.[38]

Dance and *the body* were not gender-neutral terms for Guthrie any more than for his critics, but for him the female dancing body could have very positive consequences for the church. The prominence of women as choreographers and dancers, both in Guthrie's experiments and in the broader world of modern dance, supports the thesis that, like most of his contemporaries, Guthrie primarily imagined the dancing body as female. Invoking the persistent gender dualism which identifies woman with body and man with spirit, Guthrie suggested that proper liturgical dance could ensure that the potentially dangerous power of the (female) body would bring spiritual benefit rather than harm. In a discussion of the "Ritual Dance of the Della Robbia Annunciation," Guthrie explained that the human body was "potentially divine," and it was therefore vitally important to ensure that the "rhythm of its motion . . . become a handmaiden to the spirit and not a temptress." Indeed, one of the rector's goals for eurythmic worship was to incorporate expressions of femininity back into Christian worship. As he explained:

> For those who are still likely to be scandalized at a Protestant Church showing regard for the Virgin Mary, may we state that for three hundred years Christendom paid its chief homage to her. Later, having cast out from our world of ideals and divine symbols the woman, the Protestant reformers left woman without an adequate spiritual expression, and naturally compelled the unconscious *feminization of Christ* to meet this need. If we have suffered from an effeminate Christ, it has been because the faithful have not been allowed to express their ideal of womanhood in a normal way by the cult of the Mother of Jesus.[39]

In this passage, Guthrie argued for the reincorporation of women, here in the person of Mary, as symbols of the divine. Interestingly, however, the problem he wanted to resolve was that of a feminized Christ. Complaints of a feminized Christianity and a feminized Christ were ubiquitous among early-twentieth-century Protestants, who suggested a wide variety of solutions for resolving this perceived problem.[40] The newspaper accounts of dancing girls and crowds of fainting women at St. Mark's suggest that one reason for critics' opposition to dance in worship may have been this fear of a feminized church. It is ironic that part of Guthrie's agenda in presenting the dances was to address this same concern. But rather than barring feminine images and the dancing body, Guthrie suggested that incorporating them into divine worship would actually reestablish the proper balance between male and female, allowing Protestant conceptions of Christ to become fully masculine once again.

Guthrie theorized the body, and specifically the dancing body, as crucial to the revitalization of Christianity in the modern world. He wrote:

> The dance is the most inevitable form of expression; it is the human body speaking. The body cannot be denied. An intelligent religion will idealize it. To attempt to ignore it brings disaster. What the world needs is not a frantic faith that will suppress and condemn any normal functioning of the body, for this ends in all sorts of abnormalities. It needs a faith that will control the body, put it in its proper place and make it minister to the spirit. Whatever is beautiful is good. Seize all beauty, the handiwork of God, and find a way to use it for the advantage of the spirit.[41]

Here, Guthrie implied that the church was still holding to a late Victorian cultural ideal—the suppression of the body and its desires—that outside the church had largely crumbled by the 1920s.[42] In contrast, Guthrie insisted that the beauty of the (female) body, if properly presented, would inspire a truly religious—that is, pure—aesthetic. In 1918 or so, he had a nude statue by New York sculptor Solon Borglum titled "The Little Lady of the Dew" installed in the churchyard—a very controversial move.[43] Guthrie told a reporter that he got this idea "from the figure of Venus in the garden of the Palace of the Popes at Avignon—a beautiful, chaste figure," and that Americans should not be so "filthy-minded" as to condemn such an expression of spiritual beauty.[44] Here Guthrie insisted that the body and its beauty, presented in the right way, would strengthen and not undermine religion. The body was one of God's creations, and religion should make use of all the arts to celebrate its beauty. Guthrie believed dance to be particularly effective in this endeavor because it directly displayed the rhythmic beauty of the living, moving body.

Guthrie's interest in the dancing body was further motivated by his concerns about physical degeneracy among Anglo-Saxon men. Like many of his contemporaries, he feared that modern civilization had stripped many American white men of their physical vitality, making them dangerously degenerate. Guthrie particularly admired the work of G. Stanley Hall, a psychologist best known for his proposed cure for the disease neurasthenia, or nervous exhaustion. Between the 1870s and the 1910s, physicians frequently diagnosed this disease in middle-class white men whose "nerve force" was believed to be drained by the mental overstimulation characteristic of modern civilization. Hall advocated training young boys in sports and allowing them to play at "savagery" so they could attain the physical vitality associated with "primitive" masculinity—thereby enabling them to develop into strong civilized men.[45] In keeping with this theory, Guthrie proposed that religious dance was a way to rescue "civilized men" from the degeneracy caused by an "almost complete loss of our natural and spiritually necessary bodies." He explained:

> Now, if we are to recapture the hope of the race, we must recover the old instinctive con-
> trol of our bodies. They must become a divine plastic language once more. . . . The ex-
> pressive dance, giving its steady return in joy, begun in earliest childhood, never thought
> of exhibitionistically, practiced expressively with the naivety of nature, will re-endow the
> Race with its physical mobile plastic basis for the life of the spirit.

Guthrie argued that, along with its specifically religious benefits, religious dance could avoid the self-consciousness that would inevitably accompany "any form of conscious scientific exercise." Without this self-consciousness, religious dance could be particularly effective in building the physical vitality that was so necessary for the future of the race.[46] It is important to pause here to remember that all the dances actually staged at St. Mark's were performed by a small group of (female) dancers rather than by the assembled (male and female) congregation as a whole. If Guthrie intended to expand these dance performances to include the whole congregation, he never indicated this. Apparently without noticing these discrepancies in gender and participation level, Guthrie enthusiastically proposed religious dance as his solution for the physical weakness he and others saw in civilized (white) American men.

The Essence of Religion

Guthrie believed that dance was the essence of religion and could therefore revitalize religion in the modern world. Along with other theorists of his time, Guthrie sought the essence of religion in its origins, discoverable, it was believed, through the study of "primitive" societies.[47] Guthrie argued that the harsh conditions of "primitive men" would have required group cooperation, which could only have been maintained through the creation of an "obsessive group mood." Dramatic motions such as leaping, whirling, stamping, and twisting, at first the result of spontaneous outpourings of emotion, would have created such a group mood. These motions would then be intentionally performed in order to inspire the necessary emotion—hence, the earliest dance, and also the earliest religion.[48] For Guthrie, therefore, dance and religion shared the basic original purpose of summoning the spiritual and psychological power of group unity. In other words, religion originated in dance. He found support for this thesis in the distinguished Anglican scholar W. O. E. Oesterley's *The Sacred Dance,* a comparative study of sacred dance in ancient religions and among contemporary "uncultured races," which concluded that the sacred dance was universal "among all races at one time or another of their cultural development."[49] And, with the British psychologist Havelock Ellis, Guthrie believed that all the other arts had originated "as aids to the fury of the religious Dance," in order to create "the spell-power requisite for an effective public Religion."[50] Understanding both dance and religion in this way, he wrote, "one cannot but see why the trail of every religion at least that I have so far investigated, leads back, in its first cult-utterance, to the expressive ritual dance."[51]

These theories led Guthrie to attribute particular importance to Native American religious practices. Guthrie explained that Christianity had originally incorporated "many of the best so-called pagan elements of worship from Greco-Roman times," and that "any effort to revive for the future the joyous youthful vigor and spiritual resilience of the Christian religion" must involve a renewed emphasis on "these precious pagan elements." Because the paganism of the "dead classic ages" could never truly be revived, Guthrie turned to what he saw as the living paganism of Native Americans, which he assumed to be equivalent in spirit to the paganism of the ancient Greeks and to the original rites of religion. Thus, he developed "Indian Day" at St. Mark's. The parish first celebrated Indian Day in 1915, and thereafter it was marked in early May almost every year until Guthrie's retirement. These special services involved prayers and responsive readings drawn from translations of various Native American "myths, holy songs, and secret traditions, chiefly from the 'Hako' for the Pawnees."[52] Underlining the importance of Native Americans for his work, Guthrie purchased sculptures of two "American Indian chiefs" titled "Aspiration" and "Inspiration" to flank the church doors, thereby framing the entrance to the physical space of the church with an artist's rendering of native figures.[53] Guthrie's critics predictably condemned his use of Native American materials. In 1923, Bishop Manning insisted that Guthrie immediately end any and all "American aboriginal" and "non-Christian" performances at St. Mark's, whether they included dance or not.[54] The controversy brought ongoing publicity. In November 1924, for example, a *New York Times* photographic spread of current events included an image of Guthrie and two Indian performers with the comment that Guthrie had once again "departed from the usage of the Book of Common Prayer" (Fig. 11.3).

Naturally, Guthrie was particularly interested in Native American ceremonial dancing. He staged his first Indian dance, which he called "The Ritual Dance of the Zuni Corn-maidens," an adaptation of a Zuni corn dance, at an experimental St. Nicholastide festival between 1915 and 1920.[55] On another occasion, in May 1924, a Mohawk performer, whom records refer to as "Chief Os-ke-non-ton," led the congregation outdoors into the churchyard where, accompanied by Os-ke-non-ton's tom-tom, five young women "in flowing Grecian costumes" performed "the ceremonial sacred dance of the Planting of the Seven Varieties of Corn." When Indians were converted to Christianity, Guthrie wrote, they "acted out their religion in dancing before the Blessed Sacrament, not the degenerate European dances, but dancing ex-

Fig. 11.3. William Norman Guthrie flanked by Gai-wah-go-wah (*left*) and Os-ke-non-ton (*right*). *New York Times,* 30 Nov. 1924; courtesy of Episcopal Diocese of New York.

pressive of their racial tradition."[56] Why should other Christians not relearn from the Indians the art of vital and joyful religious dance? If the origins of religion were to be found in dance, then religion without dance lacked its vital essence. In order to survive in a changing modern world, Guthrie believed, Christianity must find a way to return to this essence.

Guthrie had direct ties with a number of artists and intellectuals who shared his views of Native American dance, and he used his pulpit to support their campaign for Indian religious freedom. In 1923 and 1924, a number of prominent American modernist artists, writers, and intellectuals were involved in a fight against a U.S. Bureau of Indian Affairs circular, sent to agents on all Indian reservations, that threatened severe restrictions on Native American dancing. The controversy centered on the Pueblo Indians of New Mexico (including the Zuni), but modernist opposition came from New York, Boston, Chicago, and California as well as from New Mexico. Many of the leading figures among the New Mexico modernists, a group that included John Collier, Mabel Dodge Luhan, and Mary Austin, had formerly lived in New York. In their defense of Indian dances, these modernists, in language very similar to Guthrie's, described the Pueblo ceremonies as the essence of an ancient primal religion. They suggested that these Indian traditions—in contrast to a sterile modern Christianity—embodied the primitive essence of true religion.[57] Guthrie offered support for this modernist battle from the pulpit, and he intended a 1923 performance of the Zuni corn dance as a repudiation of the opposing publicity that painted Pueblo dances as degrading and immoral. The *New York Times* praised this service as demonstrating that "the Indian dances have an underlying religious motive."[58] Six months later, YWCA reformer Edith Dabb helped reignite the controversy by lashing out against Indian dances in several New York newspapers, and she privately cited her disgust at "Dr. Guthrie's use of primitive ritual at St. Mark's" as her inspiration.[59] Not to be outdone, Guthrie responded by denouncing Dabb in a morning sermon on "The Necessity of Paganism," followed by an afternoon "Indian service" designed to show "the beauty of mysticism" through prayers and responsive readings drawn from an assortment of Native American rituals.[60] Here, Guthrie defended the religious integrity of Pueblo dances by bringing Indian sacred ceremony into Episcopal sacred space. And indicating his ongoing interest in the Indians of New Mexico, Guthrie visited New Mexico in 1931, where Mary Austin advised him on improving St. Mark's Indian Day celebration.[61]

Saving America

Guthrie's defense of Indian religious freedom did not necessarily suggest an interest in radical political activism in his own community. To the extent that he was interested in the needs of working-class New Yorkers, Guthrie seems to have espoused a rather moderate form of the social gospel. He supported those modernist clergymen whose churches sanctioned them for preaching socialism, and he occasionally spoke out on behalf of the working class. For a few months in 1921, Guthrie provided food and housing to a group of several hundred homeless men at St. Mark's Chapel.[62] This gesture was at least partly motivated by a desire to embarrass Manning, then bishop-elect and rector of Trinity Church, a wealthy parish in Lower Manhattan. Modernist leaders in the diocese, including Guthrie, had strongly opposed Manning's nomination to be New York's bishop because of his relatively conservative stance on questions of church polity.[63] During that debate, Guthrie encouraged the homeless men housed at St. Mark's to attend Sunday morning worship at Trinity and demand additional housing at one of Trinity's chapels. When Manning insisted this was impossible due to inadequate facilities, Guthrie denounced Trinity as "lined up with the capitalists instead of with the house of God."[64]

However, Guthrie evidenced little ongoing concern for the problems with homelessness in the Bowery district, which would only become more severe with the onset of the Depression at the end of the decade. In 1924, the radical activist Urbain Ledoux, one of the organizers of the 1921 protest at Trinity, led a demonstration at St. Mark's by another band of homeless men. Ledoux explained that his goal was "to see if the man with a shovel gets the same reception as the man with a cane," indicating that he saw St. Mark's as an upper-class domain.[65] And despite the contemporary ferment of labor organizing and socialism in Manhattan, Guthrie occasionally demonstrated some hostility towards labor unions and radical socialists. He complained that when he arrived at St. Mark's, the surrounding buildings were in "shocking condition . . . tenanted by Industrial Workers of the World, Bolshevist presses and other nuisances." In response, he persuaded his vestry to buy many of the surrounding buildings in hopes of developing a sort of artists' colony around the church.[66] The rector's primary response to the poverty of the neighborhood was not to join in the socialist political struggle that was swirling around him but to try to attract a class of artists who could provide a sort of buffer around the church. Apparently, Guthrie saw cultural improvement rather than socialist politics as the best means to social betterment.

Guthrie believed that a large part of the value of socialist politics for the church was its potential to attract another portion of the unchurched. For a year, a socialist assistant rector led the Sunday evening service at St. Mark's, including an abbreviated liturgy and a short sermon followed by congregational debate on socialist topics. The vestry was less than enthusiastic about these services, and Guthrie made no further effort to incorporate socialism into the services at St. Mark's. Still, Guthrie considered his experiment with the "Socialist Pulpit" a great success—not because he wished to convert people to socialism, but because these services attracted some who were otherwise suspicious of Christianity. In his words, "people who had never entered the church came often to blaspheme, and in the course of a few months had been sweetened and persuaded to consider the claims of religion."[67] He once described his agenda for a revitalized Christianity this way: "What does matter is the evolution of the Christian religion, its control of our country and its duty to see that the proletariat doesn't run amuck."[68] In other words, Guthrie advocated what Marx condemned in the latter's characterization of religion as the "opiate of the masses." In this moderate version of the social gospel, the attractions of an artistically presented Christianity could prevent the specter of class warfare in part by wooing the workers into the fold of religion.

Guthrie applied the same logic to New York's flood of immigrants, suggesting that his liturgical program could solve this perceived problem as well. The rector shared the common commitment among progressives in his era to Americanizing immigrant populations. He frequently included readings from Shakespeare and other English classics in his liturgies, commenting that Shakespeare was worthy of special notice in the liturgy of the church as "a racial scripture." In fact, he wrote that regular performances of such masterpieces were "the most important thing we can do for the preservation of our race character. When America is being submerged with foreigners and their ways tend to supplant our way, it is our duty to see that they become acquainted with our ways so that they may be preserved as racially superior."[69]

Indeed, Guthrie described the "problem of ministering to our neighborhood" as one of "Americanizing our incoming Polish citizenship." For Guthrie as for most of his contemporaries, *race* did not signify skin color in any simplistic way but indicated an inseparable complex of culture and biology in which the "Anglo-Saxon race" was just as distinct from southern and eastern Europeans as it was from African Americans.[70] Virtually his only contact with the immigrant communities of St. Mark's neighborhood on the Lower East Side was to grant permission to a Polish Catholic congregation to use St. Mark's Chapel, a few blocks away from the main church building, for worship services. Guthrie set one condition: that the Poles gradually adopt the use of the Episcopal Prayer Book.[71] Despite Guthrie's unorthodoxies, he understood Episcopal tradition, along with Shakespeare, as part of the superior Anglo-Saxon racial heritage that must be preserved for the best fortunes of America.

The nationalism suggested in Guthrie's immigrant ministry had long been evident in his writing and in the liturgical calendar at St. Mark's, particularly during and after the First World War. In May 1917, he held a "Service of Patriotic Dedication" that featured a reading of the names of servicemen killed in action.[72] That same year, his *Leaves of the Greater Bible*, a compilation of worship resources from world literatures and religions, included a similar service "for American Public Holy Days." Here Guthrie suggested the use of the Declaration of Independence and the Star-Spangled Banner along with readings in honor of patriotic heroes and American poets, including Thomas Jefferson, Abraham Lincoln, George Washington, and Walt Whitman.[73] In 1918, Guthrie published *The Religion of Old Glory*, which elaborated on the symbolism of the American flag as a national and religious ideal. The book concluded by outlining a service of reverence for the flag, including "a dance unto and before the flag, making us look worshipfully at the flag."[74] In addition to these services, Guthrie added to the church calendar festivals to celebrate the "birthdays of great historical Americans and men of world-wide importance in every nation which is now yielding us future citizens."[75] These expressions of religious nationalism echoed widespread efforts by progressive reformers of the day, as in the pageantry movement, to reform American holidays and create new ones as a way to Americanize immigrant populations.[76] Such Americanization efforts, while they are rightly criticized as culturally insensitive and even racist, were intended as a positive way to incorporate immigrants and were in opposition to proposals to exclude them as irredeemably alien. Guthrie's patriotic services are best understood as performances of religious nationalism, sacralizing the American nation and its incorporation of new citizens from around the world.[77]

Universalizing Christianity

If Guthrie sought to incorporate immigrants into American life, he worked even harder to incorporate the religions of the world into his own practice of Christianity. Indeed, he insisted that all world religions were important for the revitalization of Christianity. The afternoon services at St. Mark's, he explained in 1921, were to be primarily devoted to "consideration of comparative religion," including positive presentations of "Vedantism, Parseeism, Bahaism, Buddhism, Taoism, Confucianism, Shintoism, ancient Roman religion, ancient Greek religion, Chaldean religion, Egyptian religion, Mithraism, etc."[78] His *Leaves of the Greater Bible* included selections, intended for liturgical use, from Hindu, Zarathustrian, Native American, ancient Egyptian, Buddhist, and Jewish, as well as Christian sacred texts.[79] In one example, Guthrie's March 1923 "Sun-God Service" was devoted to the ancient Egyptian gods of Amen-Ra and Aten. As part of this service, he led the congregation in a "responsive chant," as follows:

> Hail to thee, beautiful God of every day! Beautiful is thy arising in the horizon of the sky.
>
> Beautiful is thine arising, O living Aten, Orb of Light, O first beginning of life! When thou arisest in the easterly horizon thou fillest every land with thy beauty.
>
> Thou art beautiful to behold, great glistening high above the whole earth—Thou art Ra, the Sun-God, and thou carriest all away captive. Thou blindest them fast with Thy love.[80]

Guthrie made full use of the church's stage lighting during this service, and the *New York Times* reported that "rainbow lights" of "green, blue, red, and amber shades played here and there in the church" while a white spotlight shone on the rector himself "as he addressed the ancient god."[81] As always, Guthrie was committed to a tastefully dramatic presentation of material he found spiritually powerful, whatever its origins.

Guthrie defended his use of non-Christian materials with the contention—a familiar trope among many Christian comparativists of the day—that all the world's religions held spiritual truths in common with Christianity. Since at least the time of the Chicago World's Parliament of Religions in 1893, many liberal American intellectuals had adopted appreciative views of the world's religions and a belief in the universality of religion.[82] Guthrie traced his own interest in world religions to his cosmopolitan upbringing, his education in the classics at Sewanee, and the influence of comparative religionists such as the British rector Sabine Baring-Gould, the British sociopolitical theorist Edward Carpenter, and the American Unitarian leader James Freeman Clarke.[83] He demonstrated his willingness to move beyond simple appreciation by confirming a practicing Bahá'í into his congregation. According to Guthrie, Mountfort Mills was directed to join St. Mark's by none other than Àbdu'l-Bahá, the son and successor of Bahá'í's founding prophet Bahá'u'lláh and the leading Bahá'í missionary to the United States and Europe. Mills became a longtime vestryman at St. Mark's and an important Guthrie ally. He served as senior warden during the height of Guthrie's conflicts with Manning, though presumably Manning did not know of Mills's Bahá'í identity.[84] Both Mills and Guthrie had previously participated in Sarah Farmer's Greenacre community in Maine, where liberal Christians, Hindus, New Thought leaders, Bahá'ís, and others explored together the possibility for a universal religion.[85] Guthrie's theories of comparative religion had their roots in a transatlantic liberal search for universal religious truth. His incorporation of world religions into Christian worship can be understood, in the terms Leigh Schmidt elaborates in Chapter 10 of this volume, as another illustration of the practice of religious sympathy in the tradition of Thomas Wentworth Higginson.

Although some liberal comparativists, at least ideally, placed all the world's religions on an equal plane, Guthrie's loyalties ultimately lay with those who saw Christianity as the fulfillment of all the religions. Debates over the actual content of a nonsectarian universal religion could be quite contentious, as witnessed by Greenacre's breakup over Bahá'í claims that its revelations best represented the universal religion—claims which many liberal universalists, particularly Christian liberals like Guthrie, simply could not accept.[86] Over and over, Guthrie emphasized that Christianity was the truly universal religion, to which all of the world's religions had something to contribute. Just as Christians accepted the Hebrew Bible as the precursor to the New Testament, he wrote, they should also realize that God had spoken to every people on earth and that Christianity had something to learn from every sacred tradition.[87] For example, he explained that the purpose for his "Egyptian service" was "to draw upon the past treasures of spiritual experience and arrange them in harmony" with Christianity. He regarded the service as showing "that the people of all ages were making preparation for Christianity."[88] An element of another religion that was lacking in Christianity might be a necessary "complementary addition" for realizing the truly universal quality of Christianity.[89] Guthrie proposed a truly open appreciation of the world's religions as sources of new spiritual insights that could challenge Christianity to better fulfill its mission, but he was quite clear that these diverse expressions of spiritual truth found their ultimate fulfillment in Christianity.

Guthrie portrayed the incorporation of world religions into Christianity as the best way to secure the eventual expansion of Christianity throughout the world. In his words, the services at St. Mark's presented each religion "in the light of what it has to contribute to Christians who look forward to the inclusion of the whole earth in the kingdom of Christ."[90] The so-called "pagan" services at St. Mark's, the vestry insisted in 1924, were designed to showcase "the noblest selections from the scriptures of other religions," and all such services were "definitely intended and conducted to represent the claims of Jesus Christ on the allegiance of the world." In other words, Guthrie wrote, "All these religions must be regarded as preparatory and auxiliary to the highest and most inclusive religion, and therefore capable of contributing to a yet imperfect Christianity . . . so that Christianity may ultimately become the religion of a united world."[91] Comparing and even incorporating insights and practices from other religions would aid Christianity in becoming more "militant" and "effective," and would ultimately prove Christianity's "innate superiority as well as its greater pragmatic value in the modern world, while not denying the beauty and human value of other faiths."[92] Guthrie believed that if only Christianity would open itself up to the insights of all the world's religions, all of humanity would inevitably be brought into Christendom through sheer attraction to its superior qualities. And indeed, Guthrie's emphasis on universalizing Christianity often suggested the colonialist agenda that many recent scholars have seen as almost inevitably embedded in the Western endeavor of comparative religions.[93]

But, like many other liberal Christians, Guthrie tempered his hopes for the eventual triumph of Christianity with an explicit critique of missions, regarding them as a tool of Western imperialism.[94] In a talk on missions to the San Francisco Church Congress, Guthrie provocatively argued that the "usual concept of missions" had been motivated by "Caesarism in disguise as Christianity, pioneering for trade, creating demands for wares, disturbing the religions of the countries where we went." He told the delegates that the most positive result of foreign missions to date had been a growing interest within "the Christian nations" in the other religions of the world, so that "we might be Christianized via the Buddha and Lao-Tse." He continued:

> It sounds so very well, to make the Kingdom of Christ co-extensive with the world. But if what is really intended is the forcible conquest of other races by ours, the forcible displacement of other civilizations by ours, then I have my doubt whether the result would be Christianization. This scaring or bullying or bribing the world into attempting to "Westernize," "Europeanize," "Americanize," doesn't look to me like the work of Christ. It's attempting to build up a Caesarian uniformity, to establish a standardization, leaving Christ out and using some form of Christian dogma or Christian institution as a substitute for him. What we do in His Name is not necessarily His work.

Ultimately, Guthrie hoped that Christianity would provide a unifying force for the world, but to be true to the "spirit of Christ" it would need to be open to the beauties and truths of all the religions of the world. "The world without variety is dead," he wrote, and a truly universal Christianity would not attempt to erase that variety but would allow for all peoples to experience the spirit of Christ as a fulfillment—not a negation—of their own religions. Whether this stance functioned to support or to rein in the imperialist tendencies of early-twentieth-century America is perhaps a matter of interpretation, but Guthrie certainly intended it to do the latter.[95]

Whatever the political implications of Guthrie's comparativism, what made him unusual among theorists of comparative religion was his emphasis on liturgical practice as the way to achieve a universal Christianity. He expressed frustration with the standard texts in comparative religions because of their exclusive focus on theology rather than practice, while he believed that the latter held "primary significance" for religion. As he described the development of his own work, this early realization was a crucial step. In his words, "The comparison of theologies promised little; the comparison of devotions, on the other hand, promised much."[96] When a Baptist missionary in China wrote to Guthrie about his own "creative experimentation in the art of public worship" in the Chinese church, and requested some of Guthrie's liturgical materials, particularly those involving "various Oriental sources," Guthrie was delighted to hear from a kindred spirit.[97] For Guthrie, of course, dance was the key to this vision of universalizing Christianity through worship. "There is no question, in my mind, that if we could restore the Dance to its legitimate function (and, incidentally, all the other arts along with it to theirs) our Religion of the Incarnation might recover its sacramental power over mankind, and become catholic as it has never yet been throughout the centuries."[98] In addition to all the other benefits of liturgical incorporation of the world's religions, and in particular the bodily practice of religious dance, Guthrie believed that it could usher in the longed-for age of a truly universal Christianity.

Summary and Conclusion

The controversy over Guthrie's liturgical experiments was in part a battle over the boundaries of acceptable worship practices and who controlled them. Bishop Manning and his supporters argued that any form of dancing and any non-Christian materials were self-evidently not appropriate for the "holy offices," such as scripture reading, prayer, and the holy sacraments, outlined in the Book of Common Prayer's Service of Consecration as legitimate uses for a consecrated church building. In defense, Guthrie argued that the general term of "holy offices" allowed for rituals beyond those specifically mentioned.[99] Pointing out that two previous bishops had tentatively supported his vision of St. Mark's as an experiment station, Guthrie proposed that he, the St. Mark's vestry, and the bishop mutually select "a jury of fifty representative clergy and laymen" to judge the disputed services. This jury would attend three services: the Ritual Dance of the Annunciation to be held on March 23, 1924, and "the two Christian services composed respectively out of American aboriginal material and out of the flower of Buddhist literature," planned for May 11 and May 18, respectively. Guthrie promised that if a majority of this jury judged these services inappropriate for Episcopal use, he would suspend for one year "all the services and ceremonies" of which Manning disapproved. During that time, presumably, he would work to gain their acceptance for the future.[100] While Guthrie argued that only the body of the church as a whole could determine the boundaries of acceptable practice, Bishop Manning believed that he as bishop ultimately had the final say. Manning categorically refused this proposal, commenting, "the obedience which every Priest promises to render is to his Bishop, not to select juries, however numerous or however chosen," and that he as bishop was committed to follow existing Church prescriptions rather than the decisions of any jury.[101] Newspapers speculated that Manning would take Guthrie to trial before the Standing Committee of the Diocese.[102] Perhaps the bishop wanted to avoid giving Guthrie any more publicity, perhaps he feared that Guthrie might prove victorious, or perhaps he simply had his attention on other matters. Whatever the case, the bishop never attempted to take Guthrie to trial, confining his discipline to the refusal of episcopal visitation. The standoff continued for eight years.

Guthrie and the St. Mark's vestry were ultimately left to determine the nature of liturgical practice at the church, and these issues became increasingly contentious for the congregation in the early 1930s. Most members of the vestry had evidently supported Guthrie enthusiastically throughout the 1920s, or had at least been largely persuaded by his eloquent advocacy of eurythmic worship and his other innovations. But despite the large crowds during special events and times of particular controversy, as the years wore on it became clear that St. Mark's would never see the increases in membership and revenue that Guthrie had assured them his programs would bring. Succeeding groups of vestrymen grew increasingly concerned about St. Mark's deteriorating financial condition, and in the early years of the Depression this problem reached crisis proportions. An independent audit revealed that the parish's expenditures consistently outstripped its meager income, which was mostly derived from rental properties. In this context, it is not surprising that the vestry then in office were growing tired of Guthrie's extravagant spending on the artistic touches so necessary to his vision for an aesthetic religion, and became more and more skeptical of his overall program. In 1932, a majority of the vestry accused Guthrie of reckless mismanagement and demanded that he cancel all special programs and obtain their permission before incurring any expense whatsoever.[103] At this point, with all afternoon services including the ritual dances cancelled, Bishop Manning resumed episcopal visitation, though his relationship with Guthrie remained quite tenuous.[104]

Guthrie refused to be defeated. The following month, he called an election for a new vestry and nominated a slate of his own supporters. At the election, *he* determined who was qualified to vote, and, not surprisingly, the voting members overwhelmingly elected his candidates.[105] When the ousted vestrymen took their case to civil court, claiming a fraudulent election, the New York Supreme Court ruled that under St. Mark's ancient charter the rector had the right to determine the voting members of the congregation, and therefore the new vestry was legally elected.[106] With this victory, Guthrie continued for four more years as the rector of St. Mark's, although somewhat chastened. He soon resumed some of the "special services" at the church, eventually including occasional dance performances.[107] These services never again received the level of publicity or attendance they had gained in the mid-1920s, and Bishop Manning never again declined episcopal visitation, choosing instead to ignore the occasional dance performances and "pagan" services at St. Mark's.

In the context of early-twentieth-century American Episcopalianism, religious dance was an invented and a very controversial practice. But no matter how unprecedented this practice might have seemed in its immediate context, Guthrie argued for it not as an invention but as a recovered practice.[108] He drew on contemporary theories of religion to argue that dance was the original and therefore the most essential of all religious practices; this was precisely why dance offered the key for Christianity's revitalization in the modern world. This leading innovator of religious dance, then, understood it as an experimental retrieval of ancient and primitive religious practice for the sake of Christianity's future. Many movements have sought to recover and re-store the "primitive" or "true" practices of the earliest Christians, with hopes, like Guthrie's, of revitalizing contemporary Christian life.[109] But unlike most Christian restorationists, Guthrie combined his appeal to early Christianity with a very differ-ent variety of primitivism—a romanticized fascination, common among modernists of the day, with contemporary cultures seen as "primitive."[110] Religions he believed to be ancient, exotic, and primitive provided much of his material for liturgical ex-perimentation.

Guthrie and his vestry attributed the need for this experimentation to the demo-graphics of the city, but they expressed little direct interest in the immigrant and working-class population in the neighborhood of St. Mark's. Far from looking to these immigrants for additional worship resources, Guthrie demanded that they use the Episcopal Prayer Book as part of their process of Americanization. Perhaps it is not coincidental that Guthrie and his congregation sought inspiration from cultures quite distant in time and space, perceived as exotic, in order to respond to the pres-ence of a foreign population too close for comfort (and thus too threatening to in-clude in the practice of worship). Taken as a whole, Guthrie's program of liturgical experimentation suggests that the revitalization of Christianity he heralded was pri-marily envisioned for white middle-class Americans like himself. Subtextually, it seems that the distant exotic was invoked in order to guard against the foreigners near at hand, a way to maintain a place for St. Mark's in the modern city of New York. The practice of religious dance at St. Mark's mediated both between the familiar and the exotic and between Christianity and modern culture.

Despite its controversial nature, eurythmic worship at St. Mark's offered many people a thought-provoking experience of the creative possibilities for the develop-ment of worship, and it found receptive audiences among some liberal Protestants. *The Churchman,* a liberal Episcopal journal, gave the special services at St. Mark's ap-preciative coverage; and Guthrie corresponded enthusiastically with interested in-quirers within the Episcopal Church and beyond. His daughter Phoebe Guthrie took the St. Mark's dance group on tour in the mid-1930s to perform on the Chatauqua cir-cuit and at a variety of Protestant churches.[111] Other religious dance innovators be-gan to perform in United Church of Christ and Unitarian church services beginning in the 1930s. In 1955, the formation of the Sacred Dance Guild signaled the growth of an interdenominational liturgical dance movement; the practice had spread among Catholic as well as Protestant churches. Most of this movement's texts do not men-tion Guthrie, but one important liturgical dance leader and teacher, Margaret Fisk Taylor, praised Guthrie as the first church leader "to sponsor religious dance" and cited his work in her discussion of the place of dance in worship.[112] Like Guthrie, liturgical dance theorists use modern dance innovators such as Martha Graham and Ruth St. Denis as resources, and they too point to precedents in the Bible, in early Christianity, and in other religions of the world.[113] Guthrie's idiosyncrasies notwithstanding, his experiments with dance in worship turn out to have been forerunners of a still-growing movement for liturgical renewal in much of American Christianity. They might also provide a caution about the inevitable entanglements of even the most innovative practices with cultural prejudices of the day.

CHAPTER TWELVE

Taste Cultures

The Visual Practice of Liberal Protestantism, 1940–1965

SALLY M. PROMEY

- In 1949, a fine arts professor in Lexington, Virginia, returning from church one Sunday afternoon, paused to look at the pictures his daughter had been given in Sunday school. The father recalled his reaction to the "offending artwork," an "anemic, pasty version of our faith": he immediately destroyed it, in front of the astonished child, and provided "something better from my collection of prints [and] books."[1]
- In 1958, in Lawrence, Kansas, a Lutheran painter from Missouri and an Episcopalian sculptor from Maine discussed "good" art before an audience of 3,400 youthful delegates to the Sixth Quadrennial Conference of the Methodist Student Movement. Both artists "belted modern taste for its sentimentality and commercialism"; they singled out Warner Sallman's immensely popular *Head of Christ* for special condemnation.[2]
- In 1965 Protestant humorist Charles Merrill Smith "advised" young clergy on the decoration of parsonage walls. With tongue firmly planted in cheek, he maintained: "Every preacher should possess and display . . . a large and well-framed copy of Warner Sallman's 'Head of Christ.' That this is a badly done, repulsive piece of art is beside the point. It is the most popular Christ among American Protestants . . . it identifies your taste with about 99 per cent of your congregation, which is very good for you."[3]

Each of these short historical vignettes indicates the significance its protagonists assigned not just to art but also to the activity of art's evaluation. Like their Protestant forbearers from earliest colonial times, these mid-twentieth-century liberal Protestants framed important roles for *visual* practice in shaping American religious belief. Specifically, they sought to identify and implement a modern Protestant Christian aesthetic, to institutionalize a related stylistic practice of images, to revise the appearance of worship and religious education, and to assert the vital necessity of these new visual standards for contemporary religious experience.[4] This essay thus explicates not so much pictures as the values and weight people ascribe to them, the ways pictures are primed to work in particular contexts. For participants, this mid-century exercise in the prescriptive framing of taste was not about decoration. Quite the contrary: they maintained that the visible outcome would measure the survival of meaningful Christianity in modern America.

In advocating a theoretical shift toward studies of "practice," scholars of religion (and other disciplines) have signaled their desire to move away from the historian's customary obsessions with human cognition and texts to consider, in addition, emotion, sensation, and image—to consider, in other words, not simply the things people think in and about religion but also how people live and do religion. The most useful studies of practice altogether reject this set of bifurcations and consider human experience as their embodied sum. Even in the particular historical case examined here, where the top-down formation and reinforcement of a modernist high-cultural aesthetic set some obdurate limits, ideas, pictures, actions, and feelings were intimately connected.[5]

Immediately following the Second World War, self-described "modern" Protestants hoped that aesthetic discernment would become customary Protestant practice. For this elite group of intellectuals, art was empowered by their humanist convictions concerning its ability to incarnate individual and national freedoms at a time when global freedom seemed in short supply. In response, they sought to habituate artistic discrimination of a particular sort as an actively engaged and consistently exercised behavior, to insist (in a hyperbolic mode suited to the sense of crisis they experienced in contemporary theology, politics, and world events) that the ability to select and use appropriately the right sorts of pictures was essential to Protestant Christianity's future, and even to the future of human civilization. "Sentimental" images like Warner Sallman's *Head of Christ* (1940; Fig. 12.1), the liberal church leadership believed, could not represent a living Christianity. Modernist abstraction of an expressionist or abstract expressionist bent (Fig. 12.2) was the alternative they recommended.[6]

Aesthetics and *taste* are closely related terms. Aesthetics is a philosophy of the beautiful, or a similarly valued quality, including perception of it and responses to it.[7] Aesthetics as a philosophical system thus concerns itself with identifying, studying, theorizing about, explaining, and setting apart "valued experiences." Aesthetics, put into practice in the exercise of taste, mediates evaluation and action, ensuring that actions are valued ones and that values are enacted.[8] Taste, in this capacity, is an application of the aesthetic (philosophical) framework so as to discern, along a valuation contin-

Fig. 12.1. Warner Sallman, *Head of Christ,* 1940. Copyright 1941 Warner Press, Inc., Anderson, Indiana, all rights reserved. Used by permission.

uum, the degree to which objects and experiences of them approach the ideal. Aesthetics constitutes the framework of valuation; taste is the practical, and practiced, expression of it in the activity of aesthetic discernment or discrimination. Neither aesthetics nor tastes are shaped in a cultural vacuum; both are directly related to social and historical processes. Together they illuminate "acceptable" patterns of inclusion and exclusion in a particular time and place.

During the twenty-five years this essay documents, liberal Protestant professionals in fields of both art and religion promoted a particular system of interwoven and interdependent judgments or valuations, hoping to establish them as normative con-

Truth in Art

The end of art is not beauty but satisfaction through experience.

BY MARION JUNKIN

Perhaps no other form of religious art is more saddening than at times more nauseating than the anemic, weak, sentimentalized "likenesses" of the Christ. Neither artists nor most worthy. Remember, we do not know what Jesus looked like. We do know what he was like. Christ was not physically handsome; in fact, that Christ is shown, as being physically handsome, is open to question. Perhaps he was, but he was a Jew living in ancient Palestine some nineteen hundred years ago—a hard life. He could be both tender and powerful in this strength and terrible in his attack on the Scribes. He did not allow the money changers to stay in things in people. He died a terrible death of torture. None of these things do I find in these pictures. Instead I find a prettied portrait for the sentimental that has no character. These portraits of Christ do indicate to the degree to which we have weakened and sentimentalized our faith. We don't like the sermon that hits us, only those vague ones that hit other people.

WHEN MARTIN LUTHER threw an ink pot at the devil, the decorative splash it made on the wall was the final signature to an era of glorious religious art. For three centuries the artists of Italy, Flanders, whatever country and Spain had remained the needs of the church for altarpieces, stained-glass windows, carved pews, sculpture, illuminated books, and anything else that might make an appeal to the people. With the coming of the Protestant churches hung up a "no help wanted" sign to the artists, much of the richness and beauty of church worship was lost. For the artists served the church well and made more real those things of the spirit and soul. Today the Episcopal Church alone has retained some of the warmth and feeling of reverence which the Gothic architecture evokes.

As a Protestant, I know the causes of the Reformation and why these reforms were necessary, but I do not think so much that was good should have been surrendered to the Catholic Church. I believe that when the church rejected the artist and no longer needed his work, it lost a spiritual ally. The church needs that certain mystical quality and appeal that only the church can give. In its beginning Christianity was a mystical Eastern religion and the Western people have very cleverly turned it into a coldly ethical system which follows the exact pattern of life. No better illustration of this can be found than in the ethical imperatives of the Sermon on the Mount and in the disregard shown it by both laymen and ministers.

In many churches the Sunday worship service is held in a building devoid of aesthetic satisfaction. At times I have wondered if this was deliberate. In some denominations I am sure it is. This cold atmosphere for worship places on the minister a heavy burden. If the sermon is a flop then the entire service is

a failure, but when there is beauty, as in a Gothic chapel, and satisfying music, one is helped to feel a reverence that induces meditation and spiritual contact so that even if the sermon is not inspiring, one feels that something has been received. When I worship in an ugly church, I often feel that my religion is being received as an unpleasant medicine, something I ought to take but that actually tastes nasty.

ANOTHER and perhaps more important respect in which the church should assume a long-neglected responsibility is in helping to form the aesthetic standards of young people so as to influence their appreciation for the finer things of life. Art, music, literature, architecture, drama and poetry are forms of expression. People who love these things have inner urges that make them finer and more interesting people. I think, that Christian should make a genuine effort, possible in addition to being good. To be good but dull does not attract others to our way of life. By this I do not mean that we should turn our homes into art clubs and book review clubs. But there are many ways in which we could direct our youth toward a wider understanding of cultural things.

Take, for example, the dreadful colored pictures distributed each Sunday in the church schools. They are made by commercial hacks who have no interest in religion, and are devoid of any expressive sense. These pictures instill into the child's consciousness a feeling that in Bible times people lived in a purple and pink landscape with lovely flowers, where everything was sweet. No wonder than when these tots grow up they do not reproduce the old masters wherever possible. Second, since that the lithograph masters wherever possible. Second, since that the lithograph was sweet. No wonder than when these tots grow up they like it, there are several things that could be done to change this situation. First, if pictures must be used why not reproduce the old masters wherever possible. Second, since that the lithograph are so cheap, why not reproduce the old masters. Third, have the children draw their own versions of the story (and do not be too critical). Fourth, a few large reproductions of the old masters' works around the walls would certainly add to the aesthetic value of the room. Since there are any artists who are members of the church ask them to talk to the children about the paintings and about good art. The children could draw and paint; this develops their version of the story is in the best because it gives a creative approach. Often there is opposition to this sort of thing both in art and in music. A friend attempted to help with the music in the primary department of a large city church recently. She was actively opposed in this, however, by teachers who wished to continue in the set patterns and procedures that they had, and it was immediately to teach the children some of the older German, English and French hymns and carols with the idea that it would be well for them to know good music rather than the stupid songs so often indicated in the weekly lesson. She was activity opposed in this, however, by teachers who wished to continue in the set patterns and procedures that they had, and it was. There was no question that the children loved the better music, but tradition and habit won and my friend was obliged to give up the work.

We underestimate the importance of early impressions and I am sure that childhood contact with good art and music will go on through life. I am so convinced of this that I destroy the offending art work as soon as my child gets home from Sunday school and substitute something better from my collection of prints or books.

I SERIOUSLY doubt if much can be done about the art and music in the church and church school unless there are in each community a few people who understand and know good art and music. Many of the young people of college age are receiving fine training in the arts today and should be trained to help in these matters. For the sake of those who would like to have a clearer understanding, I would like to make a few notes that may be of help, and to show in the illustrations for the article a few comparisons of good and bad art. These examples are for adults and are not suggested for children in the church school.

It is necessary to remember that an is, after all, not a representation of what something looks like. How should it be self-evident but it is depressing to realize how many people still believe this. Again art is not beauty. Art is not what God made in nature. Art is man's way of expressing his feelings, and many mediums are used such as paint, stone, copper, wood, etc. A painting is supposed to be felt rather than looked at. This can be done with a little training and discipline. Lines for instance have many different qualities such as:

In this portrayal of the Christ Rouault is in no way attempting to show us what Christ looked like. He is trying to express what Christ suffered. This torture is a torture expressed in the very lines and colors, not something added to a similar image. The ability to feel and respond to line and color directly is fundamental to an appreciation of art and its religious or especially the feeling must be a disinterest we feel. This is higher understanding but it is worth the effort in the enrichment of our natures and the increased capacity we have for spiritual experience. The end of art is not beauty but satisfaction through experience. To him that hath ears to hear...".

October 1949

22   motive   23

Fig. 12.2. In an essay titled "Truth in Art," liberal Protestant Marion Junkin recommended the modernist abstraction of Georges Rouault's *Head of Christ*, depicted at right. From *motive* magazine, Oct. 1949; courtesy of the General Board of Higher Education and Ministry, The United Methodist Church, Nashville, Tennessee. Used by permission.

temporary practice. Theirs was a theological aesthetic: the objective was not simply the beautiful but beauty (and other valued terms) distinguished by orientation toward the ultimate value and concern of "Ultimate Reality," as phrased by existentialist theologian Paul Tillich. The degree to which this episode in Christian taste making was a true collaboration between professionals in the fields of religion and art is one of its rather remarkable features. In the case of this mid-twentieth-century initiative, a constellation of elite intellectual and artistic actors knowingly invested in the construction and dissemination of a set of aesthetic standards and related practices that they assembled, recommended, and installed. Theirs was a concerted—and, over the long run, largely unsuccessful—effort to style liberal Protestantism, its adherents and institutions, as a high-modern taste culture.

The use of the term *taste culture* in this essay elaborates on the scholarship of sociologist Herbert J. Gans—with one fairly subtle but important difference.[9] By contrast with Gans, for whom "taste publics" are people and taste cultures are things, here taste cultures include not just objects but also the processes of their selection, the rationale(s) informing those choices, and the network of values and meanings ascribed to them. A taste culture, then, is intimately tied to ways of interpreting human life and history. Examining a taste culture provides insight into a hermeneutics of taste. Implicit within the parameters of the taste culture explored in these pages was a set of expectations about the sort of identity (individual and interpersonal) and comportment it would foster. For the creators, promoters, and adopters of this perspective, the appearance of things made certain kinds of experiences and relations more or less likely; right forms would lead to right behavior and right belief, a new liberal Protestant "orthodoxy" achieved through aesthetics. "Good" taste would thus become a critical part of the visual and moral task of religion. Practitioners recommended the development of this particular sort of discernment as a replicable behavior, as one that could be learned and applied to a wide variety of activities and situations. They used the traditional religious language of vocation, or calling, to refer to the cultivation of Christian visual discernment. They assumed shared values and asserted a sharable idiom as the logical extension of their commitments.

This essay considers the construction and contours of one particular taste culture. In this context, aesthetic discernment is the "practice" under consideration. The specific visual practices in relation to which this discernment operates might helpfully be construed as its subpractices. And, finally, both practice and subpractice proceed from an overarching aesthetic/philosophical "metapractice." It is useful, in other words, to imagine many smaller or more tightly circumscribed activities, such things as liturgical decoration, annual religious arts festivals, the use of flannel boards in Sunday schools, and devotional images in the home, arrayed around the organizing practice of aesthetic discernment. This chapter's interest is to examine, first, how visual discernment was situated, within this taste culture, as religious practice and, second, in relation to this, to explore the set of specific visual subpractices drafted to spread "good" Christian taste. Finally, this interpretation ventures to account for why this Protestant appropriation of aesthetics occurred in this form at this time and to consider its success and failures.

Framing Aesthetic Discernment as Protestant Practice

In the 1940s, art and religion joined in a multipronged effort of mutual recuperation. The innovation in this initiative was both real and rhetorical. Neither partner was new to the other: art and Protestant Christianity in the United States shared a lengthy and fruitful past. Broader historical and political contingencies, however, now reinvigorated and reshaped the exchange. At this particular time, American art, no longer seen as Europe's inferior, occupied a recently attained international center stage. By 1950, the contemporary Western art world granted precedence to New York rather than Paris. American religion, for its part, after decades of assault by forces that yoked modernity to secularization, had accrued substantial cultural capital in its reconstruction as the free-world alternative to communist atheism. High art's timely approach to religion thus underscored and accentuated art's own claims to individualism, democracy, freedom, and transcendence. Liberal Protestantism's embrace of high modern abstraction, furthermore, not only distinguished it from dictatorships abroad, but also stocked its domestic arsenals in a heated exchange with evangelical Protestant "mass culture." In modernist abstraction, religious currency might be regained and social class alignment reconstituted through endorsement of a specific sort of religious art, inhospitable to sentimental and commercial interests. In the public rhetoric of the war years and the Cold War period, American abstraction and formalism held their ground opposite fascist and Soviet realisms; and pious Americans naturalized belief as the necessary interior, subjective, spiritual foil to "godless" communism. High (abstract) art and liberal (here Protestant Christian) religion closed ranks as Cold Warriors confronting a shared foe.

What the foregoing sentences seem to suggest about art and religion as parallel but separate trajectories coming together to make common cause is a bit off the mark, however, especially when applied to individuals. While it suits historians to make use of distinct, broadly configured categories of experience, in this case to put art on one side of the equation and religion on the other, things are rarely this clearly differentiated in the daily experience of human beings. Alfred H. Barr, Jr., for example, was one of the principal architects of American artistic modernism, founding director of the Museum of Modern Art in New York City, and director of museum collections there from 1947 to 1967, but he was also the observant son and grandson of Presbyterian ministers and missionaries. Barr despaired over the cultural apostasy represented in the "terrible taste of Protestantism" and, on the basis of his arts expertise, set out to help rectify the situation.[10]

Barr's highly influential book *What Is Modern Painting?* (1943) played a significant role in laying out for a large public the terms that liberal Protestantism would use in its association of expressionist styles, spirituality, and artistic freedom. The section in his book on the work of expressionist painters Georges Rouault and Max Beckmann he titled "Expressionism and the Religious Spirit." The section concludes with a statement on Hitler's aversion to Beckmann's art.[11] A decade later, when the National Council of Churches went looking for an arts authority who was also an active "churchman" to head its Commission on Art, Barr was a wise choice. From his lofty institutional and intellectual platform, he would play a key role in the mid-century liberal Protestant agenda to set high aesthetic standards for Protestant Christianity, to effect public Protestant "reconciliation" with the fine arts.

For many of those involved in this emergent taste culture, art-making itself (especially the making of *fine* art) was a spiritual enterprise. Direct contact with art provided not only a satisfying aesthetic experience but also increased the beholder's "capacity . . . for spiritual experience."[12] Expressionist and abstract expressionist artists obliged this interpretation by using conventionally religious terminologies to distinguish their activity. Abstract expressionist exhibition practices presented art as the auratic subject of contemplation, generally displaying individual canvases side by side in plain and even stark settings.[13] Amos Wilder, Hollis Professor of Divinity at Harvard University and brother of author Thornton Wilder, expressed feelings shared widely among Protestant intellectuals when he posited art as an extra-institutional custodian of religion in the modern era.[14] The gravitation of contemporary art and contemporary religion toward the discourse of the sublime refined the fit of this characterization. Art could be construed as an avenue for divine encounter, a window onto ultimate reality and ultimate concern. The right kind of art, these taste culture proponents claimed, could reconnect religion to depth, authenticity, and freedom, all qualities necessary for its survival:

> Any church that is truly concerned with nurturing the spiritual life must encourage its members to look at exhibitions of painting and sculpture and think about what is revealed there. . . . How exciting it would be if the Protestant church, so long the staunch defender of a free tradition, should become the great repository of the spirit of the creative man much battered in the secular world.[15]

In 1957, liberal church executive Marvin Halverson, writing in *Art in America,* a widely circulated secular arts periodical, celebrated the fact that,

> [a]fter centuries of alienation a renascence of interest in the arts is manifest in the churches, for in all parts of the country, there is mounting evidence that the hiatus among the arts and churches is being overcome. College and university student Christian groups, theological seminaries and individual churches are beginning to recognize their local museums and art collections as a key to the religious understanding of life.
>
> To be sure, the church bookstores and liturgical goods houses are still filled with barbarous and saccharine art. But these ecclesiastical junk shops are being challenged by a new wave of interest in serious art.[16]

The sense of retrieving long-lost pictorial habits across a great chasm in time required some tweaking of the historical narrative; the recommended transformations were actually a set of emendations and additions to continuing practices rather than the invention of altogether new ones. Undeterred by past realities, interested parties argued the case for a particular kind of art ("avant-garde," "original," "serious," "authentic," "modern") against a newly reconfigured premise of Protestant iconoclasm. Shaping to their own purposes a long-popular rhetoric about American Protestant belief and behavior, the framers of this taste culture appealed to an embellished history in their attempt to retrieve and restore a "lost" visual practice of religion. A Presbyterian pastor in Athens, Ohio, registered his conviction that "we can go forward by going backward and picking up the ancient forms whereby man has become a religious being."[17] Apprehensive, as were many of his peers, that Protestants were coming late to the game, Harry R. Garvin, editor of the *Bucknell Review,* recorded his guarded hopes for "a new golden age of Christianity," the outcome of a transformation in "aesthetic sensibilities."[18] A "study document" published by the National Council of Churches issued an institutional manifesto:

> The church should resume its ancient and proper responsibility and productivity with reference to all the arts. It could well begin by purging its own arts, educating its own members, developing standards of perception and evaluation, making clear the theological considerations that are crucial, and at all times insisting on the wholeness of the arts in the sense that they must speak to the whole man and not to some isolated sentiment or moral intention. Even those arts of the Church which derive from the great tradition have been falsified in the modern situation and become insipid or precious or esoteric or sentimental.[19]

This quotation clarifies the extent to which the castigation of past iconoclasms promoted a new iconoclastic episode, at least figuratively speaking. The new agenda was not just a recommendation of religious art-making per se. On the contrary, it asserted a new orthodoxy in Protestant aesthetics that would involve rejecting competing current visual orthodoxies. Not content with simply reclaiming art for the church by promoting its widespread practice, this effort also called for a "purging" of practices and aesthetic values perceived to be out-dated and dangerous. In an address to a constituency of liberal Protestant leaders, Alfred Barr delivered what was perhaps his most withering criticism:

> In the arts of painting, sculpture and book illustration our churches and churchmen seem, generally speaking, both ignorant and blind.
>
> Our churches do of course use art—but what art! Consider the vulgarity and banality of the pictures of Christ now in general use. "Gentle Jesus, meek and mild" is translated into art on the level of cosmetic and tonic advertisements. Yet these saccharine and effeminate images are distributed by millions with the tolerance and often the well-intentioned blessing of our churches. They look up at us from bulletins and calendars and Sunday school magazines and down at us from the walls of church houses and parsonages. They corrupt the religious feelings of children and nourish the complacency and sentimentality of their elders. They call for iconoclasm.[20]

Seeking to implement a strategy of opposition, containment, and replacement, the promoters of the new "modernist" aesthetic asked observant liberal Protestants to break and then to reform visual habits. They sought to substitute one sort of Christian image for another, denouncing the alternatives as idols of conformity and sentimentality.

Marvin Halverson's use of the paired adjectives *barbarous* and *saccharine* points directly to two major, and for these liberal Protestant culture warriors interrelated, sources of anxiety. At that time, the word *barbarous* evoked the threat of fascism and communism, while *saccharine* described American "mass culture." Throughout the 1950s, in parish, museum, and academy, Paul Tillich's Christian existential theology shaped the terms of aesthetic debate with a surprising degree of consistency; and Halverson was well-acquainted with Tillich—socially as well as intellectually. Very frequently and in one breath, Tillich indicted the "dehumanizing structure of the totalitarian systems in one half of the world and the dehumanizing consequences of technical mass civilization in the other half."[21] The fact that many were convinced that the latter (in the "conformity," "complacency," "sentimentality," and "superficiality" it urged on its audiences) veered precipitously toward the former laid the foundation for an aesthetic battle with enormously high stakes. Repeated warnings issued by secular and religious critics of mass culture pointed to *visual* similarities between the idealizing realisms of mass reproductive images in the United States and the National Socialist (Nazi) and Soviet "realist" styles.

The social fears and tensions of the late 1940s and early 1950s, then, intensified and extended the terms of a culture war that, in the United States, had begun several decades earlier.[22] United by their opposition to fascism, Soviet communism, and Western commercial culture, a generation of American sociologists, anthropologists, psychologists, cultural historians, art critics, philosophers, and theologians pursued their own versions of the critique of mass culture in the United States. In the face of authoritarian and/or commercial dehumanization, the liberal religious press evoked the idiom of the "mass" (undifferentiated, homogenous, mindless) and called on religious institutions and religious individuals to oppose "the gray-flannel uniformity of the conforming culture," to be "different, separate, special, independent characters."[23]

The material equivalent of mass culture was "kitsch." In an essay published in *Partisan Review* in 1939, art critic Clement Greenberg had defined kitsch as "ersatz culture," a sort of pseudo-art of "vicarious experience and faked sensations," insisting that "kitsch is the epitome of all that is spurious in our times."[24] Kitsch "predigested" art for the beholder, providing a "short cut to the pleasures of art that detours what is necessarily difficult in genuine art."[25] Kitsch, for Paul Tillich, was not simply a generic name, a synonym, for mass culture (although it was that too). It was, even more importantly, a stylistic designation, a name for a particular sentimental mode of art-making that characterized the worst, the most dangerous, of mass cultural representation. As he put it, he employed the

> untranslatable German word *Kitsch* for a special kind of beautifying, sentimental naturalism, as it appears in disastrous quantities in ecclesiastical magazines and inside church buildings. The word *Kitsch* points not to poor art, based on the incompetence of the painter, but [to poor art based] on a particular form of deteriorated idealism (which I like to call "beautifying naturalism"). The necessary fight against the predominance of such art in the churches . . . leads me to the frequent use of the word *Kitsch*.[26]

In direct response to Adolph Hitler's derision of modernism's "degeneracy," Tillich characterized this beautifying naturalism or kitsch, which he conflated with all forms of contemporary realism, as the "really degenerate art."

According to many "combatants" in this culture war, the development of "taste" itself vanished in mass culture, where aesthetic preference was imposed from outside the individual, not generated from within.[27] This view of mass culture provided the perfect foil for an opposing notion of individuated agency in audiences for abstract art. In the hyperbolic language characteristic of the entire debate, modern art represented, for its liberal religious promoters,

> a momentous struggle in the modern soul to recover depth and wholeness, to reaffirm personal responsibility in the face of dehumanization, to find a true order beneath our

modern anarchy, a true ground for human freedom and creativeness in a culture marked by impersonal tyrannies, and so to prepare the way for renewed human community.[28]

This engagement was to be a fight to the death. Either "authentic" art would succumb to contamination by kitsch or kitsch would be successfully "purged" from the churches and, indeed, from American culture.

Paul Tillich, Alfred Barr, and Marvin Halverson most persuasively articulated the connections between "authentic" art and "authentic" religion. Tillich's theology of culture contributed substantially to the framing and specific vocabulary of the "new" liberal Protestant aesthetics. Proponents turned most often to two of Tillich's ideas. They were, first, attracted by his notion that religious content in a work of art resides most significantly in style rather than subject matter (in "expression" rather than "depiction"); and, second, they were compelled by his expansive definition of religion as "ultimate concern for Ultimate Reality." As a *public* theologian, in a sense perhaps without parallel today, Tillich's reach was broad and his energy for this subject (and many others) apparently boundless. He lectured on art and religion not only in local churches and in Protestant seminaries but also in major institutions of art including the Museum of Modern Art, the National Gallery of Art in Washington, D.C., and the Minneapolis Art Institute. His words could be found in *Life* magazine and *Partisan Review* as well as in *The Christian Century,* in *The Christian Scholar,* and in *motive* magazine.

Over the years, Tillich proposed a number of typologies for religious art, each one a bit different but all in agreement about what was fundamentally important. In 1954 when the World Council of Churches met in Evanston, Illinois, the Art Institute of Chicago hosted an exhibition of religious painting and sculpture, attended by 50,000 people according to contemporary estimates. Tillich and Yale University philosopher Theodore Greene collaborated on the catalogue essay, "Authentic Religious Art," described in the liberal religious periodical literature as a definitive statement on religion and art. A passage from it illuminates Tillich's ideas in this regard.

> Artistically authentic art . . . can be significantly religious in two distinct ways, implicitly and explicitly. It is implicitly religious if it expresses, in whatever fashion, the artist's sensitive and honest search for ultimate meaning and significance in terms of his own contemporary culture. If religious be defined as man's *ultimate concern for Ultimate Reality,* all art which reflects, however partially and distortedly, this ultimate concern is at least implicitly religious, even if it makes no use whatever of a recognizable religious subject-matter or any traditional religious symbols. . . .
>
> Authentic art is explicitly religious if it expresses the artist's sensitive and honest search for ultimate meaning and significance with the aid of a recognizable religious subject-matter or religious symbols. . . . The mere use of such material does not, of course,

guarantee either artistic integrity or significant religious expressiveness. Indeed, much so-called religious art today is totally lacking in both artistic and religious value, despite its use of traditional religious subject matter and symbolism. . . . bogus religious art . . . is the curse of every generation.[29]

When it came to defining what he was after, Tillich used the same adjectives to describe "authentic" art, "authentic" religion, and "authentic" human identity and relations. He was looking for "depth," freedom, honesty, and timeliness or modernity.[30] In his search for authenticity, Tillich placed his confidence in "expressive," "abstract" styles, the antithesis, for him, of the beautifying naturalism of kitsch. "The predominance of the expressive style in contemporary art," he wrote, was "a chance for the rebirth of religious art."[31] For Tillich, Barr, and their compatriots in this enterprise, abstraction operated as a powerful visual metaphor for a range of desired qualities. Its "liberation" from the task of reproducing the appearance of the visible world rendered it a contemporary equivalent of "freedom." Released in this manner from subservience to the superficiality of objects as held by the eye (and the camera), abstract artists now painted out of their own inner "depths," out of "authentic" individualities. Their callings thus connected them to realities beneath the "mere surface" of things. Abstract expressionism, precisely because it made such deep realities visible, manifested "a revelatory function," according to Roger L. Shinn, professor of applied Christianity at Union Theological Seminary.[32]

Furthermore, contemporary criticism explicitly gendered the terms of mid-twentieth-century debates about taste. In 1947, arts professional Marion Junkin wrote, "Perhaps no other form of religious art is more saddening and at times more nauseating than the anemic, weak, sentimentalized 'likenesses' of the Christ." Junkin accused Heinrich Hofmann and Warner Sallman of portraying "a Christ that is not worthy," of creating "a prettified portrait for the sentimental that has no character." Such depictions of Christ indicated "the degree to which we have weakened and sentimentalized our faith."[33] Dismissing the "effeminate," "sentimental," "saccharine," "complacent," "domesticated" mass religious art of the contemporary Protestant church, Barr, Halverson, Tillich, and many others sought to legitimate, instead, the masculine, ruggedly individualistic, "virile," "serious" art world of contemporary abstract expressionism. One desired impact of these efforts was to reconfigure the interior decorative culture of the liberal church, to make it less the apparent domain of women and children, to distance it from the visual program of "home"—and then to encourage domestic religious taste to follow suit.

The configuration of mass consumer taste assumed an American household gendered female, especially as women left the wartime work force and returned to the home. Mass culture by this measure appeared to be a phenomenon related to the rapid growth of "cookie cutter" suburbs, the domain of the wife and mother. According to contemporary analysts like William H. Whyte, Jr., during the daylight hours commuting husbands vanished from suburban communities. Widely read and frequently quoted, Whyte's *The Organization Man* (1954) included a list of metaphors coined by dwellers in suburbia to describe their own suburban life. These metaphors ("a womb with a view," "a sorority house with kids," "Russia, only with money") point out the conflation of femaleness with both conformity and mass culture.[34] It is noteworthy that the church building boom of the 1950s and 1960s was largely an affair of the suburbs, and the same group of intellectuals who promoted abstract painting and sculpture for the church also urged a modernist architectural idiom for new church buildings. "Gothic" became anathema. Protestant tastemakers styled the contemporary church as an island of modern architectural masculinity in a sea of feminine consumer taste.[35]

The "masculine" antidote to "feminine" sentimentality was surface-penetrating authenticity. The trope of the sublime, retrieved, recast, and gendered masculine reinforced the dichotomy between authentic modernist culture and sentimental mass culture and formed the discursive framework of liberal theology and of abstract expressionism. The artist, at the vanguard of civilization, was what every authentic "man" should be in the face of contemporary existence: a cultural warrior, heroic, courageous, revolutionary.[36] Art should express, honestly and directly, this modern character rather than the anachronistic "nightgown nightmares," "pink and blue confections," and "warm, pink feeling" of academic art and its mass kitsch counterpart.[37] "The sentimentalized, emasculated, super-humanized (and therefore dehumanized) Jesus who often appears is thoroughly domesticated, and therefore quite incapable of bearing an ultimate revelation."[38] Alfred Barr clipped and noted with approval a letter to the editor that appeared in *Time* magazine, sent by a Catholic reader: "Well might a man grow weak in faith and careless in practice who has been reared among spineless Madonnas, saccharine Sacred Hearts, swivel-hipped St. Josephs, and gaudily garbed Infants of Prague."[39]

The use of stereotyped terminologies associated not just with women but also, and in some cases exclusively, with homosexual men suggests that these hierarchies of taste served to mark and reinforce more than one distinction in contemporary social relations and identity. The "valued" subject here was a taste culture represented as normative to the white, heterosexual, liberal Protestant male. Of Sallman's *Head of Christ* one liberal intellectual despaired:

> The line is flaccid and lifeless; color and light are artificial and jejune. The conventional upturned eyes carry the whole expression. So it has no claim to artistic power. . . . [It]

does no more than reproduce the fashionable and facile attraction of a movie star or an advertisement in a woman's magazine. The sleek and flowing coiffure is effeminate (which means a loss of the strength of the masculine without achieving the grace of the truly feminine). . . . This is not the Incarnate Word but the cult hero of a culture that can think no higher than an unsexed matinee idol.[40]

Responding to the threat of mass culture, the cultured defenders of art and religion cast up bulwarks against the specific popular prejudice that regarded the production and appreciation of art, in general, as "effeminate" activities. By assigning kitsch a feminized role and distancing high art from it, "valued" aesthetic experiences could be protected from association with culturally perceived "weakness" of many sorts. Roger Ortmayer, an advocate for Christian "good taste," sardonically assailed the typical "layman's point of view," encoded in the epigraph he selected for an article in *motive* magazine: "Art is all right for women and children: I'll take a good baseball game."[41]

The 1950s saw an upsurge of attempts to shield the American populace from numerous so-called perversions: witness contemporary efforts to root out homosexuality in Hollywood and to associate it with communism. Red-baiting went hand in hand with homophobia.[42] Liberal Protestant intellectuals generally opposed the ideologies behind these scare tactics, but they appropriated the vocabulary of contemporary cultural fears. The terminologies' crisis mode generated a strategy of matching scare with counter-scare. Protestant tastemakers asserted the "virile" masculinity of "authentic art" in an effort to reclaim the modern church for the men of America. In the battle against "godless communism," it would pay to have "real men" in the pews.

Cultivating Protestant Taste

At the National Council of Churches' inaugural conference, in Cleveland, Ohio, in early December 1950, the ecumenical organization chartered its Department of Worship and the Arts. The department, headed by the Reverend Marvin P. Halverson, would play a critical role in the liberal religious engagement of art and pursuit of good taste.[43] During Halverson's tenure at the helm, the department functioned as an institutional clearinghouse for the efforts in liberal Protestant tastemaking that had begun a decade earlier. Halverson, a charismatic individual of impressive talent and conviction, encouraged and channeled this groundswell. At Halverson's invitation, Paul Tillich spoke on art and religion at the May 1952 departmental meeting, at which Halverson was officially introduced to institutional constituents.[44] The department's six commissions (architecture, art, drama, literature, music, worship), formally appointed in 1954, came together around a mandate to study and promote the relationship of contemporary faith and contemporary aesthetics.[45] To the Commission on Art fell the task of acquainting "ministers and laymen with a heritage in art which has been neglected and ignored."[46] Halverson and the members of the commission energetically pursued this goal, arranging conferences and workshops, assisting with the organization of exhibitions, making relevant educational materials available to churches and seminaries, and instituting Christianity and the Arts Associates, an auxiliary organization to "provide a means by which individuals throughout the United States would become identified with the Department."[47] For a small annual membership fee, associates received all publications of the department and periodic invitations to departmental meetings.

Examining the work of the National Council of Churches (NCC) clarifies the extent to which the art world's engagement with liberal religion was only somewhat more cautious than liberal religion's embrace of art. The exchange also guaranteed that religion would play an active role (largely unacknowledged in the scholarly literature) in the construction of the aesthetics of American modernism, the shaping of its institutions, and the charting of the modernist canon.[48] Prominent among those who promoted a modern abstract aesthetic for liberal religion in opposition to the realist styles of "godless" communism and commercial culture were Alfred Barr, Charles Rufus Morey (historian of medieval art at Princeton University), Sumner Crosby and George Heard Hamilton (both members of the art history faculty at Yale University), Perry T. Rathbone (director, Museum of Fine Arts, Boston), David E. Finley (director, National Gallery of Art), and Duncan Phillips (director, Phillips Collection).[49] These men also numbered among the most influential leaders of the secular art world.

From its inception in 1954 and for most of its life, the NCC's Commission on Art operated under the direction of museum professional and passionate modernist Alfred Barr. When, in 1955, Barr constituted a small subcommittee to select Christian images for an article in *Life* magazine, he had no difficulty persuading three well-known art professionals (a museum director and two academic art historians) Rathbone, Hamilton, and Morey, to join him. Paul Tillich was the fifth and final member of this group. The subcommittee was charged, in Barr's words, with compiling for *Life* a "list of works of the highest artistic and religious quality which . . . would serve as an initial attack upon the banality and saccharine vulgarity of most Christian art, particularly protestant Christian art in this country."[50] The *Life* article would be designed to reach "not only several million laymen, but also tens of thousands of protestant clergy," constituencies that Barr and his committee believed to be crucial if real change was to be effected. In a 1955 letter to Rathbone, Barr noted his initial inclination to include a "page with small reproductions of typically bad Christian art now being used by protestant churches as illustrations for children's Bibles, church calendars, church papers and sunday school magazines, reproductions on the walls of parish houses, etc., perhaps also Christmas and Easter cards."[51]

At about the same time, Amos Wilder penned a "study document," titled "The Church, the Arts, and Contemporary Culture" for the Department of Worship and the Arts, to be circulated among the members of Christianity and the Arts Associates. Here Wilder outlined an agenda for churches:

> The first task of the Church in the area of the arts is to know contemporary culture and its expressions and through them to know our time more fully. . . . The second task of the Church in the area of the arts is to assess and interpret them in terms of Christian criteria [and here he explicitly recommends "Christian discrimination"]. . . . A third task . . . is to contribute directly to the health and vitality of the arts and a proper understanding of the vocation of the artist. . . . A fourth task . . . is to heal the breach that has arisen between the religious institution and those chiefly identified with the arts in our society. . . . A final task of the Church in the area of the arts is to bear witness to the common ground to which both religion and the arts refer.[52]

By the time of the document's adoption, the Commission on Art had a series of subcommittees devoted to such things as a Christian art poll (preliminary to the *Life* project on Christian art); the use of "art and illustrative material in Church publications and educational materials"; the production and viewing of films, filmstrips, and slides; the use of art reproductions and reprints; and the selection of church bulletin designs.[53]

With a father involved in theological education, Barr recognized the importance of the aesthetic training of clergy if the NCC initiatives were to succeed; he was not alone in this assessment. In 1948 the University of Chicago Divinity School started one of the first seminary programs in religion and art.[54] Other major liberal seminaries followed suit.[55] In 1952 the Religious Art Committee of the student body at Union Theological Seminary organized an exhibition of contemporary religious art and architecture (Fig. 12.3). The exhibition included paintings and sculpture as well as religious architecture displayed in architectural drawings, photographs, and models. An advisory committee guided the students' selection of works. This advisory group included an all-star roster of aesthetic luminaries: Lloyd Goodrich (associate director of the Whitney Museum of American Art), Meyer Shapiro (prominent art historian on the fine arts faculty at Columbia University), and Eloise Spaeth (American Federation of Arts).[56] Tillich, who was then on the Union faculty, wrote a short postscript on religious art for the back cover of the exhibition catalogue. The two students who co-chaired the Religious Art Committee, Miriam Dewey Ross and David H. McAlpin, Jr., introduced the show in Tillichian terms: "The criterion of choice was not necessarily traditional religious subject matter or a so-called religious style. Rather it was

Fig. 12.3. Union Theological Seminary Exhibition of Contemporary Religious Art and Architecture. From *motive* magazine, Mar. 1953; courtesy of the General Board of Higher Education and Ministry, The United Methodist Church, Nashville, Tennessee. Used by permission.

the power of each work to express something of ultimate significance."[57] McAlpin wanted to discover a "meaningful art and architecture for Protestants."[58] The show was apparently a great success; it received ample attention in the secular press. *New York Times* art critic Aline B. Louchheim noted that the exhibition divided "primarily into two parts—-works which give bold, expressionist treatment to religious subjects and works which, with abstract or even secular themes, suggest a style, a way of seeing and saying, that might lend itself to religious purposes or in itself have religious significance."[59] Catherine Linder, a Union student, interviewed artist Richard Pousette-Dart for an article to appear in *motive*. Pousette-Dart commented:

My definition of religion amounts to art and my definition of art amounts to religion. I don't believe you can have one significantly without the other. Art and religion are the inseparable structure and living adventure of the creative. Every work is potentially religious but only becomes realized in itself and meaningful when it sufficiently burns its way through into its own reality. It is this quality of penetration of intensity which I call religious in an art sense.[60]

Recognizing the necessity of shaping taste not just among clergy and professional religious educators but also among new generations of Christians, liberal Protestants used religious periodicals, and especially those aimed at youth and at Sunday school teachers, to promote their aesthetic agenda. Particularly successful in this regard was *motive*, the magazine of the Methodist Student Movement. Its first issue appeared in February 1941.[61] More completely than any other periodical, *motive* exemplified the taste culture the intellectuals sought. Moreover, its audiences of mostly college-age young adults were inclined to be susceptible to the message of artistic nonconformity. Proposing to demonstrate the centrality of vital, creative religion in the life of the college student, *motive* rapidly became one of the most important purveyors of the liberal Protestant high modernist aesthetic.[62]

As early as 1945, *motive* artist Robert Hodgell had produced a "modern" *Head of Christ*, offering an alternative to the 1940 image by Warner Sallman. His goal, Hodgell told the magazine's readers, was to "suggest something of strength, conviction, manhood, and sensitivity . . . simplicity embedded in complexity."[63] Marion Junkin's "Truth in Art" in the October 1949 issue clearly laid out the terms of the high-modern liberal Protestant taste culture. Junkin was familiar with Tillich's theology of culture and conversant with the mass culture critique. Two years earlier his essay, "Painting Faith," only slightly less strident in its commentary, had appeared in *motive*'s fourteen-page painting feature. In 1950, the journal published serially a set of "Tenth Anniversary Art Reproductions," showcasing "works from eight of the world's leading contemporary painters." With biography and commentary, one print appeared in each of eight issues over the course of the year. While all eight of the selected artists were (or became) prominent, two of them were dead by 1950 and none represented abstraction pushed to its extreme. It showed uncommon foresight, however, that the editors included among their selections two Mexican muralists (José Clemente Orozco and David Siqueriros), one woman (Käthe Kollwitz), an acclaimed painter and photographer who was Jewish (Ben Shahn), and an African American modernist (Jacob Lawrence), as well as Picasso, surrealist Peter Blume, and the Catholic expressionist Rouault.

In October 1956, *motive* sponsored a graphic arts contest, with separate categories for students and professionals, "designed to stimulate young artists to individual, creative, visual interpretations of great Christian texts."[64] Winning prints became part of *motive*'s permanent art collection, to be exhibited at their annual conferences.[65] The publicity for a *motive* sale of "original works of art" early in 1958 (Fig. 12.4) deplored the "reprehensible custom of collecting art via the printing press," saying, "we'd be perfectly happy if you never cut any art out of *motive*. What we desire is that you do your best to acquire original works of art!" After the sale, the magazine took satisfaction in reporting, "For most of the graphics the prices ranged from $5 to $35. They were gobbled up."[66] In 1953, *motive* had carried the story of the contemporary arts exhibition at Union Theological Seminary, making it one of the earliest Protestant denominational magazines to show nonobjective works. In 1957, the periodical reproduced a Jackson Pollock drip painting (*Cathedral*, 1947) as well as a Sam Francis abstraction from 1955 and a Philip Guston dated 1954. In the essay accompanying these images, art editor Margaret (Peg) Rigg quoted Tillich and wrote as one committed to his intellectual and aesthetic agenda.[67]

Protestant religious educators in the United States had long acknowledged the particular importance of pictures in the Christian upbringing of children. In an early-

Fig. 12.4. Photo taken at *motive* sale of original art shows art and managing editor, Margaret Rigg, with a delegate. From *motive*, Feb. 1958; courtesy of the General Board of Higher Education and Ministry, The United Methodist Church, Nashville, Tennessee. Used by permission.

Fig. 12.5. Use of art in a children's chapel. From *Children's Religion,* Jan. 1954; courtesy of The Pilgrim Press. Used by permission.

twentieth-century iteration, the liberal Protestant Religious Education Association, founded in 1903, included a department of religious art in its organizational structure and promoted the use of fine art reproductions as part of its educational mission.[68] By 1945, in the Christian educational literature, Sunday school teachers had for decades been describing their experiences with such exercises as decorating devotional corners, children's worship centers and chapels (Fig. 12.5), designing seasonal activities like Advent tableaux based on fine art reproductions, using pictures to elicit prayerful attitudes and to organize Bible lessons (Fig. 12.6), inviting children to participate in various creative projects of artistic production, and employing and understanding religious symbols in the classroom and at home. These same journals, furthermore, carried advertisements for all sorts of audio-visual materials, such as slides sets, filmstrips (Fig. 12.7), and movies. This long familiarity with the educational use of pictures, however, also meant prior attachments to and customary uses of pictures being censured by those who would "purge" the churches of "beautifying naturalism."

Throughout the 1940s liberal Protestant Sunday schools continued to recommend Warner Sallman's *Head of Christ* and other pictures that the liberal intellectuals wished

Fig. 12.6. Bible lesson aided by reference to artwork. From *Children's Religion*, July 1951; courtesy of The Pilgrim Press. Used by permission.

to expel. In 1944 one teacher commented, "for the first year intermediates we chose Sallman's *Head of Christ.* So rich and lovely are the colors, so strong and appealing the face in this particular picture, one sixth grade boy purportedly said to his mother, 'That's what I want for Christmas . . . a picture just like that for my room.'"[69] Writers for *Children's Religion* attempted to balance a critique of mass culture with an endorsement of Christ imagery. In November 1955, for example, Graham Hodges, writing on Christian education in the home, encouraged the use of "*good* religious pictures" and "first class religious art." "In these times," he continued, "we should have great pictures instead of sentimental ten-cent-store material for our children to look upon." He parted company with the high cultural Protestant tastemakers, however, in his selection of "good" art: "There is tremendous teaching power in a large, well-framed head of Christ by, perhaps, Hofmann, hanging in a family's living room. And

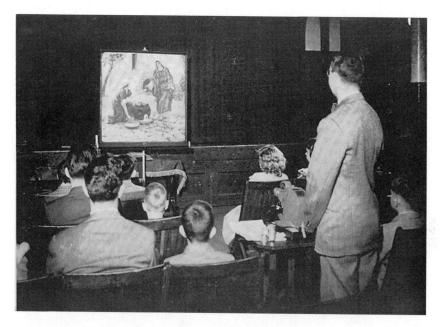

Fig. 12.7. Filmstrip being used to aid Bible study. From *Children's Religion*, Nov. 1953; courtesy of The Pilgrim Press. Used by permission.

what better picture to see as we snap off the light before retiring than Hofmann's "Christ in Gethsemane"? . . . A good picture of the boy Christ will inscribe itself in our children's memories if it hangs in their rooms year after year. Our own Pilgrim's Press has a good supply of pictures . . . in forms suitable for every need."[70]

In November 1958, Ruth L. Bishop, a Virginia-based children's worker from the Evangelical and Reformed branch of the United Church of Christ, offered a similar endorsement of "good art," noting with some urgency the necessity of helping "our children cultivate a taste for better religious art." Still, while she argued against settling for "cheap religious prints" and "gaudy religious pictures that are crude in design and garish in color," she also concluded that it was best to avoid images that represented "suffering" (as many religious expressionist works did). In addition, she compiled for the reader a resource list of companies that stocked religious pictures and similar visual aids; most of the specific images she recommended would not have met the standard established by the modernist tastemakers. There was very little overlap between her "good art" and their "good art."[71]

Despite the continued use of reproductions of paintings by Hofmann and Sallman and the distribution of such images even by liberal publishing houses, during the 1950s modern styles of several sorts made some headway in journals like *Children's*

Fig. 12.8. Cover design for *Children's Religion*, Dec. 1963. Courtesy of The Pilgrim Press. Used by permission.

Religion and the *International Journal of Religious Education.*[72] The result by the late 1950s was generally a mixture of realist and more abstract styles. At *Children's Religion*, it took a change in editors to accomplish a more comprehensive transition to "modern" design. The Reverend Betty E. Stone succeeded Frances Whittier Eastman during 1962–63 (the October 1963 issue marked Stone's formal introduction to the readership). Beginning with the November 1963 number, nonobjective painting made its debut in the pages of *Children's Religion* and in December was featured on its cover (Fig. 12.8). These years saw a redesign of the entire magazine and the introduction of art as a regular feature. During the rather brief years of her editorship (October 1963 to December 1965), Stone began most issues of the periodical with a poem of her own authorship and a highly abstract image.

In February 1959, the *International Journal of Religious Education* produced a special feature on art in Christian education. Vincent Van Gogh's highly expressive (but hardly contemporary) *Starry Night* of 1889 appeared on the cover (Fig. 12.9). The periodical had, for some time, offered regular "picture meditations," and it did so in this pictorial special. The color cover and an inserted color picture section, courtesy of Providence Lithograph Company, reproduced works by expressionists Van Gogh,

Fig. 12.9. Cover design for "Art in Christian Education" issue of the *International Journal of Religious Education,* Feb. 1959. Presbyterian Historical Society, Presbyterian Church (U.S.A.), Philadelphia.

Nolde, and Rouault, as well as by Giotto, Rembrandt, and Ribera. Prefatory notes framed the journal's intentions. Managing editor Lillian Williams decried the fact the "many fine contemporary works of art are still unsold" and encouraged churches to commission contemporary art. Editor Virgil Foster clarified three main purposes behind the arts issue: to promote "a new appreciation of the best Christian art," to demonstrate "the possibilities of creative art in Christian education," and to provide practical information that would "be helpful to families and churches in securing reproductions for framing, and in building a library of art reproductions, slides, and books." Furthermore, he maintained, "the focus of the issue is not on illustrative art, used as an aid in presenting other material, but on *Christian art as a subject of value in itself along with the Bible and with great Christian literature, music, and architecture* [italics added]."[73]

Interpretive and historical materials, replete with recommendations for exercising good Protestant taste, occupied roughly one-half of the special issue's pages. In one article, for example, University of Chicago professor John Hayward expressed his fear that kitsch might be driving intelligent people from the churches: "These weak depictions of Bible stories may well have confirmed the intuitions of the brighter students that biblical lore lacks the blood of life and the ring of truth."[74] In another article, Marvin Halverson explained expressionism's penchant for tragic subjects and feelings of alienation: "The truth is that art is not sick, but rather our age is sick and the times are out of joint. . . . it is to be expected that serious art of our times should mirror the world of the twentieth century."[75] Elsewhere in the issue, Harvard Divinity School's Samuel H. Miller called for the "re-education" of Protestant taste to fit contemporary circumstances. A well-illustrated essay titled "Young People Like Them Modern," by Charles H. Boyles, of the executive staff of the National Conference of Methodist Youth, argued the relevance of contemporary artwork to the situation of Protestant youth (Fig. 12.10).[76]

In keeping with Foster's second purpose, several experts elaborated on the value of creativity in Christian education. Articles with titles like "Co-Creators with God" and "Anyone Can Be an Artist," urged a reinvigoration of creative arts programs in the churches. The authors provided photographs to demonstrate implementation in the parishes (Fig. 12.11).[77] Finally, fulfilling Foster's third aim for the volume, an ample resources section offered information on the acquisition, display, and storage of art reproductions in the churches (Fig. 12.12).[78] In order to further demonstrate the availability and beauty of such resources, the *International Journal of Religious Education* organized an exhibition, "Great Art for Christian Education," showcasing slightly over one hundred "reproductions of great paintings." Interested parties could see the display at the annual meeting of the NCC's Division of Christian Education in Omaha,

Young people like them modern

by Charles H. BOYLES

Executive Staff, National Conference of Methodist Youth, Nashville, Tennessee

"Maze and Chi Rho."

Margaret Rigg, art editor of *motive*, has stated the same theme Nagler treats above—God with us—in a radically different way. Using two symbols, one a contemporary maze and the other the ancient Chi Rho, she has suggested that in the midst of life's conflict Christ speaks his word.

Courtesy, motive

Fig. 12.10. "Young People Like Them Modern," an article by Charles H. Boyles in the "Art in Christian Education" issue of the *International Journal of Religious Education* (Feb. 1959). Presbyterian Historical Society, Presbyterian Church (U.S.A.), Philadelphia.

Older boys and girls may discuss ahead of time the purpose of their art project. A painting of a Madonna and Child may be done to express gratitude for the incarnation of Christ. It may also have a secondary decorative purpose.

28

Fig. 12.11. A girl in Sunday school painting a picture of Mary with baby Jesus; the caption proposes uses for creative art in Christian education. *International Journal of Religious Education,* Feb. 1959; Presbyterian Historical Soceity, Presbyterian Church (U.S.A.), Philadelphia.

Nebraska, in early February 1959, or later that month in Hartford, Connecticut, when the General Board of the NCC gathered for their annual conference.[79] Given the journal's ostensible pretensions to modernity and its claims of Halverson's oversight on these matters, a curiously small percentage of the images represented the work of twentieth-century painters. Reproductions of two 1950s paintings by surrealist Salvador Dali (whose work the intellectuals generally despised for its apparently superrealist style, artifice, and "plastic" surface) were the only "contemporary" pictures. Here, in 1959, the tastemakers' ideal was still far from realized.

Throughout this period, in the Sunday schools, children's production of original art had been an easier sell than the embrace of an aesthetic of modernist abstraction. The right sort of youthful artmaking was essential to the liberal intellectuals' call for active rather than passive engagement with art. In the first half of the 1960s, the World Council of Christian Education embarked on a "period of thorough exploration of the arts in Christian Education."[80] An early outcome of this study was a series of children's art exhibitions. Representatives of the World Council collected children's art, specifically their "paintings of Bible stories," from around the world and, from these works, assembled traveling shows.[81] The Auburndale (Massachusetts) Congrega-

Fig. 12.12. Advertisement for a Sunday school picture filing cabinet to provide proper storage of art reproductions. *International Journal of Religious Education,* Feb. 1959; Presbyterian Historical Society, Presbyterian Church (U.S.A.), Philadelphia.

tional Church hosted one such display and offered a panel discussion, "Creative Arts in Christian Education," at the exhibition opening (Fig. 12.13). An educator in this parish compiled quotations from experts in early childhood psychology and education to provide further insight on the application of high-modernist thinking in the parish classroom:

- A child's work is pure expression—he is unacquainted with pretense—and teachers and parents should be awakened to the treasure before it is lost.
- Coloring books, stencils, patterns have caused more devastation than any other activity. . . . [Children] become so dependent on them they no longer enjoy their freedom and are inflexible—they lose confidence in their ability to use their imagination. It actually leads to totalitarian thinking!
- Children understand distortion! They exaggerate a feature or a part of the body that has the most meaning emotionally to them. This is more important than visual representation. They understand abstraction too. Line and color they know have lives of their own; they do not need to represent something.[82]

Over time the linkage of modern expressive style with "good" Protestant taste also influenced the design of Sunday school curricular materials. In 1955, the Episcopal

paintings of Bible Stories

· by children everywhere

· for children everywhere

Selected by

The Children's Work Advisory Committee
WORLD COUNCIL OF CHRISTIAN EDUCATION

MOSES AND THE BURNING BUSH: Margareta Sundquist, Girl, 9 years, Sweden

CHILDREN'S PAINTINGS OF BIBLE STORIES

Catalog of the Exhibition

1. JOSEPH'S DREAM: The Moon and eleven stars bow before him. Helma Kropatschek, Girl, 9 years, Austria
2. THE CREATION: The universe with shooting stars and movement. G. Kisell, Girl, 10 years, U. S. A.
3. CREATION: Laurie Clarke, Girl, 6 years, U. S. A.
4. THE GOOD SAMARITAN: Soilie Puustinen, Girl, 13 years, Finland
5. SHEPHERDS IN THE FIELD: Miwako Fukunaga, Girl, 7 years, Japan
6. DANIEL IN THE LION'S DEN. Grant Hestelow, Boy, 10 years, New Zealand
7. JESUS BLESSES THE CHILDREN; THE DISCIPLES REBUKE THEM: Lennart Karlsson, Boy, 10 years, Sweden
8. THE HARD WAY OF JESUS: Noriko Sasaki, Girl, 14 years, Japan
9. JACOB'S DREAM: Lucy Bowditch, Girl, 6 years, U. S. A.
10. THE LAST HOURS OF CHRIST: Piet van Dam, Boy, 12 years, Holland
11. THE FIGHTING OF THE PERSIANS AND THE ISRAELITES: Masako Okade, Girl, 10 years, Japan
12. BURIAL: Sengendo, Boy, 15 years, Kenya, Africa
13. CREATION (Mother-Father-Child): Anil Jumar Jeti, Boy, 4½ years, India
14. THE RESURRECTION: Marybeth Shinn, Girl, 10 years, U. S. A.
15. JESUS BEING CARRIED TO HEAVEN: Sonoko Matswi, Girl, 9 years, Japan
16. THE PRODIGAL SON WELCOMED BY HIS FATHER: Lee Kin Lee, Chinese Boy, 14 years, India
17. THE LIGHT OF THE STAR ON JESUS: Yoshiski Matsuda, Boy, 9 years, Japan
18. BEING BETRAYED BY ONE OF HIS DISCIPLES, JESUS WAS CRUCIFIED. I FEEL FOR HIM: Kazuo Ichizaki, Boy, 9 years, Japan
19. THE PRODIGAL SON: Kyoko Tateishi, Girl, 8 years, Japan
20. MOSES AND THE BURNING BUSH: Margareta Sundquist, Girl, 9 years, Sweden
21. PALM SUNDAY: Klaasde Boer, Boy, 6 years, Holland
22. THE CREATION: K. Gitija Shankar, Boy, 14 years, India
23. JOSEPH IS SOLD BY HIS BROTHERS TO MERCHANTS IN A CARAVAN: Monhan Kuruvallai, Boy, 10 years, India
24. THE FIRST COMMANDMENT: Gita Brara, Girl, 13 years, India
25. THE PRODIGAL SON: Kyoko Tateishi, Girl, 8 years, Japan

Exhibited at — THE AUBURNDALE CONGREGATIONAL CHURCH
EUGENE W. MEYER, *Minister*

APRIL 3rd TO APRIL 14th

Hours: Weekdays 3-5 P. M. and 7-9 P. M.; Saturdays, 10 A. M. to 9 P. M.; Sunday, 2-9 P. M.

Opening Wednesday, April 3rd, 8 P. M. Panel discussion
"CREATIVE ARTS IN EDUCATION" — Refreshments

Sunday, April 7th from 2-5, Demonstration classes in the Creative Arts for Children.

Fig. 12.13. Flyer for Auburndale Congregational Church exhibition of children's paintings of Bible stories. Paintings were selected by the Children's Work Advisory Committee of the World Council of Christian Education. Courtesy of Betty Herndon Meyer.

Church's Seabury Series announced "something new in religious education." In 1957, in the pages of *The Churchman*, the editors described the new curriculum: "The Seabury Series contains a goodly number of firsts in curriculum publishing. To begin at the lowest level, the set of 64 take-home cards for nursery class contain completely new illustrations drawn especially for this purpose. . . . The artist, Gregor Thompson Goethals, has skillfully executed illustrations that are modern without being modernistic, appealing but not sentimental."[83] Goethals had been a staff member at the National Council of Churches Department of Worship and the Arts in the early 1950s just as their initiatives in the arts were taking shape. While the Seabury Series was promoted as early as 1955, Seabury Press copyrighted Goethals's four-color cards (Fig. 12.14) in 1957. By the late 1960s, the press had issued a packet of large color reproduc-

Fig. 12.14. Six from a set of sixty-four cards, "All Things Created," representing "modern" design in the Christian Educational Curriculum of the Episcopal Church. Selected and designed by Gregor Thompson Goethals, published by Seabury Press, 1957; courtesy of The Archives of the Episcopal Church USA.

tions, "eleven fine art prints for preschool and elementary children in church, school, or home." Of the eleven prints, six were from the twentieth century but none represented a late 1960s avant-garde. In 1966, United Church Press commissioned seven contemporary artists (Philip Evergood, William Gropper, Jacob Lawrence, Karl Knaths, Eric von Schmidt, Reed Champion, and Doris Lee) to "translate their vision of seven concepts universal to the Christian faith into graphic messages." The resulting portfolio of lithographs, packaged as "Christian Concepts in Art" could be purchased for $20.00 from the press for use with "youth and adult courses of the United Church Curriculum" or as Christmas gifts (Fig. 12.15).[84]

Outside Christian education, elsewhere in the American liberal Protestant church, worship bulletins and liturgical aids and artifacts, too, showed the impact of high-modern taste culture on congregational life. For example, Grant Gilderhus and Wendell Mathews, two young Lutheran artists with bachelor of divinity degrees, founded a company called Sacred Design Associates to create contemporary "bulletin covers, pamphlets, brochures, posters, [and] liturgical furniture," in consultation with congregations and church architects. By the Advent season in 1959, the Lutheran Concordia Publishing House was marketing the wares of Sacred Design Associates, offering to mail samples as well as a brochure (Fig. 12.16).

Throughout the 1950s and 1960s, various denominations and their seminaries held art exhibitions and festivals, often in conjunction with annual or biennial synods or conferences that attracted large numbers of people. Many individual parishes instituted annual arts festivals; this became increasingly possible in the late 1950s and early 1960s as congregations appointed fine arts committees to oversee this work.[85] A number of churches, among them New York City's Judson Memorial Church; Auburndale (Massachusetts) Congregational Church; Hunt (Texas) Methodist Church; Central Presbyterian Church in Rochester, New York; Fairmount Community Congregational Church in Wichita, Kansas; and Shiloh Church (Congregational Christian) in Dayton, Ohio, defined their ministries in such a way as to focus considerable attention on art and artists.

To pursue just one of these examples, the Auburndale Congregational Church (now called the United Parish of Auburndale) carried out an impressive schedule of major arts initiatives under the leadership of Betty Herndon Meyer. Meyer had trained at Chicago Theological Seminary and worked with Paul Tillich during his Harvard years (1955–62). In 1962 Meyer, along with the adult education committee of the parish, organized an Easter festival of religious art.[86] For two weeks that April the church displayed this "exhibition of original paintings, prints, and sculpture by contemporary New England artists." The project began with a letter of invitation to artists who had already had their work selected for the professionally juried secular Boston Art Festival. The education committee enclosed with each letter of invitation an ex-

would you believe . . . .

contemporary artists interpreting the Christian faith?

would you believe . . . .
Philip Evergood, William Gropper, Jacob Lawrence, Karl Knaths, Eric von Schmidt, Reed Champion, Doris Lee—all in one portfolio?

would you believe . . . .
that these artists were commissioned to translate their vision of seven concepts universal to the Christian faith into graphic images?

would you believe . . . .
that they were chosen on the basis of their reputations as artists rather than their religious views? (The **New York Times** does!)

would you believe . . . .
that they weren't coached? Prodded? "Assisted"? (When you see these lithographs you will!)

would you believe . . . .
that you can own the resulting portfolio, **Christian Concepts in Art,** for only $20.00? (If you've been shopping for reproductions, let alone original lithographs lately, this will be hard to believe!)

would you believe . . . .
that you could make seven of your friends very proud this Christmas for under $3.00 each? (Haven't got seven friends? Keep some for yourself!)

Yes, its all true. **Christian Concepts in Art** was produced by the United Church Press for use with youth and adult courses of the United Church Curriculum—it is part of AV Packet 3. This brilliant portfolio of seven 18-by 24-inch lithographs (five are in color) on lustrous white paper ready for matting or framing is now available for general use from United Church Board for Homeland Ministries—Periodical, 1505 Race Street, Philadelphia, Pa., 19102

Fig. 12.15. Advertisement for "Christian Concepts in Art," a portfolio of lithographs by seven contemporary artists commissioned and produced for the United Church Curriculum. From *Children's Religion*, Dec. 1966; courtesy of The Pilgrim Press. Used by permission.

Fig. 12.16. Advertisement for Sunday bulletins in a new line of liturgical wares incorporating contemporary design. From *Response: In Worship—Music—the Arts,* Advent 1959; The Liturgical Conference, Inc., all rights reserved. Used by permission.

cerpt from the 1954 Tillich and Greene essay, "Authentic Religious Art." The invitation produced a hearty response: 136 paintings and 18 sculptures graced the church's interior spaces over the two-week exhibition. Participating artists were so intrigued by the congregation's interest that they collaborated in hanging their work and engaged in conversation with various church groups and individuals during the course of the display. Meyer and the education committee provided training for members of the congregation to serve as docents and guides to the show. Letters of thanks from members of the congregation and the community indicate enthusiastic reception of the exhibition. The congregation held a second festival in 1964 and a third in 1966. The language and content of all three festival brochures (Fig. 12.17) promoted the ideals of the liberal intellectual taste culture shaped by Tillich's theology.[87]

But not every church was like Auburndale, and few parishes had an arts educator as skilled as Betty Meyer. Many congregations experienced a degree of shock in the presence of modern, especially nonobjective, art. The liberal intellectuals' association of modern art with freedom was countered by right-wing political association of modern art with subversion and communism.[88] Many Sunday school teachers reacted with considerable anxiety to the new initiatives in religious art. These women and some men volunteered their time to educate the church's children; the average teacher's training had not included modern art education. In 1964, *Children's Religion* published a dialogue between two Congregational ministers, one in Connecticut (J. Thomas Leamon) and one in Montana (Lawrence L. Grumon).[89] In this conversation, contrived to defend high-modern Protestant taste, Grumon raised and Leamon answered a set of questions about the apparent inscrutability (for many in the

Fig. 12.17. Brochures of the Festival of Religious Art, Auburndale (Massachusetts) Congregational Church (now United Parish of Auburndale) for (*left to right*) 1962, 1964, and 1966. Courtesy of Betty Herndon Meyer.

church) of abstract and nonobjective artistic vocabularies. Regardless of such reassurances, it must have been distressing to teachers to be told: "Go through your picture file and throw out all that is inferior. I suspect this may mean almost all pictures except those issued with the new curriculum. Begin a new file including magazine articles and pictures about the use of art in education. Make your picture file compatible with the best your children see in the school or museum."[90] From the perspective of religion's cultured defenders, "purging" inappropriate images constituted an important activity in the larger effort to reform and refine liberal Protestant taste.

A substantial fissure opened in the institutional churches' engagement with the visual arts when, in 1962, Marvin Halverson resigned from his position as executive director of the National Council of Churches Department of Worship and the Arts. Halverson left in frustration over severe budgetary constraints and what he perceived as the council's repeated failure to take appropriate advantage of what artists, historians, and museum personnel had to offer.[91] In the wake of Halverson's resignation, new strategies with respect to religion and contemporary art would emerge at the national interdenominational level. These would move the conversation in new directions, but chronology puts them beyond the scope of the current essay.

Assessing the Practice of Protestant Tastemaking in the 1950s

It can hardly be insignificant that the liberal Protestant bid for contemporary religious relevance took place in a broader intellectual culture heavily saturated by a theory of secular modernity that assumed the eventual demise of religion. In 1959 *motive* published comments from a Boston University School of Theology symposium on religion in contemporary society. One participant commented on two commonly shared presuppositions: "Religious beliefs and practices are frequently regarded, by both critics and adherents, as having risen primarily in response to man's sense of insecurity and his fear of the future. The assumption that as scientific and technological advances are made our need for religion will gradually disappear is also widespread."[92] In this scenario, religion itself (and especially institutional Christianity) was in some significant danger of becoming a kind of "kitsch" (a last species of the primitive in secular intellectual discourse), a feminized, sentimental, even "emasculated" vestige, the matter of cultural detritus, drained of any real contemporary power or "authenticity." A pictorial essay in the Lutheran worship arts periodical, *Response,* delineated the "alarm[ing]," "androgynous," "Effeminate Church Type" of Christ in its 1960 survey of multiple "Faces of Christ" (see Fig. 12.18).[93] The director of one liberal Protestant missions board elaborated: "The irony of our present religious climate is that while the churches have more adherents than ever before in their history, the his-

EFFEMINATE CHURCH TYPE

"Not Herod, not Caiphas, not Pilate, not Judas ever contrived to fasten upon Jesus Christ the reproach of insipidity; that final indignity was left for pious hands to inflict." — *Dorothy Sayers*

This androgynous type of Jesus has its counterpart in the Hellenistic period of Greek sculpture. Its prevalence in Church school literature and on church bulletin covers gives cause for alarm.

Fig. 12.18. "Effeminate Church Type." From "The Faces of Christ," *Response: In Worship—Music—the Arts,* Pentecost 1960; The Liturgical Conference, Inc., all rights reserved. Used by permission.

toric faith of the church is most threatened . . . not because it is attacked, but because it is ignored." Marvin Halverson expressed deep concerns about the church's "alienation from the form-giving persons and forces in our culture. We have become the shaped rather than the shapers."[94]

From the liberal religious perspective, high culture had not surrendered (as evangelical religion had) to the contaminating forces of commerce. Religious intellectuals treated high culture as self-authenticating; in the liberal religious literature, high culture shared with authentic religion a language of ultimacy and heroic subjectivity. Boston University religion and theater expert Harold Ehrensperger explained, "Good art, like all creative activity . . . even while depicting the commonplace, . . . carries [the beholder] into another, transfigured world." "Tawdry art" (and this is a telling quotation) has "made religion look tawdry and inconsequential for everyday life."[95] The new Protestant art would be not simply didactic, not simply devotional, not simply utilitarian, but liberated and liberating in a newly subjective way and for its own sake. Thus would authentic (i.e., liberal) religion and authentic (i.e., abstract, expressive) art secure their own "universality" and "relevance" in contemporary American and global culture. "When it is recognized that genuine art is not didactic, moralistic, propagandistic, inspirational—and in this connection, not representational—then its proper universality and cultural relevance are established. . . . this same law holds for the Gospel and the arts of the Church."[96]

In the 1950s, taste competed with wealth as a marker of social hierarchies. *Highbrow, middlebrow,* and *lowbrow* supplemented the grammar of upper, middle, and lower class.[97] Liking abstract expressionism functioned in this context as an important indicator of taste-cultural distinction.[98] The mass culture wars provided the perfect terms for liberal Protestants' efforts to describe and reinforce the boundaries between liberal and evangelical Christianity, to aesthetically "purify" their own congregations by installing a new taste culture, and to elevate and promote aesthetic discrimination as an essential practice of Christian modernity. The taste hierarchies that emerged as part of the liberal agenda represented a second wave in the twentieth-century religious culture wars. If the first volleys had concerned the modernists and the fundamentalists (with little direct engagement of visual practice), this new offensive sought visually to distinguish liberal Protestantism from an evangelical Protestant "mass culture"—and art became a primary weapon in liberalism's arsenal. The third wave would not come until the late 1980s and 1990s, when the Christian Right emerged at least temporarily triumphant over a reputedly "leftist" arts establishment that had become predominantly, but not exclusively, secular.

Deliberately countering mass (taste) culture with the notion of an intellectual and artistic "vanguard," liberal Protestants at mid-twentieth century asserted their own taste culture, akin to high culture's avant-garde, as an alternative to the evangelical competition and to alarming trends they observed in their own congregations. The liberal vanguard achieved its classic expression in a study document titled "The Church, the Arts, and Contemporary Culture," adopted by the Department of Worship and the Arts of the National Council of Churches on 12 September 1955 and approved a month later for circulation to member churches and their seminaries. "The Church should have a vanguard," the document maintained,

> of men and women qualified to interpret the significance of contemporary art for the believer and able to make contact with the influential movements of our time in art, architecture, music, literature and criticism. To identify and encourage such a vanguard, to foster its common understanding of the problems involved, to build bridges of conversation for it with the appropriate secular groups, to open channels for its witness and impact in the life of the churches as well as in society at large—all this requires considered planning and organization. . . . The desired vanguard must be mobilized, its members brought into productive relationship . . . with various groups both within and without the Church.[99]

From roughly 1945 to 1965, a highly educated group of individuals sought to "restore" to the liberal Protestant church a wide-ranging set of visual (sub-)practices, each one arranged in relation to the overarching practice of aesthetic discrimination, which they styled as fundamental to modern *Christian* practice. In this context, practitioners and promoters linked the exercise of good taste to a constellation of cherished values and convictions about Christian worship, education, and daily life. Adherents did not seek a "quick fix" but dedicated enormous physical, intellectual, and emotional energy to the task of cultivating religious good taste. In the final analysis, this liberal Protestant enterprise in tastemaking reads as a bid for *cultural* reestablishment. The liberals' embrace of a politics of freedom and a spirituality of interiority and transcendence accommodated the growing pluralism of modern American culture and, especially, new Cold War "Judeo-Christian" alliances. By factoring out "realist" particularity, the aesthetic of abstraction that accompanied and communicated liberal Protestant political and religious commitments asserted universality for itself and its partners. This very abstraction, then, also framed an opportunity for liberal Protestant cultural recolonization of secular America.

While these efforts had a range of observable consequences, in the long run several obstacles proved virtually insurmountable, even within liberal Protestantism. First, for reasons examined here, liberals identified a particular *style* of high artistic production—expressionisms of both figurative and nonobjective sorts—as the solution to the problems they wished to address. The degree of stylistic unanimity was a striking feature of this episode. Scholar and churchman John Dixon, an articulate voice who spoke persuasively at various times in his career for both art and religion, was one of the few individuals who broke with Tillich on the matter of style. Dixon pointed out the difficulty of linking revelation to a single style or set of expressive styles.[100]

Artistic styles are neither static nor uniform; they change as time passes, and, especially in modernity, multiple styles—some dominant, others less so—generally coexist in any given moment. By the 1960s, German expressionism had been long gone from the contemporary scene and Abstract expressionism was becoming rapidly dated. Its high-cultural successor, pop art, deliberately offered an entirely different sort of experience and a different overt relationship to commercial culture and technologies. The legacy of Tillich and his sense of urgency about expressionism, so useful in shaping the liberals' high-modern taste culture, now contributed to its undoing, a result of changing styles. The 1960s would bring their own crises, to which both art and religion would certainly respond, but abstract expressionism, overburdened by the posture of hyperbole and never easily translatable into the Protestant parish or Sunday school, was unable to sustain its reputation as a revolutionary spiritual form of avant-garde art-making, the aesthetic bulwark of the free world.

A second obstacle to success over time had to do with the inclination of both religious and secular intellectuals to interpret the "sentimental" popular art of "mass culture" in terms of their fears about modernity rather than through any consultation with its actual audiences.[101] The promoters of the high-modern taste culture knew little or nothing about what the person in the pew made of Heinrich Hofmann or Warner Sallman (let alone Emil Nolde or Georges Rouault). The tastemakers knew the place of their own high-cultural evaluated forms within the larger ideology of mass culture, but they did not sufficiently acknowledge the actual roles and situation of "mass" evaluated forms within the day-to-day practice of Protestant Christians. And while, by urging and educating modern taste, they offered new forms to Protestant Christianity, their replacement strategy stalled at the level of parish and home. The result was a new mix of styles, not the substitution of one style for another.

The characterizations that led liberals to reject "beautifying naturalism" should not be confused with the attributes valued by this art's supporters. Barr assumed that some combination of ignorance, passivity, and captivity to commerce accounted for Protestantism's "terrible" taste. Educate the people in the pews, empower them to make a choice, and offer them inexpensive prints of "superior" art, and they would happily abandon their "kitsch." Appreciators of Sallman's *Head of Christ,* however, were not so easily dissuaded; they reported highly individual and personalized responses to reproductions of the beloved painting.

It is possible, even likely, furthermore, that abstract styles, while they could do certain things well, did other things only very poorly. Subjects of violence and agony, characteristic of twentieth-century expressionisms, seemed emphatically out of place in early childhood education, where experts in Christian pedagogy advised that it was "best to stay clear of involved theology, suffering, and symbolism."[102] Furthermore, Sunday schools needed pictures of an identifiable Jesus. A taste culture geared to adult intellectuals had little to say to kindergartners. Thus, even for those who shared the values promoted by the liberal seminaries and the National Council of Churches, some "realist" images (deemed, according to the values of this high-modern taste culture, to be substandard) were tolerated, even celebrated, because they fulfilled certain needs and expectations that abstraction did not. While, typically, the liberal Protestant culture warriors charting the course were men, overwhelmingly it was women—Christian educators and Sunday school teachers—who were charged with implementation at the parish level and who found themselves addressing the gap between prescriptions from above and the real needs of children in the classroom. (And here contemporary gender politics surely contributed to the disjunction.)

Edith Wyschogrod's clarification of the double meaning of the verb *to value* marks a fairly subtle, but nonetheless useful, distinction. The sense of *valuing* as prizing or cherishing, as affective or emotive work, operated most powerfully in the context of the Sunday schools' selection of pictures. For the intellectual elite, on the other hand, while affective response was not inconsequential, the mechanism of valuation most insistently employed was one that ranked, assessed, and assigned hierarchies of worth to the modernist artifacts of high culture in opposition to the products of so-called mass culture.[103] While the Sunday schools adopted the *rhetoric* of aesthetic hierarchy, *in practice* they accommodated a much wider range of images than the intellectuals were willing to allow; and, in the end, Christian educators were perhaps the more discerning audience for the multiplicity of alternatives available to the religious imagination. Local contentions of various sorts suggest a range of concerns about the implementation of abstraction in Protestant religious life—and about the replacement of pictures formerly valued. It would be instructive, having reached the end of this story of the 1950s efflorescence of visual practices in liberal Protestantism, to begin again and, this time, work in the opposite direction: to start with the experience of the people in the pews, to tell the story from the bottom up. The narrative would clearly differ; the trick would be to see if the "bottom-up" and the "top-down" versions ever managed to meet somewhere in the middle.

Whatever the directional perspective, however, the particular disposition of categorical relations that characterized the 1950s no longer pertained a decade later. In the 1960s, significant shifts along a number of cultural variables modified high-cultural reactions to mass culture. In the 1940s and 1950s critics connected certain kinds of elevated art to a larger humanistic vision, a vision that "lower" images—by appealing to an imagined and feared population of inert and complacent beholders—appeared to thwart. The 1960s produced a revolt against this sort of cultural pessimism. "Cultural populists" reactivated the audiences of "mass" culture.[104] In the process they retrieved and took as their subject the more benign, and here even celebratory, label *popular* culture, and they asserted their conviction of its potentially liberating possibilities.[105] Both the optimism of the countercultural New Left and the pessimism of the mass culture critique were predicated on problematic assumptions about the political and social implications of entire classes of artistic production. Both extremes asserted their own commitments to a truly democratic art. For the liberal Protestant high-modern tastemakers of the 1950s, authentically democratic art, with its accent on subjectivity and individual freedom, was mediated from above. For the cultural populists of the 1960s and 1970s, it was produced by engagement with the people rising up from below, people whose action thus constituted popular art as a subversive, grassroots phenomenon.[106]

Perhaps thanks in part to the door opened to it in the 1950s, art in the later 1960s and through the 1970s, differently inflected by the civil rights and anti–Vietnam War movements, would make significant headway in local liberal parishes through its association with social action ministries, especially for youth and in the Sunday schools (Fig. 12.19). Making the right visual choices still mattered, but this was an art tied to human activity rather than to a particularly refined way of "being," to Christian behavior rather than to Christian taste.[107] The 1960s reappropriated aspects of the social gospel movement that Tillich and his aesthetically influential contemporaries had more or less dismissed. It is indicative of this shift in emphasis and vision that in January 1968 *Children's Religion* ceased publication and *Colloquy* (a periodical of the United Church of Christ and the United Presbyterian Church) took its place. *Colloquy* would address "education in church and society" rather than "children's religion in home and church"; its professional contemporary design, consistent with the poster art of late 1960s youth culture, announced this intention (Fig. 12.20).[108] Using art to accomplish something as a Christian community, to communicate a call to social action that was informed and in some cases directed by youth culture, seemed to promise a more visible result and to offer a clearer mandate than the practice of Protestant aesthetic discernment for the sake of the more abstract concepts of human freedom and authenticity. The recommendations from liberal intellectuals had been geared to helping people select the right art: everything else, they believed, would follow from refined aesthetic discrimination. In the liberal parish, however, the message

MICAELA MYERS

Illustration for a new confirmation series to be published in January, 1968, for use in the United Church of Christ. Here photography is used "to create visual metaphor capable of calling out from the reader his own answer to the questions."

Fig. 12.19. Recommended style of illustration for the new United Church of Christ confirmation curriculum. From *Children's Religion*, Dec. 1967; courtesy of The Pilgrim Press. Used by permission.

Fig. 12.20. Projected cover design for the inaugural issue of *Colloquy,* successor to *Children's Religion.* From *Children's Religion,* December 1967; courtesy of The Pilgrim Press. Used by permission.

that replaced the one advanced by the Protestant mass culture critique, the new artistic impulse that took hold and flourished, at least for a time, was one that embraced practices of creativity and imagination newly framed in relation to the exercise of Christian agency in human society.

The shift from discernment to action was, of course, a matter of emphasis. The 1950s intellectuals were intensely concerned with individual human initiative in the world. When it came to the task of implementation, *motive* magazine, for example, from its very inception documented Protestantism's engagement in social justice, civil rights, and peace-making activities. At least as concerns the practice of Christian good taste, however, many appeared to feel fairly certain that change would be inaugurated from "above" by a small, expert, and expertly discriminating elite, and that selecting the right art, on its own, could produce the right sorts of human being, reflection, and behavior. In the 1960s and 1970s, by contrast, change would arise from "below," from the energized and newly articulate "masses" reconfigured to represent a powerful "grassroots" initiative. Art would, of course, participate in this mobilization, but right action in human society took precedence over the selection of the right objects.

Preface

1. David Hall, ed., *Lived Religion in America: Toward a History of Practice* (Princeton: Princeton University Press, 1997); Colleen McDannell, ed., *Religions of the United States in Practice*, 2 vols. (Princeton University Press, 2001); Michael D. McNally, "The Practice of Native American Christianity," *Church History* 69 (2000): 834–59; James O'Toole, ed., *Habits of Devotion: Catholic Religious Practice in Twentieth-Century America* (Ithaca, N.Y.: Cornell University Press, 2004); Robert Wuthnow, *After Heaven: Spirituality in America since the 1950s* (Berkeley: University of California Press, 1998).

Introduction

1. David Hall, ed., *Lived Religion in America: Toward a History of Practice* (Princeton: Princeton University Press, 1997), xi.

2. Pierre Bourdieu, *Outline of a Theory of Practice*, trans. Richard Nice (Cambridge: Cambridge University Press, 1977), 20; Pierre Bourdieu, *The Logic of Practice*, trans. Richard Nice (Stanford: Stanford University Press, 1990), 53. See also Michel de Certeau, *The Practice of Everyday Life*, trans. Stephen Rendall (Berkeley: University of California Press, 1984); Catherine Bell, *Ritual Theory, Ritual Practice* (New York: Oxford University Press, 1992); Sherry B. Ortner, "Theory in Anthropology since the Sixties," *Comparative Studies in Society and History* 26 (1984): 126–66; Talal Asad, "Reading a Modern Classic: W. C. Smith's *The Meaning and End of Religion*," *History of Religions* 40 (2001): 205–21.

3. Catherine M. Bell, *Ritual: Perspectives and Dimensions* (New York: Oxford University Press, 1997), 76–77.

4. Dorothy C. Bass, ed., *Practicing Our Faith* (San Francisco: Jossey-Bass, 1997); Dorothy C. Bass and Miroslav Volf, eds., *Practicing Theology: Beliefs and Practices in Christian Life* (Grand Rapids: Eerdmans, 2001); Craig Dykstra, *Growing in the Life of Faith: Education and Christian Practices* (Louisville: Geneva, 1999); Richard J. Foster, *Celebration of Discipline: The Path to Spiritual Growth, 25th Anniversary Edition* (San Francisco: HarperSanFrancisco, 1988); John Ortberg, *If You Want to Walk on Water, You've Got to Get Out of the Boat* (Grand Rapids: Zondervan, 2001).

5. Bass, *Practicing Our Faith,* xi.

6. Aristotle, Book II, chaps. 3–6, *Nicomachean Ethics,* trans. Martin Ostwald (Englewood Cliffs, N.J.: Prentice Hall, 1962).

7. Alasdair MacIntyre, *After Virtue: A Study in Moral Theory* (Notre Dame, Ind.: University of Notre Dame Press, 1984).

8. For a critical appraisal of the ways in which recent work on pastoral care and Christian practice assumes a core tradition that is "unified, essentially good, and therefore authoritative" rather than "contradictory and oppressive," see Roy Steinholl Smith, "White Man's Burden: Recent Thought about Christian Practice," *Religious Studies Review* 21, no. 3 (July 1995), 192–95.

9. For a recent summary statement about the concept of "embodied wisdom," see Trudy Bush, "A Way to Live: The Shape of Christian Existence," *Christian Century,* 24 Feb. 2004, 22–29.

10. Robert Orsi, "Everyday Miracles: The Study of Lived Religion," in David D. Hall, ed., *Lived Religion in America: Toward a History of Practice* (Princeton: Princeton University Press, 1997), 3–21; quote from 11. In the same volume, Hall surveys practice as a field that encompasses culture, custom, improvisation, and resistance: "Introduction" to *Lived Religion,* vii–xiii.

11. Colleen McDannell, ed., *Religions in the United States in Practice,* 2 vols. (Princeton: Princeton University Press, 2001). See esp. McDannell's "Introduction," 1:1–8.

12. Charles Hambrick-Stowe, *The Practice of Piety: Puritan Devotional Disciplines in Seventeenth-Century New England* (Chapel Hill: University of North Carolina Press, 1986); Susan Karant-Nunn, *The Reformation of Ritual: An Interpretation of Early Modern Germany* (Christianity and Society in the Modern World) (London: Routledge, 1997); Raymond A. Mentzer, ed., *Sin and the Calvinists: Morals Control and the Consistory in the Reformed Tradition* (Sixteenth Century Essays and Studies, vol. 32) (Kirksville, Mo.: Truman State University Press, 1994); Merry E. Wiesner, ed., *Christianity and Sexuality in the Early Modern World: Regulating Desire, Reforming Practice* (New York: Routledge, 2000).

13. For the widespread economic, social, and legal changes during the New England Enlightenment period and their connection to evangelical Protestantism, see the essays by John Walsh, Susan O'Brian, and Harry S. Stout, in Mark A. Noll, David W. Bebbington, and George A. Rawlyk, eds., *Evangelicalism: Comparative Studies of Popular Protestantism in North America, the British Isles, and Beyond, 1700–1990* (New York: Oxford University Press, 1994). For intellectual shifts, see Hugh Amory and David D. Hall, eds., *A History of the Book in America,* vol. 1, *The Colonial Book in the Atlantic World* (Cambridge: Cambridge University Press, 1999); and Daniel Walker Howe, *Making the American Self: Jonathan Edwards to Abraham Lincoln* (Cambridge: Harvard University Press, 1997). For the Enlightenment as a cultural movement, see Roy Porter, *The Creation of the Modern World: The Untold Story of the British Enlightenment* (New York: W. W. Norton, 2000). For increasing religious pluralism, see Jon Butler, *Awash in a Sea of Faith: Christianizing the American People* (Studies in Cultural History) (Cambridge: Harvard University Press, 1992).

14. On nineteenth-century revivalism, see John Corrigan, *Business of the Heart: Religion and Emotion in the Nineteenth Century* (Berkeley: University of California Press, 2001); Nathan Hatch, *The Democratization of American Christianity* (New Haven: Yale University Press, 1989); Ann Taves, *Fits, Trances, and Visions: Experiencing Religion and Explaining Experience from Wesley to James* (Princeton: Princeton University Press, 1999).

15. On academic culture and scientific challenges, see James Turner, *Without God, Without*

Creed: The Origins of Unbelief in America (Baltimore: Johns Hopkins University Press, 1985). On religious doctrine, see Robert Bruce Mullin, *Miracles and the Modern Religious Imagination* (New Haven: Yale University Press, 1996). For other religious responses around the turn of the twentieth century, see: for modernism, William R. Hutchison, *The Modernist Impulse in American Protestantism* (Cambridge: Harvard University Press, 1976); for fundamentalism, George M. Marsden, *Fundamentalism and American Culture: The Shaping of Twentieth-Century Evangelicalism, 1870–1925* (New York: Oxford University Press, 1980); for Pentecostalism, Grant Wacker, *Heaven Below: Early Pentecostalism and American Culture* (Cambridge: Harvard University Press, 2001).

One • *Writing as a Protestant Practice*

I am grateful to all the members of the History of Christian Practice Project, especially Mark Valeri, Sally Promey, and Heather Curtis for their close readings of my essay. I would also like to thank Clark Gilpin for his helpful criticisms, Sarah Rivett for sharing her fascinating dissertation research with me, and Kathryn Lofton for all of her help throughout the project.

1. Sarah Osborn, Diaries and Memoir, 1757–1769, Beinecke Rare Book and Manuscript Library, Yale University, New Haven, Conn. Diary entry for 24 Apr. 1757. The description of how Sarah wrote her diaries comes from her letter to Joseph Fish of 7 March 1767, in Sarah Osborn, Letters, 1743–1770, 1779, American Antiquarian Society, Worcester, Massachusetts.

2. Sarah Osborn, Diary #15 (1754), undated entry at end of diary, p. 129, Connecticut Historical Society, Hartford. According to Hopkins, "the least" of Osborn's fifty volumes of diaries contained "near 100 pages, the bigger part above 200, and a number 300," and she also wrote "letters to her friends, and other occasional writing." See Samuel Hopkins, ed., *Memoirs of the Life of Mrs. Sarah Osborn* (Worcester, Mass.: Leonard Worcester, 1799), 358. The approximately 1,500 pages of surviving diaries have been preserved in the following collections: Sarah Osborn, Diaries, 1753–1772, Newport Historical Society, Newport, R.I.; Sarah Osborn, Diaries and Memoir, 1757–1769, Beinecke Rare Book and Manuscript Library, Yale University, New Haven, Conn.; Osborn, Letters, 1743–1770, 1779; and Sarah Osborn, Diaries, 1754, 1760–1761, Connecticut Historical Society, Hartford; Samuel Hopkins, ed., *Familiar Letters, Written by Mrs. Sarah Osborn and Miss Susanna Anthony, Late of Newport, Rhode Island* (Newport: Newport Mercury, 1807).

3. Winthrop's annals were published in the nineteenth century as *History of New England*. John Winthrop, "Experiencia," in *Life and Letters of John Winthrop*, ed. Robert C. Winthrop (Boston: Ticknor and Fields, 1864), vol. 1, p. 73. For a full discussion of Winthrop's writings, see David Sanford Shields, "A History of Personal Diary Writing in New England, 1620–1745" (Ph.D. diss., University of Chicago, 1982), 37–78. Other good overviews of early spiritual memoirs are Charles Hambrick-Stowe, *The Practice of Piety: Puritan Devotional Disciplines in Seventeenth-Century New England* (Chapel Hill: University of North Carolina Press, 1982); Jon Alexander, *American Personal Religious Accounts, 1600–1980: Toward an Inner History of America's Faiths* (New York: Edwin Millen Press, 1983); and Daniel B. Shea, Jr., *Spiritual Autobiography in Early America* (Princeton: Princeton University Press, 1968).

4. Winthrop, "Experiencia," 79–80; Hambrick-Stowe, *Practice of Piety*, 45.

5. See Exodus 17:14, Jeremiah 30:2, and Habakkuk 2:1–2. Puritans believed that it was because of human imperfection that God had chosen to reveal himself in the written form of the

Bible, which they saw as an unchanging, objective record of his will. See Shields, "History of Diary Writing," 72.

6. John Flavel, *The Mystery of Providence* (1678; London: Banner of Truth Trust, 1963), 220.

7. Charles Hambrick-Stowe suggests that personal journals share affinities with the "literature of journey." See *Practice of Piety,* 191–93. Edmund Morgan describes Michael Wigglesworth's diary as "a kind of account-book in which he rendered up the assets and liabilities of his soul, with the debit side of the ledger receiving almost all the entries." Edmund Morgan, ed., *The Diary of Michael Wigglesworth, 1653–1657: The Conscience of a Puritan* (New York: Harper and Row, 1946), vii.

8. Cotton Mather, *Bonifacius: An Essay Upon the Good,* ed. David Levin (1710; Cambridge: Harvard University Press, 1966), 35.

9. On the influence of Bacon, see Christopher Hill, *Intellectual Origins of the English Revolution Revisited* (Oxford: Clarendon Press, 1997), 77–117. Baird Tipson, "The Routinized Piety of Thomas Shepard's Diary," *Early American Literature* 13 (1978): 66; Michael McGiffert, ed., *God's Plot: The Paradoxes of Puritan Piety Being the Autobiography and Journal of Thomas Shepard* (Amherst: University of Massachusetts Press, 1972), 117, 83.

10. Stephen E. Toulmin, *Cosmopolis: The Hidden Agenda of Modernity* (Chicago: University of Chicago Press, 1990).

11. Charles Lloyd Cohen, *God's Caress: The Psychology of Puritan Religious Experience* (New York: Oxford University Press, 1986), 110.

12. On Puritan attitudes toward assurance, see Norman Pettit, "Hooker's Doctrine of Assurance: A Critical Phase in New England Spiritual Thought," *The New England Quarterly* 47, no. 4 (Dec. 1974): 518–34; Henry Scudder, *The Christians Daily Walke* (London: I. Beale, 1631); Thomas Hooker, "The Character of a Sound Christian in Seventeen Marks," in his *Paterne of Perfection* (London: R. Young, 1640), 376–92, and Norman Pettit, *The Heart Renewed: Assurance of Salvation in New England Spiritual Life* (Lewiston, N.Y.: Edwin Mellen Press, 2004). Patricia Caldwell argues that Puritan conversion narratives were characterized by ambivalence, open-endedness, and lack of assurance. See Patricia Caldwell, *The Puritan Conversion Narrative: The Beginnings of American Expression* (New York: Cambridge University Press, 1983), 34.

13. Increase Mather, *Diary, March, 1675–December, 1676. Together with Extracts from Another Diary by Him, 1674–1687,* ed. Samuel A. Green (Cambridge, Mass., 1900), 32, quoted in Hambrick-Stowe, *Practice of Piety,* 170.

14. Shields, "History of Diary Writing," 72–73. On the new, positive idea of selfhood in the nineteenth century, see Daniel Walker Howe, *Making the American Self: Jonathan Edwards to Abraham Lincoln* (Cambridge: Harvard University Press, 1997).

15. Morgan, *Diary of Michael Wigglesworth,* 13, 20, 21, 25; Extracts from Mitchel's diaries are reprinted in Cotton Mather, *Ecclesiastes. The Life of the Reverend and Excellent Jonathan Mitchel* (Boston: B. Green and J. Allen, 1697), 56–57; Cotton Mather, *Diary of Cotton Mather* (New York: Frederick Ungar Publishing, [1957?], vol. 2, p. 2.

16. Moses Coit Tyler, *A History of American Literature, 1607–1783,* ed. Archie H. Jones (1878; Chicago: University of Chicago Press, 1967), 84.

17. McGiffert, *God's Plot,* 88. Baird Tipson notes that "even Shepard's most profound experiences left him short of the spiritual security he sought." See "The Routinized Piety of Thomas Shepard's Diary," 69.

18. Cotton Mather, *Diary,* vol. 2, p. 119.

19. Samuel Shaw, *The Voice of One Crying in the Wilderness* (1665; Boston: Rogers and Fowle, 1746), 147. Cotton Mather, *Diary,* vol. 2, p. 253.

20. William Perkins, "Directions how to Live Well, and to Dye Well," cited in Hambrick-Stowe, *Practice of Piety,* 224. McGiffert, *God's Plot,* 90. See also Sally Promey, "Seeing the Self 'in Frame': Early New England Material Practice and Puritan Piety," *Material Religion* 1, no. 1 (Mar. 2005): 10–46.

21. McGiffert, *God's Plot,* 18.

22. The quote is from Erik Seeman, *Pious Persuasions: Laity and Clergy in Eighteenth-Century New England* (Baltimore: Johns Hopkins University Press, 1999), 15. Tom Webster views "the phenomenon of diary writing as a 'technology of the self,' as a means by which the godly self was maintained, indeed constructed, through the action of writing." "Writing to Redundancy: Approaches to Spiritual Journals and Early Modern Spirituality," *Historical Journal* 39, no. 1 (Mar. 1996): 40. See also Margo Todd, "Puritan Self-Fashioning: The Diary of Samuel Ward," *Journal of British Studies* 31, no. 3 (July 1992): 236–64. James Olney argues that writing enables the creation of the self: "it is through that act that the self and life, completely intertwined and entangled, take on a certain form, assume a particular shape and image, and endlessly reflect that image back and forth between themselves as between two mirrors." See James Olney, "Autobiography and the Cultural Moment: A Thematic, Historical, and Bibliographical Introduction," in his *Autobiography: Essays Theoretical and Critical* (Princeton: Princeton University Press, 1980), 22.

23. McGiffert, *God's Plot,* 198.

24. Nathaniel Gilman's diary measures 3¾ inches by 6 inches, and Isaac Backus's 13 volumes of diaries range from 4 by 6 inches to 6½ by 8 inches. Nicholas Gilman's diary has been transcribed and edited. See William Kidder, ed., "The Diary of Nicholas Gilman" (M.A. thesis, University of New Hampshire, 1972). Kidder describes Gilman's manuscript in the Preface. For Backus's diary, see *The Diary of Isaac Backus,* ed. William G. McLoughlin (Providence: Brown University Press, 1979), vol. 1, p. xxxiii.

25. See Elizabeth Carroll Reilly and David D. Hall, "Customers and the Market for Books," in *A History of the Book in America,* vol. 1, *The Colonial Book in the Atlantic World,* ed. Hugh Amory and David D. Hall (New York: Cambridge University Press, 2000), 395. Because of the similarities between Puritan and evangelical writings, Charles Hambrick-Stowe has interpreted Sarah Osborn's diary as evidence of the persistence of older Puritan models of piety. He argues that the mid-eighteenth-century revivals marked a "'renaissance' of older traditions." Charles E. Hambrick-Stowe, "The Spiritual Pilgrimage of Sarah Osborn (1714–1796)," in *Religion in American History: A Reader,* ed. Jon Butler and Harry S. Stout (New York: Oxford University Press, 1998), 135.

26. Barbara E. Lacey, ed., *The World of Hannah Heaton: The Diary of an Eighteenth-Century New England Farm Woman* (Dekalb: Northern Illinois University Press, 2003), 48; Sarah Osborn, Diaries and Memoir, 1757–1769, 130. For more on Heaton, see Barbara Lacey, "The World of Hannah Heaton: The Autobiography of an Eighteenth-Century Farm Woman," *William and Mary Quarterly* 45 (Apr. 1988): 280–304.

27. Ross W. Beales, Jr., "The Diary of John Cleaveland, January 15–May 11, 1742," *Essex Institute Historical Collections* 107, no. 2 (Apr. 1971): 161, 155.

28. Osborn, Diaries and Memoir, 1757–1769, Diary #21, 20 July 1757, p. 77.

29. D. W. Bebbington, *Evangelicalism in Modern Britain: A History from the 1730s to the 1980s* (London: Unwin Hyman, 1989), 43. On evangelical individualism, see D. Bruce Hindmarsh, *The Evangelical Conversion Narrative: Spiritual Autobiography in Early Modern England* (Oxford: Oxford University Press, 2005).

30. Michael Crawford, ed., "The Spiritual Travels of Nathan Cole," *William and Mary Quarterly* 33, no. 1 (Jan. 1976): 92. On the new understanding of conversion as an abrupt change rather than a gradual process, see Kenneth P. Minkema, "A Great Awakening Conversion: The Relation of Samuel Belcher," *William and Mary Quarterly* 44 (Jan. 1987): 121–26.

31. T. H. Breen and Timothy Hall, "Structuring Provincial Imagination: The Rhetoric and Experience of Social Change in Eighteenth-Century New England," *American Historical Review* 103, no. 5 (Dec. 1998): 1411–39.

32. Jonathan Edwards, "An Account of the Life of the Reverend Mr. David Brainerd," in Jonathan Edwards, *The Life of David Brainerd,* ed. Norman Pettit, vol. 7 of *The Works of Jonathan Edwards* (New Haven: Yale University Press, 1984), 173. There are scores of examples of evangelicals who expressed their desire to be weaned from the world. For example, Sarah Osborn begged God, "Strip me intirely of self. Wean me wholly from the world and all things therein" (Osborn, Diaries, 1753–1772, Diary #20, 16 Jan. 1757, p. 24). Nicholas Gilman wrote in his diaries: "Let me not Seek Self any otherwise than in the gloryfing and Enjoying God in and thro' thee My Lord and Saviour" (Kidder, "Diary of Nicholas Gilman," 245.) Susanna Anthony prayed, "Lord, let nothing delight me, without thee. I know no other good, but thee; and will have no other rest, or delight, but God in Christ, as the centre of my soul. Let me never live to see the time, when any thing beside, and without God, shall satisfy my soul" (Samuel Hopkins, ed., *The Life and Character of Miss Susanna Anthony* [Worcester: Leonard Worcester, 1796], 61). And Isaac Backus exclaimed in his diary, "O that my heart were more weaned from all things here below!" (McLoughlin, *Diary of Isaac Backus,* 441).

33. Rebecca Ann Husman, ed. "The Religious Journal of Sarah Prince Gill, 1743–1764" (unpublished paper, Bard College, 1983. The original manuscript of Gill's journal is in the Boston Public Library), 25.

34. Jonathan Edwards, "Diary," in Jonathan Edwards, *Letters and Personal Writings,* ed. George C. Claghorn, vol 16 of *The Works of Jonathan Edwards* (New Haven: Yale University Press, 1998), 766.

35. For statistics on church membership in Newport, see Elaine Forman Crane, "Uneasy Coexistence: Religious Tensions in Eighteenth-Century Newport," *Newport History* 53, no. 5 (Summer 1980): 101–11.

36. Letter from Sarah Osborn to Joseph Fish, 17 Sept. 1750, Letters, 1743–1770.

37. Samuel Clarke, *A Demonstration of the Being and Attributes of God* (London: J. Knapton, 1705); Daniel Whitby, *A Discourse* (London, 1710), quoted in H. Shelton Smith, *Changing Conceptions of Original Sin: A Study in American Theology Since 1750* (New York: Charles Scribner's Sons, 1955), 12–13; Samuel Webster, *A Winter's Evening Conversation upon the Doctrine of Original Sin* (Boston, 1757); and Jonathan Edwards, *Some Thoughts Concerning the Present Revival* (1742), in Jonathan Edwards, *The Great Awakening,* ed. C. C. Goen, vol. 4 of *The Works of Jonathan Edwards* (New Haven: Yale University Press, 1972), 394. Norman Fiering has argued that by the mid-eighteenth century, most people believed that human nature was "irresistibly compas-

sionate." See Norman Fiering, "Irresistible Compassion: As Aspect of Eighteenth-Century Sympathy and Humanitarianism," *Journal of the History of Ideas* 37 (Apr.–June 1976): 195–218. On changing attitudes toward original sin, see Merle Curti, *Human Nature in American Thought: A History* (Madison: University of Wisconsin Press, 1980); Conrad Wright, *The Beginnings of Unitarianism in America* (Boston: Starr King Press, 1955), 59–90; and Smith, *Changing Conceptions of Original Sin.*

38. Shields, "History of Diary Writing," 149–50. Margo Culley notes that journal keeping is often a response to "dislocation." A major event, for example, the westward journey or marriage, creates "a sense of discontinuity of self—I was that, now I am this; I was there, now I am here. Keeping a life record can be an attempt to preserve continuity seemingly broken or lost." Margo Culley, ed., *A Day at a Time: The Diary Literature of American Women from 1764 to the Present* (New York: Feminist Press, 1985), 8.

39. Hopkins, *Life and Character of Miss Susanna Anthony,* 127.

40. Lacey, *World of Hannah Heaton,* 56.

41. Henry F. May, *The Enlightenment in America* (New York: Oxford University Press, 1976), 42–65.

42. John Locke, *An Essay Concerning Human Understanding* (1690), reprinted in *The Portable Enlightenment Reader,* ed. Isaac Kramnick (New York: Penguin, 1995), 186.

43. Bebbington, *Evangelicalism in Modern Britain,* 74. Mark Noll has pointed out that evangelicals shared with Locke a belief that "the self's personal experience was foundational for reliable knowledge." See Mark A. Noll, *The Rise of Evangelicalism: The Age of Edwards, Whitefield and the Wesleys* (Leicester: InterVarsity Press, 2004), 140. See also Bruce Hindmarsh, "Reshaping Individualism: The Private Christian, Eighteenth-Century Religion, and the Enlightenment," in *The Rise of the Laity in Evangelical Protestantism* (New York: Routledge, 2002).

44. Edwards, *Life of David Brainerd,* 143.

45. Jonathan Edwards, *A Treatise Concerning Religious Affections,* in *Religious Affections,* ed. John E. Smith, vol. 2 of *The Works of Jonathan Edwards* (New Haven: Yale University Press, 1959), 93–461.

46. Jonathan Edwards, "Personal Narrative," in *Letters and Personal Writings,* 792; Osborn, Diaries, 1753–1772, Diary #14, 8 July 1753.

47. Lacey, *World of Hannah Heaton,* 16; Edwards, *Life of David Brainerd,* 161.

48. Husman, "Religious Journal of Sarah Prince Gill," entry for 24 Mar. 1744, p. 13.

49. Ibid., entry for 28 Jan. 1764, p. 97.

50. Ellen Richardson Glueck and Thelma Smith Ernst, eds., "Diary of Experience (Wight) Richardson, Sudbury, Mass., 1728–1782," (typescript, Massachusetts Historical Society, Boston), 7.

51. Hopkins, *Life and Character of Miss Susanna Anthony,* 67–68.

52. *The Result of a Council of the Consociated Churches of the County of Windham* (Boston, 1747), 7, 17. On the Separates, see C. C. Goen, *Revivalism and Separatism in New England, 1740–1800: Strict Congregationalists and Separate Baptists in the Great Awakening* (New Haven: Yale University Press, 1962).

53. Crawford, "Spiritual Travels of Nathan Cole," 97. Emphases mine.

54. In response to the Separates' insistence that doubt was sinful, a group of ministers protested that doubt could be "a suitable and necessary means to stir up Believers to use most

diligent Endeavours to obtain Scripture Evidences for their Satisfaction." See *Result of a Council of Consociated Churches*, 13.

55. Lacey, *World of Hannah Heaton*, 139. Osborn, Diaries, 1753–1772, Diary #14, 29 July 1753, p. 25. David Brainerd remembered that at a time when he was suffering from melancholy, he "was something relieved by reading some passages in my diary." See Edwards, *Life of David Brainerd*, 158.

56. Husman, "Religious Journal of Sarah Prince Gill," undated entry, 1; Glueck and Ernst, "Diary of Experience (Wight) Richardson," 62.

57. Lacey, *World of Hannah Heaton*, 140.

58. On the role of transatlantic communication in the "First Great Awakening," see Susan O'Brien, "A Transatlantic Community of Saints: The Great Awakening and the First Evangelical Network, 1735–1755," *American Historical Review* 91, no. 4. (Oct. 1986), 811–32.

59. Hopkins, *Life and Character of Miss Susanna Anthony*, 16.

60. For more on contemporary journal writing, see Catherine A. Brekus, "A place to go to connect with yourself: A Historical Perspective on Journaling," Martin Marty Center Web Forum, University of Chicago Divinity School, http://marty-center.uchicago.edu/webforum/archive.shtml.

61. Dorothy Bass, *Receiving the Day: Christian Practices for Opening the Gift of Time* (San Francisco: Jossey-Bass, 2001); and Stephanie Paulsell, *Honoring the Body: Meditations on a Christian Practice* (San Francisco: Joseey-Bass, 2002).

Two • *Forgiveness*

1. Jonathan Edwards, "Mercy and Not Sacrifice," *The Works of Jonathan Edwards*, vol. 22, *Sermons and Discourses, 1738–1742*, ed. Nathan O. Hatch and Harry S. Stout, with Kyle Farley (New Haven: Yale University Press, 2003), 128, 130–31, 133–34.

2. Pierre Bourdieu, *Outline of a Theory of Practice*, trans. Richard Nice (New York: Cambridge University Press, 1977), 20.

3. Samuel Willard, *A Compleat Body of Divinity* (Boston, 1726), 912. For Puritans' participation in international religious networks, see Menna Prestwich, ed., *International Calvinism, 1541–1715* (Oxford: Clarendon Press, 1985); and Francis J. Bremer, *Congregational Communion: Clerical Friendship in the Anglo-American Puritan Community, 1610–1692* (Boston: Northeastern University Press, 1994).

4. For two typical and influential examples of Puritan teaching on forgiveness, see William Ames, *The Marrow of Theology* [1623; 3rd ed. 1629], trans. and ed. John Dykstra Eusden (1968; Grand Rapids, Mich.: Baker Books, 1997), esp. 314–17; William Ames, *Conscience, with the Power and Cases thereof* (n.p., 1639), esp. 114–23; and John Cotton, *The Way of Life* (London, 1641), 122.

5. For one particularly vivid example of Puritan assumptions about repentance as a condition for forgiveness (from the First Church of Boston), see James F. Cooper, "The Confession and Trial of Richard Wayte, Boston, 1640," *William and Mary Quarterly*, 3rd ser., 44 (1987): 310–32.

6. Cotton Mather, *Bonifacius: An Essary Upon the Good*, ed. David Levin (1710; Cambridge: Harvard University Press, 1966), 62. Thacher also allowed that Christians might disagree with each other, but in such cases they ought to take their complaints to church courts, where the

"Rules" of procedure encouraged "Gracious Love and Charity," "Self-denial," and other incentives to forgiveness: Peter Thacher, *Christ's Forgiveness Of True Christians, is a Preceptive Pattern of Christian Fraternal Forgiveness* (Boston, 1712), 3, 5, 41; with which was printed John Danforth, *Holy Striving Against Sinful Strife* (Boston, 1712), 110, 112, 114. For an extended discussion of the importance of speech acts, see Jane Kamensky, *Governing the Tongue: The Politics of Speech in Early New England* (New York: Oxford University Press, 1997).

7. See David D. Hall, *Worlds of Wonder, Days of Judgment: Popular Religious Belief in Early New England* (Cambridge: Harvard University Press, 1989), esp. 166–212. One example of how forgiveness was linked to frankly national political fortunes was an immensely popular 1647 work by Nathaniel Ward. Ward urged Parliament and the king (a bit too late, as it happened), in the midst of civil war, to forgive each other as a matter of national policy: Theodore de la Guard [Nathaniel Ward], *The Simple Cobler of Aggawam in America* (London, 1647), 78–80.

8. In 1542, when one Michiel, a saddler, was found to have engaged in a dispute with his nephew, the elders demanded (on pain of excommunication) that Michiel "pardon his said nephew entirely," which meant, quite specifically, to "embrace and express his love" for him (bodily and vocal acts), attend worship services with him (a communal and liturgical act), and refrain from contentious behavior (a social act of restraint). See Robert M. Kingdon, T. A. Lambert, and I. M. Watt, eds., *The Registers of the Consistory of Geneva at the Time of Calvin,* vol. 1 (Grand Rapids, Mich.: William B. Eerdmans, 2000), 45–46.

9. On church discipline in general, see Emil Oberholzer, Jr., *Delinquent Saints: Disciplinary Action in the Early Congregational Churches of Massachusetts* (New York: Columbia University Press, 1956); James F. Cooper, Jr., *Tenacious of Their Liberties: The Congregationalists in Colonial Massachusetts* (New York: Oxford University Press, 1999); and Kamensky, *Governing the Tongue.* For the cases cited here, see *Records of the First Church in Boston, 1630–1868,* ed. Richard D. Pierce, *Publications of the Colonial Society of Massachusetts,* vols. 39–41 (Boston: Colonial Society of Massachusetts, 1961), 39: 31–37, 52.

10. For the shift from religious discipline to civil litigation, see Oberholzer, *Delinquent Saints;* Mark Valeri, "Religious Discipline and the Market: Puritans and the Issue of Usury," *William and Mary Quarterly,* 3rd ser., 54 (1997): 747–68, esp. 764–67; and the stunning rise in the number of civil litigations as illustrated in "Records of the Suffolk County Court, 1671–1680," ed. Samuel Eliot Morison, *Publications of the Colonial Society of Massachusetts,* vols. 29–30 (Boston: Colonial Society of Massachusetts, 1933).

11. Relation of Thomas Jonson, Jr., 24 Mar. 1728, in "Confessions of Faith of the Members of the First Parish Church, Haverhill, Massachusetts," property of Centre Congregational Church, deposited at the Haverhill Public Library, Haverhill, Massachusetts, transcribed by Douglas Winiarski. Winiarski kindly provided copies of the Haverhill and Medfield relations (cited below).

12. Confession of John Bradley, 16 Jan. 1732, in "Confessions of Faith, Haverhill."

13. Relation of Hope Lovel, 31 Jan. 1742, Medfield Church, Medfield Massachusetts, transcribed by Ross Beales (transcription in the possession of Douglas Winiarski). For Timothy Edwards, see Kenneth P. Minkema, "The East Windsor Conversion Relations, 1700–1725," *Connecticut Historical Society Bulletin* 51 (1986): 9–63, esp. 30, 39.

14. See George M. Marsden, *Jonathan Edwards: A Life* (New Haven: Yale University Press, 2003), 341–74.

15. Jonathan Edwards, "Self-Examination and the Lord's Supper," in *The Works of Jonathan Edwards,* vol. 17, *Sermons and Discourses, 1730–1733,* ed. Mark Valeri (New Haven: Yale University Press, 1999), 268–69.

16. Jonathan Edwards, sermon on Luke 15:28–31b, Jonathan Edwards manuscripts, Beinecke Library, New Haven, Conn. (hereafter, Jonathan Edwards MSS). See Kenneth P. Minkema, "Old Age and Religion in the Writings and Life of Jonathan Edwards," *Church History* 70 (2001): 674–704, for a discussion of local social conditions that informed Edwards's preaching at this time.

17. See Jonathan Edwards, "A Farewell Sermon," in Wilson H. Kimnach, Kenneth P. Minkema and Douglas A. Sweeney, eds., *The Sermons of Jonathan Edwards: A Reader* (New Haven: Yale University Press, 1999), 212–41. For the controversy of access to the sacrament and Edwards's dismissal, see Marsden, *Jonathan Edwards,* 341–74. For examples of Edwards's social exhortations, see Mark Valeri, "The Economic Thought of Jonathan Edwards," *Church History* 60 (1991): 37–54.

18. In a 1723 entry in his private "Diary," Edwards groped for the boundary between a proper judgment that his offenders should repent and an improper desire that they be punished or harmed in some way: Jonathan Edwards, *The Works of Jonathan Edwards,* vol. 16, *Letters and Personal Writings,* ed. George S. Claghorn (New Haven: Yale University Press, 1998), 779; see also his "Resolutions" in ibid., 755, 757. For a parallel case that bears much resemblance to the pattern in New England, with its assumptions of the dependence of feelings on sacramental discipline, see David Warren Sabean, *Power in the Blood: Popular Culture and Village Discourse in Early Modern Germany* (New York: Cambridge University Press, 1984), esp. 37–60. Edwards's Puritan-like voice on forgiveness resonated with what contemporary theorists such as Bourdieu, Marcel Mauss, and Talal Asad describe as a central feature of practice: beliefs and dispositions inculcated through ritual and external regulation. See Bourdieu, *Outline of a Theory of Practice;* Marcel Mauss, "Body Techniques," in *Sociology and Psychology: Essays,* trans. Ben Brewster (London: Routledge, 1979); and Talal Asad, *Genealogies of Religion: Discipline and Reasons of Power in Christianity and Islam* (Baltimore: Johns Hopkins University Press, 1993), discussed and cited in Amy Hollywood, "Inside Out: Beatrice of Nazareth and Her Hagiographer," in Catherine M. Mooney, ed., *Gendered Voices: Medieval Saints and Their Interpreters* (Philadelphia: University of Pennsylvania Press, 1999), 78–98, esp. 78–80.

19. Edwards, sermon on Matt. 5:44, n.d. (early 1730s), Jonathan Edwards MSS.

20. Here Edwards fits into Asad's category of a misguided modern, who misconstrues practice as originating in belief or sentiment. For a discussion and critique of Asad's category of the misguided modern, see Hollywood, "Inside Out."

21. Jonathan Edwards, *The Works of Jonathan Edwards,* vol. 2, *A Treatise Concerning Religious Affections,* ed. John E. Smith (New Haven: Yale University Press, 1959), 417, 419.

22. For a general statement on revival networks, with evidence from Edwards, see Frank Lambert, *Inventing the "Great Awakening"* (Princeton: Princeton University Press, 1999).

23. Ample evidence is provided in Edwards's "Miscellanies," his private philosophical meditations (see n. 25 below), and in the secondary literature, of his engagement with Scottish figures such as Shaftesbury, Hutcheson, and David Hume, and with rational moralists such as Samuel Clarke and William Wollaston (who wielded the moral law against Calvinism without explicitly Moral Sense arguments). See, for example, Norman S. Fiering, *Jonathan Edwards's Moral Thought and Its British Context* (Chapel Hill: Univeristy of North Carolina Press for the Insti-

tute of Early American History and Culture, 1981); and Gerald R. McDermott, *Jonathan Edwards Confronts the Gods: Christian Theology, Enlightenment Religion, and non-Christian Faiths* (New York: Oxford University Press, 2000).

24. Jonathan Edwards, sermon on Matt. 5:44, n.d. (early 1730s), Jonathan Edwards MSS. Edwards's argument here parallels that of Joseph Butler, the widely read Anglican moralist and critic of deism. Butler's *Fifteen Sermons Preached at the Rolls Chapel* (London, 1726) included two sermons on resentment and forgiveness, based on the same text as Edwards's sermon, from Matthew 5. Butler argued that resentment was a natural feeling of indignation in response to injury. When it led to passions for revenge, resentment no longer served to protect the injured; it became self-defeating. Edwards added to Butler's reasoning a Calvinist incentive to forgive: confidence in divine justice. Butler argued in sum that revenge was irrational, to be checked by a natural sentiment for benevolence. Edwards contended that it was unfaithful, to be displaced by trust in divine principles. Butler, *Fifteen Sermons,* quoted in Paul A. Newberry, "Joseph Butler on Forgiveness: A Presupposed Theory of Emotion," *Journal of the History of Ideas* 62 (2001): 233–44, esp. 236.

25. Edwards, "the Miscellanies," 1023 [1744–1745], in *The Works of Jonathan Edwards,* vol. 20, *The "Miscellanies," 833–1153,* ed. Amy Planginga Pauw (New Haven: Yale University Press, 2002), 356; and "the Miscellanies," 1230 [1753], in *The Works of Jonathan Edwards,* vol. 23, *The "Miscellanies" 1153–1360,* ed. Douglas A. Sweeney (New Haven: Yale University Press, 2004), 162–64. See also from *The "Miscellanies," 1153–1360,* no. 1206, 126–31.

26. This I take from a survey of the chief works of this group: Anthony Ashley Cooper, the third earl of Shaftesbury, *Characteristics of Men, Manners, Opinions, Times* (London, 1711); Francis Hutcheson, *An Inquiry into the Original of our Ideas of Beauty and Virtue* (1725; 4th ed., London, 1738); and Adam Smith, *The Theory of Moral Sentiments* [1759], ed. D. D. Raphael and A. L. Macfie (Oxford: Oxford University Press, 1976). The American follower of this thinking, Samuel Johnson, wrote his widely used *Ethices Elementa,* eschewing the idea of pardon or release from past debts: Aristocles [Samuel Johnson], *Ethices Elementa: or, the First Principles of Moral Philosophy* (Boston, 1746), 57. Edwards's anticommercial sentiments have been documented in several places; see, e.g., Valeri, "Economic Thought of Jonathan Edwards."

27. Jonathan Edwards, *Two Dissertations: I. Concerning the End for Which God Created the World. II. The Nature of True Virtue* (Boston, 1765).

28. Edwards, sermon on Matt. 5:44.

29. See John Demos, *The Unredeemed Captive: A Family Story from Early America* (New York: Alfred A. Knopf, 1995); and Richard I. Melvoin, *New England Outpost: War and Society in Colonial Deerfield* (New York: W. W. Norton, 1989). The father's account was John Williams, *The Redeemed Captive Returning to Zion* (Boston, 1707).

30. Edwards, sermon on Ps. 119:56, Sept. 1740, Jonathan Edwards MSS.

31. Edwards, sermon on Rev. 22:5, Aug. 1756, Jonathan Edwards MSS (cite and transcription courtesy of Rachel Wheeler). See also Edwards to Isaac Hollis, 17 July 1752, in *Works of Jonathan Edwards,* vol. 16: 493–509. McDermott, *Jonathan Edwards Confronts the Gods,* 194–206, provides a suggestive reading of Edwards and Indians, with further evidence. Edwards's argument for the idea of a common human nature that crossed ethnic bounds is the subject of an essay by Rachel Wheeler, "'Friends to Your Souls': Jonathan Edwards' Indian Pastorate and the Doctrine of Original Sin," *Church History: Studies in Christianity and Culture* 72 (2003): 736–65.

32. Edwards, sermon on Luke 24:47, Oct. 1751; baptismal sermon fragment (ca. 1756); profession of faith, n.d. (from Stockbridge period): all in Jonathan Edwards MSS (cites and transcriptions courtesy of Rachel Wheeler).

33. See esp. Edwards's 1738 sermon series known as "Charity and Its Fruits," in *The Works of Jonathan Edwards,* vol. 8, *Ethical Writings,* ed. Paul Ramsey (New Haven: Yale University Press, 1989), esp. 366–97.

34. When Anglo-French hostilities resumed during the late 1740s, Edwards supported the British war effort. This was not necessarily self-contradictory; Edwards might well have reasoned that New England's enemies neither sought forgiveness nor exhibited repentance at such times. See Marsden, *Jonathan Edwards,* 306–19.

35. For the return to tradition, see esp. Craig Dykstra and Dorothy C. Bass, "Times of Yearning, Practices of Faith," and L. Gregory Jones, "Forgiveness," in Dorothy C. Bass, ed. *Practicing Our Faith: A Way of Life for a Searching People* (San Francisco: Jossey-Bass, 1997), 1–12 and 133–47 (resp.). For explicitly Christian theological arguments, see L. Gregory Jones, *Embodying Forgiveness: A Theological Analysis* (Grand Rapids, Mich.: William B. Eerdmans, 1995); Miroslav Volf, *Exclusion and Embrace: A Theological Exploration of Identity, Otherness, and Reconciliation* (Nashville: Abingdon Press, 1996); and the collection of essays in Raymond G. Helmick and Rodney L. Peterson, eds., *Forgiveness and Reconciliaion: Religion, Public Policy, and Conflict Transformation* (Philadelphia: Templeton Foundation Press, 2002), which includes Donald W. Shriver, Jr., "Forgiveness: A Bridge across Abysses of Revenge," 151–67. For critiques of theologically grounded notions of forgiveness, see Jeffrie Murphy and Jean Hampton, *Forgiveness and Mercy* (New York: Cambridge University Press, 1988); and Jacques Derrida, *On Cosmopolitanism and Forgiveness,* trans. Mark Dooley and Michael Hughes (London: Routledge, 2001); and Jacques Derrida, *The Gift of Death,* trans. David Wills (Chicago: University of Chicago Press, 1995). For the issue of forgiveness and justice, see Avishai Margalit, *The Ethics of Memory* (Cambridge: Harvard University Press, 2002).

Three • Assembling Bodies and Souls

1. George Q. Cannon, *My First Mission,* Faith-Promoting Series, no. 1 (Salt Lake City: Juvenile Instructor Office, 1879), 45.

2. S. George Ellsworth, ed., *The History of Louisa Barnes Pratt* (Logan: Utah State University Press, 1998), 107.

3. Lucy Thurston, *Life and Times of Mrs. Lucy G. Thurston* (Ann Arbor, Mich.: S. C. Andrews, 1882), 45.

4. Michel de Certeau, *The Practice of Everyday Life,* trans. Steven Rendall (Berkeley: University of California Press, 1984), xix, 23.

5. De Certeau points out the value of this exercise in which "moves, not truths, are recounted." He asserts that such examination can help us map out the wide range of possibilities for human behavior that is perceived as viable in any given situation. (Ibid., 23.)

6. For a comprehensive history of Protestant missionary ideology, see William R. Hutchison, *Errand to the World: American Protestant Thought and Foreign Missions* (Chicago: University of Chicago Press, 1987).

7. Ann Laura Stoler, *Carnal Knowledge and Imperial Power: Race and the Intimate in Colo-*

nial Rule (Berkeley: University of California Press, 2002), 141. I have adapted Stoler's phrase "colonial racial grammar" to my discussion of "religious grammar."

8. Charles W. Forman, *The Island Churches of the South Pacific: Emergence in the Twentieth Century* (Maryknoll, N.Y.: Orbis Books, 1982), 3–10; Neil Gunson, *Messengers of Grace: Evangelical Missionaries in the South Seas, 1797–1860* (Melbourne: Oxford University Press, 1978), 12–27. Although Roman Catholics gained many converts in the Marquesas, which became almost completely Catholic, they were much less successful in areas where the Protestants had entered the field first. On Roman Catholicism in the region, see Ralph M. Wiltgen, *The Founding of the Roman Catholic Church in Oceania, 1825–1850* (Canberra: Australian National University Press, 1979).

9. Henry Cheever, *Life in the Sandwich Islands: Or, the Heart of the Pacific, As It Was and Is* (New York: A. S. Barnes, 1856), 287–88. See also Hutchison, *Errand to the World,* 69–77.

10. The rich literature on Mormonism in the Pacific Basin is growing rapidly. Among the most salient for this study were Ian Barber, "Between Biculturalism and Assimilation: The Changing Place of Maori Culture in the Twentieth-Century New Zealand Mormon Church," *New Zealand Journal of History* 29, no. 2 (Oct. 1995): 142–69; R. Lanier Britsch, *Unto the Islands of the Sea* (Salt Lake City, Utah: Deseret, 1986); S. George Ellsworth, *Zion in Paradise: Early Mormons in the South Seas* (Logan, Utah: Faculty Association, Utah State University, 1959); Grant Underwood, "Mormonism, the Maori, and Cultural Authenticity," *Journal of Pacific History* 35, no. 2 (Sept. 2000), 133–46; David J. Whittaker, "Mormon Missiology: An Introduction and Guide to the Sources" (unpublished manuscript, 1998); and David J. Whittaker, with the assistance of Chris McClellan, "Mormon Missions and Missionaries: A Bibliographic Guide to Published and Manuscript Sources" (unpublished manuscript, 1993).

11. The Reverend Henry T. Cheever waxed poetic when he characterized the early missionaries as "pioneers" and "heroes," and narrated the Protestant missionary effort as the logical extension of the explorations of the intrepid Captain James Cook. On female missionary training, see Amanda Porterfield, *Mary Lyon and the Mount Holyoke Missionaries* (New York: Oxford University Press, 1997).

12. Christopher Herbert, *Culture and Anomie: Ethnographic Imagination in the Nineteenth Century* (Chicago: University of Chicago Press, 1991), 165.

13. Cheever, *Life in the Sandwich Islands,* 263.

14. Ibid., 81.

15. Thurston, *Life and Times of Lucy Thurston,* 18.

16. James M. Alexander, *Mission Life in Hawaii: Memoir of Rev. William P. Alexander* (Oakland, Calif.: Pacific Press, 1888), 75.

17. Anna Johnston, *Missionary Writing and Empire, 1800–1860* (Cambridge: Cambridge University Press, 2003), 120; Herbert, *Culture and Anomie,* 162.

18. Cheever, *Life in the Sandwich Islands,* 29.

19. William Ellis, *Polynesian Researches,* vol. 1 (New York: J and J Harper, 1833), 11.

20. A. W. Murray, *Forty Years' Mission Work in Polynesia and New Guinea, from 1835 to 1875* (London: J. Nisbet, 1876), 31, 34.

21. Cheever, *Life in the Sandwich Islands,* 128–30. See also Johnston, *Missionary Writing,* 152.

22. Much more could be said about the sociology of the gift in this context. For the classic statement on this topic, see Marcel Mauss, *The Gift: The Form and Reason for Exchange in Archaic Societies,* trans. W. D. Halls (New York: W. W. Norton, 2000).

23. Johnston, *Missionary Writing*, 123. Although it is beyond the scope of this paper, the native response to the missionary encounter offers an extraordinarily complex and suggestive area for further research. Reactions to Protestant overtures varied, obviously, but it is clear that islanders understood these negotiations differently than did their Euro-American visitors and carefully tread the treacherous boundary of "civilized practice" for their own social and personal ends.

24. Thurston, *Life and Times of Lucy Thurston*, 41–43.

25. Alexander, *Mission Life in Hawaii*, 82.

26. Cheever, *Life in the Sandwich Islands*, 271.

27. Alexander, *Mission Life in Hawaii*, 78–79.

28. Gunson, *Messengers of Grace*, 133–35, 201, 204. See also Andrew Thornley, "Religious Interaction," in Max Quanchi and Ron Adams, eds., *Culture Contact in the Pacific: Essays on Contact, Encounter, and Response* (Cambridge: Cambridge University Press, 1993), 73–82.

29. Cheever, *Life in the Sandwich Islands*, 79.

30. Johnston, *Missionary Writing*, 116.

31. Thurston, *Life and Times of Lucy Thurston*, 77.

32. Alexander, *Mission Life in Hawaii*, 77.

33. Ibid., 77–78.

34. Anna Johnston argues that the British missionary experience was similarly marked by profound unease over particular points of "cultural permeability," such as bodies, sexuality, language, and the family. See Johnston, *Missionary Writing*, 135.

35. Alexander, *Mission Life in Hawaii*, 40.

36. Cheever, *Life in the Sandwich Islands*, 97.

37. Thurston, *Life and Times of Lucy Thurston*, 126.

38. Ibid., 84, 81. On the segregation of missionary children, see also Herbert, *Culture and Anomie*, 180, and Johnston, *Missionary Writing*, 162–63.

39. Thurston, *Life and Times of Lucy Thurston*, 126–27.

40. Ibid., 102.

41. Alexander, *Mission Life in Hawaii*, 97.

42. Thurston, *Life and Times of Lucy Thurston*, 120.

43. Ibid., 80.

44. For a probing and suggestive study of intimacy and imperialism, or what she terms the "microphysics of colonial rule," see Stoler, *Carnal Knowledge*.

45. For recent explorations of the historical development of Mormonism as an ethnic marker, see Arnold H. Green, "Gathering and Election: Israelite Descent and Universalism in Mormon Discourse," *Journal of Mormon History* 25, no. 1 (Spring 1999): 195–228; and Armand Mauss, "In Search of Ephraim: Traditional Mormon Conceptions of Lineage and Race," *Journal of Mormon History* 25, no. 1 (Spring 1999): 131–73. See also Norman Douglas, "The Sons of Lehi and the Seed of Cain: Racial Myths in Mormon Scripture and Their Relevance to the Pacific Islands," *Journal of Religious History* 8, no. 1 (June 1974).

46. Ellsworth, *History of Louisa Barnes Pratt*, 149.

47. Parley Parker Pratt, *Proclamation! To the People of the Coasts and Islands of the Pacific*, in *The Essential Parley P. Pratt* (Salt Lake City: Signature Books, 1990), 155.

48. As late as the 1960s, Ian Barber concluded that many urban Maori still viewed their

church as non-European. They identified strongly with the LDS church as symbolic of an ongoing oppositional stance toward a colonizing power. Like the African American adaptation of the Old Testament theme of chosenness, the ongoing history of the Mormon people exhibited an internal logic and message of hope that distinguished this mission from all others. See Barber, "Between Biculturalism and Assimilation," 167. On resonances with the African American theme of chosenness, see Albert J. Raboteau, "African Americans, Exodus, and the American Israel," in *Fire in the Bones: Reflections on African-American Religious History* (Boston: Beacon, 1995).

49. R. Lanier Britsch, *Moramona: The Mormons in Hawaii* (Laie, Hawaii: Institute for Polynesian Studies, 1989), 14–15.

50. Cannon, *My First Mission*, 12–13.

51. Ellsworth, *Zion in Paradise*, 11.

52. Britsch, *Moramona*, 23.

53. Surprisingly, given the Mormons' emphasis on evangelism, it was not until the founding of the Church Missionary Home and Preparatory Training School in 1924 that their missionaries received any formal instruction (even then, instruction lasted exactly one week). The *Missionary's Handbook* began to be published in 1937. See Marjorie S. Newton, *Southern Cross Saints: The Mormons in Australia* (Laie, Hawaii: BYU Institute for Polynesian Studies, 1991), 63; and Britsch, *Moramona*, 28.

54. Gunson, *Messengers of Grace*, 237–38.

55. Thornley, "Religious Interaction," 78.

56. David J. Whittaker, "Early Mormon Pamphleteering" (Ph.D. diss., Brigham Young University, 1982), 282; Newton, *Southern Cross Saints*, 56; Ellsworth, *Zion in Paradise*, 20.

57. Ellsworth, *History of Louisa Barnes Pratt*, 128; Andrew Jenson, French Polynesia Mission Manuscript History, Latter-Day Saints Church Archives, Salt Lake City, Utah.

58. Ellsworth, *History of Louisa Barnes Pratt*, 161.

59. *Autobiography of Parley Parker Pratt*, edited by his son, Parley Parker Pratt (1938; Salt Lake City: Deseret, 1985), 378.

60. James Stephens Brown, *Giant of the Lord: Life of a Pioneer* (Salt Lake City: Bookcraft, 1960), 228.

61. Ellsworth, *History of Louisa Barnes Pratt*, 128, 154.

62. Gunson, *Messengers of Grace*, 229.

63. Ellsworth, *History of Louisa Barnes Pratt*, 128. Grant Underwood discusses similar resonances among the Maori in New Zealand in "Cultural Authenticity." Polygamy was perhaps the practice that most clearly distinguished Mormons from Protestants. Owing to the political battles brewing back in Utah over plural marriage, Hawaiian Saints kept a very low profile regarding the issue, and one finds very few references to it in diaries. When Smith's revelation of the new doctrine was presented to the Hawaiian Saints in 1853, church elders made it very clear that the teaching was not intended for them. Fearful that the small Mormon community in the islands would come under even more calumny from their religious opponents, the church discouraged members from marrying more than once, and the record indicates that the practice was never observed in Hawaii. But it is fair to speculate that native practices of polygamy would not have stirred the same kind of criticisms among Mormons that they did for Protestants.

64. Douglas, "Sons of Lehi," 94; and David J. Whittaker, "Mormons and Native Americans: A Historical and Bibliographical Introduction," *Dialogue* 18 (Winter 1985): 33–64.

65. On missionary ambivalence with respect to native customs and the ability to incorporate them into the faith, see Barber, "Between Biculturalism."

66. Cannon, *My First Mission*, 56.

67. Ellsworth, *Zion in Paradise*, 29; *History of Louisa Barnes Pratt*, 127.

68. Ellsworth, *History of Louisa Barnes Pratt*, 125.

69. Brown, *Giant of the Lord*, 229–30.

70. Britsch, *Moramona*, 29.

71. Ibid., 18, 20, 22.

72. Benjamin F. Johnson, *My Life's Review* (Independence, Mo.: Zion's Printing, 1947), 182.

73. Green cited in Britsch, *Moramona*, 39. For more on the settlement at Lanai, see 37–40, 74.

74. Britsch, *Moramona*, 78–79, 86, 88–89.

75. For more on the Iosepa community, see Dennis H. Atkin, "Iosepa: A Utah Home for Polynesians," in Grant Underwood, ed., *Voyages of Faith: Explorations in Mormon Pacific History* (Provo, Utah: Brigham Young University Press, 2000), 71–88.

76. On ideologies of race among Mormons, see Armand L. Mauss, *All Abraham's Children: Changing Mormon Conceptions of Race and Lineage* (Champaign: University of Illinois Press, 2003).

77. The Polynesian Cultural Center is still the subject of much debate because of the way it represents Pacific cultures. For differing views about the center, see Vernice Wineera and Rubina Rivers Forester, "The Polynesian Cultural Center: Reflections and Recollections," in Grant Underwood, ed., *Voyages of Faith: Explorations in Mormon Pacific History* (Provo, Utah: Brigham Young Univeristy Press, 2000), 239–54; and Rob Wilson and Arif Dirlik, "Introduction: Asia/Pacific as Space of Cultural Production," in *Boundary 2*, vol. 21, no. 1 (1994), 5.

Four • Honoring Elders

This chapter was significantly shaped under the direction and guidance of a circle of elders and others at the White Earth reservation, especially Erma Vizenor, Dan Kier, the late Josephine Degroat, and the late Larry Cloud Morgan. Further clarity and encouragement came from discussions during retreats with colleagues on this project, especially its directors and editors of this volume. I found personally refreshing the Lilly Endowment's support of solid historical research to nourish conversations in contemporary faith communities. It has borne fruit in this volume; it has also borne fruit at home in engaged historian-practitioner conversations with the Reverend Devon Anderson, with whom I aspire to grow old.

1. Thomas Cole, *The Journey of Life: A Cultural History of Aging in America* (New York: Cambridge University Press, 1992).

2. While one cannot speak of any golden age in the past, historians have documented how mainstream evangelical Protestantism contributed to the further diminution of the authority of old age. See Cole, *The Journey of Life*; W. Andrew Achenbaum, *Old Age in the New Land* (Baltimore: Johns Hopkins University Press, 1978).

3. On the image of the Indian in American thought, literature, and film, see Robert Berkhofer, Jr., *The White Man's Indian* (New York: Vintage, 1978).

4. John Comaroff and Jean Comaroff, *Of Revelation and Revolution: Christianity, Colonial-*

ism, and Consciousness in South Africa (Chicago: University of Chicago Press, 1991), *Of Revelation and Revolution: The Dialectics of Modernity on a South African Frontier* (Chicago: University of Chicago Press, 1997); Michel de Certeau, *The Practice of Everyday Life*, trans. Stephen Rendall (Berkeley: University of California Press, 1984). See also Pierre Bourdieu, *Outline of a Theory of Practice*, trans. Richard Nice (Cambridge: Cambridge University Press, 1987).

5. Robert Orsi, "Everyday Miracles: The Study of Lived Religion," in *Lived Religion in America*, ed. David Hall (Princeton: Princeton University Press, 1997).

6. See Michael McNally, *Ojibwe Singers: Hymns, Grief and a Native Culture in Motion* (New York: Oxford University Press, 2000), esp. 13–18, 195–205.

7. In his germinal essay "Religion as a Cultural System," Clifford Geertz privileges ritual action as that which can produce the "symbolic fusion of ethos and worldview" in which "the world as lived and the world as imagined . . . turn out to be the same world." See Clifford Geertz, *The Interpretation of Culture* (New York: Basic Books, 1973), 113.

8. I should note here that I will speak of Ojibwe tradition in the perfect rather than the past tense, emphasizing the irreducibly dynamic nature of that tradition rather than positing some pure, aboriginal form thereof. I thus establish no aboriginal benchmark by which to measure cultural change; instead I want to consider how that tradition informs post-contact cultural change even as it is drawn in distinction to the aboriginal.

9. See Christopher Vecsey, *Traditional Ojibwa Religion and Its Historical Changes* (Philadelphia: American Philosophical Society, 1983).

10. *Anishinaabe* could, in certain instances, be translated as "person" or "human" as well as a member of this particular community of persons.

11. Pauline Colby, *Reminiscences,* typescript in Minnesota Historical Society (hereafter MHS).

12. The Reverend John Johnson Enmegabowh blamed this in large part on the "impurity of the water used on the reservation." But he also blamed the social stresses and "firewater" for an epidemic of premature death. "Indian Notes," *Minnesota Missionary* 3, no. 7 (Apr. 1880).

13. See Jane Lamm Carroll, "Dams and Damages: The Ojibway, the United States, and the Mississippi Headwaters Reservoirs," *Minnesota History* 52 (Spring 1990): 2–16.

14. See Melissa Meyer, *The White Earth Tragedy: Ethnicity and Dispossession at a Minnesota Anishinaabe Reservation, 1889–1920* (Lincoln: University of Nebraska Press, 1994).

15. Pauline Colby, *Reminiscences,* p. 65. Colby is referring to reverence accorded Indian elders "in the story of Ramona," a fashionable reform novel that highly romanticizes noble savages.

16. Rebecca Kugel, *To Be the Main Leaders of Our People* (East Lansing: Michigan State University Press, 1998.)

17. Kugel observes that the many "full-blood" Ojibwe who aligned with the Episcopal mission had basically followed their elder civil leaders' strategic alliances with the missionaries and their power network for an accommodationist future. In sum, for Kugel, becoming Episcopalian was a religious repercussion of strategic political choices made by the elders whose authority they recognized. And this is in stark contrast to a faction, many of whom were of mixed descent (and thus more closely affiliated with the Roman Catholic mission heritage during the fur trade), drawn to the militancy of the warrior leaders.

18. H. B. Whipple, Account of 1862 Visitation, H. B. Whipple Papers, box 3, MHS.

19. The first Christian inroads among the Ojibwe were made by French Jesuits in the late seventeenth century. But it was in the mid and late nineteenth century, when the Ojibwe were increasingly confined to reservations and as necessity forced a traditional life based on movement with the seasonal round to keep time with the unfamiliar rhythms of sedentary agriculture and annuity payments, that Ojibwe people became more demonstrably Christian in more demonstrable numbers. In 1879, Episcopalians claimed one fourth of White Earth's population as communicants, not to speak of Roman Catholics. Among Minnesota's Ojibwe in this era, the most substantive and lasting inroads among "full-blood" Ojibwe were made by Episcopalian missionaries, and this discussion will focus on those encounters.

20. On the dexterity of practice in missionary encounters, see Comaroff and Comaroff, *Christianity, Colonialism, and Consciousness* and *Dialectics of Modernity*.

21. I develop this theme elsewhere. See Michael D. McNally, "The Practice of Native American Christianity," *Church History* 69 (Dec. 2000): 834–59.

22. See McNally, *Ojibwe Singers*, 81–122.

23. See Bloch's "Introduction" to *Political Language and Oratory in Traditional Society*, ed. Maurice Bloch (London: Academic Press, 1975), esp. 3–5.

24. J. A. Gilfillan, "Some Indians I have Known," *The Red Man by Red Men*, J. A. Gilfillan Papers, MHS.

25. Still, it should be added that a number of old people were significant in the life of the missions. Infirm and aged Ojibwe people routinely stayed behind under the care of the mission stations when others had gone off to their seasonal ricing, hunting, or fishing camps.

26. Bonnie Sue Lewis, *Creating Christian Indians: Native Clergy in the Presbyterian Church* (Norman: University of Oklahoma Press, 2003).

27. John Johnson Enmegabowh to Samuel Hollingsworth, 30 Dec. 1878, John Johnson Enmegabowh Papers, MHS.

28. J. A. Gilfillan, "Indian Notes," *Minnesota Missionary* 10, no. 1 (Jan. 1886).

29. For a discussion of his participation in the shaking tent, see J. A. Gilfillan to Rev. E. W. Cook, 3 Aug. 1882, J. A. Gilfillan Papers, folder 5, MHS.

30. J. A. Gilfillan, "Indian Notes," *Minnesota Missionary* 10, no. 1 (Jan. 1886).

31. *The Red Man* (Dec. [1886?]), in J. A. Gilfillan Papers, 7 MHS.

32. J. A. Gilfillan, "Shaydayence," *Woman's Work* (July 1882), J. A. Gilfillan Papers, Scrapbook, box 2, MHS.

33. Ibid.

34. J. A. Gilfillan to H. B. Whipple, 12 Sept. 1881, H. B. Whipple Papers, MHS.

35. Kakabishque via ibid., 25 July 1876.

36. Committee of Mazigishik's Band via Henry Selkirk to H. B. Whipple, 14 Aug. 1881, H. B. Whipple Papers, box 15, MHS.

37. "Notes from the Indian Field," *Minnesota Missionary* 4, no. 6 (Mar. 1881), MHS.

38. Committee of Mazigishik's Band via Henry Selkirk to H. B. Whipple, 14 Aug. 1881, H. B. Whipple Papers, box 15, MHS.

39. J. A. Gilfillan, "Indian Notes," *Minnesota Missionary* 10, no. 5 (May 1886), MHS.

40. Kugel, *To Be the Main Leaders of Our People*, 123.

41. Benedict to H. B. Whipple, 26 Sept. 1881. Whipple Papers, box 15, MHS.

42. J. A. Gilfillan, "Shay-Day-Ence," J. A. Gilfillan Papers, box 1, folder 1, MHS.

43. J. A. Gilfillan, *Minnesota Missionary* 3, no. 6 (Mar. 1880).

44. Ibid.

45. Gilfillan, "Shaydayence."

46. Bloch, "Introduction."

47. Gilfillan, "Shaydayence."

48. Gilfillan, "Some Indians I have Known," 463–68.

49. J. A. Gilfillan, "Shay-Day-Ence," J. A. Gilfillan Papers, box 1, folder 1, MHS.

50. Rebecca Kugel argues persuasively that the elder civil leaders' alignment with the Episcopal mission beginning in the 1850s was in large part a matter of a strategic alliance, one that resulted in disillusionment when, in the 1870s, non-Indian Episcopal authorities supported policies that further undermined the sovereignty of Ojibwe leadership. See Kugel, *To Be the Main Leaders of My People,* esp. 143 ff.

51. John Johnson Enmegahbowh, 13 Jan. 1874, to *Spirit of Missions* (Apr. 1874), 222, J. A. Gilfillan Papers, box 2, MHS.

52. Sherman Hall's diary, July 22, 1832, in ABCFM Papers, box 2, MHS.

53. Grace Lee Nute Collection, box 3, folder 1, MHS.

54. According to Gilfillan, even the Ojibwe deacon at White Earth's Pembina settlement, where Abitageshig's movement was afoot, was being "utilized" by the prophet and his Roman Catholic missionary supporters "for their own purposes." J. A. Gilfillan to H. B. Whipple, 12 Sept. 1881, H. B. Whipple Papers, MHS.

55. C. H. Beaulieu to H. B. Whipple, 17 Sept. 1881, H. B. Whipple Papers, MHS.

56. Ibid.

57. J. A. Gilfillan, *Minnesota Missionary* 3, no. 6 (Mar. 1880), MHS.

58. Francis Willis, Jr., "Red Lake Mission," *Minnesota Missionary and Church Record* 21, no. 2 (Feb. 1897).

59. Colby, *Reminiscences,* 29.

60. Visiting among the *Anami'aajig* may have reiterated the expectations of clan membership, where Ojibwe travelers could always claim the hospitality of members of their clan or *doodem.*

61. Gilfillan, "Some Indians I have Known."

62. Dr. Thomas Parker to H. B. Whipple, 12 Mar. 1880, H. B. Whipple Papers, box 14, MHS.

63. Colby, *Reminiscences,* 105.

64. J. A. Gilfillan, *Minnesota Missionary* 3, no. 6 (Mar. 1880), MHS.

65. Ibid., no. 5 (Feb. 1880); ibid., no. 6 (Mar. 1880), MHS.

66. Kugel, *To Be the Main Leaders of Our People,* p. 142. Samuel Madison Nabiquan was son of Shaydayence of Gull Lake Band; Charles Wright Nashotah was son of Waubonoquod, one of the more powerful *ogimaag;* George Morgan Kakagun, son of Ayabe of the Mille Lacs Band; Mark Hart, the son of Obimweweosh; and George Johnson, the son of Enmegahbowh. By contrast, Fred Smith Kadawabide was the orphaned son of Hole in the Day's principal warrior. See McNally, *Ojibwe Singers,* 96–99.

67. See McNally, *Ojibwe Singers,* 98–99.

68. J. A. Gilfillan to H. B. Whipple, 12 Sept. 1881, H. B. Whipple Papers, MHS.

69. Ibid., 30 Jan. 1883.

70. Ibid., 23 Sept. 1882.

71. Ibid.

72. Thomas Parker to Whipple, 2 Mar. 1880, H. B. Whipple Papers, box 15, MHS.

73. Kugel, *To Be the Main Leaders of Our People,* 149. By the conventions of Ojibwe "marriage," men and women could come and go from marital relationships with an ease and frequency that greatly irritated missionaries.

74. J. A. Gilfillan to H. B. Whipple, 21 Nov. 1882, H. B. Whipple Papers, MHS.

75. Ibid., 23 Jan. 1883.

76. This point is suggested in Gilfillan's later reflections on the affair. Ibid., 4 May 1883.

77. Ibid., 10 Jan. 1883.

78. Ibid.

79. Ibid., 4 Jan. 1883.

80. Ibid., 10 Jan. 1883.

81. Ibid., 23 Jan. 1883.

82. Ibid., 30 Jan. 1883.

83. Ibid., 8 Feb. 1882.

84. Ibid., 4 May 1883.

Five • Nurturing Religious Nationalism

The author gratefully acknowledges the invaluable assistance of the Reverend Steven Jhu, former senior pastor of the Korean Christian Church in Honolulu, and the generosity of many church members who shared with me their memories and documents. Thanks also to the other participants in the History of American Christian Practice Project for their insights and suggestions, especially Leigh Schmidt, Laurie Maffly-Kipp, Michael McNally, and Charles Hambrick-Stowe, each of whom provided written feedback that greatly aided the process of revisions to this chapter.

1. The congregation has been raising funds to restore the main sanctuary including the replica of the gate. The South Korean government has donated more than $600,000, and the church has raised a little over $1 million. The total cost of the project is estimated at $2.8 million. *Honolulu Star-Bulletin,* 14 Aug. 2000.

2. Conrad Cherry reminds us, "Two chief revelatory events for the civil religion are the American Revolution (joined with the entire constitutional period) and the American Civil War. The first was a moment when God delivered the colonies from Pharaoh Britain and the 'evils' of the Old World. . . . The Civil War was the nation's first real 'time of testing' when God tried the permanence of the Union or, in some interpretations, brought judgment upon his wayward people." Conrad Cherry, ed., *God's New Israel: Religious Interpretations of American Destiny,* rev. ed. (Chapel Hill: University of North Carolina Press, 1998), 11.

3. Albert Raboteau, *Fire in the Bones: Reflections on African American Religious History* (Boston: Beacon Press, 1995), 4.

4. Bruce Cumings, *Korea's Place in the Sun: A Modern History* (New York: W. W. Norton, 1997); Peter Duus, *The Abacus and the Sword: The Japanese Penetration of Korea, 1895–1910* (Berkeley: University of California Press, 1995), 413–23. I borrow the phrase "community of memory" from Robert Bellah et al., *Habits of the Heart: Individualism and Commitment in American Life* (Berkeley: University of California Press, 1985), 153.

5. For a general overview of Asian American history, Ronald Takaki, *Strangers from a Different Shore: A History of Asian Americans* (Boston: Little Brown, 1989); and Sucheng Chan, *Asian Americans: An Interpretive History* (Boston: Twayne, 1991). The literature on race in the United States is vast, but some helpful studies include: Alexander Saxton, *The Rise and Fall of the White Republic: Class Politics and Mass Culture in Nineteenth-Century America* (New York: Verso, 1990); Michael Omi and Howard Winant, *Racial Formations in the United States: From the 1960s to the 1990s*, 2nd ed. (New York: Routledge, 1994); Gary Gerstle, *American Crucible: Race and Nation in the Twentieth Century* (Princeton: Princeton University Press, 2001); and George Lipsitz, *The Possessive Investment in Whiteness: How White People Profit from Identity Politics* (Philadelphia: Temple University Press, 1998).

6. President Woodrow Wilson's Fourteen Points speech was delivered before a joint session of the U.S. Congress on 8 January 1918, as part of his effort to sketch out a just and lasting peace to follow World War I. For Koreans and Korean Americans, his emphasis on the self-determination of nations gave voice to efforts they had been engaged in well before Korea was annexed by Japan in 1910. For more background on Wilson and the speech, see Arthur S. Link, *Wilson the Diplomatist: A Look at His Major Foreign Policies* (Baltimore: Johns Hopkins Press, 1957); Arthur S. Link et al., eds., *The Papers of Woodrow Wilson*, vol. 45 (Princeton: Princeton University Press, 1984).

7. The reference to issues of power, negotiation, and resistance as well as disposition are drawn from the introduction to this volume and the commentary on the work of leading social theorists of practice like Pierre Bourdieu and Catherine Bell.

8. Ho-Youn Kwon, Kwang Chung Kim, and R. Stephen Warner, eds., *Korean Americans and Their Religions: Pilgrims and Missionaries from a Different Shore* (University Park: Pennsylvania State University Press, 2001); Warren Kim, *Koreans in America* (Seoul: Po Chin Chai Printing, 1971); Bong-youn Choy, *Koreans in America* (Chicago: Nelson-Hall, 1979); Won Moo Hurh, *The Korean Americans* (Westport, Conn.: Greenwood Press, 1998).

9. James Huntley Grayson, *Korea: A Religious History* (London: Routledge Curzon, 2002), 155. For general background on Christianity in Korea, see Allen D. Clark, *A History of the Church in Korea* (Seoul: Christian Literature Society of Korea, 1971); Donald N. Clark, *Christianity in Modern Korea* (Lanham, Md.: University Press of America, 1986); and Chung-Shin Park, *Protestantism and Politics in Korea* (Seattle: University of Washington Press, 2003).

10. Fred H. Harrington, *God, Mammon, and the Japanese: Dr. Horace Allen and Korean-American Relations, 1884–1905* (Madison: University of Wisconsin Press, 1944).

11. The standard work on Protestant missions in Korea is L. George Paik, *The History of Protestant Missions in Korea, 1832–1910* (Pyongyang: Union Christian College Press, 1929).

12. Kenneth M. Wells, *New God, New Nation: Protestants and Self-Reconstruction Nationalism in Korea, 1896–1937* (Honolulu: University of Hawaii Press, 1990), 16–17, 40.

13. Don Baker, "Christianity Koreanized," in *Nationalism and the Construction of Korean Identity,* ed. Hyung Il Pai and Timothy R. Tangherlini (Berkeley: Institute of East Asian Studies, University of California, 1998), 118–20.

14. Cumings, *Korea's Place in the Sun,* 157–60.

15. Wi Jo Kang, *Christ and Caesar in Modern Korea: A History of Christianity and Politics* (Albany: State University of New York Press, 1997), 39–42.

16. Wells, *New God, New Nation,* introduction. I have drawn heavily on Wells's analysis for this section.

17. It is beyond the scope of this chapter to fully examine the sources of this division. Despite their many commonalities, Rhee and Pak differed in their vision of how best to achieve independence for Korea. Rhee favored diplomacy and a close alliance with the United States, while Pak advocated a militaristic approach in which Koreans abroad would spearhead an armed invasion of the peninsula coordinated with independence efforts in Korea. Wayne Patterson provides some background on the divided nature of the Korean American community in Hawaii in *The Ilse: First-Generation Korean Immigrants in Hawaii, 1903–1973* (Honolulu: University of Hawaii Press, 2000), 100–101.

18. For more background, see Ronald Takaki, *Pau Hana: Plantation Life and Labor in Hawaii, 1835–1920* (Honolulu: University of Hawaii Press, 1983).

19. Wayne Patterson, *The Korean Frontier in America: Immigration to Hawaii, 1896–1910*, (Honolulu: University of Hawaii Press, 1988), 47–50.

20. Kingsley K. Lyu, "Korean Nationalist Activities in Hawaii and the Continental United States, 1900–1945, Part I: 1900–1919," *Amerasia Journal* 4, no. 1 (1977): 31.

21. Bernice B. H. Kim, "The Koreans in Hawaii," (M.A. thesis, University of Hawaii, 1937), 136–39.

22. Jung Ha Kim, "Cartography of Korean American Protestant Faith Communities in the United States," ed. Pyong Gap Min and Jung Ha Kim, *Religions in Asian America: Building Faith Communities* (Walnut Creek, Calif.: Altamira, 2002), 190; Patterson, *The Ilse*, 67.

23. Patterson, *The Ilse*, chaps. 2 and 5.

24. The College of Hawai'i, founded in 1907, became the University of Hawai'i in 1920, and the University of Hawai'i, Manoa, in 1972.

25. Bernice Kim, "The Koreans in Hawaii," 140–42; Lyu, "Korean Nationalist Activities in Hawaii," 47, 77.

26. Choy, *Koreans in America*, 260–61.

27. Syngman Rhee, *The Spirit of Independence: A Primer of Korean Modernization and Reform*, trans. Han-Kyo Kim (Honolulu: University of Hawaii Press; and Seoul: Institute for Modern Korean Studies, Yonsei University, 2001), 1–18. Kim provides a brief but helpful biographical sketch.

28. Rhee, *The Spirit of Independence*, 280–83, 1–14; Robert T. Oliver, *Syngman Rhee: The Man Behind the Myth* (New York: Dodd, Mead, 1954), 113–26. Oliver's biography is unquestioningly favorable towards Rhee, but he had access to Rhee's personal papers, and the work contains useful information. Richard C. Allen, *Korea's Syngman Rhee: An Unauthorized Portrait* (Jutland, Vt.: Charles E. Tuttle, 1960) is far more critical, but Allen often depends upon Oliver for details and facts about Rhee's activities.

29. Choy, *Koreans in America*, 79, 83–85; Rhee, *The Spirit of Independence*, 1–18 (translator biography).

30. Oliver, *Syngman Rhee*, 109–14.

31. Bernice Kim, "The Koreans in Hawaii," 142–43.

32. Choy, *Koreans in America*, 261–62; Oliver, *Syngman Rhee*, 123.

33. On the March 1st movement, see Ki-baik Lee, *A New History of Korea* (Cambridge: Harvard University Press, 1984), trans. Edward Wagner, 340–44; and Michael Robinson, *Cultural Nationalism in Colonial Korea, 1920–1925* (Seattle: University of Washington Press, 1988), 3–13.

34. Bernice Kim, "The Koreans in Hawaii," 143–45.

35. Lyu, "Korean Nationalist Activities in Hawaii," 48–51. Many of the Korean-language schools that operated under religious auspices also provided Korean Americans shelter from efforts by the territorial government of Hawaii to curb foreign language instruction, in hopes that students would acquire standard English language rather than pidgin English.

36. *No Chai-yon, Chai-Mi Hani Sa Rya* [Brief History of Korean Residents in America], (Los Angeles, 1951), 174, quoted in Lyu, 79. Ironically, Rhee married an Austrian, Francesca Donner, who would become the first First Lady of the Republic of Korea.

37. "Objectives and Aims of the K.C.C.," a memo with excerpts from Syngman Rhee's writings on the Korean Christian Church. It was reportedly in the possession of the Reverend Richard C. Kimm in 1945. I thank Mrs. Bessie Park, a long-time member of the Korean Christian Church, for lending me documents from her personal papers, including this item.

38. Lyu, "Korean Nationalist Activities in Hawaii," 79–85.

39. "History of Korean Missions Inc.," unpublished paper, no date, in the Korean Christian Church files, Honolulu, Hawaii. This organization continues to oversee the KCC churches in Hawaii, which now number three: in Honolulu, Wahiawa, and Hilo.

40. Warren Kim, *Koreans in America,* 67.

41. Interview with Helen Chung, 4 Apr. 2000, Honolulu, Hawaii.

42. Warren Kim, *Koreans in America,* 67.

43. Winifred Lee Namba, "Nodie Kimhaikim Sohn," in *Notable Women of Hawaii,* ed. Barbara Bennett (Honolulu: University of Hawaii Press, 1984), 356–57.

44. *Honolulu Star-Bulletin,* 23 Apr. 1938.

45. Lyu, "Korean Nationalist Activities in Hawaii," 80–81; *Honolulu Star-Bulletin,* 23 Apr. 1938.

46. The date of the dedication is taken from the program produced for the event. I thank Mrs. Bessie Park for giving me a copy of the program.

47. The large mixed race population in Hawaii (including Koreans) also complicates discussions about racial categories.

48. Ferenc Szasz, *Religion in the Modern American West* (Tucson: University of Arizona Press, 2002).

49. Because assimilation has been (and to an extent, still is) such a dominant framework for understanding immigration and settlement in the United States, historians have understudied the ways that many groups have found to engage (or not engage) in the nation. American exceptionalism has also contributed to the tendency to view the United States as somehow categorically different from other nations in the processes of nation-building, especially in relation to colonial or imperial endeavors. Works on Korean nationalism that have been helpful in thinking about the nationalisms of Korean American Christians include: Chong-sik Lee, *The Politics of Korean Nationalism* (Berkeley: University of California Press, 1963); Elaine H. Kim and Chungmoo Choi, eds., *Dangerous Women: Gender and Korean Nationalism* (New York: Routledge, 1998). An interesting trio of groups to compare in studying religious nationalism might be Indian Sikh, Irish Catholic, and Korean Protestant immigrants to the United States, since all three groups were active during the first part of the twentieth century.

Six • Re-Forming the Church

1. Richard Henry Dana, Jr., *Two Years Before the Mast: A Personal Narrative of Life at Sea* (1840; New York: Penguin Books, 1981), 101.

2. Ibid., 189. While the Santa Barbara Mission was founded in 1786, the original mission was destroyed in an earthquake in 1812 and was rebuilt in 1815.

3. Ibid.; Gerald Geary, *The Secularization of the California Missions, 1810–1846* (Washington, D.C.: Catholic University of America Press, 1934), 25–34; and William Taylor, *Magistrate of the Sacred: Priests and Parishioners in Eighteenth-Century Mexico* (Stanford: Stanford University Press, 1996), 15–17.

4. See David J. Weber, *The Spanish Frontier in North America* (New Haven: Yale University Press, 1992), 236–70.

5. "Reglamento De La Nueva California, 1773," in *Diario Del Capitan Comandante Fernando de Rivera y Moncada,* ed. Ernest J. Burrus, S.J., vol. 2, (Madrid: Ediciones Porrua, 1967), 375–89.

6. Secularization was completed and mission lands were largely redistributed and sold off by 1845, just before war broke out with the United States.

7. Dana, *Two Years Before the Mast,* 232–33.

8. Joseph Warren Revere, *A Tour of Duty in California,* ed. Joseph N. Balestier (New York: C. S. Francis, 1849), 33.

9. This editorial change in the editions of Dana's work was first noted in John Ogden Pohlman, "California's Mission Myth" (Ph.D. diss., University of California, Los Angeles, 1974), 22.

10. Elizabeth Hughes, *The California of the Padres; or, Footprints of Ancient Communism* (San Francisco: I. N. Choynski, 1875), 32. A counter-example can be found in Mary Cone's *Two Years in California* (Chicago: S. C. Griggs, 1876), 26–48. Cone makes use of Dana's writings to support a negative assessment of the mission system and its effects on California's Native American population.

11. *Our Centennial Memoir,* ed. P. J. Thomas (San Francisco: P. J. Thomas, 1877), 68.

12. Ibid., 82.

13. Ibid., 83.

14. Ibid., 91–92.

15. Ibid., 91.

16. Ibid., 118 and 120. The italics are in the original.

17. Ibid., 121.

18. Note that Vallejo's speech does, however, appear in translation in *Our Centennial Memoir.*

19. Benjamin Truman, *Semi-Tropical California* (San Francisco: A. L. Bancroft, 1874), 27.

20. *Santa Barbara Weekly Press,* 17 Jan. 1874, cited in Albert Camarillo, *Chicanos in a Changing Society: From Mexican Pueblos to American Barrios in Santa Barbara and Southern California* (Cambridge: Harvard University Press, 1996), 54.

21. *The California Missions: A Pictorial History,* editorial staff of Sunset Books (Menlo Park, Calif.: Lane, 1964), 246–47.

22. Ibid., 234.

23. Franklin Walker, *A Literary History of Southern California* (Berkeley: University of California Press, 1950), 94.

24. Ruth Odell, *Helen Hunt Jackson* (New York: D. Appleton-Century, 1939), 173.

25. "Echoes In The City Of The Angels," was originally printed in *The Century Magazine* in December of 1883. This quote is drawn from a reprint of the essay in a collection of Helen Hunt Jackson's California writings entitled, *Glimpses of California and the Missions* (Boston: Little and Brown, 1907), 177.

26. Hunt, *Glimpses of California*, 193.

27. Ibid., 180–81.

28. Helen Hunt Jackson, "Father Junipero and His Work," *Century Magazine* 26, no. 1 (May 1883): 3–18 (part one), and no. 2 (June 1883): 199–215 (part two).

29. Odell, *Helen Hunt Jackson*, 183.

30. In *Bits of Travel,* her collected travel writings from Europe, Jackson (then Helen Hunt) alternates between fascination and contempt for Catholic Rome; she displays a more positive but condescending interest in rural Catholic piety in Germany. See Helen Hunt, *Bits of Travel* (Boston: James R. Osgood, 1873).

31. Jackson, "Father Junipero and His Work," no. 1 (May 1883): 4.

32. Ibid., 18. Jackson claimed that a lonely caretaker at Mission Carmel had discovered the location of Serra's remains in the winter of 1882, but in fact the opening of Serra's grave at Carmel, on the 3rd of July 1882, was witnessed by a crowd of more than 400 people, including an honor guard of Legion of Saint Patrick cadets of the California National Guard. The remains were deemed to be Serra's and were reinterred. See Zephyrin Englehardt's *The Franciscans in California* (Harbor Springs, Calif.: Holy Childhood Indian School, 1897), for an account of the event.

33. Jackson, "Father Junipero and His Work," 201.

34. Ibid., 215, citing John Dwinelle's *Colonial History of San Francisco* (San Francisco, 1864), 44–87.

35. Karen Weitze, *California's Mission Revival* (Los Angeles: Henessey and Ingalls, 1984), 25.

36. Nadine Ishitani Hata, *The Historic Preservation Movement in California: 1940–1976* (Washington D.C.: California Department of Parks and Recreation, 1992), 4.

37. More than half of the boom towns of the late 1880s became ghost towns or were incorporated into other municipalities within Los Angeles County, see Glenn S. Dumke, *The Boom of the Eighties in Southern California* (San Marino, Calif.: Huntington Library Press, 1944), 175–99.

38. Weitze, *California's Mission Revival*, 21–23.

39. Ibid., 29–31.

40. Ibid., 38.

41. "California's Exposition Building," *California Monthly World's Fair Magazine* (Feb. 1892): 62.

42. *Official Guide to the World's Columbian Exposition,* ed. John J. Elkin (Chicago: Columbian Guide/John Anderson Printing, 1893), 147–48.

43. Two Catholic priests interested in California mission preservation were Father O'Keefe and Father O'Sullivan. Father O'Sullivan was frequently listed in Landmarks Club membership rosters published in *Land Of Sunshine.*

44. For a counter to restorationists' appeals, see "Restoration Undesirable" from the *Los Angeles Times,* 25 Dec. 1910, quoted in *Some Essays About the California Missions in Honor of the V*

Centenary of the Evangelization of the Americas, ed. Msgr. Francis J. Weber (n.p.: California Catholic Conference, 1992), 51–52.

45. See Turbesé Lummis Fiske and Keith Lummis, *Charles F. Lummis: The Man and His West* (Norman: University of Oklahoma Press, 1975), 88. The "A.P.A." to which Lummis refers was the American Protective Association, an anti-Catholic association and not a precursor to the already well-established Knights of the Klu Klux Klan.

46. Ibid., 87.

47. Ibid., 90. Note that Pala is not a mission; it is a chapel at an *asistencia,* or branch chapel. Although Lummis notes this, he continually refers to Pala as a mission.

48. *Land Of Sunshine* 6, no. 4 (Mar. 1897), 83.

49. Eliza Otis, "The Romance of the Mission Period" (1905) in *Some Essays About the California Missions in Honor of the V Centenary of the Evangelization of the Americas,* Msgr. Francis J. Weber ed., California Catholic Conference, 1992: 45. Note that the 1905 date in Weber's anthology is the date of the article's reprinting.

50. Letter from Lummis to Englehardt dated 1 April 1909, transcribed in "The Correspondence of Charles F. Lummis with Fr. Zephyrin Englehardt, O.F.M.," in *Franciscan Provincial Annals, Province of Santa Barbara* 3, no. 4 (July 1941): 52.

51. Ibid., 53.

52. In 1943, two decades after Lummis's death, a historical commission was convened by the Catholic Church in California to investigate the life and character of Junipero Serra. In 1988, amid contentious debate, Serra was beatified by Pope John Paul II. Herbert Bolton testified at the historical hearings early in the beatification process.

53. See Weitze, *California's Mission Revival,* 79–111; and Fiske and Lummis, *Charles F. Lummis,* 90.

54. Among the most damaged missions that the Landmarks Club restored were Mission San Fernando and the *asistencia* at Pala.

55. Fiske and Lummis, *Charles F. Lummis,* 90.

Seven • "Acting Faith"

1. Mrs. Edward [Sarah] Mix, *Faith Cures, and Answers to Prayer* (Springfield, Mass.: Press of Springfield Printing Co., 1882) 107–10. This text has recently been reprinted, with a critical introduction by Rosemary D. Gooden (Syracuse, N.Y.: Syracuse University Press, 2002).

2. Mix, *Faith Cures,* 107–10.

3. On the revisionist agenda of antebellum health reform movements, see Catherine Albanese, *Nature Religion in America: From the Algonkian Indians to the New Age* (Chicago: University of Chicago Press, 1990); and James Whorton, *Crusaders for Fitness: The History of American Health Reformers* (Princeton: Princeton University Press, 1982). For the relationship between "orthodox" Protestant notions of suffering and the alternatives posed by Spiritualism, Christian Science, and New Thought, see Ann Braude, *Radical Spirits: Spiritualism and Women's Rights in Nineteenth-Century America,* 2nd ed. (Bloomington: University of Indiana Press, 2001); Stephen Gottschalk, *The Emergence of Christian Science in American Religious Life* (Berkeley: University of California Press, 1973); and Beryl Satter, *Each Mind a Kingdom: American Women, Sexual Purity, and the New Thought Movement, 1875–1920* (Berkeley: University of Cal-

ifornia Press, 1999). While some of these scholars have highlighted continuities between their subjects and American evangelical religion, the tendency to characterize spiritualism, Christian Science and New Thought as "alternative" or "outsider" sects, as opposed to "mainstream" Protestant evangelicalism, remains strong. The classic statement of this categorization is Sydney E. Ahlstrom, *A Religious History of the American People* (New Haven: Yale University Press, 1972), 1019–36. R. Laurence Moore reinforced this reading in *Religious Outsiders and the Making of Americans* (New York: Oxford University Press, 1986), 105–27; and Stephen J. Stein's *Communities of Dissent: A History of Alternative Religions in America* (New York: Oxford University Press, 2003), 87–104, also reproduces this dichotomy. Although Ann Taves has drawn attention to the parallels between evangelical divine healing and "new religious movements" such as spiritualism, New Thought, Christian Science, and theosophy, in *Fits, Trances, and Visions: Experiencing Religion and Explaining Experience from Wesley to James* (Princeton: Princeton University Press, 1999), there is yet to be a book-length interpretive study that places divine healing within the broader context of late-nineteenth-century efforts to revise traditional Protestant assumptions about physical suffering and the spiritual life. Works that have contributed to the growing literature on divine healing include Jonathan Baer, "Perfectly Empowered Bodies: Divine Healing in Modernizing America" (Ph.D. diss., Yale University, 2002); Nancy Hardesty, *Faith Cure: Divine Healing in the Holiness and Pentecostal Movements* (Peabody, Mass.: Hendrickson, 2003); R. Bruce Mullin, *Miracles and the Modern Religious Imagination* (New Haven: Yale University Press, 1996); and James W. Opp, "Religion, Medicine and the Body: Protestant Faith Healing in Canada, 1880–1930" (Ph.D. diss., University of Alberta, 2000).

4. While some historians have argued that *faith cure* was a derogatory term, applied to the divine healing movement only by critics, I have found evidence of its use among participants, especially during the first two decades of the movement's history. Charles Cullis and Sarah Mix, for example, used this designation in the titles of their published collections of answered-prayer narratives. As the movement came under increasing attack in the middle to late 1880s, some of its defenders began to distance themselves from the term *faith cure* and argued that *divine healing* represented a more appropriate moniker. Given the enduring popularity of *faith cure* among many participants throughout the 1880s, I use *divine healing, faith cure,* and *faith healing*—another idiom adopted by both proponents and detractors—interchangeably.

5. For fuller biographical treatments of these figures and discussions of their participation in divine healing, see Hardesty, *Faith Cure.* Contemporary biographies and autobiographies are also available for most of these individuals. See William E. Boardman, *Faith-Work under Dr. Cullis, in Boston* (Boston: Willard Tract Repository, 1874); W. H. Daniels, ed., *Dr. Cullis and His Work: Twenty Years of Blessing in Answer to Prayer* (1885; New York: Garland, 1985); William McDonald, *The Life of Rev. John S. Inskip* (1885; New York: Garland, 1985); Mrs. [Mary M. Adams] Boardman, *Life and Labours of the Rev. W. E. Boardman* (New York: D. Appleton, 1887); Adoniram Judson Gordon, *The Ministry of Healing: or, Miracles of Cure for All Ages* (Boston: Howard Gannett, 1882); Ernest B. Gordon, *Adoniram Judson Gordon: A Biography* (New York: Fleming H. Revell, 1896); A. B. Simpson, *The Gospel of Healing,* rev. ed. (1888; London: Morgan and Scott, 1915); and A. E. Thompson, *The Life of A. B. Simpson: Official Authorized Edition* (New York: Christian Alliance Publishing, 1920).

6. Hardesty offers some biographical information on most of these women in *Faith Cure.* Like their male counterparts, many of them also authored accounts of their own experiences,

and some inspired biographies. See, for example, Mary H. Mossman, *Steppings in God; or, The Hidden Life Made Manifest* (New York: Eaton and Mains, 1909); Nathaniel Wiseman, *Elizabeth Baxter (Wife of Michael Paget Baxter), Saint, Evangelist, Preacher, Teacher, and Expositor* (London: Christian Herald, 1928); S. A. Lindenberger, *Streams from the Valley of Berachah* (New York: Christian Alliance Publishing, 1893); Sarah Freeman Mix, *The Life of Mrs. Edward Mix, Written by Herself in 1880 with Appendix* (Torrington, Conn.: Press of Register Printing Co., 1884); and Mix, *Faith Cures.*

7. On the Mixes' leadership and the participation of African Americans in late-nineteenth-century divine healing, see Gooden, "Introduction," in Mix, *Faith Cures,* esp. xlii–xlvi. For Amanda Berry Smith's involvement, see Robert L. Stanton, "Healing Through Faith," *Presbyterian Review* 5 (1884): 55; and Amanda Berry Smith, *The Story of the Lord's Dealings with Mrs. Amanda Berry Smith, The Colored Evangelist* (1893; New York: Garland, 1987).

8. Because evangelical divine healing was such a broad and diverse movement, generalizing about its constituency is difficult. In the southern and western regions of the United States, for example, divine healing evangelists often hailed from impoverished backgrounds and were rarely well educated. For a fuller treatment of divine healing in these geographical areas, consult Baer, "Perfectly Empowered Bodies," esp. chap. 3.

9. Mix mentions her indebtedness to Allen in both *Faith Cures,* 10–11, and *Life of Mrs. Edward Mix,* 17. For Allen's life and ministry, see Ethan Otis Allen, *Faith Healing; or, What I Have Witnessed of the Fulfilling of James V:14, 15, 16* (Philadelphia: G. W. McCalla, 1881).

10. *Record of the International Conference on Divine Healing and True Holiness Held at the Agricultural Hall, London, June 1 to 5, 1885* (London: J. Snow and Co. and Bethshan, 1885). In the absence of any official governing body, published treatises defending divine healing, alongside the articles and narratives printed in religious periodicals, served as the primary vehicles for developing, defining, and propagating the doctrines and practices of faith cure—a process that reflected the movement's vibrancy, vernacular base, and ambiguous boundaries.

11. Mix, *Faith Cures,* 12, 38.

12. Mix, *Faith Cures,* 38–39.

13. Judd recounts the story of her illness and healing in Carrie F. Judd, "Have Faith in God," in Mix, *Faith Cures,* 32–45; and Carrie F. Judd, *The Prayer of Faith* (1880; New York: Garland, 1985), esp. 9–21. She offers another version in her autobiography, Carrie Judd Montgomery, *Under His Wings: The Story of My Life* (1936; New York: Garland, 1985), 48–60.

14. C. F. R. Bielby's letter, dated 13 Mar. 1880, is reprinted in Judd, *Prayer of Faith,* 16–21.

15. Judd, *Prayer of Faith,* 16–21; Judd Montgomery, *Under his Wings,* 54, 59, 65–67.

16. Judd Montgomery, *Under His Wings,* 49, 53, 61.

17. For a discussion of changing perspectives on pain in this period, see Ariel Glucklich, *Sacred Pain: Hurting the Body for the Sake of the Soul* (New York: Oxford University Press, 2001), esp. 179–205. Scholarship on the waning influence of Calvinism throughout the nineteenth century is voluminous. On the specific issue of challenges to the limited age of miracles theology, see Mullin, *Miracles,* esp. 31–82; and Rick Ostrander, *The Life of Prayer in a World of Science: Protestants, Prayer, and American Culture, 1870–1930* (New York: Oxford University Press, 2000), 35–38. For the rise of the "cult of benevolence," consult James Turner, *Reckoning with the Beast: Animals, Pain, and Humanity in the Victorian Mind* (Baltimore: Johns Hopkins University Press, 1980), 1–14.

18. The literature on "heroic" medicine and challenges to this form of therapy is extensive. For one classic treatment, see Charles E. Rosenberg, "The Therapeutic Revolution: Medicine, Meaning, and Social Change in Nineteenth-Century America," in Morris J. Vogel and Charles E. Roseberg, eds., *The Therapeutic Revolution: Essays in the Social History of Medicine* (Philadelphia: University of Pennsylvania Press, 1979), 3–25. On the history of anesthesia, see Martin S. Pernick, *A Calculus of Suffering: Pain, Professionalism, and Anesthesia in Nineteenth-Century America* (New York: Columbia University Press, 1985).

19. Glucklich, *Sacred Pain*, 195.

20. On the waning attraction of self-restraint as a mark of character during the late nineteenth century, see Gail Bederman, *Manliness and Civilization: A Cultural History of Gender and Race in the United States, 1880–1917* (Chicago: University of Chicago Press, 1995). Jackson Lears also charts the growing ambivalence as to what constituted proper Protestant character and behavior, particularly in relation to the "crisis" of neurasthenia in *No Place of Grace: Antimodernism and the Transformation of American Culture, 1880–1920* (New York: Pantheon Books, 1981).

21. Bederman, *Manliness and Civilization*, esp. 10–15. The literature on late-nineteenth-century manhood is extensive and growing. In addition to Bederman's influential work, important recent studies include Mark C. Carnes and Clyde Griffen, ed., *Meanings for Manhood: Constructions of Masculinity in Victorian America* (Chicago: University of Chicago Press, 1990); R. Marie Griffith, "Apostles of Abstinence: Fasting and Masculinity during the Progressive Era," *American Quarterly* 52, no. 4 (Dec. 2000): 599–638; Donald E. Hall, ed., *Muscular Christianity: Embodying the Victorian Age* (New York: Cambridge University Press, 1994); Judy Hilkey, *Character Is Capital: Success Manuals and Manhood in Gilded Age America* (Chapel Hill: University of North Carolina Press, 1997); Clifford Putney, *Muscular Christianity: Manhood and Sports in Protestant America, 1880–1920* (Cambridge: Harvard University Press, 2001); Anthony E. Rotundo, *American Manhood: Transformations in Masculinity from the Revolution to the Modern Era* (New York: Basic Books, 1993); and Norman Vance, *Sinews of the Spirit: the Ideal of Christian Manliness in Victorian Literature and Religious Thought* (New York: Cambridge University Press, 1985).

22. Associations between true womanhood and suffering have been assiduously documented. Classic studies of the domestic ideology include Barbara Welter, "The Cult of True Womanhood, 1820–60," *American Quarterly* 18 (Summer 1966): 151–74; Nancy F. Cott, *The Bonds of Womanhood: 'Woman's Sphere' in New England, 1780–1835* (New Haven: Yale University Press, 1977); Kathryn Kish Sklar, *Catharine Beecher: A Study in American Domesticity* (New Haven: Yale University Press, 1973); Carroll Smith-Rosenberg, *Disorderly Conduct: Visions of Gender in Victorian America* (New York: Alfred A. Knopf, 1985); and Nancy M. Theriot, *Mothers and Daughters in Nineteenth-Century America: The Biosocial Construction of Femininity*, rev. ed. (Lexington: University Press of Kentucky, 1996).

23. Theriot, *Mothers and Daughters*, esp. 77–136. Martha H. Verbrugge has also made a case for the importance of the physical education movement in promoting an alternate view of female health in *Able-Bodied Womanhood: Personal Health and Social Change in Nineteenth-Century Boston* (New York: Oxford University Press, 1988).

24. Mrs. R. W. Fuller to Carrie Judd, 14 June 1883, *Triumphs of Faith* 3 (Sept. 1883): 214. Testimonies of healing were often addressed to Carrie Judd and printed in the form of personal correspondence.

25. Mrs. Mattie E. Littell, "Experiences of Spiritual and Physical Healing," *Triumphs of Faith* 5 (May 1885): 118–20; Urwin D. Sterry to Carrie Judd, 11 Feb. 1884, *Triumphs of Faith* 4 (July 1884): 164–66; and Alice M. Ball, "Following On," *Triumphs of Faith* 7 (Oct. 1887): 224–26.

26. Mrs. Sidney Whittemore, "Made Perfectly Whole," in A. B. Simpson, ed., *A Cloud of Witnesses for Divine Healing*, 2nd ed. (New York: Word, Work and World Publishing, 1887), 94–108.

27. Promoters of divine healing frequently bemoaned the rationalism, materialism, and empiricism that, in their view, increasingly characterized late-nineteenth-century American culture. For examples of this antimodernist discourse, see Simpson, *Gospel of Healing*, 68; and Gordon, *Ministry of Healing*, 9. As Rick Ostrander has aptly observed, however, the emphasis that advocates of divine healing placed upon published testimonies of answered prayer as evidence of healing for both believers and skeptics suggests that these evangelicals did not entirely reject the empiricist ethos, but instead sought to offer tangible, empirical proof of supernaturalism. See Ostrander, *Life of Prayer in a World of Science*, 35–55.

28. Elizabeth Sisson, "Faith, Fasting and Prayer," *Triumphs of Faith* 7 (Jan. 1887): 14; and Lindenberger, *Streams from the Valley*, 82–83.

29. Lindenberger, *Streams from the Valley*, 82.

30. Mossman, *Steppings in God*, 17–22, 25, 110–19.

31. Mossman, *Steppings in God*, 78; Otto Stockmayer, "The 'Look on Jesus,'" *Words of Faith* 11 (Aug. 1885): 93–96; and Anna W. Prosser, *From Death to Life: An Autobiography* (Buffalo: McGerald, 1901), 198.

32. Stockmayer, "Look on Jesus," 93. Mossman mentions a fourth means, walking in the Spirit (Gal. 5:16), see *Steppings in God*, 107, but the tripartite formulation was much more common. For example, Frederick C. Seely, "The Heritage of the Church of Christ," *Triumphs of Faith* 3 (Apr. 1883): 78–79, mentions these three practices along with the same Scripture passages.

33. S. G. C., "My Help and My Deliverer," *Triumphs of Faith* 1 (Oct. 1881): 153–57.

34. Edward Ryder, "Healing Through Christ," *Triumphs of Faith* 5 (Mar. 1885): 54; Mrs. W. J. Starr, "Touching the Hem of His Garment," *Triumphs of Faith* 2 (Mar. 1882): 39–41; Sarah Battles, "Experiences of Spiritual and Physical Healing," *Triumphs of Faith* 2 (Apr. 1882): 63–64; and Ruth S. King to Carrie F. Judd, *Triumphs of Faith* 3 (Dec. 1883): 285–87.

35. Seely, "Heritage of the Church," 78. A. B. Simpson, *Inquiries and Answers* (New York: Word, Work and World Publishing, 1887), 20; originally published as "Divine Healing, Inquiries and Answers. Concluded," *The Word, Work and World* 7, no. 6 (Dec. 1886): 338–42.

36. Gordon, *Ministry of Healing*, 32; and "Rev. John E. Cookman, D.D.," in A. B. Simpson, ed., *A Cloud of Witnesses for Divine Healing*, 2nd ed., (New York: Word, Work and World Publishing, 1887), 7.

37. Carrie Judd, "The Temple of the Body," *Triumphs of Faith* 4 (Feb. 1884): 25–27.

38. A. B. Simpson, "Himself," *Triumphs of Faith* 5 (Nov. 1885): 204–9; A. B. Simpson, "The Gospel of Healing," *Triumphs of Faith* 3 (Nov. 1883): 257–60; and Mrs. [Elizabeth] Baxter, "The Sentence of Death," *Triumphs of Faith* 5 (Oct. 1885): 217–19.

39. Carrie Judd, "Abide in Me," *Triumphs of Faith* 3 (Sept. 1883): 201–2.

40. A. B. Simpson, "Principles of Divine Healing," *Triumphs of Faith* 7 (Aug. 1887): 171–78.

41. W. T. Hogg, "'Christian Science' Unmasked," *Triumphs of Faith* 11 (Jan. 1891): 4; and K. Mackenzie, Jr. "The Devil," *Triumphs of Faith* 9 (Apr. 1889): 78. On the rise of mental therapeutics, see Rosenberg, "Therapeutic Revolution," 3–25; F. G. Gosling, *Before Freud: Neurasthe-*

nia and the American Medical Community, 1870–1910 (Urbana: University of Illinois Press, 1987); and Taves, *Fits, Trances, and Visions*, 122–26.

42. James Monroe Buckley, "Faith-Healing and Kindred Phenomena," *The Century Illustrated Monthly Magazine* 32 (June 1886): 221–36. See also James Monroe Buckley, "Faith-Healing and Kindred Phenomena (Supplementary Article)," *The Century Illustrated Monthly Magazine* 33 (Mar. 1887): 781–87. Both of these articles were reprinted along with two essays on what Buckley considered "kindred phenomena"—"Christian Science and 'Mind-Cure'" and "Dreams, Nightmares and Somnambulism"—as *Faith-Healing, Christian Science and Kindred Phenomena* (New York: Century, 1898).

43. A. J. Gordon, "'Christian Science' Tested by Scripture," *Triumphs of Faith* 6 (Dec. 1886): 276–80; and Annie Van Ness Blanchet to Carrie Judd, 15 Dec. 1884, *Triumphs of Faith* 5 (Jan. 1885): 22–23. For evidence of the ill-repute in which advocates of divine healing held Christian Science and other movements of mental healing, see E. P. Marvin, "'Christian Science' (not Christian and not Science)," *Triumphs of Faith* 9 (Mar. 1889): 52–54; and Anna Prosser, "So-Called 'Christian Science,'" *Triumphs of Faith* 10 (Mar. 1890): 49–52.

44. Edward H. Clarke, *Sex in Education; Or, A Fair Chance for Girls* (Boston: J. R. Osgood, 1873). For discussions of "scientific" discourses on women's physiology and pathology, especially with reference to late-nineteenth-century gender norms, see: Braude, *Radical Spirits*, 142–61; Ann Douglas Wood, "'The Fashionable Diseases': Women's Complaints and Their Treatment in Nineteenth-Century America," *The Journal of Interdisciplinary History* 4 (Summer 1973): 25–52; Satter, *Each Mind a Kingdom*, 21–56; Carroll Smith-Rosenberg, "The Hysterical Woman: Sex Roles and Role Conflict in Nineteenth-Century America," in *Disorderly Conduct*, 197–216; Sarah Stage, *Female Complaints: Lydia Pinkham and the Business of Women's Medicine* (New York: W. W. Norton, 1979), 64–88; and Theriot, *Mothers and Daughters*, 86. On mounting fears of "race suicide" and concerns about the advancement of civilization, see Carroll Smith-Rosenberg and Charles Rosenberg, "The Female Animal: Medical and Biological Views of Woman and Her Role in Nineteenth-Century America," *Journal of American History* 60 (Sept. 1973): 332–56; and Satter, *Each Mind a Kingdom*.

45. On Mitchell and the rest cure, see Ellen L. Bassuk, "The Rest Cure: Repetition or Resolution of Victorian Women's Conflicts?" in Susan Rubin Suleiman, ed., *The Female Body in Western Culture* (Cambridge: Harvard University Press, 1986), 141–43; and Satter, *Each Mind a Kingdom*, 54–55. Bassuk notes that while the rest cure was "theoretically used to treat both men and women, most patients described in the literature were nervous females" (141).

46. L. Etta Avery, "His Name, Through Faith in His Name," *Triumphs of Faith* 4 (Mar. 1884): 49–53.

47. Almena J. Cowles, "Made Every Whit Whole," *Triumphs of Faith* 2 (May 1882): 65–66; and Almena J. Cowles to Sarah Mix, Aug. 1881, in Mix, *Faith Cures*, 58–61.

48. On women's proclivity to hysteria, see Smith-Rosenberg, "The Hysterical Woman," 197; and Rosenberg and Rosenberg, "The Female Animal," 332–56.

49. W. T. Hogg, "'Christian Science' Unmasked," *Triumphs of Faith* 10 (Sept. 1890): 199.

50. Cowles, "Made Every Whit Whole," 66.

51. George M. Beard, *American Nervousness: Its Causes and Consequences* (New York: Putnam, 1881). The literature on male illness and therapy is less developed than the corresponding literature on female invalidism. The best treatments focus primarily upon the late nineteenth

century, with an emphasis on the diagnosis and treatment of male neurasthenia. See, for example, Hilkey, *Character Is Capital*, 76–68; Tom Lutz, *American Nervousness, 1903: An Anecdotal History* (Ithaca: Cornell University Press, 1991), 31–37; and Rotundo, *American Manhood*, 185–93.

52. Buckley, "Faith-Healing and Kindred Phenomena," 236.

53. A. P. Moore, "The Walk on the Waves," *Triumphs of Faith* 4 (Jan. 1884): 10; Sophia Nugent, "Where is the Guest-Chamber," *Triumphs of Faith* 4 (May 1884): 108; and Sophia Nugent, "He Shall Live," *Triumphs of Faith* 5 (Apr. 1885): 89–92; and A. B. Simpson, "How to Receive Divine Healing," *Triumphs of Faith* 8 (Feb. 1888): 35–40.

54. "Rev. T. C. Easton, D.D." and "Geo. P. Pardington," in A. B. Simpson, ed., *A Cloud of Witnesses for Divine Healing*, 2nd ed., (New York: Word, Work and World Publishing, 1887), 63–66, 118–28, resp.

55. In one measure of women's predominance in the movement, James Opp has found that women authored 86 percent of the gender-identified testimonials that appeared in *Triumphs of Faith* from 1890 to 1898; see Opp, "Religion, Medicine, and the Body," 79.

56. David B. Morris, *The Culture of Pain* (Berkeley: University of California Press, 1991), 1–2, 20, 4; and David B. Morris, "Placebo: Conversations at the Disciplinary Borders," in Anne Harrington, ed., *The Placebo Effect: An Interdisciplinary Exploration* (Cambridge: Harvard University Press, 1997), 188, 190–91. For the term *culturogenic*, see Harrington, *Placebo Effect*, 9. Other recent discussions of the relationship among culture, personal belief, and the experience of pain include: Thomas J. Csordas, *Body/Meaning/Healing* (New York: Palgrave, 2002); Glucklich, *Sacred Pain;* Mary-Jo DelVecchio Good et al., *Pain as Human Experience: An Anthropological Perspective* (Berkeley: University of California Press, 1994); Arthur Kleinman, *The Illness Narratives: Suffering, Healing and the Human Condition* (New York: Basic Books, 1988); and Cheryl Mattingly and Linda C. Garro, eds., *Narrative and the Cultural Construction of Illness and Healing* (Berkeley: University of California Press, 2000).

Eight • Observing the Lives of the Saints

1. Zora Neale Hurston, *The Sanctified Church* (New York: Marlowe, 1981), 103. Hurston, well known as a writer, was also trained at Barnard College in anthropology by Franz Boas, and her work for the Works Progress Administration and writings such as *The Sanctified Church* are most informative about African American religion and folklore.

2. W. E. B. DuBois, *The Souls of Black Folk* (New York: Penguin Classics, 1903, Penguin reprint 1996), 154. DuBois's formulation of the preacher, the music, and the frenzy, I feel, led later interpreters of black church traditions to focus merely on emotional manifestations and not on the intellectual or theological reasoning behind ecstatic practices. DuBois would probably have been quite upset about this, but the work of Carter G. Woodson later made such descriptions even more popular, and other chroniclers of African American religious practices followed suit.

3. For more historical information on COGIC, see Ithiel Clemmons, *C. H. Mason and the Church of God in Christ* (Bakersfield, Calif.: Pneuma Life, 1996); and Anthea Butler, "Church Mothers and Migration in the Church of God in Christ," in *Religion in the American South:*

Protestants and Others in History and Culture, ed. Donald Mathews and Beth Barton Schweiger (Chapel Hill: University of North Carolina Press, 2004), 195–218.

4. Studies of COGIC congregations include Arthur Huff Fauset, *Black Gods of the Metropolis: Negro Religious Cults in the Urban North* (Philadelphia: University of Pennsylvania Press, 1944); Hortense Powdermaker, *After Freedom: A Cultural Study in the Deep South* (n.p.: Russell and Russell, 1936); and St. Clair Drake and Horace A. Cayton, *Black Metropolis: A Study of Negro Life in a Northern City* (Chicago: University of Chicago Press, 1945).

5. Dorothy Bass, *Practicing Our Faith* (San Francisco: Jossey Bass, 1997), 5.

6. William A. Clark, "Sanctification in Negro Religion," *Social Forces* 15, no. 4 (May 1937): 545.

7. Michel de Certeau, *The Practice of Everyday Life,* trans. Stephen Rendall (Berkeley: University of California Press, 1984), 39–42.

8. For a more complete explanation of sanctification, see Douglas Jacobsen, *Thinking in the Spirit: Theologies of the Early Pentecostal Movement* (Bloomington: Indiana University Press, 2003), 41–44.

9. Donald Dayton, *Theological Roots of Pentecostalism* (Metuchen, N.J.: Scarecrow Press, 1987), 18. Dayton's explanation of three-stage, two-stage, and Oneness Pentecostalism neatly summarizes the place of sanctification within the different groups. Three-stage Pentecostal and Holiness churches tend to place their emphasis on the sanctification experience, while two-stage and Oneness Pentecostals focus on the baptism of the Spirit, or speaking in tongues.

10. *Official Manual with the Doctrines and Disciplines of the Church of God in Christ* (Memphis: Church of God in Christ, 1973), 58. Many Scripture passages are cited in the manual, including Rom. 6:4, 1 Cor. 6:15–20, Jer. 31:34, and Titus 1:15.

11. Some of the women of COGIC may also have been involved in black chapters of the Women's Christian Temperance Union. See Anthea Butler, "A Peculiar Synergy: Matriarchy and the Church of God in Christ" (Ph.D. diss., Vanderbilt University, 2001), 79.

12. In Mary C. Mason, *The History and Life Work of Bishop C. H. Mason* (Memphis: n.p., 1924), 53.

13. Pearl Page Brown, *Sewing Circle Artistic Fingers* (n.p.: Church of God in Christ, Women's International Conventions, n.d., private collection of Anthea Butler), 15.

14. Jack T. Hunt and Leila Mason Byas, *From Priors Farm to Heaven, Bishop C. H. Mason* (Memphis: Hunt/Fam Publishing, 1995), 25. Mason continued to carefully monitor his diet until the end of his life.

15. *Yearbook of the Church of God in Christ,* 1926 (n.p.: n.p.), 148.

16. In "Bishop R. F. Williams's story," (n.p., n.d., in University of Michigan Library). Sister Carter was one of Bishop Williams's nieces. I think, given other clues, that her testimony is from the early 1930s.

17. Brown, *Sewing Circle,* 4.

18. Purity Resource Book (n.p., n.d., in Dupree African-American Pentecostal and Holiness Collection, Schomburg Center for Research in Black Culture, New York Public Library, New York, N.Y.). This is internal material used in the training of purity class teachers within the COGIC denomination.

19. Mary Mason, *History and Life of C. H. Mason,* 61. This admonition is taken from 1 Cor. 7:5.

20. In Mary Mason, *History and Life of C. H. Mason,* 57

21. Lucille J. Cornelius, *The Pioneer History of the Church of God in Christ* (Memphis: Church of God in Christ, 1975), 52.

22. Laurence Iannaccone, "Why Strict Churches Are Strong," *American Journal of Sociology* 99, no. 5 (Mar. 1994): 1180–1211.

23. Quoted in Hiley Hill, "Negro Storefront Churches in Washington, D.C." (Ph.D. diss., Howard University, 1947), 102.

24. Cornelius, *Pioneer History of Church of God in Christ,* 55.

25. Butler, "Peculiar Synergy," 100–101.

26. Pearl McCollum, "Purity" column, *The Evangelist Speaks,* Nov. 1954, 2–3.

27. Pearl Roberts McCullum, *Historical Sketches of Pioneer Women in the Church of God in Christ Inc.* (n.p.: n.p., 1975), 40. E. J. Dabney, *What It Means to Pray Through* (Philadelphia: E. J. Dabney, 1945), 49.

28. Ann Taves, *Fits, Trances, and Visions: Experiencing Religion and Explaining Experience from Wesley to James* (Princeton: Princeton University Press, 1999), 334. Early Holiness believers from the Keswick tradition, Taves relates, did not think of yieldedness and obedience as matters of emotion. Pentecostals, of course, thought otherwise.

29. David Hall, *Lived Religion in America: Toward a History of Practice* (Princeton: Princeton University Press, 1997), xi. Hall speaks of practices as bearing the marks of both regulation and resistance. I think that in COGIC's case it is also revealing and concealing—and compelling and repelling—persons who are engaged, or not, in these manifestations.

30. The Scripture passage is as quoted in COGIC materials.

31. Mary Mason, *History and Life of C. H. Mason,* 58.

32. Clark, "Sanctification in Negro Religion," 547.

33. In Mary Mason, *History and Life of C. H. Mason,* 58.

34. "Church Celebrates Founder's 50th Anniversary as Leader," *Ebony,* May 1958, p. 58.

35. Judith Weisenfeld and Richard Newman, eds., *This Far by Faith: Readings in African American Women's Religious Biography* (New York: Routledge, 1996), 34.

36. Ford's Holy Spirit baptism provided her with a tactic to use against those who would keep women from preaching.

37. Mary Mason, *History and Life of C. H. Mason,* 88.

38. Henrietta Sellers, WPA interview, Jacksonville, Fla., 19 May 1939. Federal Writer's Project Papers, University of North Carolina, Southern Historical Collection.

39. David Daniels, *The Cultural Renewal of Slave Religion: Charles Price Jones and the Emergence of the Holiness Movement in Mississippi* (New York: Union Theological Seminary, 1992), 185.

40. C. H. Mason, "Doctrinal Subjects of the Church of God in Christ," in *Yearbook of Church of God in Christ,* 29; and in Mary Mason, *History and Life of C. H. Mason.* For Mason's understanding of the dance, see Daniels, *Cultural Renewal of Slave Religion,* 187.

41. Hurston, *Sanctified Church,* 92.

42. Ibid., 91.

43. Clark, "Sanctification in Negro Religion," 546.

44. Quoted in Mary Mason, *History and Life of C. H. Mason,* 54.

45. Quoted in ibid., 55–56.

46. Taves, *Fits, Trances, and Visions,* 336. The Azusa Street revival and its proximity in Los

Angeles to the spiritualist campgrounds made for some interesting interactions between the two groups.

47. "Church Celebrates Founders 50th Anniversary as Leader," *Ebony* (June 1958): 54.

48. Jerma A. Jackson, *Singing in My Soul: Black Gospel Music in a Secular Age* (Chapel Hill: University of North Carolina Press, 2004), 29–30.

49. Jerma A. Jackson, "Testifying at the Cross: Thomas Andrew Dorsey, Sister Rosetta Tharpe, and the Politics of African-American Sacred and Secular Music" (Ph.D. diss., Rutgers University, 1995), 125.

50. Jerma Jackson relates that it may have been Tharpe's mother who encouraged her foray into the nightclub circle, the move that eventually led her to be estranged from COGIC. See Jackson, *Singing in My Soul,* 100–101.

51. Mahalia Jackson, with Evan McLeod Wylie, *Movin' on Up* (New York: Hawthorne, 1967), 58–59.

Nine • *The Practice of Prayer in a Modern Age*

1. *Moody Bible Institute Monthly* (Apr. 1925), 363–64; James Gray, "Modernism a Revolt Against Christianity," *Moody Bible Institute Monthly* (Oct. 1924), 57. The "fundamentalists" studied here constitute one particular strand of a complex web: that part of fundamentalism found in Bible institutes and so-called "faith" missions, and characterized by Keswick holiness themes of absolute surrender and divine power for service. Members of this group would not necessarily have matched the stereotypical image of fundamentalists that emerged from the Scopes "monkey trial" in the 1920s, but they probably formed the heart of the movement. And while such fundamentalists were undoubtedly alarmed by the rise of modernism in the churches, as George Marsden observed, "militancy was not necessarily the *central* trait of fundamentalists. Missions, evangelism, prayer, personal holiness, or a variety of doctrinal concerns may often or usually have been their first interest" (*Fundamentalism and American Culture* [New York: Oxford University Press, 1980], 231).

2. Harry Emerson Fosdick, *Adventurous Religion and Other Essays* (New York: Harper, 1926), 233, 311; Harry Emerson Fosdick, *The Living of These Days: An Autobiography* (New York: Harper, 1956), 67. The liberals dealt with here are for the most part those early-twentieth-century Protestants studied by historians such as Kenneth Cauthen and William Hutchison. Reared largely in evangelical Protestant homes, many of them came to be heavily influenced by philosophical idealism and its religious corollary, divine immanence. Believing that God could be revealed in human cultural development, they sought, in varying degrees, to adapt Christian orthodoxy to modern thought. Though never synonymous with mainstream Protestantism, liberalism did achieve a large measure of influence in the northern mainline denominations and came to dominate most northern Protestant educational institutions. Union Theological Seminary in New York and the University of Chicago Divinity School were particularly well known bastions of the movement. Liberal views were promulgated in journals such as Lyman Abbott's *Outlook,* the University of Chicago's *Biblical World,* and most notably the *Christian Century.*

3. Of course, prayer was only one of a constellation of religious practices of concern to liberals and conservatives. Liberal prayer occurred within a context of practices such as liberal social action, devotion to science, and commitment to intellectual fellowship. Fundamentalist

spirituality included practices such as evangelism, Bible reading, and hymn singing. However, for the sake of space limitations this paper will focus on the particular practice of Christian prayer.

4. Catherine Bell, *Ritual: Perspectives and Dimensions* (New York: Oxford University Press, 1997), 77, 83.

5. Trudy Bush, "A Way to Live" (interview with Dorothy Bass), *Christian Century* (24 Feb. 2004), 22.

6. William Adams Brown, *The Life of Prayer in a World of Science* (New York: Scribner's, 1927), 5, 18; Frederick Spurr, "The Place of Prayer in Life," *The Baptist* 5 (1924): 96.

7. Charles Blanchard, *Getting Things From God* (Wheaton, Ill.: Sword of the Lord, 1915), 57.

8. Donald Meyer, *The Protestant Search for Political Realism, 1919–1941* (Berkeley: University of California Press, 1960), 116; Sinclair Lewis, *Babbitt* (New York: Harcourt, Brace, 1922).

9. Robert Lynd and Helen Lynd, *Middletown: A Study in Contemporary American Culture* (New York: Harcourt, Brace, 1929), 331.

10. Ibid., 337–38.

11. Ibid., 339, 383.

12. James Bennett, *Religion of the Closet* (Andover, Mass.: Flagg and Gould, 1818), 7; Reuben Torrey, *The Power of Prayer and the Prayer of Power* (New York: Fleming Revell, 1924), 16; Harris Hale, "Why I Keep Praying," *The Baptist* 4 (1923), 840.

13. Benjamin Trumbull, "An Address on the Subjects of Prayer and Family Religion" (Northampton, Mass.: William Butler, 1805), 2; W. S. Tyler, *Prayer for Colleges* (New York: M. W. Dodd, 1855), 56.

14. E. M. Bounds, *Power Through Prayer* (Grand Rapids, Mich.: Zondervan, [1912]), 117; Reuben Torrey, "The Duty and Worth of Prayer," *Christian Workers Magazine* 18 (Sept. 1917), 21.

15. S. D. Gordon, *Quiet Talks on How to Pray* (Chicago: Fleming Revell, ca. 1910), 12; Reuben Torrey, *How to Pray* (Chicago: Moody Press, [1900]), 90, 54.

16. Robert Harkness, *Reuben Archer Torrey, The Man, His Message* (Chicago: Bible Institute Colportage Association, ca. 1929), 24–30; Reuben Torrey, "The Duty and Worth of Prayer," *Christian Workers Magazine* 18 (Sept. 1917), 21.

17. Lillie Oliver, *Richard Oliver: A Challenge to American Youth,* in Joel Carpenter, ed., *Sacrificial Lives: Young Martyrs and Fundamentalist Idealism* (New York: Garland, 1988), 41, 49, 80.

18. Ibid., 129–30, 149.

19. *Good News* (weekly newsletter of the Moody Church) (1 Feb. 1919); *Moody Church News* (May 1923); *Good News* (24 Nov. 1917); Nominating Committee document, 12 Jan. 1927); *Moody Church News* (Jan. 1927).

20. *Good News*, 11 Feb. 1920, 11 May 1921); *Moody Church News* (Jan. 1929); *Moody Church News* (May 1923).

21. *Moody Church News* (May 1926, Jan. 1927).

22. Ibid., Sept. 1928; Dec. 1926.

23. D. L. Moody, *Thoughts for the Quiet Hour* (Chicago: Moody Press, ca. 1900), foreword.

24. Mark Sidwell, "The History of the Winona Lake Bible Conference," (Ph.D. diss., Bob Jones University, 1988), 56, 90, 139, 251.

25. *Winona Herald,* May 1918.

26. Quote from a 1929 Bible conference pamphlet; "Winona Program Number," 1928.

27. Minutes of the Great Commission Prayer League, in the Moody Church Archives, box 42-2; *Good News* (Dec. 1921); Virginia Brereton, *Training God's Army: The American Bible School, 1880–1940* (Bloomington: Indiana University Press, 1990), 115.

28. Lettie Cowman, *Streams in the Desert* (Grand Rapids, Mich.: Zondervan, [1925]), fore-word.

29. Herbert Willett and Charles Clayton Morrison, *The Daily Altar* (Chicago: Christian Century Press, 1918), foreword; James M. Campbell, *The Place of Prayer in the Christian Religion* (New York: Methodist Book Concern, 1915), 257.

30. Harry Emerson Fosdick, *The Manhood of the Master* (1913); *The Meaning of Prayer* (1915); *The Meaning of Faith* (1917); and *The Meaning of Service* (1920). All volumes were published by the Association Press, New York; also William Adams Brown, *The Quiet Hour* (New York: Association Press, 1926).

31. Fosdick, *Meaning of Prayer*, 84–85; Brown, *The Life of Prayer in a World of Science*, 53–54, 173–74.

32. Marilee Scroggs, *A Light in the City: The Fourth Presbyterian Church of Chicago* (Chicago: Fourth Presbyterian Church, 1990), 72, 77, 100.

33. *Fourth Church Monthly*, Mar. 1926, Sept. 1926, Apr. 1928.

34. Charles Harvey Arnold, *God Before You and Behind: The Hyde Park Union Church Through a Century, 1874–1974* (Chicago: Hyde Park Union Church, 1974), 20–34; *Hyde Park Baptist Review* (Jan. 1923).

35. *Hyde Park Baptist Review* (Oct. 1926, Nov. 1928, Dec. 1929). *Hyde Park Baptist Church Calendar* (25 Oct. 1925, 1 Dec. 1929, 1 Nov. 1925).

36. Borden Bowne, *The Immanence of God* (Boston: Houghton, Mifflin, 1905), 149; Campbell, *The Place of Prayer*, 201.

37. William Adams Brown, *A Teacher and His Times* (New York: Scribner's, 1940), 153; Brown, *The Quiet Hour*, 48.

38. Brown, *A Teacher and His Times*, 147.

39. Fosdick, *Adventurous Religion*, 87.

40. *Fourth Church Monthly* (Jan. 1924); *Hyde Park Baptist Review* (Sept. 1921); *Fourth Church Monthly* (May 1918).

41. Henry Nelson Wieman, *Methods of Private Religious Living* (New York: Macmillan, 1929), 18–23; Shailer Mathews, "Putting Religion to the Test," interview by Neil M. Clark, *American Magazine* 109 (June 1930), 50–51.

42. Lyman Abbott, *What Christianity Means to Me* (New York: Macmillan, 1922), 6–7; Morgan P. Noyes, *Henry Sloane Coffin: The Man and His Ministry* (New York: Scribner's, 1964), 118.

43. *Good News* (21 July 1917).

44. Brown, *Life of Prayer in a World of Science*, 173–74; Bell, *Ritual*, 77.

Ten • Cosmopolitan Piety

1. Thomas Wentworth Higginson (hereafter TWH) letter to editor William Lloyd Garrison, 19 Mar. 1856, published in *Liberator*, 9 May 1856; TWH, 17 Mar. 1856, Houghton Library, Harvard University, bMS Am 784, box 4, #546. (Unless otherwise stated, TWH documents, unpublished and published, are in the Houghton Library collection.)

2. Mary Thacher Higginson, *Thomas Wentworth Higginson: The Story of His Life* (Boston: Houghton Mifflin, 1914), 328, 411–12.

3. Sympathy is the subject of a considerable literature, especially in the history of moral philosophy. For two accounts that are particularly helpful, see Jennifer A. Herdt, *Religion and Faction in Hume's Moral Philosophy* (Cambridge: Cambridge University Press, 1997); and David Marshall, *The Surprising Effects of Sympathy: Marivaux, Diderot, Rousseau, and Mary Shelley* (Chicago: University of Chicago Press, 1988). I take Herdt's reading, in particular, to be a helpful corrective to the more suspicious readings of sympathy current among many interpreters on the American side. For an incisive examination of the extensions—and limits—of sympathy in nineteenth-century America, see Robert S. Cox, *Body and Soul: A Sympathetic History of American Spiritualism* (Charlottesville: University of Virginia Press, 2003).

4. TWH, "The Sympathy of Religions," *Radical* 8 (Feb. 1871): 2, 20.

5. Annie Payson Call, *As a Matter of Course* (Boston: Roberts Brothers, 1898), 82.

6. "Reality in Christian Sympathy," *Congregationalist* 14 (1885): 187.

7. Elizabeth B. Clark, "'The Sacred Rights of the Weak': Pain, Sympathy, and the Culture of Individual Rights in Antebellum America," *Journal of American History* 82 (Sept. 1995): 463–93, Clarke's quotation on 464 and Garrison's on 476. See also Andrew Burstein, "The Political Character of Sympathy," *Journal of the Early Republic* 21 (Winter 2001): 601–32; Roy R. Male, "Sympathy—A Key Word in American Romanticism," in *Romanticism and the American Renaissance*, ed. Kenneth Walter Cameron (Hartford: Transcendental Books, 1979), 19–23.

8. TWH, "Cheerful Yesterdays," *Atlantic Monthly* 79 (1897): 251.

9. The best biographical account of Higginson as activist and reformer remains Tilden G. Edelstein, *Strange Enthusiasm: A Life of Thomas Wentworth Higginson* (New Haven: Yale University Press, 1968). Edelstein is skimpy in his attention to Higginson's religious thought and does not discuss "The Sympathy of Religions."

10. TWH, "The Return of Faith," file for 1854–1856, Houghton Library, Harvard University, bMS Am 1081.3 (12). The manuscript is scattered through 13 folders, some of which include other early religious writings and sermons of TWH. The collection has not been reordered to fit TWH's short outline of 11 chapters in folder 7, #91, so it takes some careful reconstruction in reading the chapter notes that do survive. See folders 7, #94–95; 8, #113; 11, #169; 12, #177, 179 for the cited quotations.

11. TWH, "Scripture Idolatry" (Worcester, Mass.: John Keith, 1854), 7–8, 11–12, 14–15; TWH to Garrison.

12. TWH, "Scripture Idolatry," 16; TWH, "Extra-Christian or Anti-Christian," *Index* 3 (1872): 37.

13. TWH, "My Creed So Far As I Have One," bMS Am 784, box 6. The manuscript is undated, but TWH himself later added a note that it was "written probably between 1870 & 1880." It resembles in some details a short piece he published in 1874. See TWH, "Law and Love," *Index* 5 (1874): 187.

14. TWH, *The Results of Spiritualism* (New York: Munson, [1859]), 19, 21; TWH, *The Rationale of Spiritualism* (New York: Ellinwood, 1859), 3–4.

15. TWH, diaries, 24 Jan.–19 Feb. 1870; 5 Jan. 1871, bMs 1162.

16. TWH, clippings on "The Sympathy of Religions," in scrapbooks, bMS Am 1256.2.

17. TWH, 15 Dec. 1871, bMS Am 784, box 6, #1077; frontispiece inscribed from TWH to Eva

S. Moore in *The Writings of Thomas Wentworth Higginson,* 7 vols. (Boston: Houghton, Mifflin, 1900), *AC85.H5358.C900wb v.7.

18. Mary Higginson, *Thomas Westworth Higginson,* 268. The standard work on the Free Religious Association remains Stow Persons, *Free Religion: An American Faith* (New Haven, 1947; Boston: Beacon, 1963). Also very helpful on the FRA's importance as a link between transcendentalism and the World's Parliament of Religions is Carl T. Jackson's *The Oriental Religions and American Thought: Nineteenth-Century Explorations* (Westport, Conn.: Greenwood, 1981), 103–22.

19. TWH, *The Sympathy of Religions* (Boston: Free Religious Association, 1876); *Unity Church-Door Pulpit,* 16 June 1885.

20. TWH, "Sympathy of Religions," 1–2.

21. TWH, "Sympathy of Religions," 2–5.

22. TWH, "Sympathy of Religions," 3, 12–13, 16, 18, 20–22. TWH prefaced his inclusion of "Galla Negroes" with the condescending adjective *ignorant.* That word was probably intended as descriptive of their lack of formal knowledge of "technical Christianity" (which might well have been, in Higginson's view, a good thing). Elsewhere he spoke of "the beautiful prayers of the Gallas" and attributed "an inspiration akin to genius" to their songs. See TWH, "The Use of Religion," *Index* 4 (1873): 209.

23. TWH, "Sympathy of Religions," 3, 12–13, 16, 18, 20–22.

24. See David Wasson, *Christianity and Universal Religion* (Boston: Parker Fraternity, 1865); Samuel Longfellow, "The Unity and Universality of the Religious Ideas," *Radical* 3 (1868): 433–57; Samuel Johnson, "The Natural Sympathy of Religions," *Proceedings at the Third Annual Meeting of the Free Religious Association* (Boston: Wilson, 1870), 59–83. Wasson and Higginson later modestly disagreed over the sympathy of religions, and Wasson returned to a more Christ-centered view of the universal religion. See TWH, "Bread Alone," *Index* 2 (1871): 165.

25. John W. Chadwick, "Universal Religion," *New World* 3 (Sept. 1894): 405, 416, 418; M. J. Savage, *Life* (Boston: Ellis, 1890), 211–23; C. A. Bartol, "Cosmopolitan Religion," *New World* 2 (Mar. 1893): 51–60; Ednah Dow Cheney, *Reminiscences* (Boston: Lee and Shepard, 1902), 162–65; L. Maria Child, *Aspirations of the World: A Chain of Opals* (Boston: Roberts, 1878), 257–58.

26. William J. Potter, "'Sympathy of Religions,'" *Index* 3 (1872): 329; W. Creighton Peden and Everett J. Tarbox, Jr., eds., *The Collected Essays of Francis Ellingwood Abbot (1836–1903), American Philosopher and Free Religionist,* 4 vols. (Lewiston, N.Y.: Mellen, 1996), 1:321–24; Francis E. Abbot, "A Study of Religion: The Name and the Thing," *Index* 4 (1873): 109; Joseph Henry Allen, "The Alleged Sympathy of Religions," *New World* 4 (June 1895): 312, 320; William Wallace Fenn, "The Possibilities of Mysticism in Modern Thought," *New World* 6 (June 1897): 201. Potter's sermon manuscripts contain recurrent reflections on these themes. See William J. Potter, "The Bibles of the World as Showing the Antipathies & Sympathies of Religions," 4 Nov. 1877; "One Spirit, Many Manifestations," 10 July 1870; "Unity of the Spirit: The Progress of Mankind toward Spiritual Unity," 9 Oct. 1870; "The East & the West in Religion," 1 Nov. 1874; all in New Bedford (Massachusetts) Free Public Library, Archives.

27. Potter, "'Sympathy of Religions,'" 329; Peden and Tarbox, *Essays of Francis Abbot,* 1:321–24.

28. TWH, "Sympathy of Religions," 23; TWH to Garrison; TWH, 22 Nov. 1855, bMS Am 784, box 4, #528; TWH, "Fayal and the Portuguese," *Atlantic Monthly* 6 (Nov. 1860): 533–35. "Faial" is now the accepted spelling, but for historical purposes I have retained the nineteenth-century

spelling. On Higginson's interest in health regimens, see TWH, "Saints, and Their Bodies," *Atlantic Monthly* 1 (Mar. 1858): 582–95.

29. S. G. W. Benjamin, *The Atlantic Islands as Resorts of Health and Pleasure* (New York: Harper, 1878); Albert L. Gihon, *The Azores and Madeira Islands, the Great Sanitarium of the World: Sketches of Interest to Tourists and Travelers* (Boston: Bartlett, [1877]); Herman Canfield, "The Azores as a Health Resort," *Around the World* 1 (1893–1894): 163–64; C. Alice Baker, *A Summer in the Azores with a Glimpse of Madeira* (Boston: Lee and Shepard, 1882), 3–4.

30. TWH, 23 July 1855, bMS Am 784, box 4, #505; TWH, "Fayal," 526.

31. TWH, 9–13 Nov. 1855, bMS Am 784, box 4, #520, 525, 527.

32. Henrique de Aguiar Oliveira Rodrigues, ed., "The Diary of Catherine Green Hickling, 1786–1788," *Gávea-Brown* 15–16 (Jan. 1994–Dec. 1995): 122–123, 130, 141, 145–46, 148, 160, 178.

33. Silas Weston, *Visit to a Volcano: Or, What I Saw at the Western Islands* (Providence, R.I.: E. P. Weston, 1856), 12–15, 25. A more sympathetic travel guide, the only one written by an emigrant from the Azores to the United States, came later with Borges de F. Henriques, *A Trip to the Azores or Western Islands* (Boston: Lee and Shepard, 1867).

34. Robert Steele, *A Tour through Part of the Atlantic; Or, Recollections from Madeira, the Azores (or Western Isles), and Newfoundland* (London: Stockdale, 1810), 42, 52–54, 103, 118–19; Edward Boid, *A Description of the Azores, or Western Islands* (London: Bull and Churton, 1834), 57–58; John Fowler, *Journal of a Tour in the State of New York, in the Year 1830; with Remarks on Agriculture in those Parts Most Eligible for Settlers: And Return to England by the Western Islands* (London: Whittaker, Treacher, and Arnot, 1831), 269–70.

35. Joseph May, ed., *Samuel Longfellow: Memoir and Letters* (Boston: Houghton Mifflin, 1894), 24–37; Roxana Lewis Dabney, comp., *Annals of the Dabney Family in Fayal, 1806–1871*, 3 vols. (Boston: Mudge, [1892]), 1:456, 476–79; 2:533, 608, 643, 649–51, 715–16; 3:1364, 1398, 1483.

36. May, *Samuel Longfellow*, 38–40; TWH, "Fayal," 540–41. For analysis of Protestant spectating of Catholicism, see especially Jenny Franchot, *Roads to Rome: The Antebellum Protestant Encounter with Catholicism* (Berkeley: University of California Press, 1994).

37. TWH, 13 Nov. 1855, #527; 25 Nov. 1855, #529; 8 Dec. 1855, 16 Dec. 1855, #531; 26 Dec. 1855, #533; 31 Dec. 1855, #536; 5 Feb. 1856, #543; 14 Mar. 1856, #549.

38. TWH, 18 Feb. 1856, #546; 20–22 Mar. 1856, #550; TWH, "Fayal," 541.

39. TWH, 18 Feb. 1856, #546.

40. TWH, "Fayal," 533, 540–43; TWH, 5 Mar. 1855, #499; 6 Dec. 1855, #531. The religious elements of his nature writing were especially evident in an 1858 essay on water-lilies, which offered reflections on the plant's significance in Hindu and Buddhist symbolism. See Howard N. Meyer, ed., *The Magnificent Activist: The Writings of Thomas Wentworth Higginson (1823–1911)* (New York: Da Capo, 2000), 414–26.

41. TWH, "Sympathy of Religions," 23.

42. TWH, "Sympathy of Religions," 18, 23; TWH, "Fayal," 543.

43. TWH, *Army Life in a Black Regiment* (Boston, 1870; New York: Norton, 1984), 122. Another practical instance in which Higginson took the Catholic side against Protestant opinion was on composition of the Boston School Board, from which Protestants tried to exclude Catholics. See TWH, "Roman Catholics on the Defensive," *Index* 6 (1885): 146–47. The opposite relationship between practice and profession no doubt remained equally, if not more, common. See, for example, Grant Wacker, "A Plural World: The Protestant Awakening to World Religions,"

in *Between the Times: The Travail of the Protestant Establishment in America, 1900–1960,* ed. William R. Hutchison (Cambridge: Cambridge University Press, 1989), 273.

44. TWH, *Army Life,* 41, 71. Higginson was acknowledged as "above all others" in his support of the first book-length collection of spirituals: William Francis Allen, Charles Pickard Ware, and Lucy McKim Garrison, *Slave Songs of the United States* (New York: A. Simpson, 1867), xxxvii. His contributions to the work are especially evident in the notations to the songs (pp. 4–6, 19–21, 38, 45, 48, 72, 93, 114–15).

45. TWH, *Army Life,* 41, 45, 48, 55, 70–72, 187–213, 241; TWH, "Negro Spirituals," *Atlantic Monthly* 19 (June 1867): 685–94; TWH, "Use of Religion," 209; TWH, "Remarks," in Free Religious Association, *Report of Addresses at a Meeting Held in Boston, May 30, 1867 to Consider the Conditions, Wants and Prospects of Free Religion in America* (Boston: Adams, 1867), 51; Christopher Looby, ed., *The Complete Civil War Journal and Selected Letters of Thomas Wentworth Higginson* (Chicago: University of Chicago Press, 2000), 218. Higginson apparently added the comparisons to mysticism and transcendentalism upon further reflection. Note their absence from the relevant passage in Looby's critical edition of Higginson's wartime journal (86) versus Higginson's published version in *Army Life* (70–71).

46. TWH, "A Correction," *Index* 6 (1875): 697; Octavius Brooks Frothingham, "Address of the President," FRA, *Proceedings at the Third Annual Meeting,* 16, 22; Johnson, "Natural Sympathy," 60–61; TWH, "Address," FRA, *Proceedings at the Sixth Annual Meeting* (Boston: Cochrane and Sampson, 1873), 60–61.

47. TWH, "Address," in FRA, *Proceedings at the Tenth Annual Meeting* (Boston: Free Religious Association, 1877), 86–88.

48. FRA, *Proceedings at the Twenty-Sixth Annual Meeting* (Boston: FRA, 1894), 12–13, 22–23; TWH, "The Sympathy of Religions," in *The World's Parliament of Religions,* ed. John Henry Barrows, 2 vols. (Chicago: Parliament Publishing, 1893), 1:780–84.

49. Lewis G. Janes, "Address," in FRA, *Proceedings at the Thirtieth Annual Meeting* (New Bedford, Mass.: FRA, 1897), 6–14; "Program of the Summer Lectures at Greenacre-on-the-Piscataqua," 1897, box 6, Sarah J. Farmer Papers, National Bahá'í Archives, Wilmette, Ill.

50. Swami Sârâdananda, "The Sympathy of Religions," *Journal of Practical Metaphysics* 1 (Aug. 1897): 318–19.

51. "The Greenacre Lectures," *Boston Evening Transcript,* 4 Sept. 1897; Alfred W. Martin, *Great Religious Teachers of the East* (New York: Macmillan, 1911), 3–4; Alfred W. Martin, *Seven Great Bibles* (New York: Stokes, 1930), v–viii.

52. William Norman Guthrie, "Whitman and the American of the Future," 31 May 1912 noted in *Walt Whitman Fellowship Papers* (Philadelphia: The Fellowship, 1912); William Norman Guthrie, *Modern Poet Prophets* (Cincinnati: Clarke, 1897), 246, 250, 254, 257, 331; William Norman Guthrie, *Offices of Mystical Religion* (New York: Century, 1927), xxiv; William Norman Guthrie, ed., *Leaves of the Greater Bible: A Spiritual Anthology* (New York: Brentano's, 1917).

53. Guthrie, *Offices,* xxiii; Guthrie, *Leaves,* unpaginated foreword.

Eleven • The Practice of Dance for the Future of Christianity

The author wishes to thank Leslie Callahan and Bryan Bademan for their comments on earlier versions of this essay.

1. Minutes of Meeting of Rector, Wardens, and Vestrymen of St. Mark's-in-the-Bouwerie, 15 Feb. 1932, St. Mark's Episcopal Church Vestry Minutes, 1793–1937, New York Historical Society (hereafter cited as St. Mark's Vestry Minutes).

2. On the history of American Christian opposition to dance, see Ann Louise Wagner, *Adversaries of Dance: From the Puritans to the Present* (Urbana: University of Illinois Press, 1997).

3. For a detailed account of the evolution of Episcopal liturgy, see Michael Moriarty, *The Liturgical Revolution: Prayer Book Revision and Associated Parishes: A Generation of Change in the Episcopal Church* (New York: Church Hymnal Corp., 1996).

4. William Norman Guthrie (hereafter WNG), *A Tentative Statement of the Principles Involved in the Work at Present Conducted at St. Mark's-in-the-Bouwerie* (New York: St. Mark's-in-the-Bouwerie, 1921), 12, 22; WNG, *St. Mark's-in-the-Bouwerie: A Vital Expression of Present-Day Religion in New York City* (New York: St. Mark's-in-the-Bouwerie, 1929).

5. This biographical information is drawn from Geoffrey T. Hellman, "Profiles: Lights, Please!" *New Yorker* (31 Jan. 1931), 22–25; and Cynthia Alice McEvoy, "When Seraphim and Muses Met: Some Aspects of the Ministry of William Norman Guthrie, Rector of St. Mark's-in-the-Bouwerie, New York, 1911–1937" (M.A. thesis, New York University, 1955).

6. WNG, *Tentative Statement*, 12–17.

7. Hellman, "Profiles: Lights, Please!", 25; and *St. Mark's-in-the-Bouwerie,* (New York: St. Mark's-in-the-Bouwerie, 1932). The latter booklet reprinted an article that originally appeared in the *New York Sun,* 11 Apr. 1931.

8. Robert A. Orsi, ed., *Gods of the City: Religion and the American Urban Landscape* (Bloomington: Indiana University Press, 1999), 63.

9. "Dr. Guthrie Stirs Throng by Defense," *New York Times,* 17 Dec. 1923, 1.

10. WNG to Mr. Shipler, 14 Apr. 1928, box 1, folder 53, William Norman Guthrie Papers, St. Mark's-Church-in-the-Bowery Archives, New York City (hereafter Guthrie Papers).

11. A prominent example is William R. Hutchison, *The Modernist Impulse in American Protestantism* (Durham, N.C.: Duke University Press, 1992).

12. "Girls Dance under Spotlight at Church," *New York Times,* 27 Mar. 1922; WNG, *The Pageant in Honor of the Blessed Virgin Mary on the Sunday Nearest to the Feast of the Annunciation, St. Mark's-in-the-Bouwerie, 1920–1924* (New York: St. Mark's-in-the-Bouwerie, 1924).

13. "Lights in Church Reflect Emotions," *New York Times,* 16 Oct. 1921; "Play Lights to Aid St. Mark's Service," *New York Times,* 17 Oct. 1921.

14. "Women Faint in Jam at Mystic Service," *New York Times,* 19 Nov. 1923. The article indicates that some of the women in the audience, overcome by the crowd and the spectacle, fainted during the service.

15. McEvoy, "When Seraphim and Muses Met," 41, 67. Isadora Duncan's topic in the aborted 1922 lecture was to be "the moralizing effects of dancing on the human soul," suggestive of her interest in religion and dance. For more on Duncan's life and career, see Ann Daly, *Done into Dance: Isadora Duncan in America* (Bloomington: Indiana University Press, 1995); and Peter Kurth, *Isadora: A Sensational Life* (Boston: Little, Brown, 2001).

16. McEvoy, "When Seraphim and Muses Met," 73. On Graham's life and career, see Julia L. Foulkes, *Modern Bodies: Dance and American Modernism from Martha Graham to Alvin Ailey* (Chapel Hill: University of North Carolina Press, 2002); and Agnes De Mille, *Martha: The Life and Work of Martha Graham* (New York: Random House, 1991).

17. Phoebe Guthrie to Ruth St. Denis, 15 Aug. 1932, folder 409, Ruth St. Denis Letters, 1914–1959, New York Public Library Performing Arts Library, New York City (hereafter Ruth St. Denis Letters).

18. Ted Shawn, *Every Little Movement: A Book About François Delsarte,* 2nd ed. (New York: Dance Horizons, 1974), 87; cited in J. G. Davies, *Liturgical Dance: An Historical, Theological and Practical Handbook* (London: SCM Press, 1984), 78; and Margaret Fisk Taylor and Paula Nelson, *A Time to Dance: Symbolic Movement in Worship* (Philadelphia: United Church Press, 1967), 138.

19. Cited in Nancy Lee Chalfa Ruyter, *Reformers and Visionaries: The Americanization of the Art of Dance* (New York: Dance Horizons, 1979), 67.

20. Naima Prevots, *American Pageantry: A Movement for Art and Democracy* (Ann Arbor, Mich.: UMI Research Press, 1990), 131–48. See also David Glassberg, *American Historical Pageantry: The Uses of Tradition in the Early Twentieth Century* (Chapel Hill: University of North Carolina Press, 1990).

21. A few examples of this literature are: Episcopal Church Commission on Church Pageantry and Drama, *The Production of Religious Drama: A Primer* (New York: Presiding Bishop and Council, Department of Missions, 1922); Committee on Religious Drama Federal Council of the Churches of Christ in America, *Religious Dramas* (New York: Century, 1923–1926); William V. Meredith, *Pageantry and Dramatics in Religious Education* (New York: Abingdon Press, 1921); Division of Plays and Pageants Methodist Episcopal Church, *Seven Dramatic Services of Worship* (New York: Methodist Book Concern, 1928); and Mary Russell, *Pageants for Special Days in the Church Year* (Garden City, N.Y.: Doubleday, Doran, 1928).

22. WNG to Canon J. W. Dwelley, 23 Jan. 1931, box 1, folder 19, Guthrie Papers.

23. Phoebe Ann Guthrie to Ruth St. Denis, 15 Aug. 1932, folder 409, Ruth St. Denis Letters; Phoebe Ann Guthrie to Ruth St. Denis, n.d., 1938, folder 510, Ruth St. Denis Letters.

24. "Girls Dance under Spotlight at Church," (*New York Times,* 27 Mar. 1922); "Women Faint in Jam at Mystic Service," (*New York Times,* 19 Nov. 1923.)

25. "Bishop Summons Guthrie to Explain Dance at St. Mark's," *New York Times,* 13 Dec. 1923; "Manning Command to Rector Divulged," *New York Times,* 16 Dec. 1923.

26. "Dr. Guthrie's Brother against Church Dance," *New York Times,* 15 May 1924, 12.

27. "Barefoot Dancing May be Barred by St. Mark's Rector." *New York Evening Post,* 14 Dec. 1923.

28. John D'Emilio and Estelle B. Freedman, *Intimate Matters: A History of Sexuality in America,* 2nd ed. (Chicago: University of Chicago Press, 1997), 223–26, and plates 47–51.

29. Cited in McEvoy, "When Seraphim and Muses Met," 37.

30. WNG, *Pageant in Honor of the Blessed Virgin Mary,* 7.

31. See Ann Taves, *Fits, Trances, and Visions: Experiencing Religion and Explaining Experience from Wesley to James* (Princeton: Princeton University Press, 1999).

32. "Women Faint in Jam at Mystic Service."

33. "Many Queer Cults Are Outgrowth of Sects' 'Modernism,'" *The (Los Angeles) Tidings,* 4 Jan. 1924.

34. WNG, *Pageant in Honor of the Blessed Virgin Mary,* 7.

35. WNG, *Tentative Statement,* 15.

36. WNG, *Evangelical Offices of Worship and Meditation* (New York: Schulte Press, 1930), vi–ix.

37. WNG, *Pageant in Honor of the Blessed Virgin Mary*, 22.

38. Hellman, "Profiles: Lights, Please!" 22–25. Sally Promey's essay in Chapter 12 of this volume offers an insightful discussion of the politics of taste cultures in a slightly later period.

39. WNG, *Pageant in Honor of the Blessed Virgin Mary*, 8. Emphasis in original.

40. For a few examples, see Janet Forsythe Fishburn, *The Fatherhood of God and the Victorian Family: The Social Gospel in America* (Philadelphia: Fortress Press, 1981); Margaret Bendroth, "Women and Missions: Conflict and Changing Roles in the Presbyterian Church in the United States of America, 1870–1935," *American Presbyterian* 65, no. 1 (Spring 1987); Gail Bederman, "'The Women Have Had Charge of the Church Work Long Enough': The Men and Religion Forward Movement of 1911–1912 and the Masculinization of Middle-Class Protestantism," *American Quarterly* 41, no. 3 (1989); and David Morgan, *Visual Piety: A History and Theory of Popular Religious Images* (Berkeley: University of California Press, 1998).

41. WNG, *Pageant in Honor of the Blessed Virgin Mary*, 15.

42. On religion and the body at the turn of the century, see Beryl Satter, *Each Mind a Kingdom: American Women, Sexual Purity, and the New Thought Movement, 1875–1920* (Berkeley: University of California Press, 1999); and Marie Griffith, *Born Again Bodies: Flesh and Spirit in American Christianity* (Berkeley: University of California Press, 2004).

43. The Rector, Wardens, and Vestry of St. Mark's-in-the-Bouwerie, "The Popular Statement of the Platform of St. Mark's-in-the-Bouwerie," The Feast of the Epiphany, 1924, Special Programs, 1923–1947, Pagan Rituals and Eurythmic Dances, Parish Records Series, box 59, Episcopal Diocese of New York (hereafter EDNY). Solon Borglum was the brother of Gutzon Borglum, famous for sculpting Mt. Rushmore.

44. "Churches as Play Places," *New York Times*, 29 Feb. 1921.

45. Guthrie praised Hall's work in WNG to Mr. Easton, 20 Apr. 1928, box 1, folder 53, Guthrie Papers; and WNG, *St. Mark's-in-the-Bouwerie and the Problem of Liberalism in Modern Religion* (New York: Wardens and Vestrymen of St. Mark's-in-the-Bouwerie, 1931), 16. My discussion of Hall's work relies on Gail Bederman, *Manliness and Civilization: A Cultural History of Gender and Race in the United States, 1880–1917* (Chicago: University of Chicago Press, 1995), 77–120.

46. WNG, *The Relation of the Dance to Religion* (New York: Petrus Stuyvesant Book Guild, [1923]), 25–27.

47. One classic example of this method is Emile Durkheim, *The Elementary Forms of Religious Life*, trans. Karen E. Fields (1912; New York: Free Press, 1995). Guthrie's work shares with Durkheim's an emphasis on the social function of religion. For an insightful critique of the search for origins in Durkheim and in religious studies more broadly, see Tomoko Masuzawa, *In Search of Dreamtime: The Quest for the Origin of Religion* (Chicago: University of Chicago Press, 1993).

48. WNG, *Relation of the Dance to Religion*, 12–13.

49. W. O. E. Oesterley, *The Sacred Dance: A Study in Comparative Folklore* (Cambridge: Cambridge University Press, 1923), iv–x. Guthrie's *Relation of Dance to Religion*, 9, referred readers to both Oesterley and Havelock Ellis (see next note).

50. WNG, *Pageant in Honor of the Blessed Virgin Mary*, 6; WNG, *Relation of the Dance to Religion*, 15. Havelock Ellis, in *The Dance of Life* ([Boston: Houghton Mifflin, 1923], 34–62), argued that dancing was the "source of all the arts," the original expression of love, and the most "essential . . . part of all vital and unregenerate religion," including early Christianity.

51. WNG, *Relation of the Dance to Religion*, 13. Guthrie's insistence on the primacy of ritual in religion, along with his emphasis on origins, suggests influence from the Cambridge Ritualists—an influential group of classicists who developed similar ideas between 1900 and 1915. There is no direct evidence for this, though Guthrie's criticism of James Frazer's *The Golden Bough* (from which the Cambridge Ritualists borrowed the comparison between ancient Greece and contemporary "primitives") demonstrates his engagement in ritual studies debates (see *Relation of the Dance to Religion*, 5–8). On the Cambridge Ritualists and their relation to Frazer, see Robert Ackerman, *The Myth and Ritual School: J. G. Frazer and the Cambridge Ritualists* (New York: Garland, 1991).

52. "St. Mark's Church Plans Indian Dance," *New York Times*, 4 May 1924; WNG, *Tentative Statement*, 37.

53. McEvoy, "When Seraphim and Muses Met," 30.

54. "Manning Command to Rector Divulged."

55. Referred to in "Feast of the Annunciation Observed in Old New York Parish with Impressive Festival Service," n.d. 1921, Special Programs, 1923–1947, Pagan Rituals and Eurhythmic Dances, Parish Records Series, box 59, EDNY.

56. "St. Mark's Stages Aboriginal Dance," *New York Times*, 12 May 1924.

57. Tisa Wenger, "Modernists, Pueblo Indians, and the Politics of Primitivism," in *Race and Religion in the American West*, ed. Fay Botham and Sara Patterson (University of Arizona Press, 2006).

58. "Preserving Indian Dances," *New York Times*, 8 May 1923.

59. Edith Dabb, "Indian Dances Degrading, Says Y.W.C.A. Leader," *New York Tribune*, 25 Nov. 1923; Edith Dabb, "Evils of Tribal Dances," *New York Times*, 2 Dec. 1923.

60. "Dr. Guthrie Enlists Aboriginal Ritual," *New York Times*, 26 Nov. 1923.

61. Mary Austin to WNG, 25 June 1931, box 1, folder 24, Guthrie Papers.

62. "St. Mark's Church Shelters Jobless," *New York Times*, 2 Jan. 1921.

63. "Praise of Bishop Led by Dr. Grant," *New York Times*, 28 Jan. 1921. Bishop Manning was widely recognized as a leader in the Anglo-Catholic or "high church" movement, which emphasized the importance of episcopal succession and authority, the sanctity of the sacraments, and liturgical and sacramental continuity through time. Manning opposed fundamentalism, which never gained a significant following among Episcopalians, as well as modernism, and so the Anglo-Catholics represented the conservative end of the Episcopal spectrum. See William H. Katerberg, *Modernity and the Dilemma of North American Anglican Identities, 1880–1950* (Montreal: McGill-Queen's University Press, 2001), 124–27.

64. "St. Mark's Church Shelters Jobless."

65. "Zero's Band to Visit St. Mark's," *New York Times*, 28 Dec. 1924.

66. WNG, *Tentative Statement*, 22. According to McEvoy ("When Seraphim and Muses Met," 73), some of St. Mark's tenants included artists like Archibald MacLeish, Rachel Field, James Gould Cozzens, and Edna St. Vincent Millay.

67. WNG, *Tentative Statement*, 16.

68. "The Christ Myth in Dr. Guthrie's Text." *New York Times*, 31 Dec. 1923, 4.

69. WNG to Dr. Dettinger, 21 Nov. 1927, box 1, folder 54, Guthrie Papers.

70. The emerging field of "whiteness" studies documents how this conception of race developed over the nineteenth and twentieth centuries as European immigrants such as the Irish

and the Italians increasingly claimed the privilege of "white" identity to clearly distinguish themselves from the perennially disenfranchised blacks. Foundational texts in this literature include David R. Roediger, *The Wages of Whiteness: Race and the Making of the American Working Class* (New York: Verso, 1991); Noel Ignatiev, *How the Irish Became White* (New York: Routledge, 1996); Matthew Frye Jacobson, *Whiteness of a Different Color: European Immigrants and the Alchemy of Race* (Cambridge: Harvard University Press, 1998).

71. WNG, *Tentative Statement,* 19.

72. *New York Times,* 14 May 1917, cited in McEvoy, "When Seraphim and Muses Met," 22.

73. WNG, *Leaves of the Greater Bible: A Spiritual Anthology* (New York: Brentano's, 1917), 48–77.

74. WNG, *The Religion of Old Glory* (New York: George H. Doran Co., 1918), 400.

75. WNG, "Letter from William Norman Guthrie in *The Churchman,*" n.d. 1924, Special Programs, 1923–1947, Pagan Rituals and Eurythmic Dances, Parish Records Series, box 59, EDNY.

76. Ellen M. Litwicki, *America's Public Holidays, 1865–1920* (Washington, D.C.: Smithsonian Institution Press, 2000).

77. David Yoo, in Chapter 5 of this volume, analyzes the practice of religious nationalism among Korean American Christians and illustrates the complexities of nationalistic religion for an immigrant group.

78. WNG, "A Liberal Church in Practice," in WNG, *Tentative Statement,* 14.

79. WNG, *Leaves of the Greater Bible.*

80. "Sun-God Service Held in St. Mark's," *New York Times,* 19 Mar. 1923.

81. Ibid.

82. On religious pluralism and the World's Parliament of Religions, see Richard Hughes Seager, *The Dawn of Religious Pluralism: Voices from the World's Parliament of Religions, 1893* (La Salle, Ill.: Open Court, 1993). Grant Wacker, "A Plural World: The Protestant Awakening to World Religions," in *Between the Times: The Travail of the Protestant Establishment in America, 1900–1960,* ed. William R. Hutchison (Cambridge: Cambridge University Press, 1989), 253–77, provides a useful map of the American Protestant encounter with world religions.

83. WNG, *St. Mark's and the Problem of Liberalism,* 7–9; WNG, *Tentative Statement,* 27. Sabine Baring-Gould (1834–1924), a prolific writer on theology and comparative religions, is best remembered today for his hymnody and study of English folk songs. Edward Carpenter (1844–1929) was an Anglican priest who renounced his ordination in 1874 because of his developing identity as a feminist, socialist, and outspoken homosexual. His book *Pagan and Christian Creeds,* 1921, reviewed a wide variety of ancient pagan traditions to argue (like Guthrie) that Christianity had pagan origins and needed to "adopt and recreate the rituals of the past" in order to become a true "Church of Humanity." James Freeman Clarke (1810–1888) was an influential Massachusetts Unitarian minister, social reformer, and scholar whose books *Ten Great Religions* (2 volumes, 1871 and 1883) and *Events and Epochs in Religious History* (1881) argued that all religions included partial truths and were fulfilled in the universal religion of Christianity.

84. WNG to Kenneth Sylvan Guthrie, 14 Apr. 1925, box 1, folder 21, Guthrie Papers; WNG to Mr. Mountfort Mills, 24 Mar. 1932, box 1, folder 21, Guthrie Papers; William Thomas Manning to Mountfort Mills, Esq., 13 Mar. 1924, William T. Manning box 11, folder 19, Diocese of New York Bishops' Papers, EDNY.

85. WNG, *St. Mark's and the Problem of Liberalism*, 11.

86. On Greenacre, see Chapter 10 in this volume.

87. Guthrie repeatedly makes the point that Christianity had much to learn from other religions. Among the earliest references is WNG, "A New Offense Advertised," *The Lion of St. Mark's-in-the-Bouwerie* 3 (Dec. 1916), 4–5.

88. "Sun-God Service Held in St. Mark's."

89. WNG, *St. Mark's and the Problem of Liberalism*, 10.

90. WNG, *Tentative Statement*, 14.

91. St. Mark's, "Popular Statement of the Platform."

92. WNG, *Two Letters to the Bishop of New York Concerning the Policy of St. Mark's-in-the-Bouwerie* (New York: St. Mark's, 1924), 8–9.

93. This scholarship, heavily influenced by postcolonial theory, includes John P. Burris, *Exhibiting Religion: Colonialism and Spectacle at International Expositions, 1851–1893* (Charlottesville: University Press of Virginia, 2001); David Chidester, "Colonialism," in *Guide to the Study of Religion*, ed. Willi Braun and Russell T. McCutcheon (New York: Cassell, 2000); David Chidester, *Savage Systems: Colonialism and Comparative Religion in Southern Africa* (Charlottesville: University Press of Virginia, 1996); Timothy Fitzgerald, *The Ideology of Religious Studies* (New York: Oxford University Press, 2000); Richard King, *Orientalism and Religion: Postcolonial Theory, India and 'the Mystic East'* (London: Routledge, 1999); and Russell T. McCutcheon, *Manufacturing Religion: The Discourse on Sui Generis Religion and the Politics of Nostalgia* (New York: Oxford University Press, 1997).

94. Hutchison, *The Modernist Impulse*, 147–55.

95. WNG, "Notes of an Address Delivered at the San Francisco Church Congress," n.d., 1928, box 1, folder 52, Guthrie Papers. In this talk, Guthrie claimed that he had preached essentially the same message in a sermon on missions given twenty years earlier. He certainly expressed the germ of this message in WNG, *Tentative Statement*, 23.

96. WNG, *St. Mark's and the Problem of Liberalism*, 10.

97. WNG to Mr. Dryden Linsley Phelps, 28 Mar. 1932, box 1, folder 38, Guthrie Papers; Dryden Linsley Phelps to WNG, 5 Feb. 1932, box 1, folder 38, Guthrie Papers.

98. WNG, *Relation of the Dance to Religion*, 34–35.

99. "St. Mark's Dances Vetoed by Bishop," *New York Times*, 16 Mar. 1924, 14, 25.

100. WNG, *Two Letters to the Bishop*, 32–33.

101. William Thomas Manning to Mountfort Mills, Esq., 13 Mar. 1924, William T. Manning box 11, folder 19, Diocese of New York Bishops' Papers, EDNY.

102. "St. Mark's Dances Vetoed by Bishop," 14.

103. Minutes of Meeting of Rector, Wardens and Vestrymen of St. Mark's-in-the-Bouwerie, 20 Oct. 1931, St. Mark's Vestry Minutes.

104. WNG to William Thomas Manning, 23 Jan. 1932, Individual Files: William Norman Guthrie, EDNY; Minutes of Meeting of Rector, Wardens and Vestrymen of St. Mark's-in-the-Bouwerie, 15 Feb. 1932, St. Mark's Vestry Minutes.

105. "Guthrie Triumphs as Hot Words Fly," *New York Evening Post*, 18 Apr. 1933; WNG to William T. Manning, 19 Apr. 1933, William T. Manning box 25, folder 9, Diocese of New York Bishops' Papers, EDNY; Minutes of Meeting of Rector, Wardens and Vestrymen of St. Mark's-in-the-Bouwerie, 19 Apr. 1933, St. Mark's Vestry Minutes; "Guthrie Wins Church Vote, Ousts

Vestry," *New York American*, 19 Apr. 1933; "Dr. Guthrie Ousts St. Mark's Vestry," *New York Times*, 19 Apr. 1933.

106. "Ousted Vestry Goes to Court," *New York Sun*, 25 May 1933; Boyd L. Bailey, "Press Release: Supreme Court Sustains New Vestry of St. Mark's-in-the-Bouwerie," 24 July 1933, box 1, folder 56, Guthrie Papers; "Court Upholds Dr. Guthrie and His New Vestry," *Herald Tribune*, New York, 24 July 1933; "St. Mark's Vestry Upheld by Court," *New York Times*, 24 July 1933.

107. WNG, "Concerning the Crowning Endeavor in Liturgical Worship," 9 Feb. 1936, Special Programs, 1923–1947, Pagan Rituals and Eurhythmic Dances, Parish Records Series, box 59, EDNY; WNG, "Ritual Dance of the Della Robbia Annunciation," 7 Mar. 1937, Special Programs, 1923–1947, Pagan Rituals and Eurythmic Dances, Parish Records Series, box 59, EDNY.

108. Eric Hobsbawm and Terence Ranger, *The Invention of Tradition* (London: Cambridge University Press, 1983), point out that invented practices draw much of their power not from pure innovation but from the extent to which they can be presented as retrievals.

109. Richard T. Hughes and Crawford Leonard Allen, *Illusions of Innocence: Protestant Primitivism in America, 1630–1875* (Chicago: University of Chicago Press, 1988) suggests that such primitivism has been an intrinsic feature of American religious culture.

110. The literature on primitivism is vast. One might begin with Elazar Barkan and Ronald Bush, eds., *Prehistories of the Future: The Primitivist Project and the Culture of Modernism* (Stanford, Calif.: Stanford University Press, 1995); Leah Dilworth, *Imagining Indians in the Southwest: Persistent Visions of a Primitive Past* (Washington, D.C.: Smithsonian Institution Press, 1996); T. J. Jackson Lears, *No Place of Grace: Antimodernism and the Transformation of American Culture, 1880–1920* (Chicago: University of Chicago Press, 1994); and Marianna Torgovnick, *Gone Primitive: Savage Intellects, Modern Lives* (Chicago: University of Chicago Press, 1990).

111. Phoebe Guthrie to Ruth St. Denis, 15 Aug. 1932, folder 409, Ruth St. Denis Letters; Phoebe Ann Guthrie to Ruth St. Denis, n.d., 1938, folder 510, Ruth St. Denis Letters.

112. Taylor and Nelson, *A Time to Dance*, 143, 41.

113. See, for example, Maria-Gabriele Wosien, *Sacred Dance: Encounter with the Gods* (London: Thames and Hudson, 1974); Davies, *Liturgical Dance*; James L. Miller, *Measures of Wisdom: The Cosmic Dance in Classical and Christian Antiquity* (Toronto: University of Toronto Press, 1986); and Doug Adams and Diane Apostolos-Cappadona, eds., *Dance as Religious Studies* (New York: Crossroad, 1990).

Twelve • *Taste Cultures*

1. Marion Junkin, "Truth in Art," *motive* 10, no. 1 (Oct. 1949): 23; see also Junkin, "Painting Faith," *motive* 8, no. 3 (Dec. 1947): 41.

2. "What Is 'Good' Art?" *motive* 18, no. 5 (Feb. 1958): 29.

3. Charles Merrill Smith, *How to Become a Bishop Without Being Religious* (New York: Doubleday, 1965), 31.

4. Some descriptive material in this essay is adapted from Sally M. Promey, "Interchangeable Art: Warner Sallman and the Critics of Mass Culture," in David Morgan, ed., *Icons of American Protestantism: The Art of Warner Sallman* (New Haven: Yale University Press, 1996): 148–80.

5. The term *practice*, as employed in this essay, refers to repeated *purposeful* behavior or ac-

tivity; there is thus a cognitive dimension to practice; cf. Catherine Bell's discussion of "strategic" activity in *Ritual: Perspectives and Dimensions* (New York: Oxford University Press, 1997), 76–83.

6. Though specific preferences varied significantly and though an attachment to abstract expressionism formed early on, the church was generally at least a bit behind the times, attracted most frequently to yesterday's avant garde.

7. The Greek root of the term *aesthetics* concerns perception and the senses.

8. Kris Hardin usefully proposes an anthropological aesthetics that is more tuned to "recognition and acceptance" than to beauty or pleasure. Hardin's thinking sets the stage as well for my discussion of "evaluated forms." Kris L. Hardin, *The Aesthetics of Action: Continuity and Change in a West African Town* (Washington, D.C.: Smithsonian Books, 1993): 2–3 and 268–69. I thank Leslie Brice for recommending Hardin's book.

9. Herbert J. Gans, "American Popular Culture and High Culture in a Changing Class Structure," *Prospects* 10 (1986): 17–37; and Gans, *Popular Culture and High Culture: An Analysis and Evaluation of Taste* (New York: Basic Books, 1974).

10. The phrase "terrible taste of Protestantism" belongs to Elwood Ellwood, and debuted in "Return from Miltown: The Terrible Taste of Protestantism," *motive* 18, no. 1 (Oct. 1957): 14–17. On Barr's religious affiliation see Editorial Notes, "Christmas 1955," *Presbyterian Life*, 24 Dec. 1955, 2; Museum of Modern Art (hereafter MoMA Archives): Alfred H. Barr, Jr., Papers (hereafter AHB Papers), [Archives of American Art microfilm (hereafter AAA): Reel 3261; Frames 1280–1281]. As early as 1941, Barr proposed a Museum of Modern Art exhibition he called "The Religious Spirit in Contemporary Art" ("The Religious Spirit in Contemporary Art," summaries of meetings, Dec. through Apr. 1941, preparatory to exhibition, MoMA Archives: AHB Papers, [AAA Reel 3154; Frame 1296]. While this exhibition never materialized, Protestant Barr invited Catholic Agnes Mongan, of the Fogg Art Museum at Harvard University, and Jewish Meyer Schapiro, a prominent art historian on the faculty of Columbia University, to contribute expertise. This inclination toward religious inclusivity was characteristic and, while this essay focuses on the liberal Protestant situation, Catholic and Jewish intellectuals in the first half of the twentieth century, and on both sides of the Atlantic Ocean, actively (though somewhat differently) promoted a modernist aesthetic of abstraction and decried "sentimental realisms." Important periodicals, providing insight into the larger interfaith aspects of religion's conversations with modern art include *Liturgical Arts, Catholic Art Quarterly, L'Art Sacré, Menorah Journal.*

11. Alfred H. Barr, Jr., *What Is Modern Painting?* (New York: Museum of Modern Art, 1943), 20–21.

12. Junkin, "Truth in Art," 23.

13. Cécile Whiting, *A Taste for Pop: Pop Art, Gender, and Consumer Culture* (Cambridge: Cambridge University Press, 1997), 7–8.

14. Amos Wilder, quoted in Nathan A. Scott, Jr., "Poetry, Religion, and the Modern Mind," *Journal of Religion*, 32, no. 3 (July 1953): 196.

15. Margaret Cogswell, "Christian Education and the Lively Arts," *Children's Religion* 25, no. 6 (June 1964): 24.

16. Marvin Halverson, Foreword to "Religious Art: Pre-Holiday Feature," *Art in America* 45, no. 3 (Fall 1957): 12.

17. Fred A. Luchs, "To Religious Experience By Pathways of Art," *Religious Education* 65, no. 6 (Nov.–Dec. 1950): 352; see also Junkin, "Truth in Art," 22.

18. Harry R. Garvin, "Religion and the Arts: The Coming Dangers," *Christian Scholar* 42 (1959): 280.

19. [Amos Wilder], "Christianity and the Arts: The Church, the Arts, and Contemporary Culture" [hereafter NCC Study Document], p. 4, MoMA Archives: AHB Papers [AAA: Reel 3148; Frame 587].

20. Typescript dated 9 Nov. 1957 recording Barr comments delivered at Oct. 1957 meeting of the Executive Board of the Division of Christian Life and Work on behalf of the Department of Worship and the Arts, National Council of Churches, MoMA Archives: AHB Papers [AAA: Reel 2184; Frame 1148].

21. Paul Tillich, "Prefatory Note," in Peter Selz, *New Images of Man* (New York: Museum of Modern Art, 1959), 9.

22. See, for example, Janice Radway, "The Scandal of the Middlebrow: The Book-of-the-Month Club, Class Fracture, and Cultural Authority," *South Atlantic Quarterly* 89, no. 4 (Fall 1990): 703–36; and Theodor Adorno and Max Horkheimer, "The Culture Industry: Enlightenment as Mass Deception," in Simon During, ed., *The Cultural Studies Reader* (New York: Routledge, 1993), 29–43.

23. Editorial, "The Lonely Crowd at Prayer," *Christian Century* 73, no. 22 (30 May 1956): 663. See also Jackson Lears, "A Matter of Taste: Corporate Cultural Hegemony in a Mass-Consumption Society," in Lary May, ed., *Recasting America: Culture and Politics in the Age of the Cold War* (Chicago: University of Chicago Press, 1988), 38–57. Between 1944 and 1953, Dwight Macdonald revised his essay, "A Theory of Popular Culture," as "A Theory of Mass Culture." In an illuminating study, Paul R. Gorman points out that the words *mass* and *culture* were rarely used together in English before the 1930s. Only in the wake of the Second World War did the term *mass culture* enter common usage; see Gorman, *Left Intellectuals and Popular Culture in Twentieth-Century America* (Chapel Hill: University of North Carolina Press, 1996), 2.

24. Clement Greenberg, "Avant-Garde and Kitsch," in *Art and Culture* (Boston: Beacon Press, 1961), 10–12. Greenberg first published this essay in *Partisan Review* in 1939.

25. Ibid., 15.

26. Paul Tillich, "Contemporary Visual Arts and the Revelatory Character of Style," in John Dillenberger and Jane Dillenberger, eds., *Paul Tillich: On Art and Architecture* (New York: Crossroad, 1987), 132–33, n3; and see Martin Jay, *The Dialectical Imagination: A History of the Frankfurt School and the Institute of Social Research, 1923–1950* (Boston: Little, Brown, 1973). A large literature exists on the relationship between the art of the 1940s and '50s and the ideology of the free world. See, for example, Annette Cox, *Art-as-Politics: The Abstract Expressionist Avant-Garde and Society* (Ann Arbor, Mich.: UMI Research Press, 1982); Serge Guilbaut, *How New York Stole the Idea of Modern Art: Abstract Expressionism, Freedom, and the Cold War* (Chicago: University of Chicago Press, 1983); Eva Cockcroft, "Abstract Expressionism, Weapon of the Cold War," in Francis Frascina and Jonathan Harris, eds., *Art in Modern Culture: An Anthology of Critical Texts* (New York: Harper Collins, 1992), 82–90; Cécile Whiting, *Anti-Fascism in American Art* (New Haven: Yale University Press, 1989); Erika Doss, *Benton, Pollock, and the Politics of Modernism: From Regionalism to Abstract Expressionism* (Chicago: University of Chicago Press, 1991); and

Deborah Martin Kao, "Radioactive Icons: The Critical Reception and Cultural Meaning of Modern Religious Art in Cold War America" (Ph.D. diss., Boston University, 1999).

27. Jay, *Dialectical Imagination,* 178; and see Nathan A. Scott, Jr., "Art and the Renewal of Human Sensibility in Mass Society" in Finley Eversole, ed., *Christian Faith and the Contemporary Arts* (New York: Abingdon, 1957), 27.

28. NCC Study Document, p. 5, MoMA Archives: AHB Papers [AAA: Reel 3148; Frame 588].

29. Paul Tillich and Theodore Greene, "Authentic Religious Art," *Masterpieces of Religious Art,* Art Institute of Chicago, 15 July to 31 Aug. 1954, 9; this essay, despite joint authorship, clearly represents Tillich's thought.

30. According to Livingston, for Tillich, religion was the "*depth dimension* in all man's cultural and spiritual life," the "ultimate concern"; it directed adherents to "those conditions which undergird and give meaning to . . . existence"; James C. Livingston, *Modern Christian Thought: From the Enlightenment to Vatican II* (New York: Macmillan, 1971), 357 (italics in original).

31. Paul Tillich, "Protestantism and the Contemporary Style in the Visual Art," *Christian Scholar* 40, no. 4 (Dec. 1957): 311.

32. Roger L. Shinn, "The Artist as Prophet-Priest of Culture," in Finley Eversole, ed., *Christian Faith and the Contemporary Arts* (New York: Abingdon, 1957), 72 and 77; see also Paul Tillich, *The Courage to Be* (New Haven: Yale University Press, 1952), 147–48; and Tillich and Greene, "Authentic Religious Art," 9.

33. Junkin, "Truth in Art," 22.

34. See Whiting, *A Taste for Pop,* 60–61; also A. Huyssen, *After the Great Divide: Modernism, Mass Culture, Postmodernism* (Bloomington: Indiana University Press, 1986), chap. 3, "Mass Culture as Woman: Modernism's Other," 44–62.

35. The literature charting the mid-century Protestant modernist aesthetics for architecture is at least as voluminous as that for the visual arts and literature. On modernism's purging of "gothic" see, for example, Otto Spaeth, "Worship and the Arts," *Architectural Record* 118 (Dec. 1955): 162–67; and Fred Smith, "What Has Protestantism to Do with Gothic?" *The Churchman,* 15 May 1954.

36. See, for example, Finley Eversole, "The Brave New World of the Modern Artist," in Eversole, ed., *Christian Faith and the Contemporary Arts* (New York: Abingdon, 1957), 46.

37. Harold Ehrensperger, "The Search for the Creative Image," *Christian Century* 73, no. 21 (23 May 1956): 644; John Dixon, "Protestant Art and the Natural Order," *motive* 18, no. 2 (Nov. 1956): 25; Ellwood, "Return from Miltown," 15.

38. Tom F. Driver, "The Arts and the Christian Evangel," *Christian Scholar* 60, no. 4 (Dec. 1957): 334.

39. "Yawns and Nausea" in "Religion" column, clipped from *Time,* 21 Apr. 1947, 70, filed in MoMA Archives: AHB Papers [AAA: Reel 3264; Frame 933].

40. Dixon, "Protestant Art and the Natural Order," 25.

41. Roger Ortmayer, "Layman's Point of View," *motive* 19, no. 8 (May 1959): 18–19.

42. See, for example, David K. Johnson, *The Lavender Scare: The Cold War Persecution of Gays and Lesbians in the Federal Government* (Chicago: University of Chciago Press, 2004); and Robert J. Corber, *Homosexuality in Cold War America: Resistance and the Crisis of Masculinity* (Durham, N.C.: Duke University Press, 1997).

43. "Minutes of the Initial Meeting of the Department of Worship and the Fine Arts, National Council of Churches of Christ in the U.S.A., Hotel Hollenden, Cleveland, Ohio," 1 Dec. 1950, National Council of Churches of Christ in the U.S.A. Division of Christian Life and Mission Records, 1945–1973, NCC RG 6, box 53, folder 9, Presbyterian Hisotrical Society, Philadelphia.

44. "Minutes of the Meeting of the Department of Worship and the Fine Arts, 297 Fourth Avenue, New York," 1 May 1952, NCC RG 6, box 53, folder 9.

45. Marvin Halverson, "Two Experiments in Correlation: Department of Worship and the Arts," *Christian Scholar* 40, no. 4 (Dec. 1957): 345–52. See also Robert A. Schneider, "Voice of Many Waters: Church Federation in the Twentieth Century," in William R. Hutchison, ed., *Between the Times: The Travail of the Protestant Establishment in America, 1900–1960* (Cambridge: Cambridge University Press, 1989), 95–121.

46. Marvin P. Halverson, "Department of Worship and the Arts, Report to the Division of Christian Life and Work on the Triennium 1954–1957," 3, NCC RG 6, box 53, folder 7.

47. "Minutes of a Meeting of the Department of Worship and the Arts," 20 Oct. 1953, 2, NCC manuscript folder RG 6-53-9. See also NCC RG 6, box 55, folder 2, for correspondence on "Christianity and the Arts Associates."

48. Secular arts periodicals featured articles on and reviewed exhibitions of religious art. Major secular museums, like the Art Institute of Chicago, mounted religious art exhibitions; theologians of aesthetics were invited to address large audiences in prestigious secular venues, like the National Gallery of Art, where two of the first four Andrew W. Mellon Lecturers in the Fine Arts were neo-Thomists Jacques Maritain (1952) and Etienne Gilson (1955).

49. See Halverson to Barr, 20 May 1955, MoMA Archives: AHB Papers [AAA: Reel 2184; Frame 1203], regarding the recommendations of the nominating committee of the National Council of Churches Commission on Art.

50. Barr to Rathbone, 21 Mar. 1955, MoMA Archives: AHB Papers [AAA: Reel 2180; Frame 329].

51. Ibid., frame 330. The article, "The Life of Christ as Seen by Great Artists," appeared in a special issue of *Life* devoted to the subject of "Christianity," dated 26 Dec. 1955.

52. NCC Study Document, p. 5, MoMA Archives: AHB Papers [AAA: Reel 3148; Frame 584]. *Time* magazine published a précis of this document under the headline "Art Needs the Church" (Henry Luce, the owner of *Time,* was also associated with the NCC's Department of Worship and the Arts) (*Time,* 13 Feb. 1956: 72).

53. Halverson to Barr, 20 May 1955, MoMA Archives: AHB Papers [AAA: Reel 2184; Frames 1203–1207]. In 1960, Barr called for the "sponsoring and producing of films on art," and suggested artists to be considered and narrators to employ; among these latter he included Jacques Maritain, Paul Tillich, and Meyer Schapiro.

54. See Preston Roberts, "Two Experiments in Correlation: The Field of Religion and Art at Chicago," *Christian Scholar* 40, no. 4 (Dec. 1957): 339–45.

55. Union Theological Seminary, Harvard Divinity School, and Boston University School of Theology, for example, instituted programs in religion and the arts.

56. Goodrich was Protestant, Schapiro Jewish, and Spaeth Catholic.

57. "An Exhibition of Contemporary Religious Art and Architecture," exhibition catalogue, Union Theological Seminary, 1–16 Dec. 1952, especially "Introduction" and Tillich's words on

the back cover. Adolph Gottlieb, Marc Chagall, Morris Graves, Rico Lebrun, Mark Tobey, Richard Pousette-Dart, Ad Reinhardt, Jacques Lipchitz, and Henry Moore numbered among contemporary artists whose work was selected by the student committee. See also David H. McAlpin, Jr., to Agnes Mongan, 8 Nov. 1952, Archives of the National Gallery of Art, RG 17, Rosenwald Collection, Alverthorpe Files, box 52, Union Theological Seminary file.

58. McAlpin as quoted in Catherine Linder, "Something New Between Art and Protestant Theology," *motive* 13, no. 6 (Mar. 1953): 24.

59. Aline B. Louchheim, "Religious Art in Many Manners," *New York Times,* 14 Dec. 1952.

60. Pousette-Dart quoted in Linder, "Something New," 28.

61. H. D. Bollinger, "The Methodist Student Movement in Higher Education," *Religious Education* 45, no. 6 (Nov.–Dec. 1950): 353–56.

62. See *motive*'s own claims to being "the leading Protestant publication in the field of the arts"; "Words into Images: *motive*'s Permanent Art Collection," *motive* 18, no. 5 (Feb. 1958): 20–27.

63. Robert Hodgell, "The Artist's Note on His Drawing," *motive* 6, no. 3 (Dec. 1945): 4. Other artists frequently involved with *motive* included painter Siegfried Reinhardt and sculptor Clark B. Fitzgerald.

64. "A Graphic Arts Contest: Words into Images, for All Students and Professionals," *motive* 17, no. 1 (Oct. 1956): 28.

65. "Announcing the *motive* Art Exhibit, Sixth Quadrennial Conference of the Methodist Student Movement, Lawrence Kansas," *motive* 18, no. 3 (Dec. 1957): 15.

66. "Purchase Some of Your Own. Original Works of Art!" *motive* 18, no. 5 (Feb. 1958): 28.

67. Margaret Rigg, "The Message of the Artist for Today," *motive* 17, no. 6 (Mar. 1957): 14–19.

68. Waldo S. Pratt, "The Field of Artistic Influences in Religious Education," *Proceedings of the Second Annual Convention,* 510, as quoted in David Morgan, *Protestants and Pictures: Religion, Visual Culture, and the Age of American Mass Production,* (New York: Oxford University Press, 1999), 324–25; see also Sally M. Promey, *Painting Religion in Public: John Singer Sargent's "Triumph of Religion" at the Boston Public Library* (Princeton: Princeton University Press, 1999), chap. 7.

69. Graham Wisseman, "For Eye to Admire and Heart to Desire," *Children's Religion* 5, no. 8 (Aug. 1944): 4.

70. Graham Hodges, "Religious Art in Our Homes," *Children's Religion* 16, no. 11 (Nov. 1955): 20–21.

71. Ruth L. Bishop, "Pictures Say Something Too!" *Children's Religion* 19, no. 11 (Nov. 1958): 16–17, 32.

72. In the case of the *International Journal,* one might well have expected a more rapid transition since it was produced under the auspices of the Division of Christian Education of the National Council of Churches. *Children's Religion* was a publication of the Pilgrim Press and the Christian Educational Press of the Congregational Christian Churches and, subsequently (after the 1957 merger with the Evangelical and Reformed Churches), the United Church of Christ. *Children's Religion* also had a wide Presbyterian readership.

73. Lillian Williams, "Editorial Introduction," and Virgil E. Foster, "Editorial Introduction," *International Journal of Religious Education* 35, no. 6 (Feb. 1959): 4.

74. John F. Hayward, "The Heritage of Christian Art," *International Journal of Religious Education* 35, no. 6 (Feb. 1959): 6.

75. Marvin Halverson, "What Is Art? When Is It Christian?" *International Journal of Religious Education* 35, no. 6 (Feb. 1959): 13.

76. Charles H. Boyles, "Young People Like Them Modern," *International Journal of Religious Education* 35, no. 6 (Feb. 1959): 18–19.

77. Dorothy Virginia Bennit, "Anyone Can Be an Artist," *International Journal of Religious Education* 35, no. 6 (Feb. 1959): 26–32; and "Co-creators with God," *International Journal of Religious Education* 35, no. 6 (Feb. 1959): 38.

78. At least twenty-four pages of the special arts issue represent a resources section to guide educators in acquiring reproductions and art materials of many sorts; *International Journal of Religious Education* 35, no. 6 (Feb. 1959): 39–63.

79. See exhibition pamphlet, "Great Art for Christian Education," an exhibition arranged by the *International Journal for Religious Education*, in MoMA Archives: AHB Papers [AAA: Reel 2184; Frames 1251–1254].

80. See Cogswell, "Christian Education and the Lively Arts," 24.

81. For more on this project, see Vivian Russell, "From the Children of the World," *Children's Religion*, 25, no. 6 (June 1964): 20–23.

82. "Quotes on Art Education that May Prove Helpful," assembled by Betty Herndon Meyer, undated (ca. 1960), Betty Herndon Meyer Papers, collection of the author.

83. Randolph Crump Miller, "Something New in Religious Education: The Seabury Series Marks a New Era," *The Churchman*, 15 May 1955: 11–12; and "New Tools for Teachers: Filling a Need of Many Years in the Field of Religious Education," *The Churchman*, June 1957: 11, see also 17.

84. While each of the seven artists was indeed "contemporary," only three of them had any degree of name recognition in the secular art market.

85. An article in *Children's Religion* provided detailed discussion of how to shape a parish fine arts committee, as well as encouragement to congregations that wished to commission original works of art as an integral part of new building projects; see Mildred C. Widber, "Art and the Educational Building," *Children's Religion* 25, no. 6 (June 1964): 16–17.

86. Betty Herndon Meyer, "The Artist as Teacher," *Children's Religion* 25, no. 5 (May 1964): 17–18.

87. Harvey Cox wrote the preface to the 1966 exhibition brochure and Meyer organized "An Art Experience for Children" to coincide with the festival.

88. See, for example, Robert Hodgell, "Freedom and the Artist," *motive* 14, no. 2 (Nov. 1953): 13–15; Arthur Miller, "Reaction and Censorship in Los Angeles," *Art Digest*, 15 Nov. 1951: 9; and "Art Summoned Before the Inquisition," *Arts and Architecture*, Dec. 1951.

89. Lawrence L. Grumon and J. Thomas Leamon, "Modern Art: A Dialogue," *Children's Religion* 25, no. 5 (May 1964): 3–8.

90. Betty Herndon Meyer, "So You Can't Teach Art?" *Children's Religion* 25, no. 6 (June 1964): 19.

91. See, for example, Truman B. Douglass to Roy G. Ross, 16 Jan. 1962, MoMA Archives: AHB Papers [AAA: Reel 2198; Frame 239]; and Douglass, "The Responsibility of the Churches for the Arts," *National Council Outlook*, Jan. 1959: 7–8. See also a clipped letter from Barbara Sargent

(Bath, Maine) to the ditors of *Christianity and Crisis,* 17 Oct. 1955, MoMA Archives: AHB Papers [AAA: Reel 2184; Frame 1191].

92. Harrell F. Beck, in "Symposium: The Place of Religion in the Satellite Era," *motive* 19, no. 4 (Jan. 1959): 10.

93. "Kitsch is the contemporary form of the Gothic, Rococo, Baroque" [Frank Wedekind, 1917]. Viewed this way, Kitsch is a replicated form of something past, it is always derivative, always imitative, always "second," always looking back to something else, always the "past" in comparison to the "modern" "original's" present. Wedekind is quoted in Matei Calinescu, *Five Faces of Modernity* (Durham, N.C.: Duke University Press, 1987), 225.

94. Marvin P. Halverson to Roy G. Ross, General Secretary of the NCC, 21 Mar. 1962, marked "personal and confidential," quotation from pages 3–4, NCC RG 6, box 53, folder 1.

95. Ehrensperger, "Search for the Creative Image," 644, explicitly mentions "the familiar sentimental and insipid paintings of Jesus."

96. NCC Study Document, MoMA Archives: AHB Papers [AAA: Reel 3148; Frame 588].

97. Many believed that the United States, in the 1950s, was actually approaching classlessness. In 1949 Russell Lynes, editor of *Harper's,* asserted the obsolescence of economic class and its replacement by "taste cultures." See Russell Lynes, "Highbrow, Lowbrow, Middlebrow," *Life* (11 Apr. 1949), 99–102. Paul Tillich feared that the emerging classless society would too closely resemble the "vulgar materialism" of the middle class. Dwight Macdonald voiced a similar concern that the high and low would be swallowed by the middle. Art historian Cécile Whiting is especially helpful on this subject; see Whiting, *A Taste for Pop,* 62–64.

98. Hardin provides an illuminating discussion of abstract expressionism in this regard in *Aesthetics of Action,* 279; On the particular appeal of abstract expressionism for liberal Protestant intellectuals, see Eversole, "Brave New World," 45–55.

99. NCC Study Document, pp. 1, 6, MoMA Archives: AHB Papers [AAA: Reel 3148; Frames 584, 589].

100. John Dixon, "On the Possibility of a Christian Criticism of the Arts," *Christian Scholar* 40, no. 4 (Dec. 1957): 303.

101. Paul Gorman has made a similar point about the mass culture debate; Gorman, *Left Intellectuals,* 9–11, quote on 9.

102. Bishop, "Pictures Say Something Too!" 16.

103. Edith Wyschogrod, "Value," in Mark C. Taylor, ed., *Critical Terms in Religious Studies* (Chicago: University of Chicago Press, 1998): 365.

104. The terms *cultural pessimism* and *cultural populism* are John Clarke's; Clarke, "Pessimism vs. Populism: The Problematic Politics of Popular Culture," in Richard Butsch, ed., *For Fun and Profit: The Transformation of Leisure into Consumption* (Philadelphia: Temple University Press, 1990), 28–44.

105. The cultural criticism of Susan Sontag and Marshall McLuhan figured prominently in this revaluation of popular culture. See Ronald Edsforth, "Popular Culture and Politics in Modern America: An Introduction," in Ronald Edsforth and Larry Bennett, eds., *Popular Culture and Political Change in Modern America* (Albany: State University of New York Press, 1991), 3–6.

106. The critical engagements of the 1950s and '60s represented a relatively late manifestation of the longstanding concern with reconciling notions of democracy, class, and aesthetic quality in the United States.

107. Michele Bogart's illuminating thinking on the subject of twentieth-century distinctions between art as activity, on the one hand, and art as a history of major painters and "great" works (and, I would add, great styles), on the other hand, contributes helpfully to this line of thought. Michele H. Bogart, *Artists, Advertising, and the Borders of Art* (Chicago: University of Chicago Press, 1995), 7, 13. Robert Wuthnow's *All in Sync: How Music and Art Are Revitalizing American Religion* (Berkeley: University of California Press, 2003) is one example of a recent recommendation of the activity of artistic production as Christian practice.

108. While the editors of *Children's Religion* were all women, *Colloquy's* first editor was the Reverend John H. Westerhoff III. The reconfigured journal would seek "a wide-ranging ecumenical audience" and be a "lively, contemporary, responsibly controversial magazine," dealing with such issues as the "relationship between love and justice." See John H. Westerhoff III, "Colloquy," *Children's Religion* 28, no. 12 (Dec. 1967): 26.

CATHERINE A. BREKUS is associate professor of the history of Christianity in the Divinity School and the Department of History at the University of Chicago. She is the author of *Strangers and Pilgrims: Female Preaching in America, 1740–1845* (1998).

ANTHEA D. BUTLER is assistant professor in the Department of Religion at the University of Rochester. She holds a Ph.D. in religion from Vanderbilt University, and her areas of scholarly interest include African American religion and culture, evangelicalism, and Pentecostalism.

HEATHER D. CURTIS is a postdoctoral fellow and lecturer on American religious history at Harvard Divinity School. She holds a doctorate in the history of Christianity from Harvard University. Her current research focuses on the intersections of health, spirituality, and gender in nineteenth- and twentieth-century American culture.

ROBERTO LINT SAGARENA is assistant professor in the Departments of Religion and American Studies at the University of Southern California. He is currently at work on a book about how religious historical tropes have worked to define place in Southern California.

LAURIE F. MAFFLY-KIPP is associate professor in the Department of Religious Studies at the University of North Carolina, Chapel Hill. Her current research and teaching focus on African American religions, religion on the Pacific borderlands of the Americas, and issues of intercultural contact.

MICHAEL D. MCNALLY is associate professor in the Department of Religion at Carleton College. Author of *Ojibwe Singers: Hymns, Grief, and a Native Culture in Motion* (2000), he is currently at work on a book about the significance of age and eldership in Ojibwe tradition and history.

RICK OSTRANDER is dean of undergraduate studies and associate professor of history at John Brown University in Siloam Springs, Arkansas. He has researched and written in the areas of American Protestant spirituality, fundamentalism and liberalism, and the history of higher education.

SALLY M. PROMEY is professor and chair in the Department of Art History and Archaeology and affiliate faculty member in the Deparmtent of American Studies at the University of Maryland. She teaches and publishes on American art and visual culture from the seventeenth century to the present, with a specialization in the visual cultures of American religions.

LEIGH E. SCHMIDT is professor in the Deparment of Religion at Princeton University. He has written on Protestant revivalism, popular religion, ritual and the consumer culture, the history of perception, spirituality, and the history of the study of religion.

MARK VALERI is the E. T. Thompson Professor of Church History at Union Theological Seminary in Virginia. He has written on Puritan culture, early American economic practice, and the writings of Jonathan Edwards.

TISA J. WENGER is assistant professor in the Department of Religious Studies at Arizona State University. Her reasearch interests include the cultural histories of race, religion, and Christian missions in America.

DAVID K. YOO is associate professor in the Department of History at Claremont McKenna College and a core faculty member in the Intercollegiate Department of Asian American Studies at the Claremont Colleges. His current research includes a book project on the early history of Koreans in the United States as well as a co-edited volume on Korean American religion and spirituality.